T0385680

EVERYTHING IS POSSIBLE

EVERYTHING
IS
POSSIBLE

Antifascism and the Left
in the Age of Fascism

Joseph Fronczak

Yale
UNIVERSITY PRESS
NEW HAVEN AND LONDON

Published with assistance from the Louis Stern Memorial Fund
and from the Kingsley Trust Association Publication Fund
established by the Scroll and Key Society of Yale College.

Yale University Press books may be purchased in quantity
for educational, business, or promotional use. For information, please email
sales.press@yale.edu (U.S. office) or sales@yaleup.co.uk (U.K. office).

Set in 10.5/15 Yale New type by Newgen North America.
Printed in the United States of America.

Library of Congress Control Number: 2022941752
ISBN 978-0-300-25117-3 (hardcover : alk. paper)

A catalogue record for this book is available from the British Library.

This paper meets the requirements of ANSI/NISO Z39.48-1992
(Permanence of Paper).

10 9 8 7 6 5 4 3 2 1

To W. A. W.

CONTENTS

EVERYTHING IS POSSIBLE

THE HISTORY OF THE LEFT

When no one's asking, I know very well what the left is.
But then I'm asked, and I don't know anymore.

—JACQUES JULLIARD

"What is it? A revolutionary movement? But all is calm." The questions, and the complication, belonged to Simone Weil. She was in Paris, writing in early June 1936 about the factory occupations then sweeping through the city and its surroundings. Weil, a twenty-seven-year-old philosopher who wrote on topics ranging from work and strikes to revolution and war, had just visited several of the occupied factories, including the Renault plant where she herself had once worked while on leave from a teaching post. Now that the Renault workers had grabbed control of the grounds and were occupying the plant, Weil had returned, hoping to soak up what one of the strikers called the "pleasant feeling of being lords and masters" of a place where they usually toiled, their immediate world momentarily turned upside down.[1]

Weil found the scene inspiring, and she found it puzzling. How to square the perfusive sense of revolutionary possibility—not to mention the outright seizure of the means of production—with the emotional calm? And how to square the calm with the explosion of "sitdown strikes," as they came to be called, across Paris's industrial landscape? By the time Weil wrote out her questions, the movement, revolutionary or not, had brought the region's manufacturing to a standstill, hitting the largest firms and smaller operations alike. And by the time her words appeared in published form a couple of weeks after the

—

1

Renault strike, the sitdown movement had spiraled from the factories into all sorts of workplaces splayed across the city: the cafés, hotels, and department stores; the grocery stores and markets; boutiques, bakeries, and workshops. Weil thought that the suddenness and thoroughness of the movement suggested something fundamental, something transformative, but she still could not shake the sense that all around her the mood was too light, as if those waging the revolution — again, if that's what it was — didn't understand that it shouldn't be all smiles, songs, and affection for those who embraced each other as equals.

The puzzlement was not Weil's alone. "It was a slapstick sort of revolution, dealing in comedy instead of blood," a close observer in Paris suggested in the wake of the strike wave, "but its results were far-reaching enough to make French workers date their calendars from the day of strike settlements just as Mussolini tallies history in terms of the years since his march on Rome." The *Écho de Paris*, a daily paper popular on the right, felt it necessary to warn readers not to be fooled by the façade of "good humor," songs, and "innocent diversions." Make no mistake, the newspaper insisted, all those strikers occupying their workplaces meant that "a revolution has begun." Indeed, the *Écho* went so far as to claim, "All revolutions begin like this."[2]

Two months later, Weil boarded a train bound for Barcelona, a city by then in the midst of a revolution of its own. The revolution in Barcelona, to be sure, had not begun with good humor or innocent diversions. It had begun with deadly street battles involving swarms of the city's people fighting against soldiers of the Spanish army. The fighting had taken place in late July during the first few days of the Spanish Civil War. It had left as many as 500 dead and countless more wounded. Yet, somewhat miraculously, when it had ended, in control of the city were the common people of Barcelona — syndicalists and anarchists, the women who kept the working-class neighborhoods running, the community-based militias, rowdy teenage laborers, the local barbers and factory workers in faded blue overalls. And in the days that followed the violence, even as they buried their dead, the people of Barcelona threw the city into a state of social revolution much like what Weil had witnessed in Paris about eight weeks before, only more so: they seized the factories, the hotels, shops, and cafés; and then they collectivized them. They spoke to each other now as equals, and they looked each other in the eye as they walked down the Ramblas. There, in the heart of the city, they gathered and sang revolutionary songs (of the sort that George Orwell, when he arrived four months after Weil, would find "the naïvest kind, all about proletarian brotherhood and the wickedness of Mussolini"). Everything in the streets of Barcelona in those extraordinary days was, as one young socialist put it, "dreamlike," everyone "hallucinating" with happiness. One spectator speculated that it was "like the day of festival in older times."[3]

Weil arrived in early August, three weeks after the city's liberation. When she arrived the social revolution was still in full force. Yet as when she had visited the occupied factories near Paris earlier in the summer, she was struck in Barcelona by the calm and good spirits surrounding her: in her journal she wrote of stepping out of the train station and strolling along the city's "happy streets," the cafés and shops open and serene. "Nothing has changed, really," she suggested, "except for one little thing: now the people have the power." But from that exception much ramified. She wrote that as she scrutinized her surroundings more carefully—noticing, for example, "so few police and so many kids with guns"—she came to realize that, surface calm notwithstanding, "this truly is revolution."[4]

Weil had come to Barcelona, however, not to soak up the scene but rather to fight in the war. She had done so because she saw it not as only a Spanish civil war but also as a global one. She saw the war as a great scission splitting all humanity into enemy camps and impassioning partisans the world over with hatreds for newfound nemeses, even among old neighbors. And she saw the war's implications extending across vast overlapping ideological, political, and moral terrains. Weil was far from alone in seeing things so, as more than 40,000 people from beyond Spain left their homes—in Ethiopia, the United States, Cuba, Palestine, and many other countries—to join in a struggle that they interpreted as their own. In even those parts of the world most distant from Spain, the war worked to accelerate an ideological sorting out already underway, intensifying changes already begun in how people imagined the world's politics and in how they imagined that they themselves could shape and turn those politics. When the war had begun in late July, Weil had been at home in Paris, away from the fighting, and yet nonetheless she had already felt

—

implicated because, "despite my best efforts, I couldn't keep from subjectively participating in this war."[5]

In the end, whether she had been right or wrong in Paris to see the war as her own, her choice "to engage," as she put it, worked to make it so.[6] By engaging, Weil — and all of the thousands of others who went — made sure that the war would indeed hold just the sort of global implications that she had sensed were there when she'd decided to catch the train to Barcelona.

Consider another personal political trajectory, contemporaneous with Weil's and converging with hers in Spain: follow Oliver Law from the South Side of Chicago to the battlefields of Jarama.

On a pleasant Saturday afternoon at August's end, 1935, Law stood on a roof near Chicago's 47th Street L station and gave a speech. Below, an excitable crowd filled the street, assembled in protest of the Italian fascist regime's ever-escalating threats to invade Ethiopia. Law had put considerable work into organizing the demonstration, and after the police had rejected the organizers' application for a parade permit, he had been among those who insisted on holding the event regardless. Now, on the roof, he had a lot to say. A black veteran of the United States Army, he had become politically engaged during the earliest, most desperate days of the Great Depression. He had taken part in 1930 in Chicago's unemployed movement (both before and after officers from the police department's "red squad" beat him senseless with blackjacks), and he'd taken part the following year in local protests against the incarceration of the "Scottsboro boys," the nine black youths unjustly accused of rape in Jim Crow Alabama. He had joined the Communist Party U.S.A. the year after that and had risen quickly in the local branch's ranks, even running for office on the party ticket in 1934. Meanwhile, he had driven a cab, loaded ships along the docks, worked construction for a spell, and also opened an undercapitalized restaurant, which quickly failed. A profile of him in the *Daily Worker* suggested that he considered his political engagement during these early years of the Great Depression "a turning point in his life, protecting him against defeatism and demoralization as a result of the failure of his business."[7] By the summer of 1935, when he threw himself into the local effort to protest the Italian dictator Benito Mussolini's warmongering, he already had a sizable reputation in Chicago's radical circles.

The mass march down 47th Street was far and away the largest of the anti-war demonstrations in Chicago that summer, with some estimates suggesting that 10,000 took part. In fact, it was one of the largest of all the many "Hands Off Ethiopia" protests that swept through the world's major metropolises in 1935, everywhere from Melbourne to Calcutta and London to Rio de Janeiro. And in addition to the thousands of protesters who showed up on 47th Street for the march, hundreds of police officers also showed up — to break it up. One observer even felt that the officers with their patrol wagons "made a bigger and far more spectacular parade as white and black citizens of both sexes were herded indiscriminately into the vehicles and hurried off to precinct police station cells."[8] While Weil the following summer would find herself struck by the surprising calm of a factory occupation near Paris, Law in the summer of 1935 had to handle the predictable pandemonium of a street demonstration in Chicago.

Indeed, that was why he was on the roof. A few bold protesters attempted speeches down in the street, but they did so at their own peril. As Law and the other organizers had expected, as soon as anyone in the crowd popped up her or his head with an eye toward giving a speech, the police began to make their way through the mass of people to arrest the offender, clubbing marchers along the way. This meant that street-level speakers had to melt back into the crowd before they could make much of a point, leaving it to someone else, somewhere else, to pick up where the last speaker had left off.[9] That kept the oratory on the street somewhat impressionistic. It also made the oratory something of a cooperative act of speech, one improvisational discourse blending into the next. This had its own expressive elegance to it, and its implications (most of all in their material form, that of the police clubs) had a way of leading participants to draw solidarity-generating connections between the dangers faced by the people of faraway Ethiopia and the dangers that were their own right there in Chicago.

But on the roof Law had time to pursue his point. It appears that nobody documented what he said that Saturday afternoon, but he inevitably spoke out against the growing menace of fascism. If other speeches given during the Hands Off Ethiopia campaign provide any guide, he said something to the effect that the Ethiopian people's fight against Italian fascism belonged to all people everywhere who opposed fascism anywhere, much like what Weil implied one summer later when she considered why she felt that she had to take the Spanish people's fight as her own. What is known about Law's speech is that, his rooftop remove notwithstanding, it ended with the Chicago police hauling him off to jail.[10]

Sixteen months later, Law left Chicago for Spain. Like Weil, he saw the Spanish Civil War as a fight that belonged to all, and he saw it as a fight over the greatest of stakes, the choice between fascism and the possibility of a better world. Along with five others, he caught a train to New York sometime after Christmas 1936 and set out across the Atlantic on a steamer on January 16, 1937. Only weeks later, in the Jarama valley east of Madrid, he took command of a racially integrated machine gun company, an accomplishment, it was pointed out, that hadn't been possible when he had served in the U.S. Army. His choice of solidarity with people far away had opened possibilities of empowerment for himself. And as he had in Chicago, he achieved recognition and respect at Jarama. A reporter who interviewed him on the front in the spring of 1937 observed that "Oliver Law stands out for his leadership, his coolness and his gallantry." In the interview, Law spoke openly of the possibility of dying in Spain, but, again like Weil, he thought that taking part was incumbent upon him, and he explained that he fought not out of humanitarian sympathy for the Spanish people but rather out of human solidarity with them, the civil war ultimately as much his own concern as theirs. He explained, "We'll do it here in Spain, maybe stopping fascism in the United States, too, without a great battle there."[11]

Weil and Law; Paris, Barcelona, Chicago, and Jarama; the sitdown strikes, the Hands Off Ethiopia movement, and the Spanish Civil War. Explaining the connections between such people, places, and events and explaining the possibilities opened by those connections are two of this book's central aims. That Weil's and Law's life stories converged in Spain serves as a nicely illustrative geographical representation of a much larger story of convergence, that of the left during the middle years of the Great Depression. The left in these years came together across divisions of political geography, race, nationality, empire and colony, language, political affiliation, and ideology to achieve a fleeting and fragile — but meaningful — semblance of unity.

This book maps out that convergence.[12] It is a history of the left at a moment of its remaking into something new and more substantial than what it had been before, and into something more familiar to our notions of what the left means today. Indeed, one of the more general claims of the book is that much of what we now think of as the left turns on what happened in this short historical period. This is so in even the most fundamental of ways. For the mid-Depression years — those years leading up to and culminating in the Spanish Civil War — were when the basic idea of the left as some great aggregate of people who find common cause with each other the world over finally took form. There had been, to be sure, other notions of "the left" in political rhetoric for a long time before these years. But those were smaller and less consequential conceits; only when the generation of Weil and Law took to the political battlefield in the 1930s did the idea of the left swell into the distinctive shape and size that it has had since.[13] Only then did people take to reckoning that the left was something at work the world over, something that included masses of people in different countries all over the world all at once. And, indeed, for the most part, only then did the left transform in people's minds into the sort of thing that could be imagined to be at work anywhere, or to do anything at all: that it could be imagined to act, in the simple sense of possessing and exercising an agency all its own, as if "the left" were a sentient being like you and me.

It is the sort of political fiction usually taken for granted. It is today, and has been for a long time, quite commonplace in political talk for abstractions like "the left" somehow to act on their own, to perform even audacious acts, to hold specific beliefs, and to make clear-voiced declarations. Listen to everyday political chatter and hear that the left fights for certain causes and battles against others; that the left takes stands and makes demands; that it keeps the faith or loses faith; that the left occasionally wins great victories, even though its usual lot has seemed to be to suffer terrible defeats. The left argues, insists, struggles, demonstrates, and remonstrates; it organizes, mobilizes, dreams, pleads, and protests. It is, again, as if the left were alive, flesh and blood. How to explain

—

this being so? How did it come to be that people today would reflexively express such belief, time and again in everyday political discourse, in the agency of a mere metaphorical figure? Why is it such common sense that the left *is* something at all, let alone something capable of taking part in the great political contests of the day, contests over the fate of humanity?

One way of explaining it is to suggest that we have learned to think of the left as a political collectivity. Our politics teems with such collectivities, which is at least noteworthy and perhaps alarming, because they are all fictions of a sort, inventions of the mind that only exist to the extent that people believe them to. And yet we allow these fictions considerable power to shape our lives, to shape our world. In part, this book tells the story of how people around the world came to believe in the left, the same as they could be said to believe in any of the other great phantasmic collectivities that inhabit our political world — strange and inevitably mystifying creations such as "the people" and "the working class," or any given nation or social movement or political party; or any and all of our most familiar ideological specimens, those such as the "progressives," "liberals," "socialists," "populists," and "conservatives"; or, of course, the collectivity that is the left's natural corollary, "the right." Like the left, the right and all of the rest of these political collectivities first needed people to imagine them into being for them to exist at all, and they will last only so long as people persist in believing in them.[14]

Beware them all, warned the newspaper intellectual Dorothy Thompson in the final days of the 1930s. Thompson, a widely syndicated columnist for the *New York Herald Tribune,* insisted that many an intellectual problem — and, it followed, many a political problem — stemmed from faith in "abstractions like 'masses,' 'proletariat,' 'liberals,' 'progressives,' 'tories,' 'CIO.'" They were all, to her mind, illusions: "phonies," she called them. And yet even Thompson, the shrewd skeptic of ideological abstraction, had learned by the 1930s' end to trust subconsciously in the veracity of at least one collectivity: only a few lines after she warned against putting any stock in those phony abstractions, she then invoked the left as if it were as solid as cement.[15]

In our time as in Thompson's, it's a question worth asking: how is it that people would put so much faith in these abstractions — these "phonies" — to signify actual political creatures living among us? The various stories of these

—

8

political collectivities' makings, taken together, tell an important part of a larger story, the story of the making of the modern political world. In this book, I relate one of those stories with an eye toward that larger one.

There are endless ways to relate the history of the left. The historical moment at the heart of this book, the middle period of the Great Depression, is far from the only point of origin for the left as we know it today, and this book's narrative is far from the only origins story for the left that could be told about even this historical moment.[16] Any political formation such as the left — or the right, or communism or liberalism or conservatism or any of the other "phonies" — is necessarily complex and has multiple origins, and any one of its points of origin can be narrated in any number of ways.[17] Nonetheless, this book relates the origins story for the left that I thought I could tell and that I thought made sense to tell in our time.

The most familiar origin story for the left that could be told is a much older one. That story, explaining the spatial metaphor behind the name "the left," reaches back to the first year of the French Revolution.[18] The episode — only later invoked as the left's origin — unfolded as part of one of modernity's most myth-laden political dramas, the excited debate in Paris and Versailles over the rights of man during the extraordinary summer of 1789. In the weeks that followed the storming of the Bastille in Paris, deliberations in France's revolutionary National Constituent Assembly at Versailles became so intense that the deputies who were most taken with the metaphysics of rights, liberty, and equality gradually took to sitting together, on the chamber's left side, so as to make their case more forcefully, physically unified.[19] It may seem like an inconsequential habit, but it had force. Right away, it made those congregating on the left into a collectivity, however small and impromptu, and they sensed this to the point that it altered their behavior in the chamber. What was most noticeable was that their heckling and hissing now drove their adversaries — those protective of social hierarchy and the authority of church and crown — over to the room's right side. By August's end, after those on the left had won their greatest triumph with the issuance of the world-historic Declaration of the Rights of Man and Citizen, those who felt themselves "cast to the right," and much aggrieved by it, "began," as one of them put it, "to recognize ourselves."

—

In a way, that self-recognition was the origin of the right; in a way, then, the left had not only been present at its own making amid the fabled events of the summer of 1789, it had compelled the making of the right, by reaction, as well.[20]

And it was precisely in this way that many later political actors and thinkers took to seeing the matter. They looked back at the clamor at Versailles and found in it a parable of collectivity-making fit for their own times. Small-scale and situational as the affair had been, it nonetheless looked to them like an origin story for the left and the right, and it looked as well like an origin story for the whole of modern politics, in all its factious, collectivity-driven, and grievance-ridden glory.[21]

But only in retrospect. Neither the left nor the right had sprung forth fully formed in 1789. At the time nobody in the assembly had imagined that the occasional gesture to the left as the side of equality, the rights of man, and social justice would someday be projected beyond their chamber, let alone beyond France. The periodic, single-room, face-to-face gathering of deputies during assembly sessions was a thing of a different kind from what the left has meant since the day of Weil and Law.

Only since then, since the middle years of the Great Depression, has it made sense to people to imagine the left as not just a collectivity, such as that congregation of revolutionary deputies at Versailles, but as what you might think of as a mass collectivity—that is, as a vast aggregation of people likely never to meet each other and whose solidarities rely always on their imagining themselves and each other into a common vessel, such as the left. And, in a parallel way and for parallel reasons, only since the middle years of the Great Depression has it made sense to people to imagine the left as what you might think of as a global collectivity—that is, not only composed of many people, but moreover composed of people in many places, all over the world. The left as we know it today, and as it has been known since the generation of Weil and Law, is something dramatically universal, something seemingly at work in any and all of the world's political provinces all at once.[22]

By contrast, before those middle years of the Great Depression, the left meant only smaller and disparate things. And indeed throughout most of the nineteenth-century world, people made only sparing use of the French revolutionaries' imagery sorting out political beliefs between left and right. More to

---

my point, though, is that on those occasions when people in the nineteenth century did invoke the left, they did so not to conjure anything like a global or mass collectivity. They did so, rather, to refer to one of a few specific parliamentary factions at work in only a few particular countries. Considered against how easily people in our own age think of the left as a sweeping universal, as a political phenomenon encompassing multitudes and effortlessly reaching over national boundaries the world over, nineteenth-century constructions of the left look peculiarly cramped. Three distinctions stand out. First of all, people who talked of "the left" in the nineteenth century imagined only disparate lefts, each separate and nation-bound. Those lefts, quite tellingly, didn't at all add up in sum to any composite or multinational left, or any larger left at all. Nineteenth-century political actors certainly had no notions of a global left, or even of a European left or anything of the sort. Rather, each of the lefts they knew was locked into its own particular nation's political culture — and into that nation's formal political system at that. Second, then, those nineteenth-century national lefts were peopled only by professional politicians, the deputies themselves in parliament, not the masses they represented. In this way, each nineteenth-century left remained rather like the original at Versailles, a countable collectivity that could be fit into a single large room (and into just half of the room, at that, the left half, of course). The third distinction between then and now worth pointing out is that those nineteenth-century lefts — nation-bound and countable — existed always in only a handful of specific countries, all of them in Europe and all of them countries where mass politics had taken root early. Throughout much of the century, the countries most widely understood to have a left were France, Spain, and Italy. Depending on where one was, at times one could hear talk that there was a left as well in Prussia and the German Empire. And by the very end of the century, one could even hear talk here and there of a left in Norway or in some other specific European country.[23] But the label "the left" remained a particularism of these few countries' political domains, not at all a generic term to be applied willy-nilly elsewhere.

In other words, even as the assorted ideologues, partisans, and political scribes of the late nineteenth-century Atlantic world grew familiar with an idea of the left, they still didn't generalize that idea. Instead, they pointed time and again to the same few European countries — no matter where they themselves, those discussing "the left," happened to be. As such, newspaper readers in Panama City could read of the left in 1880, but it would have been in reference to Léon Gambetta's radical republicans in faraway France; and readers of the *Nation,* the New York–based political magazine founded by veterans of abolitionism, could read of the left as well in 1892, but it would have been in reference to secularizing democrats in the style of the late Giuseppe Garibaldi in distant Italy. Even at the century's close, by which time chatter about the left ricocheted across the full expanse of the Atlantic zone — showing up in newspapers everywhere from Edinburgh, Scotland, to Cochabamba, Bolivia — it still didn't follow that anyone thought that the left itself had spread everywhere in between, from the shores of the North Sea to the highlands of the Andes. To the contrary, no matter where talk of the left bounced about in the nineteenth century — throughout the Atlantic world and on occasion beyond, as when word of the 1870 "Manifesto of the Left," written up in Paris, reached newspaper readers in Allahabad, or when word of the left's 1893 protests in the Spanish parliament over postponed elections in Madrid reached newspaper readers in Cairo — all the time the left in question remained one or another of those discrete parliamentary factions in those same few European countries.[24]

This all needs saying because it is easy to assume that the idea of the left has always worked generally the same as it does in one's own time. And historians of modern politics who have written in the decades since the 1930s have described the left's nineteenth-century history in a way that would lead one to think that the left has always been the sweeping universal that it has been since the mid-Depression years.[25] The great historian Eric Hobsbawm, for example, writing during the Cold War, explained to his readers that the string of revolutions in 1848 had realized, however briefly, "the dreams of the left" and the "nightmares of the right." For Hobsbawm, it was as if there had been a left fused together already in 1848 into a single vast transnational continuum — and as if the right had been as well. And the great historian Geoffrey Eley, writing during the neoliberal era that followed the Cold War, similarly explained that the storied nineteenth-century International Working Men's Association (the organization later remembered teleologically as "the First International") had been in the 1860s and 1870s "the main forum" of "the European Left."[26] For Eley, it was as if the left of those decades already had been one sprawling entity spread across the continent, spilling over national and imperial boundaries. My point is that such ways of seeing the left—such generalized and transnationalized understandings of the left—had more to do with the authors' own twentieth- and twenty-first-century political cosmologies than they did with the political universe of the nineteenth century.

For those alive at the time, the left had not dreamt of 1848 and it had not organized itself internationally in the 1860s and 1870s. Neither could it have done the one or the other, in part because there had been no one big thing that was "the left" or even "the European left." The only lefts that people had imagined into being were those nation-bound parliamentary lefts. What's more, at the time those separate lefts hadn't housed the century's most committed revolutionists and socialists, or its greatest emancipators, social egalitarians, and utopians.[27] For instance, the expansive, transnationally circuited working-class solidarity and socialism of the International Working Men's Association had existed as if in a realm of life entirely sealed off from the parliamentary republicanism of the French left or the representative liberalism of the Spanish left.[28] Karl Marx, who took part in the association, thought very little about the left and thought even less *of* it. For Marx, the left didn't mesh with socialism or communism or any working-class internationalism. When he did once mention the left in his writings, while commenting on Prussian politics in 1856 for Horace Greeley's *New-York Tribune,* it was to decry the left for having "betrayed the revolution of 1848" in the German states. What Marx wrote of as the left was not the most dreamy-eyed revolutionaries of the "springtime of peoples" but rather particular Prussian deputies who had proven themselves treacherous bourgeois counterrevolutionaries and who, worse, were always being outwitted by the outright reactionary Junkers to their right. The Junkers would then "laugh in the faces of the gentlemen of the Left." The revolution to come, Marx insisted, had "as heavy an account to settle" with "the gentlemen of the Left" as it did with the reactionaries.[29] His understanding of the left in his own day, then, had little in common with what the left would become in the next century.

But even in the new century, the pieces that would, eventually, make up the left as we know it were slow to fall into place. What had been true in 1848 was still true in 1917, when the Russian Revolution shook the world: people at the time did not at all think of the revolution as the realization of the left's dreams.

—

This was in no small part because in 1917 what they meant by "the left" was still predominantly what people had meant by it in the nineteenth century: one of those parliamentary blocs in only a few specific European countries.

That was so in Spain, where revolution also rippled in 1917. In Spain, the partisans and political talkers of the day did not think of either the Russian or the Spanish revolution as the left's handiwork. In Spain, liberals and republicans in parliament had struck up a "Bloc of the Left" or "Bloc of the Leftists" in 1908, and even though the coalition had foundered shortly thereafter, it had since come to pose a potent memory—"the famous Bloc of the Leftists," the press was already calling it by 1911.[30] And, indeed, the memory of this short-lived parliamentary alliance was powerful enough that it continued to define the idea of the left in Spain throughout the crisis-plagued years of the First World War. By contrast, when people in Spain in 1917 talked revolution—whether they pointed to the seemingly promising one in Russia or to the quickly quashed one in their own country—they didn't frame it as something that struck from the political left but rather as something that sprang from entirely outside of the political sphere, out in a much more expansive atmosphere of social life well beyond politics.[31] The home of the left remained the parliamentary floor; the revolution splashed through the streets and the factories, the rail yards, the working-class neighborhoods, the mines, and even Madrid's notorious prison the Cárcel Modelo.[32] The unrest climaxed in August with a country-spanning general strike, immediately recognized by the press as revolutionary in nature.[33] Yet even though historians have depicted its protagonists as Spain's "revolutionary left," those who made the strike weren't seen by their contemporaries as a left of any sort.[34] In the failed revolution's aftermath, for instance, when the keen political connoisseur Óscar Pérez Solís set about detailing what he called his "panorama of the leftists," he didn't think to look anywhere other than squarely at the country's republican and socialist politicians in parliament, politicians who had recently revamped the famed "Bloc of the Leftists."[35] Likewise, the Spanish revolutionaries of 1917 didn't see themselves as the "revolutionary left" either—the left for them, in its entirety, was made up of politicians in parliament, most of whom kept to fence sitting while the revolution thundered all around. For all practical purposes, the furthest-reaching Spanish revolutionaries of the moment were the anarchists and the

—

anticapitalist syndicalists of the Confederación Nacional del Trabajo, the up-start labor organization known popularly by its initials as the CNT. At the time, and throughout the 1910s and 1920s, the anarchists and syndicalists insisted on posing themselves entirely apart from politics, opposed to it, antipolitical. Indeed, the revolutionaries of the CNT notoriously abstained from even voting in these years. Not until the period accentuated in this book—not until 1936 and the eve of the Spanish Civil War, when the left's meaning would inflate and take flight—would the CNT's revolutionaries consciously join the left, and in doing so take part in its remaking.[36]

Like the Spanish revolution of 1917, the Russian revolution of the same year had little to do with anything then called the left. Vladimir Lenin and the Bolsheviks, whom the revolution catapulted to power in the new Soviet Russia, certainly did not see themselves as part of any larger transnational collectivity called the left, let alone as its vanguard. To be sure, Lenin's capacious political imagination had room in it for vast imagined collectivities such as "the proletariat," "Bolshevism," and "the world revolutionary movement." These, for Lenin, were immense, messianic figures visible the world over. But he didn't envision any analogous, world-spanning left. He knew only small and separate lefts, similar in size to what nineteenth-century political actors had known. However, the lefts that Lenin knew best were quite different in nature from parliamentary factions. He mostly talked about lefts as errant cliques inside of recognized po-litical organizations and movements. Unlike the nineteenth-century notions of the left, then, Lenin's notion lent itself to indiscriminate application—he even seems to have accepted as a rule that any complex group anywhere on the face of the earth would inevitably be plagued by both a left and a right within it. He saw, for example, a left within the working-class movement, and he saw a left within Bolshevism: both of those lefts were cabals always resisting central command's orders. He was, to be clear, far from the first to think of lefts like this. The socialists who bucked their parties' leaderships and rallied to the Bol-sheviks after the October revolution became known in some countries, from the United States to Norway, as their parties' "Left Wingers." Similarly, in Russia, the left wing of the populist Socialist Revolutionary Party split off in November 1917 and, for a short while, allied with Lenin and the Bolsheviks under the name the Left Socialist Revolutionary Party.[37]

—

Hardly his own invention, then, Lenin's idea of the left nonetheless brimmed with novelty, with a fresh modernity, in its generic, abstractive quality. Yet if he saw lefts everywhere, the left that interested him most was the one inside of his own house, inside of the communist movement. And this left, once it took form, became for Lenin his greatest internal enemy, as he conveyed with even the title of his main statement on the matter, the 1920 treatise translated into English the same year as *The Infantile Sickness of "Leftism" in Communism*. The previous year, Lenin had played a dominant role in establishing the Communist International (or Comintern), which historians have seen as — in the words of one eminent scholar — "the only centralized international organization of the Left in history." The irony of such an assessment is that Lenin himself saw the Comintern as an institutional instrument with which to vanquish "the 'Left,'" or "the 'lefts'" (depending on which contemporary translation of his words you prefer). Lenin wrote *Infantile Sickness*, the last of his major intellectual works, in preparation for the Comintern's second congress, in the summer of 1920, and he did so with the aim of cutting down "the 'Left.'" He condemned the "'Left' Communists" as "doctrinaires of revolution" of the worst sort, stubborn anti-authoritarian idealists too childish and naive to accomplish what the Bolsheviks had. And worse than their own ineptitude, Lenin charged, was their insistence on attacking the Bolsheviks for the very virtues that, he knew, had won them the revolution: "iron proletarian centralism," "the strictest discipline," "complete centralization," and "the fullest comradely confidence of all party organizations in the party center." As long as the communist left — as long as any left — stood in opposition to such things, Lenin insisted, it remained an enemy to be buried. But, of course, for him, if the communist left were to outgrow such "infantile" notions it would no longer be the left.[38]

And so Lenin's idea of the left was a provocative paradox. He had gone along with the very modern way of treating "the left" as a general concept that could be applied sociologically to the interior of seemingly any political party, any organization, any movement. Yet he had also made the idea of the left as small as ever. Lenin's communist left was a cluster of schismatic sectarians splitting what he was determined to turn into an obedient and unified fighting force.

Which is to say: even if it quivered with the energy and excitement of conceptual recomposition, Lenin's idea of the left was no nearer to a view of the

———

left as a global, mass collectivity than were the older ideas handed down from the century past. The origins of the left made global and inclusive of the masses remained yet to come. The key years for understanding how the left became a sweeping and combinative universal as grandiose as any of those phony abstractions that by the final days of 1939 could make Dorothy Thompson's stomach turn were the few years just before then, the middle years of the decade, when the likes of Weil and Law set out to make sense of, and to set right, a political world that seemed suddenly and entirely undone. When they tried to piece it together anew, they put together the left anew.

So what had changed? What had happened that people would start to imagine "the left" as a universal of political life on earth? And that they would do so with such deep belief that it would come to seem, almost overnight, as if things had always been so?

Why, that is, did Weil and Law and their generation craft a new sort of politics? Why, in the first place, did their political world seem undone? And why did they then embrace a wider solidarity, a solidarity beyond one's own party, beyond one's own country, and beyond one's own favored ideological "ism"? There's never only one reason for such a great historical swing, and a satisfying answer would not be a short one. But the main reason can be stated straightaway.

The main reason was fascism.

The decade between Adolf Hitler's rise and Benito Mussolini's fall marked the age of fascism.[39] In these years, running from January 1933 to July 1943, images of Hitler and Mussolini and their uniformed enforcers flashed out to the world, dominating daily news, penetrating popular culture, signifying for even far-off people something much more immediate and elemental than "foreign affairs" or "international politics." Hitler and Mussolini, brownshirts and blackshirts, the Nazi regime and the Fascist state: around the world they became known by their performative militarism, their brutalist and ultrastylized aesthetics, their rhetoric of conspiracy and grievance and scapegoats, and — above all else — their violence. "Not little individual, sporadic acts of violence, uselessly spent," as Mussolini had once put it, "but the great, the beautiful, the inexorable violence of the decisive hour."[40]

17

When Mussolini had said this, shortly before the "March on Rome" of October 1922, to speak of fascism had generally meant to speak of his own particular political movement rooted within Italy. By the time Hitler gained power a little more than a decade later, fascism's meaning had escaped the confines of Italy and had begun to run free in the wider world. In the age of fascism that followed, it became commonplace — for people of all sorts of political persuasions, and in places all around the world — to envision fascism as a boundless political force, a global presence with global effect.

There was no shortage of reasons for seeing things so. Later, after World War II, the general sentiment was that much of the talk of fascism before the war had stemmed from mass delusion, the hyperbole of the left run riot — a "brown scare," as some historians would put it later, born of propaganda without any basis in reality.[41] The sentiment depended on a certain kind of political amnesia about just how far and wide fascism had been put to work in the years before the war.

In those years, people had put fascism to work not just in Italy and Germany — and not just in continental Europe — but in a dizzying assortment of places around the world. During the age of fascism, black-shirted men calling themselves fascists patrolled the streets of London, assaulting Jewish pedestrians and unemployed demonstrators, while black-shirted men also calling themselves fascists prowled the streets of Córdoba, Argentina, hunting their political enemies and speaking of their desire to bring about the "violent restitution of the spiritual." In Havana, green-shirted bands of the secretive group known as the ABC took part in gun fights in the city center and took to the streets to break strikes. In industrial Michigan around Detroit, an even more secretive group known as the Black Legion terrorized local labor organizers and made plans to stage a coup d'état to overthrow President Franklin D. Roosevelt. Those known in Peking as the blueshirts organized themselves into what the press called "assassination bodies" to carry out a campaign of political murder, with an eye toward making Chiang Kai-shek into a fascist dictator over China. Uniformed paramilitary squads in Beirut and Damascus — the grayshirts — were quick to fight in the streets and also to straighten their arms into that distinctive gesture that witnesses had no trouble identifying as "the fascist salute."

—

In Johannesburg and Cape Town there were grayshirts as well, running the streets organized as what a local correspondent called "storm-troop battalions," challenging pedestrians — "yelling for the blood," as one report out of Johannesburg put it, "of the natives and Jews." And in Nairobi, white settler colonists held fascist meetings and organized to the point that, as one local described the scene, "the Fascist movement in East Africa is spreading rapidly with the slogan, 'Make Kenya a White Man's Country.'" In São Paulo and Rio de Janeiro, the greenshirts of the paramilitaristic political party the Ação Integralista Brasileira marched in goose step wearing leather boots, offering straight-armed salutes and shouting antisemitic slogans at passers-by; they became notorious most of all for their brutal, even fatal, street violence.[42] Silvershirts in Minneapolis; greenshirts in Cairo; blueshirts in Paris; goldshirts in Mexico City; and, yes, brownshirts in Berlin and blackshirts in Rome — there was no limit to the local improvisations on what became a global theme. And there was no telling where it all was going to end. For all the arguments, then and since, about who specifically was a fascist and who was not, the larger pattern was clear.

And it was the larger pattern that presented the much more urgent political problem for those fearful of fascism and outraged by its rise, those like Weil and Law and all of the others around the world who perhaps thought of themselves as socialists or liberals or communists or anarchists or syndicalists or something else entirely and yet now found that they all had common cause with each other on what, suddenly, mattered most to them in the moment: making sure that, as the slogan of the day had it, fascism shall not pass.

This book is a history of the left's remaking, and more than anything else it was antifascism that remade the left.

Antifascism was the central idea pulling the left together in the years leading up to the Spanish Civil War and then pushing leftists to go to Spain to fight together there. Like any of Thompson's "phonies," antifascism is in a way just a word, meaning only what people make of it and meaningful only to the extent that we make it so. To say that antifascism drove the left's transformation in the mid-1930s is only to begin to explain what that might entail. Still, it is a good way to begin. To understand the left of the middle Depression years — the

—

years when people came to speak of "the left" as a multitude sharing in common some sort of ideological affinity and some sort of political solidarity the world over—what is most important to understand is antifascism.

And it's my contention that to understand the left *since* then, it's also the case that what is most important to understand is antifascism. It certainly does not explain everything about the left, but antifascism has often re-energized the left, and it has consistently unified the left. It has served the left as a political myth and as a promise of moral clarity amid the more typical disillusionment of political commitment. Whereas so much else persistently divides the left, antifascism has often served as its common denominator, both across the world's borders and across the left's internal ideological divides. Antifascism's significance for the left, then, runs both wide and deep.

The pages that follow tell a story of how antifascism first became a global political cause and how that in turn put the left into the form in which it is familiar today. Implicit in the telling is another story as well about how antifascism, and its spectacular clash with fascism during the Great Depression, contributed to the creation of today's political world, despite the many times over the decades since that political observers have held forth on how we've left behind all the ideological extremes and illusions "both right and left" of those ill-fated years.[43] The book, then, is in part about what the history of antifascism has to teach us about the troubled political world we find ourselves still inhabiting in the twenty-first century.

And of all the political ideas that animated the twentieth century and haunt the twenty-first—most of all, those intractable isms, such as fascism, populism, socialism, nationalism, liberalism and neoliberalism, conservatism, and so on—it is antifascism that stands out for remaining so little understood and so little studied.[44] This is so even of the most eventful and consequential phase of its history, the middle Depression years, when countless people turned to antifascism to counter fascism. The turn to antifascism began in the months following the Nazis' rise to power in early 1933 and culminated in the months following the Spanish Civil War's outbreak in mid-1936, by which time the still new and always fragile transnationalized left's antifascist solidarities were already so intensely felt as to compel tens of thousands of people like Weil and Law from around the world to go to Spain and take part there in the great antifascist cause.

Explaining how Weil, Law, and the others came to do so is one way to think of the book's task. The narrative follows these early antifascists ("premature antifascists," they were labeled later) across those deeply formative years that followed the establishment of the Third Reich, the years when antifascism first burst onto the global scene and forthwith waged what remain its most fabled political wars. Antifascism did not, however, score any clear victories in these years; the political age remained defined by fascism. Yet if the era was the age of fascism, you could call these few years within it the antifascist moment, the flash of time when antifascism squared off against fascism and offered humanity a countervision of its fate. To be sure, antifascism has a wider history than just this moment. But nonetheless, looked back upon from today, these few years—the ones I'm suggesting that we think of as the antifascist moment—stand out as the one historical point that is necessary for understanding what antifascism has meant since and why it pulls at political imaginations still.[45]

At the center of the story this book tells is what this antifascist unity brought about during the short period it was sustained. The first two chapters, though, explain the early makings of antifascism in the years before the antifascist moment, beginning in Italy even before the March on Rome. Then the book's attention turns, in the third chapter, to the start of the antifascist moment and the start of the left's transformation. The reach of the left's new solidarities became apparent in the world-spanning Hands Off Ethiopia protests of 1935, the subject of the book's fourth chapter. The mass march that Oliver Law took part in organizing in Chicago in the summer of that year may have stood out by its size, but otherwise it was of a kind with demonstrations in global cities as far flung as Paris, London, New York, Buenos Aires, Havana, Port-au-Prince, Cape Town, and Calcutta. The depth of the left's new solidarities was apparent in the working-class revolt of the following year, when a world-spanning contagion of sitdown strikes—as Weil noted, with revolutionary implications—saw millions of workers on six continents occupy their workplaces. In no small part because of the sitdowns, in 1936 the world seemed suddenly turned upside down, upended by one of modernity's recurrent outbursts of global revolutionary possibility, as in 1789 or 1848 or 1917–1920 or 1968. The social revolutions that the left made in 1936 put center-left parties in power and fueled the making of the welfare state; they also, I argue, acted out new claims of political legitimacy and popular sovereignty that still animate our understandings of politics and the political today. The sitdowns and the broader social revolutionary possibilities of 1936 are the subject of Chapter 5. Then in the last chapter, Chapter 6, the book's narrative concludes by following the likes of Weil and Law to Spain, where they attempted to dig fascism's tomb.

The brief spell of revolutionary promise that was the antifascist moment gave antifascism its enduring imagery of crowds assembled in the streets of the world's metropolises, flashing defiant closed-fisted salutes, chanting "fascism shall not pass," singing, signifying "the people," and forging the solidarities that bound antifascists around the world to each other. One of the reasons why leftists were able to spark a season of social revolution was that they made antifascism in such an unruly fashion, as a street politics of protest, parades, riots and public violence, mass demonstrations, and extralegal occupations. Popular politics such as all this holds a deep, enigmatic power to crack open great transformative possibility. The political theorist Aristide Zolberg once described 1936 as one of modern history's "moments of madness," akin to 1789 or 1848 or one of the other better-recognized years of upheaval. Such moments of madness, Zolberg suggested, are the times when humanity, with sudden energy, revels in a carnival of social liberation.[46] These flash points of possibility then inevitably end with a return to normal politics: popular politics recede and formal politics – institutional and procedural – return.

But after such a rupture the political order does not revert to what it was before. And as illuminating and fascinating as these fleeting outbursts are in their own right – because of how they offer manifest proof of the possibility of other, more deeply democratic and direct, egalitarian, and autonomous ways of political life – their ultimate historical significance lies in how they lastingly transform political life, in how they serve as new beginnings. The capacity of sudden explosions of popular politics to smash established political orders and recompose political beliefs, values, and categories has led the political theorist Andreas Kalyvas to depict such activity as "the politics of the extraordinary."[47]

—

In a moment of political rupture, when formal politics falls apart and extraordinary acts of popular politics fill the public square, basic political concepts begin to slide about. Because of this, the following chapters are organized around spectacular mass events made in the shadows of formal politics, in the places where popular politics rules. By paying close, ethnographical attention to these mass events, you can begin to see how lasting shifts in conceptual meaning sprang forth from the raucous, often hieroglyphic, and unpredictable events in the streets. Riots, brawls, strikebreaking violence, street meetings and mass marches, demonstrations and counterdemonstrations were all political spectacles that continually gave new form and force to the nascent political language of fascism and antifascism. Such episodes often seemed at first glance local events, but their cumulative effect was to alter political imaginations throughout the world. During the social upheavals of 1936 — whether in Paris or Barcelona or Port-au-Spain; Santiago, Flint, or Beirut — unruly spectacles of popular politics solidified fascism and antifascism in people's minds as concepts with global meaning. They did so more emphatically and more directly than did the formal politics of government and parties. The complexity and contingency of the spectacular events in the streets help to explain their power to reshape the meanings of basic political keywords — not just "fascism" and "antifascism," and "right" and "left," but also words such as "democracy" and "revolution." Both the right and the left in the mid-1930s fleshed out their ideas as crowds in the street, in motion, thinking on the go, capturing ideas from perceptions absorbed in action. Which is to say, the street did not simply provide crude force to impose political ideas already sorted out beforehand and from above by recognized thinkers and leaders; the street was where the ideas of the new politics first took form, where the cognitive piecing together and the experimenting in utterance, syntax, gesture, and imagery all took place and drew witness.

It all required considerable efforts of imagination. At the antifascist moment's end, Simone Weil looked back and suggested that recent times had had about them an unreal quality, as if everyone had been living out dreams and nightmares and the starriest hopes in their heads. The political world that people could see and hear around them was transformed, and, Weil thought,

—

it had all come about as a gift of imagination. Accordingly, the book's main title comes from an exclamation of outsize political imagination uttered by the free-spirited polemicist Marceau Pivert at the height of antifascist hopes, in the suddenly revolutionary atmosphere of Paris amid the outburst of sitdown strikes that so impressed Weil. Staged in the aftermath of the newly unified French left's sweeping victories at the polls, the Paris sitdowns filled newspapers and newsreels with scenes of jubilant strikers occupying the factories, reveling in song and dance, and throwing up their arms into the pose still novel enough to prompt explanations in photo captions of what an "antifascist salute" was. Pivert wrote to rebut others' anxious claims that the very qualities of the sitdowns that were inspiring imaginations were also impeding the discipline and organization needed to negotiate what tangible gains were possible. Pivert countered that such concerns suggested a failure to grasp the most valuable lesson offered by the sitdowns, that in such extraordinary moments the scope of the possible is no longer fixed as it was before, that it is no longer even finite. Instead, he insisted that the sitdowns had shown, to anyone who would take their lesson, that "for the audacious EVERYTHING IS POSSIBLE!"[48]

CHAPTER 1

HOW TO FIGHT FASCISM

To fight fascism, you need to know what it is, you need to trace it
back to its genesis, back to before all this profusion of chatter.

—GUIDO MAZZALI, "Come combattere il fascismo," 1924

"Their assailants, numbering two or three, were described by the police
as anti-Fascist," explained one of the news reports out of New York City on
Memorial Day 1927. Police are political theoreticians, as are news reporters,
poets, cranks writing letters to the editor, and anyone else who interprets the
political world around them: anyone, for instance, who politically identifies
oneself, and also — in the way of the police describing utterly unknown assailants as "anti-Fascist" — anyone who politically identifies anyone else. In making
claims of such sorts, all the time in everyday life, people rely on and rearrange
political theories left and right. Which seems very democratic, and it can be,
but it is more to the point that political language is an ungovernable babel of
confusion and cross-purposes. It isn't dictated by the dictionary or any other
particular authority; people use political words how they will, and those words'
meanings are then jostled about in a world's worth of claims and counterclaims,
opinions both knowledgeable and uninformed, and arguments made in both
good faith and bad, not to mention your typical honest misunderstandings.
Did those two or three unknown assailants think of themselves as antifascists —
or "anti-Fascisti," to use another phrasing from the news report — or was this
political identity only a shorthand of the police officers' own reckoning? The
answer isn't entirely clear, but my point is that all of the political words people

———

use – including both the ones they use to identify themselves and the ones they use to identify others – comingle out in the world of political discourse, and they all carry weight. They shape people's political consciousness, their sense of what has happened, and their sense of what might happen next.[1]

What did it mean to be "anti-Fascist" in New York City on Memorial Day 1927? Among other things, one can say that it meant something quite different from what it would mean to be an antifascist, in New York or anywhere else, a decade later. The key difference was that in 1927 antifascism (or "anti-Fascism," as it was then still more commonly written out in English) remained overwhelmingly thought of as a particularism of Italian politics. Whether one was, yes, in Rome or Milan or, otherwise, in New York or Buenos Aires or Algiers or anywhere else in the wider world, the idea of antifascism meant pointing a finger at the Italian regime. In this it operated a bit like how "the left" had in the nineteenth century, when, as I've said, no matter where in the world one was while speaking of the left, the idea of it always meant pointing out one of those same few parliamentary blocs in those same few specific countries (one of which, of course, was Italy). But the parallel isn't perfect. Unlike anything called the left in the nineteenth century, the antifascism of 1927 could indeed take place anywhere, even in places far away from Italy, such as New York. Still, regardless of where one practiced antifascism in 1927, that practice nonetheless served first and foremost as a critique of the totalitarian state ruling over Italy. Little surprise, then, that where this early antifascism materialized outside of Italy it did so largely among the Italian diaspora. In the years between 1921 or 1922 and 1933 or 1934, one almost always had to care in an especial way about the fate of the Italian people to be an antifascist.

However, even then, in the time between those years, it already was becoming clear that to be an antifascist meant in practice not only to defy the Mussolini regime but also to defy all of the millions of people, in Italy and elsewhere in the world, who championed the regime – all of those who, regardless of where they were in the world, were likely to call themselves, or find themselves called, fascists.

Two of whom were the men assailed, and killed, in New York City on Memorial Day 1927. At around eight o'clock in the morning, Joseph Carisi and Nicholas Amoroso ("both members of the Fascisti movement in this country,"

—

26

as the one news report phrased the matter) approached the train station at 183rd Street in the Bronx along with thirteen fellow fascists – or "Fascisti," to use the language of the report. They, the fifteen Fascisti, were all headed to Manhattan to march with "their black shirted brethren" in the city's main Memorial Day parade. As the thirteen others made their way up the stairs to the elevated train station, Carisi and Amoroso lagged behind, Carisi buying an Italian-language newspaper on the sidewalk, Amoroso farther back. One has to guess that they were already wearing their black shirts and that it was this that marked them for attack; it was not made clear in the one report, though some of the other news stories about the incident implied that this was so. Regardless, the two or three anti-Fascisti, if it is indeed fair to call them that, somehow marked Carisi and Amoroso and attacked them. They stabbed them both, Carisi perhaps six times to the neck and more than a dozen times in all, and Amoroso once in the chest. Then one of the anti-Fascisti pulled out a revolver and shot Amoroso through the heart. Both died there in the street, and the anti-Fascisti ran away.[2]

The killing of two Fascisti in the Bronx was but one of three incidents that marred the city's Memorial Day ceremonies with violence. The second occurred just after the end of the city's main parade, the parade that Carisi and Amoroso never made it to. According to that same news report, "400 Fascisti," having marched in the parade, made their way back to their headquarters on West 45th Street, where "three anti-Fascisti" audaciously sprang upon one of the 400. As soon as they struck their victim, "a hundred of his comrades set upon attacking the trio." Somehow, like the two or three anti-Fascisti in the Bronx, these three got away. Later on, the third incident – "in point of numbers and disorder, the most serious," again according to the same news report – took place in Jamaica, Queens, where perhaps 1,000 or more klansmen wearing the white robes of the Ku Klux Klan, along "with 400 women relatives and friends," pressed their way into one of the city's other parades of the day, despite efforts by the police to fend them off. "The result," the report suggested, "was a riot." This was a fair assessment, as after the police tried and failed to keep the Klan from marching, a great brawl broke out among the police, the spectators, the klansmen, and the women marching with the Klan. The ensuing riot lasted longer than ten minutes. "Women fought women, and spectators fought the

---

police and the klansmen as their desire dictated," the report noted. "Combatants were knocked down, klan banners were torn to shreds and at one point the Stars and Stripes was trampled under foot."[3]

What to make of such violent spectacles?[4]

In part because of the violence and in part because of the spectacle, the day's events drew considerable public attention. They became national news overnight and then within a matter of days became international news as well.[5] That was the way of it in the interwar era, when a great cultural acceleration was underway, and events could become news within hours and could be on the front page of newspapers halfway around the world within a day. Nobody famous or powerful, in the typical sense of the word, had been involved, and yet common people practicing popular politics, playing with the form offered by a day of public ritual and civic symbolism, had collectively pieced together a political statement that proved newsworthy even at great distances.[6] It was, to be sure, a messy statement, and not one that any of the various people involved could control. And yet those who had taken part in the day's marching, murder, assault and battery, fisticuffs, and rioting had all ensured that political words such as fascism and antifascism would make their mark on the following day's political discourse and shape the ways that people reading their morning newspapers of choice would set about the daily task of imagining the world they lived in. But the influence of those who had made the day's news in New York shouldn't be exaggerated. It was also the way of news in the interwar era that the span of attention, and the proportion of attention, for any one news story was contracting—almost in inverse relation to the way that, spatially, news stories' reach was expanding. There were limits on how much, and for how long, any one day's events in any one city could exert direct influence on the larger political world.

And so from a historical perspective, the 1927 Memorial Day events in New York City were less influential than they were indicative. They were indicative of their specific time and place, showing what it meant, then and there, to speak of fascists and antifascists, fascism and antifascism. And while the news they made was mostly ephemeral, the day's events have endured in that they have made their way into at least a few history books.[7] Beyond that, they were given something of a second life when they came under an unexpected public scrutiny many decades after the fact, well into the twenty-first century, in 2015. That was when it was noticed that among those arrested when the police had squared off against the klansmen of Queens was the father of Donald Trump, who was at the time running for president of the United States of America.[8] Had his father, the press wanted to know, been a klansman? Even minor events in history are like buried landmines, waiting to explode years, even decades, later. What's more, even those that don't blow up offer us, if we carefully unearth and examine them, a glimpse of the age that produced them. We can begin to acquire a sense of what political keywords such as fascism and antifascism and fascist and antifascist—and "Fascisti" and "anti-Fascisti"—meant in a particular time and place.

In this case, "Fascisti" meant Carisi, Amoroso, the blackshirts who marched in Manhattan, and others like them; "anti-Fascisti" meant the two or three assailants at the 183rd Street station, the trio who took on the 400 near Times Square, and others like them; and "klansmen" meant those who marched in the white-robe uniform of the Ku Klux Klan. There is no hint at all in what was written at the time that anyone, friend or foe, imagined that the klansmen were themselves fascist in any way. Neither was there in the moment any sense that fascists and klansmen belonged together within any larger collectivity that could be called "the right." Or that the anti-Fascisti were "leftists," belonging to anything called "the left." In 1927, the drawing of such connections was still yet to come.

Fascism at this point was not what it would become by the age of fascism. And fascism at this point was also already no longer quite what it had been at its birth. It is an odd thing: more so, I think it is fair to say, than with any of modernity's other grand ideological isms, scholarly discussion of fascism over the decades has centered on how to capture its meaning by fixed definition. A generation of historians, studying fascism comparatively, sought to discover a "fascist minimum"—a "common denominator," as one scholar put it, among diverse political actors.[9] This common denominator, it was suggested, would reveal an immutable and generic essence at fascism's core. And yet, born amid the ideological uncertainty and political disorder wrought by World War I, fascism from the beginning has been exceptionally, radically protean.

—

Which was part of Guido Mazzali's point when he wrote that if you wanted to know what fascism was, you had to trace it back to its genesis. For Mazzali, all of the contestation that had accumulated since fascism's origin regarding the concept's meaning — all of that "profusion of chatter" — had tangled fascism into a theoretical mess. And this he could write already in 1924! His essay on how to fight fascism ("Come combattere il fascismo") appeared in the September issue that year of the Turinese antifascist review the *Rivoluzione Liberale*. It was still less than two years since the March on Rome. Mussolini at the time was still months away from making his move, in January 1925, toward outright dictatorship. He had yet to embrace, and revel in, the label given to his rule by his antifascist enemies: "totalitarian." Likewise that epithet had yet to morph into noun form: the first widely observed accusation of "totalitarianism" would also appear in the coming January — written by an antifascist, in the pages of the *Rivoluzione Liberale*.[10]

Just how early in the history of fascism it was when Mazzali already felt trapped by all the contradictory talk is all the more apparent when one looks beyond Italy. Most of the people in other countries who cared about the world's politics were at that point just beginning to imagine what fascism might mean. It certainly wasn't yet the obsession of global politics that it would be a decade later. What's more, even for those to whom fascism had begun to mean something, what it meant was still something very peculiarly Italian. When blackshirts practiced fascism in the Bronx or Manhattan, it was well understood that they were acting out a specifically Italian form of politics. After all, by no means did the New York Fascisti themselves think of fascism as a political universal even in 1927, three years after Mazzali wrote; rather, even then it was precisely because of their own place in the Italian diaspora, because of their own sense of community-grounded belonging, that they thought themselves entitled to take up the political form.

And yet, as Mazzali pointed out, already in 1924 fascism meant so many things to so many people as to confound anyone trying to make sense of it all. Already it had become an impossible task to sort fact from fiction in what was said about fascism. And already fascists were producing such a barrage of mutually inconsistent claims as to shell-shock anyone trying to construe their ideological aims from what they said. All of which meant, Mazzali concluded,

—

that the thing to do was to wind back time. Study what fascism was at the start. Not because that would show you any fixed essence at fascism's core but because it would allow you then to comprehend fascism's great capacity to change, to calculate and adjust, to twist and shift shape. It would help you to see through all the verbiage thrown about. All those words just got in the way. Only when you know the beginning, Mazzali was saying, can you know what fascism is. More to his point, good antifascist that he was, only when you know what fascism is can you know how to fight it.

So the question then is, how did fascism begin? It is customary to date the birth of fascism to March 23, 1919. That was the day Benito Mussolini — thirty-five years old, a World War I veteran, the firebrand editor of his own polemical newspaper — addressed an indeterminate number of men and women gathered inside a hall facing the Piazza San Sepolcro of Milan. Later, as dictator, Mussolini would put his own stamp of approval on this birth date, even going so far as to make March 23 a national holiday. A volume of some of his early speeches and writings, authorized by Mussolini himself and published in Milan in the eleventh year of his rule, concludes with the text of the speech he gave that morning, and in the volume it is written that this speech marked "the birth of fascism."[11] Historians have tended to agree.[12]

Yet an oddity of this is that, judging by what is documented of the meeting, neither Mussolini nor anyone else made any mention of fascism in the day's speeches.[13] The closest he himself got to expressing any idea of fascism that day was to refer — once — to "the fascisti." Toward the end of his speech, he pronounced that the day's meeting would "commit the fascisti to sabotage, by any means," the campaigns of their political enemies.[14] By "fascisti" Mussolini meant those who joined a local branch — a "fascio" — of the new organization that the meeting was intended to launch, the Fasci di Combattimento, "fasci" being the plural form of "fascio."[15]

The vocabulary, though, wasn't original. When Mussolini spoke at San Sepolcro it was about four months since the armistice had gone into effect to end World War I, which is to say that it was almost five years since the war had begun in the summer of 1914. Already in the fall of that first year of war political pressure groups calling themselves fasci had sprung up in Italy, demanding that the country abandon its neutrality and intervene in the war.[16] In

—

May 1915, when agitation for war was at its peak, various fasci throughout the country staged dramatic and volatile mass demonstrations in the name of "interventismo." These demonstrations attracted thousands of pro-war protesters, by then well known as "the interventisti." In Milan, the demonstrations were particularly theatrical and emotionally charged, marked by crisp choreography and haunting chants in the streets of the city center. Mass protest went on there for several days in a row in the middle of the month. An observer of the immense May 15 march, though unsympathetic to the cause, couldn't help but acknowledge that "the spectacle offered by the demonstrators — all members of the Fasci interventisti — had something lugubrious and impressive about it."[17]

Among those who addressed the mid-May crowds in Milan was Mussolini himself. He had spoken two days before the big march, at an open-air mass meeting in the city's central square, the Piazza del Duomo. And yet he had come late to the movement. When war had broken out abroad the previous summer, he had been a prominent member of the Italian Socialist Party and the editor of its main daily newspaper, *Avanti!* At the time, he had conformed to the party line backing the government's policy of neutrality, and he had stuck to it even as the fasci interventisti began to stir in early autumn. But by the end of October he had gone over to interventismo. In response, the executive committee of the Socialist Party — still staunchly "neutralista" — stripped him of his post at *Avanti!* Unabashed, Mussolini promptly started up his own newspaper, the *Popolo d'Italia.* From its very first issue, on November 15, 1914, the new daily prosecuted the interventista case with brio. What stood out by far about the paper, though, was the ferocity of its attacks on "the neutralisti" — Italian liberals and Mussolini's fellow socialists, too; all of those who opposed war, and who did so, Mussolini charged, for the basest of reasons. Only nine days after the *Popolo d'Italia* first went to press, a new fascio in Rome saw fit after its inaugural meeting to send a telegram to Mussolini praising not only his paper's pro-war rhetoric but also, more to the point, its "courageous anti-neutralista campaign." On the same day, November 24, at a rowdy meeting in Milan's Teatro del Popolo, Mussolini watched on as he was expelled from the Socialist Party. Within days, he was exhorting his paper's readers to form fasci of their own.[18]

—

And by the following May, when he spoke in the Piazza del Duomo, he was wholly dedicated to the fasci's cause – or, as he and others had already started calling it: "the fascist movement."[19]

It was, to be sure, far from the most common way to identify those who were aggressively agitating for war in late 1914 and early 1915. But nonetheless there it was, fully recognized, alive and in action in the streets of Italy in the spring of 1915, before the country had even entered World War I: the fascist movement. It was, no matter what name one put to it, a sprawling, effective, and violent force of popular politics. Aside from Mussolini's set in Milan, the movement could also produce crowds in Rome, Ferrara, Turin, Genoa, Venice, Naples, Parma – in cities all over Italy. Everywhere the crowds generated a palpable energy. The day before his speech, Mussolini had alluded to this in the *Popolo d'Italia* with his observations on what made for a "'fascist' demonstration." At times that week, the crowds turning out in Milan chanted for the death of the neutralista political bloc's leader, the legendary liberal parliamentarian Giovanni Giolitti. Early in the week, Mussolini had written that the deputies in parliament could not be trusted and that the people must take matters into their own hands; he had added that he was becoming "more and more firmly convinced" that "a few dozen of the deputies need to be shot, SHOT, I say, in the back." Parliament, he had charged, had become a "pestiferous plague poisoning the blood of the Nation. It must be exterminated."[20] And so amid the dynamism of fascist demonstration, Mussolini's ideas of nation were congealing, as were his ideas of violence.

For his speech in the Piazza del Duomo, Mussolini stood in front of the cathedral's main door. The crowd faced him in the piazza. He gave a short speech, as was his way in those days, and finished by exclaiming, "Long live the war! Long live the revolution!" Those who made and joined the fasci did so for many different – even clashing – reasons, but for Mussolini and others like him, the premise of a certain relationship between war and revolution was the determining one. A small fascio in Milan, the Fascio Rivoluzionario d'Azione Internazionalista, had laid out the premise clearly in an October 5, 1914, manifesto. The thirteen men who signed the document were, generally speaking, revolutionary syndicalists, though in their text what they did was to take precepts familiar to revolutionary syndicalism and rework them into something new. Typical revolutionary syndicalist theory had it that a general strike would trigger the great social revolution to come; now the manifesto writers claimed that a general *war* would. Just as much of a twist, and just as crucial to the making of fascist ideology, was a second claim. It was no longer the proletariat that would make the revolution, it was the nation. Instead of rushing into a proletariat-driven world revolution, the manifesto's authors sought first of all what they called "national revolutions." These they depicted as great moral trials that would reveal who truly belonged to the nation—and who did not. Theirs was a sharply exclusionary nation, an enclosed community "formed," the manifesto read, "by language and race." These were all ideas that would stick to fascism: there would be a revolution, and it would be a national revolution; war abroad would trigger the revolution at home; the nation, and not the proletariat, would make it; and language and race determined who made up the nation. All of this was subtext to Mussolini's cry of "Long live the war! Long live the revolution!"[21]

The crowd took up the exclamation as a chant, and then another orator rose and took over. In truth, Mussolini's speech wasn't the main draw; none of the speeches was. The crowd itself was the thing—the "spectacle" of it, as Mussolini had put it in his speech. The energy to shape the movement, and to direct it, didn't lie in the discourse of demagogues in May 1915; it was in the theatrics of the gathered crowd. The movement's nature remained mutable, quicksilver and indefinite; the quotation marks Mussolini had used to qualify "fascist" when he had nodded to "'fascist' demonstration" had captured well the ambiguous state of the movement—and also his own ambivalent relation to it. In the moment, he could tell that a fascist vocabulary was spinning through the air, and yet he also remained hesitant to claim it as his own or to validate it fully. He spoke of the fascist movement, yes, but he didn't swear by its name. And he didn't presume to lead it. He certainly didn't claim—yet—to have created it. The fascist movement, however, was indeed being created in the spring of 1915; it was being created in motion, in the streets and piazze, its makers experimenting on the fly and trying to figure out how to throw the country into war. Everything about it was urgent and unruly.[22]

And generative: already by mid-May 1915, the most radicalized among the protesters had created a basic grammar of fascist politics. Not only were they calling their organizations "fasci" and suggesting that they had made a "fascist movement" and that certain demonstrations were "fascist" as well, they were also already speaking of themselves as "the fascisti." Such was the case, for instance, at a fascio's meeting in Milan on the evening of May 18, a few days after Mussolini's piazza speech. Mussolini went and delivered another of his brief speeches, but more noteworthy for the history of fascism than anything he said was how those in attendance spoke to each other. They expressed weariness from the past week's tumult; and they expressed confidence that they were cudgeling the country toward war. No one at the meeting that evening knew that the Italian government had already entered into a secret agreement—the "Pact of London"—with Britain, France, and Russia, establishing the terms of Italy's entrance into the conflict. Indeed, the government had done so before all of the unrest of May. Only five days after the fascio's meeting, Italy declared war on Austria-Hungary. But those present believed they still had more work to do in the streets. One of them pleaded with the others not to become discouraged by how few in number they themselves were but rather to take satisfaction and find joy—"virile joy"—in knowing that, few as they were, they had already led "the people of our city" to a glorious victory with the past few days' "action in the piazza." The glory of the mass demonstrations had proven just how much they themselves, they the few, could accomplish. And as the scene was depicted in the next day's *Popolo d'Italia*, this person had called them, the few, "the fascisti."[23]

Yet for all the talk of fasci, the fascist movement, fascist demonstration, and fascisti in the spring of 1915, there was no talk of "fascism" itself. This was so even though there was no shortage of abstract political speech in Italy at the time. Discourse on the classical nineteenth-century isms—liberalism, socialism, conservatism, anarchism, republicanism, and the like—abounded. By 1915 these were all longstanding universals of global politics, familiar not only in Italy but throughout much of the world. This was apparent in how people talked of them, as if they were indeed the very elements of all political life on earth. What's more, as much talk of the grand universals as there was in Italy in 1915, there was even more talk of interventismo and neutralismo, the two novel abstractions particular to the country's political circumstances. It's not, then, as if people talking politics in Italy at the time shied away from abstraction. It's closer to the truth to say that they were political theoreticians all. Even so, in all that day-to-day political theorizing there still was no discussion of anything called fascism. That, however, would still largely (though not entirely) be the case four long years later when Mussolini addressed another Milanese fascio, at San Sepolcro on March 23, 1919. To think of that date as marking the birth of fascism, then, is to point to a date both too late and too soon.

Time plays tricks. This is well known. Look to remember a moment in the past, and layers of intervening time will stand in your way and stymie your view. This was much of Mazzali's point. So consider what the genesis of fascism looked like from the vantage point of 1938, when one of the foundational histories of fascism went to press in Paris, written by an antifascist living there in exile from Italy. Angelo Tasca called his book a history of "the birth of fascism." He wrote that the birth had taken place at San Sepolcro. And he wrote (in French) that most of those who had gathered there were "former 'interventionists' of the left" from 1914 and 1915. What did it mean, for Tasca in 1938, to say that certain interventisti had been "of the left"? Or, if you prefer the English translation of his book that also went to press in 1938, that they had been "former left-wing 'interventionists'"? What did that mean, that they had been "left-wing"? The answers to these questions should help to clarify why no small number of historians have assigned "left-wing revolutionary origins" to fascism and seen it, at birth, as part of Italy's "interventionist Left," or its "nationalist left." Or, to pose the problem in a more general way, the answer should help to clarify just what the role of the left was, and was not, in the birth of fascism.[24]

In the era of World War I, Tasca had still been in Italy, active in politics, a member of the Italian Socialist Party. After the war, he took part in the creation of the Communist Party of Italy, in 1921, and then he was expelled from it as well, in 1929, for practicing what was yet another new ism of the times: anti-Stalinism. Lenin had died in 1924, and Josef Stalin had taken command of the considerable machinery of transnational political power that was the Comintern. When Tasca went to Moscow to represent the Italian party in Comintern discussions, he made the mistake of questioning Stalin's eminently questionable

—

maneuvers to consolidate his own control over the German Communist Party. Stalin responded by accusing Tasca of siding with what he called "the Right danger" in the German party. Stalin, like Lenin before him, spoke of the left and right as internal factions to be scrubbed out of communism — communism was still not yet part of the left; a left and a right (lamentably for Stalin, or, perhaps, conveniently for him) were parts of communism. When Stalin spoke against Tasca, the Italian party leadership listened, and promptly expelled him. Among the charges that the leadership leveled against Tasca was that he had tried to mobilize "democratic components" of the Italian petite bourgeoisie "for a so-called antifascist struggle." And of this Tasca was surely guilty. He had never accepted the Comintern's doctrine of the day that petit bourgeois social democrats were "social fascists," fascism's special enablers. The claim was too abstract, too unconcerned with historical specificity, and too much at odds with his own witness of fascism's rise. Indeed, one way of looking at Tasca's book is to see it as his historically grounded explanation of just how unfounded was Stalinist high theory of fascism.[25]

Not only did Tasca intend his book as a work of anti-Stalinist scholarship, though, he also intended it as a work of antifascist scholarship. By teaching his readers fascist history, he meant to inspire in them antifascist commitments. Which is not to idealize Tasca's scholarship or his politics. A few years later he would take a post in the Vichy regime, answering to its ministry of propaganda and writing for a collaborationist newspaper. More to my point, however, is that the antifascism Tasca knew and practiced in Paris in 1938 wasn't the same antifascism that he had known and practiced in Italy in the 1920s. Antifascism had changed, in large part because fascism had changed. Even more to my point is that Tasca's understanding of fascism — and of the general makeup of the political world — in his present of 1938, as he finished writing his history, had stymied his view of the past. In Paris, in the early 1930s, he had begun writing on international politics for the French Socialist Party's newspaper, and by the time of the Spanish Civil War, he was writing of fascism as a universal force, very much at work in Spain and beyond. Likewise, he wrote about the war effort to save the Spanish Republic as if it were obvious that it was a universal fight against fascism: he wrote of it as, flat out, "the antifascist war."[26] It was

—

at this point, after he had come to see fascism and antifascism as unmistakably universal political forms, easily practiced wherever, that he tried to look back in time to write his history of fascism's birth.

That timing begins to explain his mention of "left-wing" interventisti. Tasca had in mind the interventisti who had arrived at their interventismo from ideological backgrounds of socialism and revolutionary syndicalism. In 1938, with the Spanish Civil War well underway, rank-and-file socialists and revolutionary syndicalists were all obvious left-wingers, very much a part of the global, mass collectivity that was – by 1938 – the left. It largely had been the new, universalized forms of fascism and antifascism that had made this so. The new far-reaching antifascist solidarities made it easy for Tasca in 1938 to imagine "the left" as a catchall term for any and all socialists and revolutionary syndicalists, not to mention social democrats, anarchists, and communists everywhere, and a good many liberals, democrats, and republicans around the world as well. But go back to 1914 and 1915 or 1919: examine the pages of the *Popolo d'Italia* from those years, read through the texts of early fascist speeches, or even look at what the interventisti's enemies said of them at the time. As Mazzali implored, go back to the beginning. You'll see that at the time the idea of affixing the rubric "left-wing" to interventisti in the streets would have made little sense. At the time "the left" still had a much smaller range of meaning: either the politicians in parliament who took their seats on the left side of their chamber (that customary meaning handed down from the nineteenth century) or else the members within a political organization who pushed the group to adopt more radical aims (the meaning of left put to use by the likes of Lenin and Stalin). There hadn't been any grand notion of "the left" as a mass social collectivity that would include any of the people who gathered in the piazze and cried for war; the only interventisti that were in any way "left-wing" in the Italy of World War I had been a handful of pro-war parliamentary politicians, not anyone who would go to San Sepolcro.[27]

The same sort of skip in time occurs when historians point to Mussolini's youthful socialism and revolutionary syndicalism to suggest that before World War I he had been, as one scholar has put it, "the head of the revolutionary Left." It has followed that much of the debate over Mussolini's ideological trajectory has turned on the question of whether he was, as has been argued, "still

—

a man of the left" after his expulsion from the Socialist Party — and whether he was, more to the point, still a man of the left when, it is supposed, he "founded" fascism.[28]

But Tasca, consciously or not, had written his present into his past. Which is something we all do; it is, again, one of time's tricks. Does it matter? It's no sin to use a word in a way that is meaningful to you in the present to describe something in the past. But it can lead you to assume that the word was already meaningful in the same way; it can keep you from seeing the creative work that people had to do in the meantime to fill the word with the meaningfulness that it now affords you. And it can confuse cause and effect, make you think that one thing shaped another, when really it happened the other way around. To say that fascism had "left-wing revolutionary origins," or that the first fascists were "of the left," or that Mussolini himself was "a man of the left": these phrasings all take a meaning of the left that only came about later and transpose that meaning onto the earliest history of fascism. Such phrasings can make you think there's something about the left that birthed fascism. Such a thought presents a problem of historical understanding. Because cause and effect ran the other way. Fascism emerged first; then, after that, and in large part because of it, people who didn't have any particular solidarities with each other — people who *didn't* see themselves and each other as sharing any big collectivity called "the left" — started to make common cause with each other. They chose to begin imagining themselves bound together; they eventually began to imagine that there *was* a mass, global collectivity called the left. Socialists, communists, liberals, labor radicals, revolutionary syndicalists, anarchists, and people of other ideological sorts, too; people in one party or another, people without a party; people in one country or another, people strewn about the world: they didn't all add up to "the left" or anything else when fascism began. Rather, fascism gave them all cause to form unfamiliar solidarities with each other. The name for that cause, the name for those solidarities, in sum, was antifascism.

A monster had been slain. So proclaimed the venerable Turinese liberal daily the *Stampa* one day in the summer of 1919. In the pages of the era's newspapers, such things happened with some regularity. Politics took place, then as now, in a world of enchantments, mystery, and fabulous creations.

—

Those creations included those gargantuan isms, yes, but even beyond the likes of liberalism, socialism, conservatism, and so on, abstract forms lived — and died — alongside humans day after day in the particularly strange and fantastical realm that was the political world of the interwar era. The political discourse of even the era's soberest newspapers was full of divers fanciful figures. There was nothing entirely new in this; throughout modernity people have described their political world as a place where specters haunt, fates interfere, furies rage and terrorize, heavens darken, and monsters stamp about. And in the third week of June 1919, the *Stampa* announced that one of those monsters, undoubtedly one of the worst ever to prey upon the land, had been struck dead. It was explained that the beast had shown itself in life to be a "monster of political immorality," an "unnatural hybrid creature." The monster's name, the paper said, was fascism. It had been very young when it died, and it had only existed at all because the war had disordered the times. But now the monster was dead, and the people could rejoice and live in peace under liberal government once more.[29]

This was almost three months after San Sepolcro, but the monster of fascism that the *Stampa* knew and loathed in the summer of 1919 wasn't at all defined by Mussolini and the Fasci di Combattimento. They remained a negligible danger; what's more, for his part, Mussolini was proving surprisingly slow to pick up on this new word "fascism." He usually had a fine ear for novel political language, but he couldn't quite absorb the possibilities of this particular new word. The fascism that the *Stampa* was suggesting had just died was a much larger beast than Mussolini's fasci. Fascism, in the summer of 1919, meant the whole of interventista politics. The fasci had not melted away when Italy intervened in the war but instead had grown in power. Indeed, it hadn't taken long for the fascist movement to extend beyond the popular politics of the streets and to make its way into the preserves of formal politics in parliament.[30] During the war, in December 1917, more than 200 deputies and senators sympathetic to the fasci and the cause of interventismo had established a parliamentary caucus known popularly as "the Fascio." The politics that the Fascio practiced became known as "fascism" ("fascismo" in Italian). But now, in June 1919, the *Stampa* could crow that fascism was a carcass, because Italy's chamber of deputies, the Camera dei Deputati, had voted to affirm the liberal

—

order — to abandon "the politics of war" and restore an atmosphere of normalcy. Finally, the paper assured its readers, "the Fascio and fascism are dead and buried."[31]

The deputies who joined the Fascio had come to it from all ideological quarters. But once they organized the caucus, they chose as the group's home the benches on the far right of the deputies' chamber. No one went further than Edoardo Giretti, a deputy of the Italian Radical Party. He was an industrialist and free-trade liberal from the north, a brave antiwar voice during the Libyan campaign of 1911, and a pacifist of international renown for years before that. In World War I, though, he had embraced interventismo. In 1917 he became one of the first "fascist deputies," as they were called, and he quickly gained notoriety for his ferocious denunciations of neutralismo. Now in the deputies' hall those on the room's left side heckled him as he took his place, as one observer put it, "among his new friends" on the room's right side.[32]

His new friends were as prone as he was to denounce their ideological enemies sitting on the left. The most sensationalistic of the parliamentary fascisti's attacks came less than two weeks after the armistice that ended the war on November 11, 1918 (Italy had formalized its victory over Austria-Hungary one week earlier). In a floor speech in the chamber of deputies, a fascist frontbencher named Carlo Centurione accused Giolitti, a few other liberals, and several socialists of treason. The accusation was a retort to an earlier one leveled by socialist deputies against Centurione: that he had spied on them. Now he admitted that, yes, he had. And he was, he said, proud to have done so. He explained that he had disguised himself as a porter and kept a close watch over them; in his spying he had become convinced (and, he said, he had documentation proving) that they had plotted to betray the nation. It was because of them, he charged, that in August 1917 there had been an insurrection in Turin. And it was because of them that the country's military forces had lost the catastrophic battle of Caporetto in November of the same year. As soon as he voiced his accusations, a predictable tumult overtook the chamber. Those on the left rose in outrage; those on the right cheered him on.[33] It was a dramatic scene; only later would it be established that his accusations were baseless. They were cynical, opportunistic lies. Yet they were lies of the sort that can draw long-lasting, unswerving belief because they seemed, for those who believed them,

—

to tap into something like a deeper form of truth with a power to expose the falsity of what others took to be true.[34] Belief among the Italian fascist faithful that liberalism and socialism had conspired to betray the nation at Caporetto persisted throughout the fascist era. More to the point, the belief—the very word "Caporetto"—came to serve as a meta-explanation for why socialism and liberalism were never to be trusted again.

Centurione didn't accomplish that on his own, of course. But nonetheless the coverage in *Avanti!* of the "spectacular day" in the chamber of deputies noted the fabulous quality of his speech. More than one news report suggested that an aura had settled over the room as soon as the session opened, as if to foretell that something extraordinary was going to happen. As the *Avanti!* correspondent explained, "It was clear that something was in the air."[35]

Centurione's shamelessness, though, took everyone by surprise. In the days that followed, *Avanti!* described the fascist deputy as a "semi-aristocratic" young scoundrel, "notoriously amoral" and corrupt. The paper also called him "the most ardent champion of fascism."[36]

That last word—"fascismo" as it appeared on the printed page of the November 24, 1918, edition of the socialist newspaper—was very new. It wasn't one that any of the fascist deputies appear to have ever used in their parliamentary oratory. It wasn't a word used before much at all. This was only days removed from the armistice. The peace conference in Paris hadn't even begun yet. San Sepolcro was still four months in the future. And yet it was true, as the correspondent from *Avanti!* had sensed when the deputies' session had opened the day before, the day of Centurione's speech, that something was in the air.

Such was the nature of fascism when sundry fascisti gathered at San Sepolcro. Many had been, as Tasca would later note, interventisti in 1914 and 1915, when they had begun piecing together a fascist politics. Fascism wasn't born in the trenches. It didn't come about because rough experience at the front hardened the hearts of young men. And it didn't come about because soldiers came home and applied military order and discipline to political life. It can't be stressed enough: by the time Italy joined the war, the fascist movement was already underway. The source of fascism was not the experience of the war but rather an expectation for it. The first fascisti were those who, before any of

—

them went off to fight in the World War, craved its coming. Fascism came of their yearning for a warrior ethos; it came from a mythic vision of war's transformative powers. Sublime and revelatory — "the horrible and necessary holocaust," Mussolini once called it — war was to deliver the revolution of nations.[37]

If you see the fascist movement taking form before Italy entered the war, certain aspects of its nature, otherwise obscured, become clear. If fascisti were in the streets in the spring of 1915, it means that they had already taken up their struggle before Caporetto. It means they had taken up their struggle before the October Revolution in Russia. Contrariwise, accept Mussolini's premise that he delivered the speech of fascism's birth on March 23, 1919, and it is easy to accept other premises instead: such as the familiar claim that fascism came into being as a counter to bolshevism; or that the recklessness of "the left" led, pendulum-like, to the fascist reaction of "the right." But look to 1915 and you can see the fascisti waging their revolution while Lenin sat reading books in Switzerland. Call it premature fascism if you like, but the fascisti had fashioned a singular vision of revolution and power and truth before they experienced the war, and well before they had to reckon with the idea of bolshevik revolution.

The idea of revolution — their own idea of it — was crucial for the first fascisti. In the days before the San Sepolcro meeting, as Mussolini tried to drum up enthusiasm, he boasted, "We interventisti are the only ones in Italy who have the right to speak of revolution." He explained, "We have already made the revolution. In May 1915." Whether what the interventisti had accomplished amounted to revolution is debatable, but his words capture a certain irony: believing that war would deliver revolution, interventisti had agitated in such a way that they themselves delivered something at least akin to it. That they'd delivered it from political agitation at home and not from war abroad was crucial to the making of fascism: if the war had made fascism, then fascist nationalism very well might have faced outward and identified its enemies far afield; as it was, formed from the political struggle inside Italy over the question of intervention, fascist nationalism looked inward. The most hated enemy wasn't Germany, and it wasn't Austria-Hungary. It was those who sought to deny the fascisti their war. The enemy was within. In May 1915, one of the most ferocious voices of the fasci, Maria Rygier, insisted this was the "moral" revealed by the moment: that interventisti must "watch out" for "the worst internal

—

enemies."[38] Because the enemy was within, the fascisti would conduct politics as if politics were war. Much about fascism has changed over the decades since, but it has always been so that to become a fascist is to incite civil war, wherever one is. The enemy is always near.

Throughout this all, though, the enemy for the fascisti was "the neutral-isti."[39] It wasn't "the left" and it wasn't "antifascism." Antifascism, and a new conception of the left, came only when many disparate political actors, scattered far and wide, consciously decided to reach out to each other and work together, despite all their many real differences, to fight fascism.

May Day 1921: it's reasonable to say that by this day's end fascism had spread beyond Italy's borders out into the wider world. Even so, that's not how I want to say it. How does an abstraction move around in the world? Does it truly "spread"? Outward from a source of origin to the rest of the world? Does it "diffuse," as the timeworn phrase about "the diffusion of knowledge" would have it? Or does it "circulate" like blood, money, and rumor? "Spread," "diffuse," "circulate," and the like—such explanations by metaphor all carry their own theory of how something immaterial gets from one place to another. An apt metaphor, Orwell once wrote, "assists thought by evoking a visual image."[40] The danger of metaphors, though, is in what they presuppose. Because they have such vivid explanatory powers, they risk making their presuppositions our own. Because they shine such bright light on some questions, they throw others into the dark.

All metaphors involve magic of some sort. When they truly do assist our thought, it is, as Orwell said, because they have conjured before us an image (an imaginary image) that somehow helps us to see something else (something real, yet somehow hidden from our eyes without the assistance of the meta-phor's magic). But metaphors can also be magic tricks, sleights of hand lead-ing our eyes away from what's actually happening. They can make us presume something when we should question everything. Already, I've fallen for the trick: I asked how an abstraction moves around in the world. What if it's a mis-take even to picture it "moving"? Don't trust the metaphor, don't presuppose. Take a step back and ask the question again in a more elementary way, stripped of as many assumptions as you can manage. Instead of assuming abstractions "move" from place to place, let's ask the question again like this: how does an abstraction appear someplace new? Which is to say, since an abstraction is an invention of the mind, how do people come to imagine that an abstraction has appeared someplace new? How do they come to believe that it is now present where they had once believed it was absent?

One simple point worth stressing is that people have to do the work of making an abstraction seem present someplace new. That alone complicates any idea that fascism "spread" from Italy to the wider world. Abstractions don't spread themselves; people spread them. It's better, then, to say that fascism *was* spread than to say that fascism *did* spread.

But then there's the further point that I want to stress. Even to say that fascism was spread from Italy to the wider world suggests a scenario of people in Italy pushing fascism outward, casting fascism – premade – out into a passive, receptive world. By shining a bright, tight beam on the question of what people in Italy might have done to put fascism out in the wider world, the metaphor throws into darkness what people elsewhere might have done to pull it out.

It's the wrong metaphor: by the end of May Day 1921 it had been a small number of people in New York City, and not anyone in Italy, that had done the crucial work to make fascism's presence felt in the city. It isn't clear who all was involved, but it does seem safe to say that on May Day or the day before several people held a meeting at the Associazione Politica degli Italiani Redenti, in a building, long since demolished, at 17 Charles Street in Greenwich Village. At the meeting, the attendees declared that they were forming a fascio of their own. They announced the founding with a telegram to Milan stating, "The first Fascio Italiano di Combattimento of the United States has assembled today and salutes all of the Fasci of Italy." Three men's names were given as signatories at the telegram's end: Agostino De Biasi, Umberto Menicucci, and Cesare Passamonte.[41] De Biasi, the editor of the local Italian-language journal the *Carroccio*, appears to have done much of the spadework that led to fascism's appearance in New York, though he himself took no title in the new fascio's official hierarchy.

As the trio likely intended, their message ended up in the hands of Mussolini, who at the time was campaigning for a seat in the chamber of deputies; the March on Rome was still almost a year and a half in the future. Mussolini

—

promptly threw up a front-page headline in the *Popolo d'Italia:* "Fascism has crossed the Atlantic."[42]

This, again, was a reasonable way to see it: fascism's presence in New York made it easy to imagine that the once Italy-bound abstraction had set out on a voyage across the ocean and made landfall in New York. But, once more, fascism doesn't spread itself. And neither had Mussolini or anyone else in Italy spread fascism to New York. It cuts closer to the truth to say that those now self-identifying fascisti in New York had reached out into the world and pulled fascism in toward them, into New York. However one sees it, though, it's worth remembering just how interpretive and abstract the whole affair was. In a material sense, what had crossed the Atlantic hadn't been fascism east to west but rather a telegraphic signal sent west to east.

Mussolini exclaimed that the dispatch filled him "with joy." He lavished his "comrades in New York" with praise, even if he couldn't quite bring himself to call them fascisti. He also claimed that this was not the first time that fascism had gone out into the world beyond Italy: he wrote that fascism had completed a Mediterranean crossing even earlier, that a fascio was already anchored in Tripoli. Whether or not that was true isn't clear; regardless, the fascisti of New York soon took to suggesting that they themselves had created the first fascio outside of Italy. Mussolini, meanwhile, proclaimed that other fasci were presently being organized "in the main cities of Egypt," and, what's more, he promised "hundreds" of new fasci before the year was out—"in all of the republics of North, Central, and South America." Before the end of the month, an international banker and self-described "Italian officer with four years at the front" organized a fascio in Cleveland. Before the end of the year, a set of Italian emigrants organized another in Philadelphia. There were not, to be sure, hundreds of fasci in the Americas by year's end, as Mussolini had hyped. But new groups did soon take form, and there were fasci from Schenectady and Boston to São Paulo and Buenos Aires by the middle of 1923.[43]

By then the fascio in New York had become a fighting force. By then fascisti launched forth from their headquarters on East Fourteenth Street in black-shirt uniform. By then De Biasi was prepared to "transform the Fascio in America into an organ of attack and defense against all the forces unfurled against Fascism." And by then he knew to call those forces "the anti-fascist movement." On

—

that point, the people in New York who made up those forces and made that movement entirely agreed. By the spring of 1923, they were calling themselves "anti-Fascisti."[44]

As had happened with fascism, it hadn't taken very long for antifascism to show up far from Italy. But also as with fascism, antifascism in its earliest days was thought of as something decidedly, even inherently, Italian. Antifascism — again, just like fascism — had very quickly proved itself a protean and unpredictable political idea.

Well before the March on Rome, unmoored notions of antifascism had begun to drift about in Italian political talk. Their drift followed the wake made by fascist violence. More so than any other of modernity's major ideologies, fascism has drawn its meaning from violence. The interventisti's desire for war, their idealization of a warrior ethic, and their eagerness to see political adversaries as their mortal enemies had all steered fascism from the beginning toward an emphasis on violence. While it's fair to say that all of the ideologies that have shaped modern political history have been aided by violent acts of various sorts, fascism stands out as the one whose practitioners have elevated violence — above all, physical, unmediated, face-to-face violence — beyond the instrumental and into the transcendent.

The ultimate experience for the early fascisti was the "punitive expedition," a military-style, large-scale raid carried out by squads of blackshirts. Marcello Gallian, one of the blackshirts too young to have fought in the war, described the sensation of setting out by truck on an expedition "to 'cleanse'" a neighborhood or town. The fascisti's "hatred," he explained, "became enchanted" upon the truck's arrival. Years later, looking back, he remembered the expeditions as surreal scenes of blood, thirst and bricks, ruins, extended idleness and bursts of predation, vomit and spit, endless walls and gates, fatigue, and a "frenzy that made us sing out loud," all followed by the quiet of the return, "our comrades a few fewer in number than before," and those still standing possessed by "the same fantasy of action" as before. "The idea of romping, breaking, splitting open, transforming the physical frontier," he wrote, "became a spiritual need."[45]

The point, though, was to let the spirit of the punitive expeditions bleed into everyday life. In 1920, 1921, and 1922, fascism happened in the form of

—

beatings in the street, brawls in the square, buildings burnt in daylight, public humiliations and beards ripped out, victims dragged by rope, bullwhippings, purgations, and public executions, some of them mock and some actual. The fascisti were endlessly experimental with their violence. They were also always visually and aurally provocative. Squads marched in the streets; they wore black and shouted out songs; they exchanged stylized salutes and hollered war cries. They harassed passers-by and then sang some more. Their arsenal included revolvers, cudgels, castor oil, sticks, and the spiked trench clubs favored by the soldiers of Austria-Hungary in the war.[46] Much of the violence was meant to terrorize. And to display the expansive impunity with which they could stab, bully, cudgel, kick and punch, kidnap, humiliate, and murder as they pleased. But it all was also ever an expedition into the interior of one's self, to create the need within that Gallian called spiritual.

Modern politics wasn't peaceful before the fascists came along, certainly not in Italy, but they nonetheless revolutionized political violence by making violence their primary political act. "There was," Gallian boasted, "in all the world no precedent for us; comparisons are useless."[47]

And so the first thing antifascism meant was fighting back. Very quickly, though, the idea of antifascism came to mean more than meeting fascist violence with antifascist violence. Almost right away, the idea started to include the whole body of political and ethical debate over *how* to fight back — by outright collective violence? by subtler methods? by some combination of the two? Mazzali's essay in 1924 was one contribution to the debate. The axiom from which the first antifascisti worked, the axiom that went a long way toward making them antifascisti, was that it went without question that, one way or another, fascism had to be *fought.*

Their proclivity for fighting drew many a rebuke. Even before anyone expressed any explicit notion of antifascism as a general idea, even before anyone talked of themselves as antifascisti, there was talk of "antifascist violence." By January 1921, after a run of bloody incidents between socialists and fascisti, a contributor to the *Stampa* chastised the socialists for having "accepted and attempted battle on the same terrain as fascism." Faced with "fascist guerrilla warfare," the socialists were now, the author charged, quite unfortunately conducting their own "experiment in antifascist violence."[48]

—

Much of the "antifascist violence" was informal and spur-of-the-moment. This would still be so even as talk of "antifascism"—the thing itself, outright and in noun form—began to be worked into Italy's political discourse. Like early fascism, early antifascism took the form of popular politics, often as nothing more than an effervescence of impromptu public confrontation. In Parma early in the spring of 1922, for example, an uneasy crowd assembled in the Piazza Garibaldi in the center of the city, outside a courtroom where six fascisti were on trial, accused of beating a local syndicalist to death in front of his eleven-year-old child. Unable to get into the courtroom—there had been a fight inside—the crowd stayed in the piazza and voiced various opinions, "all in tune," as a local correspondent wrote, "with anti-fascism."[49] Here the abstraction, antifascism, already had ideological properties: it wasn't the violence about to ensue that provided the "tune" but rather the gist of the crowd's opinions that did. The correspondent, in effect, had recognized antifascism as the crowd's politics. Still, though, it was likely the violence about to break out that led the correspondent to write a news story at all.

The city was on edge, and the crowd's invective toward the fascisti became "more violent than usual." The words went on until "some squads of fascisti decided to go over to the place" where the crowd stood. When they tried to disperse the crowd, violence began, "on all sides." Gunfire ended the brawl in the piazza, but even then squads of fascisti spilled into the surrounding streets, forcing shops to close and laying siege to a local newspaper, the *Piccolo,* which, the correspondent explained, the fascisti (quite correctly) had "accused of anti-fascism."[50]

That episode was only a skirmish. A few months later, in the summer, Parma became the site of one of the first epic battles in the long and entwined histories of fascism and antifascism. With a strike underway in the city, the young and ruthlessly effective blackshirt Italo Balbo arrived with his squadristi to visit upon the people of Parma a punitive expedition. The Arditi del Popolo awaited him.

Historians have recognized the Arditi del Popolo as "the first militant anti-fascist organization," even "the first anti-fascist movement in the world."[51] And it is uncanny how well the group's core qualities exemplified much of what has remained the heart of antifascism. To begin, the Arditi del Popolo was

—

determinedly cross-ideological: anarchists, republicans, socialists, communists, and the occasional revolutionary syndicalist all took part. Because the Italian mass parties were ideologically based, it followed that the group drew its ranks from rival parties, all with their own institutional strategies and interests to guard. The Arditi del Popolo's founders, by contrast, specifically designed their organization for popular politics; the logic behind every step of its creation prioritized movement making and mass mobilization over institution building. The Arditi del Popolo quickly proved that it could put feet in the street, by the thousands: its antifascism worked very differently from, say, an assassination by two or three anti-Fascisti in the Bronx or an assault by an antifascist trio near Times Square.

In all these ways the Arditi del Popolo prefigured much of what antifascism as a whole would become by the time of the Spanish Civil War. The group epitomized as well the antifascism to come in the performative, stylized politics that its members practiced—full of dramatic gesture and heroic presentation, imaginative in song and slogan and the subtleties of movement culture. The "arditi" also presented themselves to the world in absolute collectivity: there was little talk of any one individual "ardito"; more to the point, there was no demagogue on the balcony, no leader figure licensed to speak for all. As a group, though, the arditi did presume to speak for "the people" (as even the "popolo" in the group's name suggested). Theirs was an anti-authoritarian politics of equals, and it was also a populistic politics posed as the will of all humanity. A final point worth making about how the arditi embodied certain constants of antifascist history has to do with their fanatical focus on fighting fascism. Presenting themselves as the people's army engaging the enemy of all humankind, the arditi communicated a mythic vision of a battle to the death. One's own death was glorious and deserving of memory (and indeed it was in death that an ardito's individuality finally surfaced); and fascism was no foe simply to be defeated or overcome; rather, it was the enemy to be destroyed. Such notions were all to become ABCs of antifascism.

The Arditi del Popolo had emerged from what one 1921 pamphlet on the subject called "the convulsions of arditismo." Arditismo—yet another novel abstraction in Italian political life—had shaken the country at the war's end much as interventismo had done at the war's beginning. Late in the war, the

Italian army had created elite assault units of shock troops, in part inspired by the German Sturmtruppen, and the troops in these units became known as "gli arditi," meaning "the daring ones." They seemed to fulfill what the earliest fascisti had foreseen: that war would generate a bold, modern warrior type capable of revolutionizing the nation. These arditi took pride in swift, perilous action; they wore dashing, colorful uniforms; they swaggered and sang in combat. After the war, rather than demobilize quietly, thousands shifted to political mobilization—many to fascism. They were, as one ardito turned fascist said, "the first prototype of a 'political army,'" waging "war on two fronts . . . against the enemies without and those within."[52] Some were at San Sepolcro, and some were behind the notorious assault a few weeks later on the press of *Avanti!* But other arditi turned to socialism, or to republicanism and anarchism. The influence of arditismo on early fascism is well known; less so is how arditismo also fueled early antifascism.

The Arditi del Popolo first marched in Rome, on "Proletarian Day," July 6, 1921, a year and a month before the group's great battle at Parma. Veterans such as Argo Secondari, an anarchist, had established the organization a few weeks before with the aim, as recorded in a police spy report, "of fighting fascism." The idea behind Proletarian Day was for Rome's working-class and radical organizations to unify against fascist violence with a mass protest in the city center. The event's organizers included socialists, communists, republicans, and anarchists. In retrospect, historians have looked at the roster of organizers and seen their demonstration as a gathering, as one historian has put it, of "left-wing organizations." In 1921, however, the fact that organizers had socialist, communist, republican, and anarchist beliefs did not make them part of the left. The communist weekly run by Tasca and Antonio Gramsci, the *Ordine Nuovo,* instead described the demonstration's principals as the country's "four subversive political parties." To be sure, one might have spoken of socialist, communist, and republican deputies as part of the left in parliament, but such talk didn't extend to the parties' matters beyond the chamber doors. When the parties turned outward to the public and engaged in protest and mass politics, talk of "the left" dissipated. For their part, the anarchists in 1921 still occupied a universe apart from any idea of the left. Indeed, the *Ordine Nuovo*'s description of the anarchists as even a party was likely meant only in the looser sense of the word. My point, though, is that the day's events were a stab at creating some sense of common collectivity where it didn't yet exist. If you think the organizing parties and their bases already existed as the left, then that common collectivity didn't need creating. Call the July 6 rally an event of the left and you miss that you are looking at an early effort to create something new. Likewise, call the Arditi del Popolo "the left's militia," as at least one historian has done, and you miss some of its originality.[53]

The language of an eternal left—always already formed before the story at hand—is deeply impressed into our narratives of modern political history. If you accept the left as preordained, then the story of the Arditi del Popolo—and the larger story of antifascism—can hardly be but a tragedy. The great collective labor that was the left's creation is made invisible. Instead, the history of the left becomes that of a long political tradition defined by a puzzlingly large number of grim betrayals from within by those who should—everyone belonging to the left, after all—have played much more nicely with the others. For example, if the left is thought of as already having been in 1922 a finished product, then when considering fascism's rise to power in Italy historians are left only to ponder "why the left failed to fight."[54] Lost in such a tragical trope is all the work that was still needed to go into crafting a politics of unity in the first place. Many of the most familiar chapters in the long version of the left's history—the history in which the left is always already there on page one, the history in which it had emerged from the French Revolution fully constituted—teach the lesson of the left's falling apart; the narrative shows solidarities always fraying and splitting. But take away the notion of a pre-assembled left, and those episodes can be seen as the opposite: as instances when people who started out with little historical reason to expect solidarity from each other nonetheless began to work together to build up a store of it.

Regardless, the organizers of Proletarian Day in 1921 meant for the rally to serve as a promise that the subversive parties, and the labor unions, had left behind the hostilities of the past. The rally wasn't proof that unity had in fact solidified; rather, the idea behind the day's events was that the act of demonstrating together might somewhat solidify what pools of unity there were. The many thousands of rally-goers who showed up that afternoon (one observer estimated 60,000) did just that.[55]

Yet no doubt the most magnificent manifestation of a new politics of unity was the Arditi del Popolo itself. The antifascist army's premiere made for a stirring scene: 3,000 young people bearing pennants, organized into three battalions, all marching with an aesthetically smart precision. Many were veterans of the war, and some of them were even veterans of the actual arditi units; many others of the "people's arditi," though, were young radicals who had never been to war. The battalions started marching from the foot of the Arch of Titus, just west of the Colosseum, and made their way to the Botanical Garden across the Tiber, where the rally was to be held. Along the way, the arditi stared down a government cavalry unit that had swept into their path and tried to scare them into retreating. They didn't take fright or flight, and onlookers cheered them onward to the garden. The rally included oratory by an anarchist, by socialist and republican politicians, and by a communist schoolteacher. The common themes were to deplore fascist violence as the most urgent problem faced by all and to prescribe muscular proletarian unity as the solution for all. Throughout, the people's arditi stood as the physical embodiment of such militant and forceful collaboration. "I saw the Arditi del Popolo at the meeting drawn up into companies," the correspondent Giovanni Giglio wrote. "I saw them in serried ranks around the meeting mounting guard over it," ready to defend "their fellow-workers."[56]

After the rally, though, the arditi were more vulnerable to attack. The police and soldiers tried with mixed success to break up crowds leaving the garden. Meanwhile, squads of fascisti set out from their headquarters to the north, on Via Laurina, looking for a fight. They made their way down Via del Corso, fighting arditi along the way. Some of the fascisti rushed to the city's central hub, the Piazza Venezia. Years later, beginning in 1929, the Mussolini regime would hold mass rallies here. The piazza, a great flattened and whitened emptiness of a cityscape, lay under the palace balcony where Mussolini would give many of his most memorable speeches. When filled with throngs singing the fascist anthem, saluting, and responding as one to Mussolini's window-framed theatrics, the piazza would transform into a grand stage for fascist symbolism of state power, militaristic messianism, and participatory dictatorship. But in the summer of 1921, the place's political significance remained as yet undefined. The fascisti, coming into the piazza, saw small groups of the people's arditi by

—

the Vittoriano – the colossal white-marble monument of Vittorio Emanuele the Second. The fascisti sprinted at them. The arditi took off around the corner, down Via San Marco and around to the far side of the palace. They turned, fired their revolvers at the fascisti, and ducked into the unlikeliest of sanctuaries, the palace that Mussolini would one day make his own.[57]

Over the year that followed the Arditi del Popolo's eventful debut on Proletarian Day, the group grew in number and in reputation. In November 1921, when fascisti converged on Rome for a national congress, the Arditi del Popolo similarly appealed to its adherents to come and defend the city. The result was five days of block-by-block barricaded warfare in the streets of Rome.[58] Many other battles followed, culminating in the defense of Parma in August 1922, the greatest antifascist triumph of the era before the March on Rome.

It was also the most improbable. After Proletarian Day, the leaderships of both the Socialist Party and the Communist Party had denounced the Arditi del Popolo's method of radical unity. The leadership of each party had done so for a variety of narrowly self-interested and outright foolhardy reasons, and each had then repeatedly sought to keep its members from joining the people's army.[59] Thousands of socialists and communists signed up all the same, seeing promise – seeing necessity – in the Arditi del Popolo's unalloyed antifascism. How startling it is to look back in retrospect, knowing what was to come, and to see how unfocused on fascism the officials of both parties were in these years, and how uninterested in fashioning an antifascist politics they were. And yet antifascism did take form. By midsummer fascist violence had become pervasive enough that the country's unions were ready to declare, as a way of protesting the onslaught, a nationwide general strike beginning August 1. It didn't go well. Mussolini and the fascisti seized on the strike as a justification for escalating their terrorist campaign and for demanding that the government prove it could rule – or else they would prove they could. The strike crumbled within a day and the fascisti romped.

Except in Parma. The punitive expedition into the city commenced the night of August 1. The blackshirts arrived in trucks, and they came, as the Arditi del Popolo's local general, Guido Picelli, put it, "equipped and armed with new rifles, revolvers, bombs, and daggers, and provisioned with great stores of ammunition; these were select squadristi, proven and experienced

---

in the tactics of the punitive expedition." The street battles the next day went on for hours; the blackshirts succeeded in destroying the press of the *Piccolo*. But they couldn't advance into the working-class quarters, where barricades stuffed the streets. By dawn on August 4, Balbo himself had arrived along with thousands more blackshirts. Balbo, cunning and strategically gifted, was determined to break Parma; he saw the showdown as a chance to set an example for all the country.[60] The fighting went on for five days in a row. The bloodiest battles centered on the working-class neighborhood of Oltretorrente, where Picelli commanded arditi forces; ferocious fighting also took place in Naviglio, where Antonio Cieri commanded. Picelli was a socialist – indeed, he was at the time an elected deputy in parliament, despite organizing for the Arditi del Popolo in defiance of party leadership – and Cieri was an anarchist. Under fire, antifascist solidarity held.

And on the sixth morning of the battle – August 7 – fascist discipline broke down. Right away the Arditi del Popolo's field report that day discerned "discontent among the blackshirts over the losses they've suffered" and suggested that the "orders of their leaders are not always carried out. Panic is spreading." Sure enough, soon thereafter, according to Picelli's account, the fascisti fell out of military formation and began to flee "in trucks, on bicycles, or on foot," scurrying off "as if they feared being chased."[61] Was Picelli, no doubt a proud commander, exaggerating? Perhaps, but neither Balbo's nor anyone else's account suggested much to undermine his version of events. The people's army had held its ranks together under siege. Fascism could be defeated on its own battlefield of organized mass violence. The Arditi del Popolo had shown how.

That's one lesson to take from the defense of Parma. The Arditi del Popolo proved the worth of a crack organization, one with a clean structure and a clear sense of institutional purpose. But Parma provided other lessons as well. In Parma entire neighborhoods had taken part in fending off the fascisti throughout the first week of August 1922, and in doing so they had also taken part in the making of antifascism. Rather than let the Arditi del Popolo define these early days of antifascist history, consider also how the informal antifascists of Oltretorrente and Naviglio provided antifascism – still nascent, still so persuasible – with some of its initial shape and substance. Doing so opens up the cast of early antifascist history. One of the reasons it's so restrictive to wall in

—

political history as the domain of recognized political parties and formal organizations is that it can lead you to naturalize whatever limits on political recognition various social orders have imposed. Consider in particular the distance
between the limited role offered to women in the Arditi del Popolo, on the one
hand, and the expansive role that women worked out for themselves in Parma's
defense, on the other. There were only a few women in the Arditi del Popolo; it
was overwhelmingly an organization for young men.[62] And yet, without formal
recognition, women did much of the work of fortifying and fighting.[63] "How
did the barricades come about?" Virginio Barbieri, one of Parma's defenders,
asked, rhetorically, years later. He said they came about from rock and wood,
from cobblestones dug up from the streets and tables carried out into the same.
And the barricades came about, Barbieri added, also from the work of all in the
working-class quarters: "Since everyone had so much to do there, not only the
so-called Arditi del popolo but the whole population participated, the women
and the kids, everyone did something." Balbo, from across the divide, also could
see that women were taking part in the defense; and he saw his chances to take
the city slipping away: "Hour by hour, their trenches are deepened and per-
fected." Women ran supplies, took sentinel duty, and ran the perilous ground
between the antifascist strongholds; Picelli recalled a woman who "managed to
make it through" from Naviglio to the command in Oltretorrente, "a message
hidden in her hair." She went back with orders to hold the line at all costs and
with all the ammunition she could hide in her clothes. Not only at the barricades but above, in the windows, women stood guard, cans of gasoline at hand
to dump on any enemy forces that made it through the barricades. The plan was
to burn the blackshirts alive. It never came to that; the barricades held, and the
blackshirts fled. But the efforts of working-class women in Parma, combined
with their general exclusion from the Arditi del Popolo, point to just how much
greater of a political movement than the arditi alone was at work in the making
of antifascism. Picelli put it well how the defense captured an antifascist ideal
of a larger politics: "Men and women, the old and the young, those of all the
parties and those without any party were there; they were fused together into
a single will of iron: to resist and to fight."[64]

It was a glorious victory, and it was hard won. It was also the exception in
the years before the March on Rome, which is one explanation for how it came

to pass that Mussolini took the helm of state only twelve weeks after. Not all heroic efforts pay out, not even the wins. Nonetheless, they offer lessons.[65] The story of Parma can be seen as a counterpart to Mazzali's idea of peeling away the layers of time to understand fascism at its genesis: it can be seen as the idea's application to antifascism. Look at Parma and see *antifascism* before all the profusion of chatter. Look at Parma and see antifascism still in genesis.

And yet no later than the following spring, labor radicals in far-off New York were already calling themselves "anti-Fascisti." With an April 10, 1923, meeting on East 14th Street, they began in earnest to make the presence of anti-fascism felt in the city. It was just over five months since the March on Rome; and it was less than two years since the small group of self-described fascisti had gathered on Charles Street and started to make the presence of fascism felt in New York. Even before the April 1923 meeting, locals had begun making antifascist noise in the city. Carlo Tresca had made much of the earliest noise. Even before the March on Rome he had held meetings near Union Square to further what he had begun calling — again, even before the March on Rome — "our antifascist agitation." A seasoned radical from the Abruzzo region of Italy, he had previously agitated for the Industrial Workers of the World (IWW) in Lawrence, Massachusetts, in the aftermath of the 1912 textile strike, and then in Paterson, New Jersey, during the following year's silk strike. "He liked to call himself an Anarchist," recalled his dearest friend Arturo Giovannitti, the charismatic labor organizer and poet, "and if that term connotes a man who is absolutely free, then he was an Anarchist."[66] By the early 1920s, Tresca was living in New York, publishing an Italian-language newspaper, the *Martello*. This was the primary tool with which he hammered into shape people's perceptions of antifascism as something that could happen not just in Italy but also right there in New York. He showed that it *was* happening in New York with relentless speeches, demonstrations, and public meetings.

He also set out on the road; his nonspeech in Waterbury, Connecticut, on March 25, 1923, quickly became part of the region's antifascist mythology. The "Waterbury incident" began at the door of the Old Concordia Hall, where 125 police officers, some armed with shotguns, physically barred Tresca from entering. He had tried to speak there two weeks before; turned away by the

---

police, he had sworn to return. Also, a recent antifascist speech of Tresca's in New York had attracted the attention of the U.S. government's Bureau of Investigation, which then encouraged the Waterbury police to run him off. All signs pointed to trouble in Waterbury on March 25. Tresca never spoke that afternoon, and the comrade who spoke in his stead was arrested for supposedly saying words that witnesses swore he never spoke. Still, the theatrics of the scene were enough to prompt even the English-language press in the following days to relate stories of the "anti-Facisti leader in this country," representing an "anti-Facisti league," being muzzled by the authorities while an "anti-Fascismo orator" was arrested on dubious sedition charges.[67] In such bedlam, and in its depiction in the press, antifascism took hold of new terrain. As it did so, its substance began to alter. Still very much, generally speaking, a particularism of Italian politics, antifascism was now a little less peculiarly Italian nonetheless. Much as when the likes of De Biasi, Menicucci, and Passamonte had reached out and pulled fascism out from Italy and into the wider world, so too now it was a New Yorker, self-identifying as an antifascist, doing the same for antifascism.

The irony is that Tresca then kept his distance from the first large-scale act of antifascist organizing in the city, the meeting on East 14th Street on April 10, sixteen days after the Waterbury incident. Causes are not made in straight lines; political ideas bounce around, and no one controls their trajectory. This is especially worth pointing out in a history of antifascism because so often the antifascist politics of the interwar era has been portrayed as the fee simple property of the Comintern. Tresca, as Giovannitti pointed out, was an anarchist, not at all a Comintern agent; and neither was he wary of the first mass antifascist campaign in New York because he feared it would be Comintern-dominated; rather, he thought that the labor union officials taking part, whom he saw as timid social democrats, were too cautious and procedural to know how to fight fascism.

And yet the April 10, 1923, meeting that gave antifascism in New York an institutional home, and all the public recognition that goes with that, was the idea of his friend, the poet Giovannitti. What had driven him to create a mass antifascist organization was something that had happened the previous month: the New York fascio had reconstituted itself under a new formal name and, more to the point, had also established a new headquarters — very pointedly placed across the street from the Italian Labor Center where Giovannitti was the secretary of the Italian Chamber of Labor. It was at the labor center — 231 East 14th Street, in a building that still stands, "Italian Labor Center" still engraved above the door — that Giovannitti hosted the April 10 meeting and there orchestrated the founding of the Anti-Fascisti Alliance of North America, soon known as AFANA. Participants came from the Workers Party, the Socialist Party, the IWW, and several mass-membership unions. In retrospect, it could look as if, as one historian has suggested, the Anti-Fascisti Alliance was "a coalition of leftist groups," established at a time when any attempt at unity was vexed, as another historian has claimed, by "the infighting so prevalent in the Italian-American Left."[68] Look at things as those in the moment did, though, and the Anti-Fascisti Alliance's founding was the opposite of leftists attempting antifascism: by choosing to be antifascisti, they were taking an early step toward eventually becoming leftists.

The April 10 meeting produced a lyrical manifesto, drawn at least in part from the speech Giovannitti gave that evening. The manifesto made clear that the antifascist alliance didn't look only to protest the new fascist regime's repressions of labor in distant Italy, but that it also would challenge the presence of fascism already felt in New York: "already the black shirt decorated with the death symbol of piracy has made its public appearance in the slums of New York" and "already the first depredations have taken place and the first blood of the workers has been shed." Another irony, then, is that part of what antifascist organizing was doing was to make people in New York recognize fascism's conceptual presence — and in doing so, solidifying it. This was, after all, still very early in the history of fascism. The first anniversary of the March on Rome was almost seven months in the future. But already blackshirts were in and out of their 14th Street fascio; when the anniversary came, New York's blackshirts celebrated by going to Carnegie Hall.[69]

Of course, the earliest antifascisti in New York didn't see their own hand in establishing fascism's presence in the city. Neither did they see local fascisti as responsible for fascism's materialization there. They saw fascism as being

—

spread from Italy, coming at them. Which is one more irony: they didn't see the power of their own actions, and their own imaginations, to shape the political world in which they lived. Instead the manifesto warned, with a vivid metaphor, "The Fascist octopus is now attempting to extend its tentacles across the ocean."[70]

The police eventually arrested two men for the murders of Carisi and Amoroso. Officers raided the *Martello* and arrested one antifascist there, Mario Buzzi; beaten, brutally, he still wouldn't help frame the two men charged. Those two men, Calogero Greco and Donato Carillo, freely described themselves as anti-Fascisti ("admitting" to it, as the *New York Times* put the matter). Both had come from Italy and both were veterans of the Italian army; both denied being anywhere near the 183rd Street train station at eight o'clock on the morning of Memorial Day 1927. When they were put on trial for murder at the year's end, the legendary labor lawyer Clarence Darrow defended them, hoping to avoid another pair of death penalties like those that the anarchists Nicola Sacco and Bartolomeo Vanzetti had just paid in Massachusetts in August.[71]

Radical politics was about to change. The very method of antifascism chosen on Memorial Day 1927—assassination—spoke to an older sort of political action, quite different from the mass politics of antifascism to come, the antifascism of crowds, chants, and marches in the street—the antifascism of, say, 1936. It wasn't the antifascism of the Arditi del Popolo, either. It was, rather, an antifascism of interpersonal conspiracy, national identity, and propaganda by deed. But it also was, quite obviously, not the work of Greco and Carillo. The case against them was a shoddy frame-up, and the jury acquitted two days before Christmas.[72] The identities of those two or three assailants that were so readily identified as anti-Fascisti by the police back on Memorial Day have remained a mystery.

For their part, Carisi and Amoroso received burial rites in Italy. First, though, hundreds attended a visitation at the Bronx fascio headquarters— there were multiple fasci in the city now—and fascisti guarded the bodies (the *New York Times* reported them to be wearing what the paper called—already in 1927!—"the traditional black shirts"). A cablegram from the fascist regime in Italy saluted the Bronx fascisti: "All the ferocity of the anti-Fascisti cannot do anything against the glorious march of the idea." The fallen were, the note praised, "pure martyrs." True to that belief, their bodies were then shipped to Italy and laid to rest alongside two fascist martyrs — two other fascist martyrs — who had fallen in the March on Rome.[73]

—

CHAPTER 2

A PREHISTORY OF ANTIFASCISM

Antifascism? Such novelties in this land!

— Anonymous anarchists in Montevideo, 1924

"Antifa" badges on their chests, marchers made their way through Berlin's dark streets all through the evening of January 25, 1933. A cold front had moved over Europe, and some of the bitter worst of it had hit Berlin. Someone who had come out that evening suggested with confidence that it was the coldest the city had been since before the onset of the Great Depression. And yet one estimate had it that 80,000 people took part in the demonstration; another put the number at 100,000; some guesses were even higher. When the crowds converged on the Bülowplatz, in the middle of Berlin, the many thousands couldn't all fit into the square, so one way or another it was decided that the marchers would walk through, past the German Communist Party's headquarters, the Karl-Liebknecht-Haus on the square's east side, and continue on back into the streets of the city. Three days earlier, on a Sunday afternoon, Adolf Hitler had led 16,000 brownshirts through the Bülowplatz, directly past the Liebknecht-Haus, on the way to the grave of the brownshirt martyr Horst Wessel in the cemetery nearby. A militant of an illegal Communist paramilitary group had murdered Wessel three years earlier; since then, the Nazis had sacralized his memory and taken to singing the battle hymn he had written a short while before his death. The brownshirts had meant their march as a provocation. As they paraded past the Liebknecht-Haus, they had hollered

—

"Hail Hitler!" and "We shit on freedom, and we shit on the Jew republic!" Now the Communists, along with a good many other antifascists, meant their parade as a show of defiance.[1] They knew what was coming and so they had come out to demonstrate their recalcitrance. Five days later, Hitler became chancellor.

The two marches didn't mark the first time that the German Communists and the Nazis had battled for supremacy over public space in Berlin. Rather, the January 25 march ended up marking the last time that the Communists would hold a mass demonstration in the city before the Third Reich banned their party. They made an impressive showing. Not only did the turnout surprise the press, all the more so because of the cold, but also the composure and dignity with which the marchers carried themselves affected all who witnessed their performance. They marched for hours. Young Eric Hobsbawm, many years before he became a renowned historian, was among those who took part, fifteen years old and active in the Communist Party's youth movement. Decades later, he recalled the "mass ecstasy," as he called it, that he had felt in the streets — "the merger of the individual in the mass, which is the essence of the collective experience," physical and emotional, intensely sensory. All he could remember with specificity was the singing of songs that made him feel a sense of belonging and a sensation of solidarity in motion. Such marches weren't only offensives for control of the city's streets; they were also schools, teaching participants a way of politics passed on from march to march; and they were laboratories, too, for inventing new practices for the cause. As one intuitive observer pointed out, for hours the thousands who took part in the march heard and rehearsed revolutionary songs and slogans; for hours, they played with language and gesture and came up with things to say and do; and so for hours "fascism was extravagantly jeered, leaving no doubt that in this evening Berlin's proletariat has enriched the antifascist vocabulary."[2]

Yet whatever lessons of political education or acts of political invention were to be found in the affair, the onset of the Third Reich soon cut them all short. Less than a month after the antifascist procession, and a few days before the Reichstag fire, the new regime's police raided the Karl-Liebknecht-Haus. Then the Hitler government banned the German Communist Party altogether. And by the end of May the new government had decreed that the Bülowplatz was thenceforth to be known as the Horst-Wessel-Platz.[3]

—

All of which points to the likelihood that, despite what there was to learn from such a moving demonstration, the larger lessons of antifascism in Germany before the Third Reich were of the negative sort: how not to fight fascism. Institutional self-interest, ideological contrivance, and wishful thinking had all played a part in impeding whatever sort of antifascism might have denied the Nazis power. To be sure, there was considerable talk of the need for antifascist unity in the final years of the Weimar Republic. After all, the organizers of the January 25 march had framed the event as not for Communist Party members alone but rather for all "the proletarian united front against fascism."[4] By that, they meant working people of multiple ideological faiths and competing party affiliations nonetheless joined together in common cause to overcome fascism. The appeal to walk together, despite differences of ideology and party, spoke to something that had figured into antifascist politics at least since the creation of the Arditi del Popolo in the summer of 1921. However, an intense faith in the institution that was the German Communist Party — and behind it, the Comintern — complicated the appeal a great deal.

When dealing with the history of antifascism, though, it's worth stressing from the start that those who put their faith in the Comintern and its parties weren't alone in handing over to an institution a sum of authority to shape and direct their own personal politics. You would be forgiven if you were to read a good share of the historiography influenced by the Cold War and come away thinking that only the Comintern's parties had exploited causes such as antifascism for brute party-building purposes. Or that only the Comintern's parties had had leaders who built up their own party at the expense of such causes, all the while jawing about how their party-building labors had been done selflessly in the service of the very causes that they had instrumentalized. During the years of the Weimar Republic, after the First World War, the German Communist Party's main rival was the Social Democratic Party. And just as there were in the Communist Party those who sought to have their party be seen as the dynamo of antifascism while they actually prioritized narrow institutional interests instead, so too were there in the Social Democratic Party those who sought to do the same regarding their own party. Throughout the years of the Nazis' rise, the leaders of both parties wielded the idea of antifascist solidarity rather cynically, so as to boost their own party and bury the other.

—

The "Antifa" badges seen in the streets of Berlin throughout the evening of January 25 stemmed from this interinstitutional war. The badges signified the militant direct-action organization that the Communist Party had set up the previous summer, Antifaschistische Aktion, or Antifa for short. Antifaschistische Aktion was actually the second group organized by the German Communist Party that went by the nickname Antifa. The first had been the short-lived Antifaschistische Junge Garde, or Young Antifascist Guard, created in Berlin in July 1929; its members had worn blue-shirt uniforms (which the authorities had quickly banned, along with the organization altogether) and had understood their Antifa as very much "a fighting organization." And therein lie the origins of "antifa" as a political concept. It wouldn't take long for antifascists elsewhere (beginning in Palestine in 1934) to rework the concept and make "antifa" into a more general idea, but in the final months before the Third Reich, its meaning was utterly particularistic, grounded in the goings-on of a specific organization of the German Communist Party—the party's second "Antifa," established in Berlin in 1932. The party's head, Ernst Thälmann, left no doubt that he saw Antifa as a tool for building the party—and for chipping away at the Social Democracy, which was then enjoying success with the militant antifascist coalition that it had helped to forge in December 1931: the Eiserne Front, or Iron Front. Made up of socialist, republican, and labor organizations, the Iron Front sought to create a mass politics of antifascism. But not by any and all means. Its organizers had very deliberately left out the Communist Party.[5]

Now Thälmann sought to counter with Antifa. Just as the Social Democratic Party had excluded the Communist Party from the Iron Front, so too Thälmann now excluded the Social Democratic Party from Antifa. What's more, Thälmann and his inner circle used Antifa as a cleaver with which to sever common Social Democrats from their party; Antifa organizers encouraged them to join Antifa and even to take local leadership posts: to build an antifascist politics of unity from the bottom up.[6] The idea, though, was to draw them in, not to reach out in collaboration. Thälmann's intent throughout was never to overcome the limitations put on mass antifascism by the Iron Front; he sought to replicate them, with the Communist Party replacing the Social Democracy as the party that would benefit.

—

And so this early Antifa had a complicated legacy. It was a top-down initiative to experiment with, and to control, bottom-up antifascism; it was established by the German Communist Party's central committee, and it encouraged and relied on decentralized community organizing in the working-class neighborhoods; party leaders hoped for Antifa to capture the energy of informal street politics, and they also hoped to impose order and discipline on those who practiced such politics. The central committee's charter for Antifa insisted that "Antifaschistische Aktion is not a fixed organization, but a movement" — and yet, the following line doubled back: "The masses united by the movement, however, should be united more firmly than has been the case regarding the party's periphery in the past."[7]

The indelicacy of the motives behind Antifa was visible even in its emblem, which appeared in all sorts of Communist Party propaganda in 1932. It showed two flags flying together inside a circle: one flag represented the Communist Party — and the other the Social Democratic Party. This, of course, was an affront. The Communist Party's leaders weren't at all seeking a politics of unity between the two parties; they meant to raid the Social Democracy's membership — and here they were doing so under the Social Democracy's own flag. The awkward justification was that the second flag "naturally," as one historian has put it, "meant the Social Democratic Party's base, not the party itself." Thälmann told Social Democratic representatives to their faces in the summer of 1932, amid Antifa's recruiting successes, that any show of unity between the parties proper would "only add to the confusion" and present "a false view of unity of the working class." He was explicit in adding, "We Communists do not want 'unity at any price.'"[8]

Thälmann wouldn't have gotten it at any price at all. Institutional prerogative ruled just as surely in the Social Democracy. In 1932, the propagandist Sergei Chakhotin crafted a striking image for the Iron Front that would later acquire great and enduring significance for antifascists: the three arrows. He envisioned them all targeting a swastika (his inspiration had come from graffiti: he had seen a thick white stripe chalked over a Nazi swastika on a streetside wall; much of the three arrows' enduring value for antifascists has been in how well the arrows work as countergraffiti when superimposed over fascist signs, subverting the fascist graffiti's messages).[9] Part of the idea behind Chakho-

Figure 1. A 1932 campaign poster of the German Social Democratic Party. The poster makes use of the antifascist "three arrows" symbol but inverts its meaning. *Poster GE 1702, Poster Collection, Hoover Institution Library & Archives.*

tin's imagery was to envision a plurality of figures (the three arrows) all aimed together at a common enemy (one swastika). That was how he thought of the Iron Front. Once he fashioned the image, though, the Social Democratic Party printed up campaign posters with the three arrows each aimed at a different target: one aimed at a crown symbolizing the reactionary monarchism of Chancellor Franz von Papen; one aimed at a swastika symbolizing the Nazi

—

Party led by Hitler; and one aimed at a hammer and sickle symbolizing the Communist Party led by Thälmann (fig. 1). This inverted the original symbolism; instead of three different arrows (the Iron Front's socialist, republican, and labor elements) striking as one, it sent the message of one heroic party (the Social Democracy) able to slay three foes all at once. The posters' headline further diminished any antifascist message: it read, "Against Papen, Hitler, Thälmann," as if to equate the three, Hitler lumped in the middle.[10]

None of that, though, negated the genuine antifascist commitments of the people in either party who acted out of conviction more than calculation — people, for example, like the antifascists willing to risk being caught by brownshirts as they scratched graffiti of arrows over swastikas on the walls of the city; and people, as well, like the common Social Democratic Party members willing to show up for a procession past a rival party's headquarters so as to take part in a protest against fascism. Underneath the instrumental antifascism of the two parties coursed a popular antifascism made of real determination and feeling. The party propagandist Chakhotin himself recognized something like this when he wrote, "The antifascist doctrine doesn't need to be invented: it exists already and it grows larger, inexorably and all on its own, each day."[11]

And yet neither did the genuine antifascist commitments of those who marched through the Bülowplatz negate the undeniable pathos of January 25, 1933: the sense of shortcoming and failure that haunted the evening, no matter how marvelous the marchers' militancy; and the sense of ending and loss that hung over the event as well. The date could even serve as a marker for the end of the first era of antifascism's history, the era before the great outburst of antifascist passions to come. The gifted historian of French antifascism Gilles Vergnon has called the years before 1934 the "prehistory of antifascism."[12] Vergnon meant in France, but it's worth cracking his idea open and casting it over a much wider political landscape. Antifascism as a whole was transformed in the years after Hitler gained power. The question of who or what made that transformation happen is a difficult one, and answering it will take some explaining, as it relates to other questions about even larger transformations in the nature of the political world. For now, though, it's useful to think of the final days of Weimar as a moment of reckoning, for antifascists in Germany and for antifascists everywhere.

—

It's also useful to recognize that what was to come next would be a different sort of politics. The rise of Nazism shook the world every bit as violently as had the October Revolution of 1917. One epoch of global politics now ended and another began. For antifascism, the years that followed marked a heroic age, when its classical images came into focus, when multitudes of people remade antifascism into a mass politics and spoke of antifascism as a global cause. But the antifascist moment that began by 1934 didn't come out of nowhere. The years before helped to shape the moment — they provided, just as Vergnon suggested, a prehistory that the antifascists of the new era could draw on and learn from. In that way, the school and the lab of marches like the antifascist parade through the Bülowplatz weren't entirely knocked down by the Third Reich. In that way, January 25 didn't only mark an end, and its effect wasn't only one of pathos.

As those antifascist marchers made their way past the Karl-Liebknecht-Haus that evening, they raised their fists into the cold.[13] It was a fierce, defiant gesture. And it was a gesture that compacted into a clenched hand's thrust an unspoken promise of solidarity. When performed in a crowd, as at the Bülow-platz, it worked to draw people into a state of collectivity — like how Hobsbawm described singing and marching as a merger of the one into the many. But just what that collectivity was that such practices worked to create remained something always open to interpretation and alteration. At first, it had been members of a German Communist paramilitary organization, the Roter Front-kämpferbund, or Red Front Fighters' League, who had exchanged closed-fisted salutes. They had done so from the group's origin in 1924. By then, the Nazis had absorbed the Italian fascisti's open-palmed salute, altering it a touch as they did; if the Nazis' salutes weren't known to the Red Front Fighters when they took up the closed-fisted salute in 1924, they became so soon enough. The meaning of the Red Front Fighters' salute became that of a foil to the Nazis.' This became the case all the more as others in and around the German Communist Party picked up the practice; and when the government banned the Red Front Fighters' League in 1929, the salutes remained a part of party life. What's more, by the time of the march through the Bülowplatz, Social Democrats had, with Chakhotin's prodding, taken up the closed-fisted salute as well, exclaiming "Freedom!" as they threw up their fists.[14] Doing so had peeled the

—

meaning of the clenched fist out of the German Communist Party's grip. What was left was the practice's expressive power as a counter to the fascist salute.

And also that power to generate a sense of collectivity. It was just that the collectivity generated was now no longer quite so tightly bound by party affiliation, no longer quite so sharply defined by the difference between official Social Democratic and Soviet Communist ideology. Which is to say, antifascism already was more than what those who put their faith in building their party wanted it to be. The salute embodied the broader paradox of antifascism. Thälmann had encouraged the clenched fist as a device by which to strengthen commitment to the party; Chakhotin had encouraged Social Democrats to adopt the practice because he saw how well it had worked for the Communists. Somehow, though, the power of it spun away from them both. Given how people made use of the practice in the streets, men and women alike, to express sincerely their defiance of fascism, the clenched fist couldn't help but encourage a new sort of solidarity.[15] Whatever the auspices of any one demonstration were, and no matter how cynical the institutional motive behind the decision to invite people from a rival party may have been, the shared experiences and practices in the streets brought common Communists and Social Democrats together and pushed them toward a sense of common cause.

Even if no one had taken to calling it an "antifascist salute" quite yet, the practice was gaining a meaning that centered more and more on the antifascist faith kept in both parties' camps. Its effect was becoming more and more to push its practitioners toward a solidarity based on an antifascist politics that they all shared. That isn't at all to say that separate party loyalties vanished or that the common cause of antifascism always overcame them. It didn't. But antifascism in the streets had been shown as something more than an instrument of the parties. People practicing politics are never puppets, and the politics they practice are always at least in part their own. Communists and Social Democrats march together and holler and sing and curse together in good faith, and they make a politics together, regardless of institutional designs. It's worth emphasizing how much of a challenge it was for them to do this in 1933. There was little political language available to them to describe their efforts. The language of the left, as it existed then, was no help: those who marched and those who commented on the march didn't see it at all as a showing of Berlin's left.

—

It wasn't, then, that the marchers belonged to an older iteration of the left that the parties were tragically dividing; the marchers weren't in "the left" at all. Any suggestion that common Communists and Social Democrats practicing street politics in tandem somehow represented the left would have struck people as quite odd in January 1933, in Berlin or anywhere else. But the physical example of a shared antifascist popular politics hinted at the need for a new political vocabulary as well as new definitions for familiar political words. And so if the march of January 25 marked the end of one era of antifascist history, it was still the case that the closing era had had in it elements that antifascists could piece together and put to use in the age to come.

It's no secret when the new age began. Five days later. January 30, 1933, the day Adolf Hitler took charge in Germany. No small number of people living in the moment knew that the world had just changed. No small number saw the triumph of Nazism in Germany as the ascent of fascism before all the world. But why? How could the appointment of one man to the German chancellery swing all the world? And why, for so many, did Nazism mean fascism?

Consider the scene that played out that night in Berlin as it looked to a newspaper correspondent about to send off a dispatch of the day's events across the Atlantic Ocean by wireless telegraph. The thousands of brown-shirted men marching down the Wilhelmstrasse in torchlit procession, searchlights flashing across their chests, were "Fascists" and "Fascist Brown Shirt marchers." Not once in the correspondent's report were they National Socialists or Nazis—just "Fascists," time and time again. Their party, Hitler's party, was simply "the Fascist Party," which had campaigned on "the highly revolutionary Fascist program." The closest the report got to conveying anything particularistic or Germany-specific about the scene was, oddly enough, to label Hitler's flagpole-stiff salute, offered from his window in the Reich Chancellery to the brown-shirts marching below, a "National Socialist salute." Without any reference to the party by its formal name or to Hitler's ideology as national socialism, the reference to a "National Socialist salute" seemed a little out of place: otherwise, the thrust of the story was to use the vocabulary of fascism to universalize the scene's meaning—to convey how the "struggle between democracy and Fascism" had entered "a new stage."[16] All this talk of fascism then appeared, half of

—

a continent and an ocean away, in the next day's edition of the *Christian Science Monitor* of Boston: certainly not a reactionary outlet, but not a revolutionists' organ, either.

Such was the extent to which the idea that Hitler and his ilk were fascists had flooded political discourse by the advent of the age of fascism. Newspapers around the world imparted the same lesson: that Hitler's rise was fascism's advance. In Rio de Janeiro, readers of the popular *Correio da Manhã* could look at *two* front-page pictures of Hitler saluting "á romana" ("in the Roman way") as they read the accompanying report about fascists in Italy celebrating Hitler's triumph as "an exalted example for all the world." Claims of Hitler and the Nazis as exemplars of fascism swept over the reportage of world affairs. And yet, decades later, part of the premise for the Cold War–influenced historiography that would see antifascism as at root Comintern propaganda—even as, in the words of the distinguished historian Annie Kriegel, "a Stalinist myth"—was a broad notion that in the interwar era it had been the Comintern's high theorists alone who had meaningfully developed the idea of Nazism as a form of fascism.[17] On the contrary, at the time of Hitler's ascent, the idea was a commonplace of general political discourse.

Actually, it had been from the earliest days of Nazism. The first time the Nazis had drawn the attention of the outside world had been in the weeks that followed the March on Rome, back in 1922, when they were still organizing themselves into a political movement in Munich. The city at the time was a furnace of nationalist anger, antisemitic grievance, and general counterrevolution. During the German Revolution, at the end of World War I, Munich had stood out for the bohemian, anarchical, and ideologically heterodox nature of its upheaval: its revolutionaries had been artists, poets, and idealists from the Café Stefanie in the center of the city.[18] It hadn't taken long for the paramilitaries known as the Freikorps to break the Munich revolution and set its makers on the run. And now in the aftermath, a rough nationalistic and militaristic popular politics ruled the city.

By late 1922, Hitler and his band had begun to stand out. But they were still figuring out the basics of political identity: what they were as a collectivity and what their aims were. Hitler had yet to attempt the "Beer Hall Putsch." He had yet to write *Mein Kampf.* It's not clear whether they had begun at all to

—

throw up open-palmed salutes as the Italian fascisti did; by January 1923, Hitler, at least, had picked up the practice, but it wouldn't be until 1926 that the Nazis would make the salute their standard form of address.[19] They didn't wear brown-shirt uniforms yet.[20] Only later in the 1920s would that practice spread through the movement and lead the Nazis to become known, metonymically, *as* brownshirts, "Braunhemden." In autumn 1922, they were known to wear gray (and, indeed, were even on occasion called grayshirts). One witness wrote from Munich of "'storm troops' with gray shirts," wearing armbands with the swastika, "armed also with blackjacks and, it is popularly whispered, revolvers." The Hungarian polymath Andrés Révész commented in November that after the recent March on Rome "the first act of the fascist chief in Bavaria, Hitler, had been to introduce the required wearing of the 'gray shirt.'"[21]

Révész was far from alone at the time in thinking of Hitler as a "fascist chief." Both within and beyond Germany it became typical in late 1922 to identify Hitler and the grayshirts of Munich as fascists. Before the year was out there was talk in the German press of "the south German fascist movement," and likewise the international press began to fill with reports of "Fascisti bands" in Bavaria, "German Fascisti," "Adolph Hitler's Fascisti," "Bavarian Fascisti," and "the Fascisti movement in Bavaria led by Herr Hitler." Such rhetoric wasn't at all the special domain of the Comintern's theorists. It was the grammar of the Associated Press, the *Times* of London and New York and Los Angeles, and other big dailies such as the *Crítica* of Buenos Aires and the *ABC* of Madrid. The language stuck. As the Nazis readied themselves for the Beer Hall Putsch the following fall, just after the first anniversary of the March on Rome, the international press broadcast far and wide warnings that the "Fascisti extremists" and "the fascist bands of Hitler" in Bavaria were looking to make trouble.[22]

It's worth asking: did this mark the beginning of "fascist" as an empty epithet, a meaningless pejorative thrown around with abandon? Quite the contrary, what's most striking about how so many people, with such different politics, collectively came to think of Hitler and his movement as fascist in 1922 and 1923 was how sparingly the identity was applied to others elsewhere beyond Italy. This was so even though the Italian blackshirts and the Bavarian grayshirts were far from the only paramilitarized groups on the prowl in those years. The aftermath of World War I made for an unsettled and uncertain time.

—

Many of the new paramilitaries took it upon themselves to put down industrial labor uprisings, to repress racial and religious minorities, and to counter revolutionary politics. Their ranks included the American Legion in the United States; the Comité Nacional de la Juventud, and then the Liga Patriótica, in Argentina; the Heimwehr in Austria; the Prónay detachment in Hungary; and the Einwohnerwehren, the Orgesch, and the Freikorps in Germany. Such groups— nationalistic, counterrevolutionary, and violently opposed to labor radicalism and social unrest—were "white guards" to their enemies; they were "Cossacks" and "terrorists."[23] But the idea of calling them all fascists didn't make sense, not even for their most polemical foes.

Pay close attention to the political language of an age and you start to see how people at the time conceived the political world they inhabited. You start to see how they perceived that world to work and what they understood, even subconsciously, as its laws and logic. If there were Bavarian fascisti, it was because fascism had somehow become a political form that someone other than Italian fascisti could practice. As close as Bavaria was geographically to Italy, this was a conceptual step beyond what De Biasi and the other fascisti of New York had pulled off in 1921—they had rooted their insistence that they were fascisti in a broader claim that they still belonged to the Italian nation; Italy, they had said, was greater than what showed up on a world map. The notion of Bavarian fascisti didn't presuppose an outright universalized fascism—a fascism so elemental and unencumbered by context as to exist in pure abstraction, manifestable anywhere the world over—but it did tug at the roots of the idea that fascism was peculiar to Italy.

At the time, though, the norm was to think of fascism as inherently Italian. All the talk of Bavarian fascisti aside, fascism remained anchored to Italian specifics. Liberalism, conservatism, socialism, nationalism, and the like—those grand isms handed down from the nineteenth century—had all long since come to float above in political discourse, unhindered by particulars of place. *Those* isms seemed obvious universals. No matter how ferociously people might argue over the contents and merits of any one of them, the way that people talked about them made them all seem to slide about effortlessly. As if they naturally existed to be shared, distributed, shuttled, transferred and circulated, toted here

—

and there unchecked and regardless of any of the formal political borders projected onto the earth's surface. Liberals and liberalism: where couldn't they be? Conservatism, anarchism, and socialism: wherever people talked about these, they talked about them as if they were some of the fundamentals of political life. But not fascism, not yet. And certainly not antifascism.

By the age of fascism, things had changed. By then, visions of fascism and antifascism as universals abounded. For a sense of how great the change was, consider how fixed and bound fascism appeared to the chairman of the Comintern's executive committee, Grigory Zinoviev, near the end of 1921. Quite typical of the time, he understood fascism as one specific nation-contained project in Italy. When he thought about how it related to the larger political world, he didn't begin to conceptualize any transnational extension of fascism outward; he turned instead to explanation by comparison. For Zinoviev, fascism was an Italian campaign of paramilitarism, one of many similar—but distinct—such national campaigns. He warned: "Fascism, the Orguesch, etc., are active and flourishing." Such groups, he added, were all "reactionary." But beyond that the only general identity for them all that he applied was that of "white guards." He didn't argue that the paramilitaries all shared their politics with each other; he didn't imply that they influenced each other or exchanged ideas with each other. When Zinoviev wrote of fascism in Italy, the Orgesch in Germany, and similar groups elsewhere, all active and flourishing, he depicted a world of parallels. He compared. One group was *like* another. Similar things happened in separate lands. There was, to be sure, some talk of transnational influences and exchanges in the world of politics at the time; the communism Zinoviev practiced was well understood to course over borders and connect people in distant lands. Nonetheless, such talk didn't dominate people's political imaginations in the way that it would in the age of fascism when, for antifascists and fascists alike, the world would seem all thrown together into a single civil war that cut through and split societies and that cut across and tore open frontiers. The change between the era of the paramilitaries' rise and the age of fascism was more than a switching of political labels, new bottles for old wine. The underlying scheme in people's heads about how the political world worked, about how one place's politics related to another's, had been rewired. By the age of

—

fascism, visions of comparative politics had given way to those of transnational politics. Assumptions of nationally contained case studies fell away; intuitions of connectivity and cross-influences came to the fore.[24]

The ways that people used even some of the most familiar political words changed. When Zinoviev had written in 1921, he had had no reason to think of all those violent, reactionary paramilitaries as fascist. That shouldn't surprise. But less obvious, from today's perspective, is that he also had had no reason to call them right-wing. Looking back from later times, it has seemed quite sensible to historians to explain the paramilitarists of Zinoviev's day as "right-wing militants." Which does help to give us, today, a sense of those paramilitary groups' political implications in language familiar to us. The risk, though, is in thinking that such language would have made sense in the paramilitarists' own world. Such thinking leads one to assume that the paramilitarists had inherited a world of stable political language — when, rather, they were creating the very politics that provoked the making of the political language that is now familiar. The paramilitarists after World War I themselves made a distinctly modern, novel sort of popular politics. It defied easy identification in their own day. It was quite different, certainly, from the old-fashioned formal politics of any right wing in any of the world's republican parliaments. Zinoviev himself didn't at all think of the paramilitaries as right-wing. He didn't see them as opposed to the left, either. He did, however, see himself as quite opposed to the left. Which is to say that when he wrote he understood right and left quite contrary to how the paramilitaries' historians would later understand the words, writing on the other side of the age of fascism. Zinoviev, after all, was writing a year after Lenin had put out *The Infantile Sickness of "Leftism" in Communism* for the Comintern's second congress in 1920. And Zinoviev was writing in 1921 not only to warn of the rise of white guards throughout the world but also to share news from the Comintern's third congress, which had just been held. Zinoviev wrote that at the congress the Comintern had reaffirmed Lenin's antagonism toward the left. Unless checked, "the 'left'" (as Zinoviev put it, caustically, in quotation marks) would undo all the Comintern's great work.[25] His left was not ours; his right was not what historians write of; and his fascism wasn't what it would become within a dozen years' time.

—

He saw his political world as befitted the moment. A year later, the commander of one of the era's largest paramilitary organizations, Alvin Owsley of the American Legion, relied on a comparative logic very similar to Zinoviev's when he warned, "Do not forget that the Fascisti are to Italy what the American Legion is to the United States."[26] Owsley's emphasis was on a resemblance between the two groups' circumstances and social roles. His emphasis wasn't, for example, on flows of ideas or aesthetics between one and the other, or crosscurrents of influence, or overlapping networks, or interconnections of any sort between Legionnaires and Fascisti. Their fates, he suggested, were parallel, not entangled. Zinoviev and Owsley were, of course, not political friends; they simply saw their political differences in the same way.

And so the talk of Hitler and the grayshirts as fascisti stuck out oddly at the time. It was an early venture into using ideas of fascism to convey transnational connectivity rather than international comparison. It was far from inevitable that people would be so quick to label Hitler and his grayshirts as fascists, and "fascist" was far from the only name that people gave them. In 1922, the Nazis were alternately "Hitlerites," "nationalists," "Bavarian National Socialists," "the Bavarian Social Nationalists," and "Hakenkreuzlers." So many names, such a multiplicity of identities. To a degree, that's indicative of just how loose and liquid political identity always is. But it's also true that the years after the war were a time when all was especially scattered and open to interpretation. Political identity seemed a less fixed matter than before the war. It certainly wasn't riveted to any sturdy party affiliation: after all, parties in these years popped up, changed names, and fell apart in quick succession, and political discourse was left to keep up and make sense of the mess. But for a sense of how foundational fascism was to the making of Nazism's meaning in global politics, consider that all through the rest of the 1920s Hitler and the Nazis appeared in the daily press the world over, again and again, as fascists, whereas not until 1930 did the public outside of Germany start to make use of the diminutive handle "Nazi" that now, in retrospect, sounds to many an ear like a much less provocative, or controversial, identity to apply to them. The idea that there was an ism to go with "Nazi" – "Nazism" – only became a part of the discourse of global politics even later. And when newspaper correspondents started in the early 1930s to cable news of "Nazis" out of Germany into the wider world, how did they decode the new word for readers? By parenthetically explaining that the new word "Nazi" meant fascist.[27]

The mass antifascism about to boom drew on all this pulp political theorizing. Yes, all the while the Comintern's high theorists were holding forth on the nature of German fascism and the roots of its appeal; but they were far from alone in doing so. The chatter about German fascists and Hitler's fascist party, diffuse and cacophonous, came from many ideological corners.

All the same, the first sustained effort at antifascism to come out of Germany did indeed come from deep within the labyrinth of the Comintern.

No one did more to make antifascism's presence felt in Germany than Clara Zetkin. How she did so, then, was consequential. She was almost sixty-seven years old when, in the summer of 1923, she wrote her defining statement on the nature of fascism and the necessity of antifascism. It was telling that she put her statement in the form of a report, and that it was a report delivered to the Comintern's executive committee, of which she herself was a member. Much of Zetkin's antifascism, and much of the early antifascism in Germany in general, took place within the organizational architecture of the German Communist Party and the Comintern. Much of it had to do with theorizing fascism in a way that fit the Comintern's ruling doctrines, and much of it was communicated in conferences, bureaucratic reports, and committee resolutions.[28] It was very different from the antifascism of, say, Carlo Tresca and the antifascisti of New York, and very different from the antifascism of the Arditi del Popolo in Italy.

There was an irony in how Zetkin now poured her political labors into the Comintern's institutional mold. In the years before the Great War, when she had been in the Social Democratic Party, she had decided to "take her stand," as one comrade put it later on, "with the left wing." That faction, the left wing of the Social Democracy, had been openly hostile to the party's bureaucratic method, critical of the centripetal force it induced. That criticism, exacerbated by the party's pro-war line in 1914, had led Zetkin to take part during the war (in between spells of imprisonment) in the creation of the revolutionary Spartakusbund, known in English as the Spartacus League. She had been skeptical of Spartacism at first, concerned that it would amount to little more than a

—

few intellectuals' show of their own ideological purity, but she was won over, largely by the arguments of Rosa Luxemburg, who also hailed from the Social Democracy's left wing and with whom Zetkin shared an uncommonly deep and trusting friendship. The creation of the Spartacus League led in turn, at the war's end and in the middle of the German Revolution, to the creation of the German Communist Party, which Zetkin promptly joined. And almost right away in the new party yet another of those interminable little "lefts" took form. This left, the German Communist left, was the one that did the most to provoke Lenin to write *Infantile Sickness* in 1920; Zetkin, elected as a Communist that year to the Reichstag of the new Weimar Republic, likewise condemned leftism in the party.[29]

She could do so with considerable gravitas. She had been a committed socialist as far back as 1878 — the very year that the chancellor of the German Empire, Otto von Bismarck, imposed the first of his notorious Anti-Socialist Laws, compelling her (at the time, still Clara Eissner) to flee the country. In exile, she agitated for socialism and women's emancipation, and after the Anti-Socialist Laws lapsed in 1890 she returned to Germany and rose quickly in the Social Democratic Party during the years that it became famous as the archetypal mass party of modernity, the largest socialist party in the world. Zetkin edited its feminist journal, the *Gleichheit*, and in Copenhagen in 1910, while presiding over the Second International Conference of Socialist Women, she introduced the proposal that led to March 8 becoming International Women's Day.[30] In short, few radicals alive in 1923, in Germany or anywhere else, could match Zetkin's legacy.

Now she became, for a season at least, the Comintern's great authority on fascism and its architect of antifascism. In early January 1923, the executive committee, which Zinoviev still chaired, decided to establish an international committee dedicated to fighting fascism, and Zetkin was appointed, by the executive committee, to chair a provisional committee tasked with the construction of said committee. It was a little over two months since the March on Rome, and the Comintern hierarchy had begun already to piece together an institutional response to fascism. Indeed, the response was already underway by the time Zetkin began her task. And it was already muddled by then, as well. Which leads to a point about the Comintern that should be stressed:

—

it was, even in these days when it wasn't yet four years old, an elaborate and mazy edifice, an organization of organizations, complex, convoluted, and inevitably self-contradictory. Throughout its history, the Comintern was a political arena as much as a political agent. To say at any given time that it had taken this stance or made that decision—to say that it, "the Comintern" itself, ever actually did anything at all—always oversimplifies. When it came to the Comintern, difference and dispute always eddied just below the surface of any institutional act.[31]

That was decidedly so regarding its response to fascism. When Zetkin set about her work, the Comintern's fourth congress had just taken place, in November and December 1922. The proceedings had begun at the People's House in Petrograd only a few days after Mussolini had taken power in Italy. Zetkin herself had called the congress into session, with her customary salutation, "Sister comrades and brother comrades!"[32] But it was not Zetkin who had given the big report on fascism at the congress. It was Amadeo Bordiga, the head of the Communist Party of Italy. And it was his report that muddled the Comintern's early antifascism the most.[33]

Speaking in the afternoon of November 16, he began with a brief history of fascism. This was before Mussolini could cultivate much of his mythology over San Sepolcro, and so Bordiga could still see "the origin of the fascist movement" in "the years 1914–1915, the period before Italy's intervention in the World War." Even so, already in late 1922 Bordiga used certain keywords of basic political grammar in ways subtly different from how people in Italy had used them back in 1914 and 1915. He didn't do so in any systematic way or at any length. He didn't even do so directly. And yet, tucked away in his speech were small hints of how to blend together the separate realms of parliamentary politics and popular politics.

How did he do this? It was when he tried to explain who it was that had created the fascist movement in Italy that he turned to a language of left and right. The interventisti who made fascism included, Bordiga briefly explained, some who were "of the right" and others who were "of the bourgeois left." Then there were some others involved whom he called "the extreme left." These, he said, were "ex-anarchists, ex-syndicalists, and ex-revolutionary syndicalists." That was a rendering of "the extreme left" very different from Italian politi-

---

cal talk during the war. Anarchists, syndicalists, and revolutionary syndicalists had had no place in parliamentary politics, and it had followed at the time that they were not at all part of what was then the left or its extreme end. Even in 1919, when Mussolini himself had inveighed against "the extreme left," he had meant only the "republicans, radicals, independents [which was to say, independent, or reformist, socialists], and constitutional democrats" in the Italian parliament—a collectivity totaling no more than 150 men with mostly bourgeois principles, a world apart from any anarchists and revolutionaries causing trouble in the streets.[34]

And that was it. Bordiga didn't go on about it; it's conceivable that he never even realized how the picture of the left in his head had changed. It's conceivable as well that the effects of the change were all the more penetrating for it. He hadn't gone nearly as far as Tasca would go later on; he certainly hadn't made the left into a universalism, or any sort of global collectivity—his left was still very much nation-bound, encased in Italy. Still, however briefly and offhandedly, he had pushed the left out into the social realm of popular politics and agitation. In doing so he had taken an early step—a step, generally speaking, very much out of place with the general discourse of the time at which he spoke—in what would soon enough become a great collective reimagining of the left and its place in the political world.

But that had not been his intent in speaking at the congress. And it was not how he had confused the matter of the Comintern's stance on fascism. His intent had been to argue that fascism was no more than a new word for the old familiar bourgeois racket. And it was this that confused the matter so that Zetkin would have to clear it up in the months that followed. To his own mind, though, Bordiga had made things quite clear: despite all the fuss, there was nothing new or exceptional about fascism. And, he added, it wouldn't last long anyway. Keep your eyes, he told his comrades, on the old class enemy, the bourgeoisie. What's more, he warned, beware of political entanglements, however convenient any alliances may seem now; they'll only cause problems after fascism disappears. Keep your distance from the socialist parties, the liberals, the democrats, and the like. These, he insisted, are not our friends. Let us cut our own path, alone. It had been Bordiga, after all, who had articulated the Communist Party of Italy's fiercest critiques of the Arditi del Popolo. In the summer of 1921, Tasca's collaborator at the *Ordine Nuovo*, Gramsci, had seen promise in the antifascist arditi and had spoken up for them. The Communist Party of Italy, only founded that January, had two wings, one led by Bordiga, vanguardist and committed to iron discipline, and the other led by Gramsci, who romanticized the revolutionary possibilities of workers' mass actions in the factories. He saw something similar in the movement making of the Arditi del Popolo. When Gramsci made his appeal in the arditi's favor, it was Bordiga who ensured that the party denounced the people's army all the same.[35]

Against Bordiga, Zetkin argued throughout 1923 that fascism posed an extraordinary threat. It was "an exceptionally dangerous and frightful enemy." So dangerous and frightful that Communists had to reach out and ally with all those antifascist elements that Bordiga had scorned. Hence the need, she said, for bodies like the proposed antifascist committee. By early March, Zetkin was introducing herself as the chairwoman of the "provisorische internationale Komitee zur Bekämpfung des Faschismus" — the "provisional international Committee to Fight Fascism." By late March, she was speaking on its behalf, at a Comintern-sanctioned international conference in Frankfurt. There she prosecuted her case against Bordiga.[36]

Not only, Zetkin argued, was fascism a distinct political force in Italy, it was on the move. "Italian fascism is already extending its web into Germany," she said at Frankfurt, pointing to the "Hitler gangs who reign in Bavaria." Zetkin had fashioned a diffusionist theory of fascism; she envisioned it spreading, "extending," from source to site of reception. She had fashioned an early transnational theory of fascism as well — it didn't replicate country by country so much as it sprawled over the border, creeping first into Bavaria, likely to grow farther into Germany soon. The fascism the Hitler gangs practiced was not sophisticated. Their program, she said, "is exhausted by the phrase 'beat up the Jews.'" But it unmistakably was fascism. This she concluded from all the cheap "pseudo-revolutionary phrases," devoid of substance and "cloaked in the steel armor of the national ethos." Above all else, she concluded that Hitlerism was fascism because of the terror of it. Her arguments in Frankfurt seem to have won over her audience. She seems also to have picked up at Frankfurt an advantageous cochair, Henri Barbusse, the French author of the magnificent and ambiguous 1916 war novel *Le feu*.[37]

———

Zetkin's committee didn't last long, and its historical significance is every bit as ambiguous as the message of Barbusse's novel. In several ways, it prefigured a certain sort of antifascist organization that became familiar in the mid-1930s. Zetkin's committee was to be international; it was to welcome members of any ideological tendency; and it was to include representatives from a wide array of parties and political organizations.[38] Each of those three characteristics was to become familiar during the antifascist moment, when a parade of international, cross-ideological, and interorganizational congresses and committees and leagues and bureaus and alliances would all march together under the banner of antifascism. And each of those three characteristics pressed toward a wide sense of solidarity — across national boundaries, across ideological divides, and among people in different parties and organizations. Such a wide-ranging and multilayered sense of solidarity was what by the time of the Spanish Civil War people would try to capture by repurposing the phrase "the left," to gesture to the unwieldy sum of those swept up by it all, the world over.

But in 1923 to propose organizing along these lines wasn't an attempt to build "the left." Rather, the language of the day — itself quite novel — had it that Zetkin was proposing to "create the united front."[39] In this way, her committee had something in common with the Antifa that Ernst Thälmann would create nine years later; Thälmann was to see his Antifa as a way to build the United Front, led by the Communist Party, to counter the Iron Front. Which points to a fourth way, more disquieting than the others, in which Zetkin's committee prefigured certain antifascist politics to come: the problem it posed of the Comintern's relation to antifascism. All the inclusive rhetoric notwithstanding, her antifascist committee was to remain always a Comintern-run operation, no matter who joined, of whatever ideological bent, representing whichever political organizations. Whereas the first three prefigurations were later to serve as glue, sticking people together, this fourth one was to tear at antifascist solidarities for the rest of the interwar era. Since then, it has set historians against each other as they've tried to sort out what antifascism ultimately meant in the era — whether it was, at bottom, a genuine commitment or a tool of the Comintern's devising, used for its institutional interests. Right away, this presented a problem for organizing antifascist politics. And as Antifa would show, the problem didn't soon go away.

—

83

After Frankfurt, Zetkin no longer chaired a German provisional committee formally within the purview of the Comintern; instead, she cochaired a formally independent and fully established international body: the Action Committee Against War Danger and Fascism. And yet there was little doubt that the Comintern hierarchy still drove the agenda. In late April 1923, a month after the Frankfurt conference, one of Zetkin's longtime comrades from the Social Democratic left and the Spartacus League, now a prominent member of the German Communist Party, asked to take on some of the committee work; understanding how the committee worked, he asked Zinoviev. Sure enough, by the end of May the Action Committee Against War Danger and Fascism had a new, duly appointed secretary. His name was Willi Münzenberg. It's a name that figures large in the historiography of antifascism. For the historian François Furet, who wrote the most renowned of the anticommunist accounts of antifascism that flourished around the time of the Cold War's end, Münzenberg had played the leading part in taking antifascism global. For Furet, Münzenberg was unsurpassed in maneuvering through "the vast jesuitical bureaucracy of Moscow." More than that, though, he was the sly propagandist who could dupe intellectuals and sway public opinion in multiple countries at once, "the great conductor of the 'fellow traveler,' that classic figure of the communist universe – or, more to the point, given the epoch, that classic figure of a fascist world."[40] He got his start in antifascist politics with Zetkin's committee.

It was not a success. Even in his first month on the job, Münzenberg could see the trouble. He saw that the Frankfurt conference hadn't drawn in anyone from beyond the Comintern's own organizations. As the year wore on, enthusiasm in the upper levels of the Comintern for antifascism deteriorated. Directives from above tinkered with the committee's purpose, even its identity. "Action Committee Against War Danger and Fascism" gave way to "International Antifascist League," and then to "Antifascist World League." By the end of September 1924 the Comintern's executive committee had given up on the whole enterprise and shut it down.[41]

What came of it? Oddly enough, the most significant consequence of the committee's history was Zetkin's report. She delivered it to the executive committee at a June 1923 meeting. What was most intellectually nimble about the report – indeed, what the report had that showed the sort of intellectual cre-

—

ativity that even a dear friend like Luxemburg had thought Zetkin lacked—was the recognition that fascism in Italy had come about from a mash of hopes, half-intuitions, and outright mixups. No one person, or organization or class, had intended the fascism that ended up ruling the country. There was no grand strategy, certainly not one that came to fruition. Neither had fascism come about because of any mechanistic forces grinding away at history, yielding inevitable consequences. Happenstance, contingency, and human mystery had all played parts. This all was what Bordiga, as mechanistically minded as he was narrowly dogmatic, could never have grasped. Zetkin realized that this volatility made fascism a danger even to those who had initially benefited from its triumph over socialism, communism, anarchism, and the old liberal order in Italy. There was much that was awkward and pretentious about Zetkin's analysis, much that seems to have been intended to show off her facility for historical materialist theory. But even so, the writing makes implicit a big wondrous world of human imagination and ideological enchantment. In Zetkin's report to the Comintern's executive committee, abstractions drive and push, leap about, make demands, and hold hands with other abstractions; crises reverberate, contradictions find unexpected expression, and then in the end the proletariat itself finds its voice and speaks out full of optimism, proclaiming rather piously, "The future is mine!"[42]

Regardless, the institutional inertia of the Comintern leaned the other way. One of those moments in the Comintern's history approached when the dissenting beliefs eddying below came to the surface and submerged what had been afloat. It became clear that something more like Bordiga's way would be the Communist International's way for the time to come. The culmination of that way was to be the Stalinist era known as the "Third Period," epitomized by the social fascist thesis. Those whom Zetkin had seen as potential allies in the fight against fascism were to be recognized as enemies who enabled fascism.

In only a short spell, the Action Committee Against War Danger and Fascism had fallen flat. But it's worth remembering. Why? First of all, because it offers an example of Comintern-driven antifascism before Stalin's rise.[43] This matters because much of the anticommunist historical writing on antifascism has emphasized how Stalin beat antifascism into a shield with which to hide his deceit. It's useful to know that the Comintern engaged, albeit ambivalently,

—

with antifascism before Stalinism. A second reason is that the history of the committee offers a reminder that Münzenberg himself took part in antifascist politics before he served Stalin. And yet the third reason the committee is worth remembering is that it was a major Comintern-initiated project of antifascism that was already underway when Münzenberg signed on. It was Zetkin who steered the way in the Comintern's first foray into antifascism, not Münzenberg. An understanding of what Furet called "Communist antifascism," already in action before Münzenberg began plying his craft, helps to release some of the excess air in the reputation of the man Furet called a "genius of propaganda," a mastermind who "invented" a "new face for Stalinism: that of antifascist communism."[44] The fourth reason is the flip side of the third. While Münzenberg is the key figure in Furet's narrative — the man who by force of personal charm, willful duplicity, and boundless exertion provided Stalin with an impenetrable shield of propaganda — Zetkin doesn't appear in Furet's book at all. The legacy of the Comintern's antifascism is an equivocal thing, but Zetkin deserves whatever credit there is to be had for her part in crafting it. Still, that she crafted it holds less significance in the end than how she went about it.

For all that it should be remembered for, the Comintern's trial of antifascism in 1923 should not be remembered as the origin of antifascism beyond Italy.

Not only had the likes of Carlo Tresca already taken up antifascist politics in New York, other experiments in antifascism were underway as well. In London, antifascisti already had engaged local fascisti by the summer of 1922 — months before the March on Rome. The historiographical tendency to funnel the origins of transnational antifascism through German communism has likely derived from two points of preconception — that the origins must have come from within the Communist International and that they must have come from continental Europe. Already in its earliest days, though, antifascism beyond Italy wasn't contained within the Comintern, and it wasn't contained within continental Europe. It's a mistake to think of transnational antifascism as begun by Communists and only later joined by "fellow travelers," and it's a mistake to think of transnational antifascist history as spiraling outward from Italy into Europe and only later being "received" by the wider world.

—

Events in London had hardly lagged behind those in New York. A small group of self-described fascisti established a fascio in London on June 12, 1921, only six weeks after De Biasi and the others had announced theirs in New York City. Antonio Cippico, a professor of Italian studies at the University of London, held the founding meeting at his home in Kensington. Soon the fascisti established a base in Noel Street in Soho. The early London fascisti included the intellectual, and *Popolo d'Italia* contributor, Camillo Pellizzi and the hotel worker Achille Bettini. Pellizzi was, Bettini said, the fascio's "mental motor." Bettini himself was its physical embodiment. His brooding figure drew comment whether he was in blackshirt uniform or not. Striding the streets of Soho, he wore on his chest a badge marked with a skull and crossbones (the New York fascisti wore the same symbol) and the word "Disperata" (Desperate). He claimed to have been one of the first 100 fascisti of the Fascio di Combattimento in Milan; in London, he said, he and the fascisti were "not preaching revolution" but were "determined to achieve" what the British government wouldn't do for "our people." That and, he added, "we combat Bolshevism."[45]

When a procession of fifty or so London fascisti marched into Westminster Abbey, Bettini bore the group's flag—an Italian tricolor with the fascist symbol of a Roman lictor's fasces at its center instead of the cross of Savoy. It was Saturday, November 4, 1922, only days since the March on Rome (and the day before Zetkin was to open the Comintern's fourth congress in Petrograd). It was Italian Armistice Day, the fourth anniversary of Italy's victory over Austria-Hungary (and one week before most people in London were to commemorate the armistice). Westminster Abbey housed the Unknown Warrior's grave, the British martyry to "the fallen soldier" of the Great War. Likewise in Rome, one year prior, on November 4, 1921, an unknown soldier's remains had been entombed with much ceremony at the Vittoriano, next to the Piazza Venezia. The fascisti arrived as the afternoon service in the abbey was finishing. As the London *Times* recounted, "Few in the crowd realized what was happening when the great door was thrown open, and through the quiet lane of people advanced three young men in black shirts." The three laid a green-white-and-red wreath on the tomb, offered straight-armed salutes, and prayed. Then they "leaped to their feet" and returned to Bettini and the others. The

—

fascisti left the abbey and "swung up Whitehall" to where stands the Cenotaph, the "empty tomb" monument erected in 1920 to memorialize the war dead and, authorities hoped, instill some nationalistic sentiment in the people at a moment when bolshevism seemed to be spreading into the country. It made the perfect symbolic setting for the blackshirts. Standing in front of the Cenotaph, they extended another round of fascist salutes and cried out "A noi!" ("To us!"). Then they sang the fascist anthem, "Giovinezza," and marched away, back up to the fascio in Noel Street.[46]

The procession was an audacious act. It spoke to just how transformative of fascism acts outside of Italy had been from the start. Fascisti in Rome wore black, threw up straight-armed salutes, and shouted "A noi!" But what a difference it made to do the same in London. (Or in New York City, where it was also exclaimed: "Fascisti, a noi!") Historians of Italian fascism have translated the exclamation into English as "Italy belongs to us."[47] But crying out the same ambiguous "To us!" in the middle of Whitehall revealed the greater ambitions of the fascisti.

By the time of their march up Whitehall, the London fascisti had local enemies. A small set of Italian anarchists lived in London, all of whom seemed to frequent the King Bomba, the Italian produce shop a few blocks away from the Soho fascio, at 37 Old Compton Street. The grand old anarchist Emidio Recchioni ran the King Bomba, and he ran it as a base for anarchist, and now antifascist, agitation. With fascisti strutting about the neighborhood, Recchioni and his circle started up a weekly magazine, the *Comento,* meant in no small part to defy fascism, both in Italy and in town. The first issue went to press in July 1922. Recchioni and his anarchist coconspirators, including Silvio Corio and Pietro Gualducci, had begun by this point to see themselves as antifascisti. Their commitments deepened over the summer amid tensions in Soho, amid even assaults and street fights between fascist-minded and antifascist-minded locals. Everything intensified once Mussolini took power. Before March 1923 was out, Gualducci and Corio were involved in organizing antifascist meetings around London; the first took place on March 25 at the Italian Bowling Club at 24 Eyre Street Hill in Clerkenwell. Gualducci led the meeting along with a rather notorious British radical who had been writing against fascism since the March on Rome. Her name was Sylvia Pankhurst.[48] She had been among those named in *The Infantile Sickness of "Leftism" in Communism* as an intransigent "Left." And she was to become, with time, one of the most intransigent antifascists in Britain.

Meanwhile, in New York City, Elizabeth Gurley Flynn looked into the future and saw an America overrun by fascism. When she did so, she was speaking at the Civic Club, on West 12th Street just off Fifth Avenue. It was April 6, 1924. A racially integrated club, founded and frequented by renowned figures such as W. E. B. Du Bois, the Civic Club had just two weeks before hosted a grand dinner of literary figures, a dinner that would later be mythologized as the launch of the Harlem Renaissance. On April 6, Flynn — a white labor organizer, feminist, and socialist — spoke to a much smaller gathering and delivered a much more ominous message. Tomorrow in America, she said, fascisti would smash working people's unions, demolish the press, shackle speech, force-feed castor oil to radicals like her, and burn down the libraries. It wasn't the blackshirts of New York who worried her the most. It was the American Legionnaires and the klansmen. They weren't fascist yet, but they had the numbers, and, she warned, they were working to make "a Fascist party in this country." Elizabeth Gurley Flynn, already in 1924, envisioned a less Italy-centric fascism. She posed it less as a form of ideology and more as a technique of domination — "the Fascist method," she called it.[49] All in all, she was working out a more expansive idea of fascism.

And she was practicing a more expansive idea of antifascism. Flynn had already been speaking out against fascism for a while: during the previous summer she had given sidewalk speeches everywhere in the city from the corner of Bleecker and MacDougal streets in Greenwich Village to the corner of 150th Street and Morris Avenue in the Bronx. She had also gone on the road, having delivered provocative antifascist speeches as far away as Baltimore. Her antifascism showed how radicals from beyond the diaspora of Italian émigrés might pick up the political form and put it to use. In this, she was akin to Pankhurst or Zetkin. More like Pankhurst in that they both sought to ground their own antifascism in lateral collaboration with the Italian-born antifascisti around them. In the spring of 1924, Flynn was thirty-three years old; her reputation as a spellbinding orator stretched back over more than half of her

—

life, back to when she had been only sixteen. That was when she dropped out of school and joined the IWW. Before she turned eighteen, she already was known as the "Anarchistic Joan of Arc" and the "Girl Orator of the Bowery." She went on to agitate for the IWW during its free speech campaigns in cities such as Missoula and Spokane. By the time she took part in organizing the union's 1912 textile strike in Lawrence, she had become one of the most notorious "Wobblies" (as the IWW's members were popularly called) in the country. Arturo Giovannitti led the strike effort in Lawrence; when the local police threw him in jail, Flynn took over along with the legendary Wobbly Big Bill Haywood. And in Lawrence she met Carlo Tresca. The two fell in love (fig. 2).[50]

They were still together when Flynn spoke at the Civic Club twelve years later. She gave a typically ferocious speech. After she finished, Mario Pei, a precocious twenty-three-year-old language instructor at City College, challenged her. Pei wore, as a reporter present described it, "the Fascista emblem" on his lapel—likely the skull and crossbones like Bettini wore in London. Pei was an active fascist, militant and highly ranked in the New York fascio. Two others who wore the emblem marking themselves as fascisti were with him. Pei insisted that Italian fascism had begun only as a defensive reaction against red radicalism and, as the reporter recounted it, he hammered away at "instances of anti-Fascista violence."[51]

That Pei, a young man born in Rome to Italian parents, would practice fascism in New York fit the pattern of early transnational fascism. But Flynn, a young woman born in Merrimack County, New Hampshire, to Irish parents, stood apart as an antifascist in 1924. What had made her one, then? It's fair to say that her familiarity with Italian antifascisti in New York shaped her thought. Even besides Tresca, her closest political comrades were Italian-born antifascisti, such as Giovannitti. But it would be wrong to say that she absorbed their politics. In general, she found their analysis overly simple. It's closer to the truth to say that Elizabeth Gurley Flynn saw in the particular struggle between fascism and antifascism a political fable that captured and clarified in small something about all the modern political world. Her antifascism was in a way metaphorical, even pedagogical: she railed against fascism so as to make clear to the crowd in front of her what forces in the world weighed on them and tried to

Figure 2. Elizabeth Gurley Flynn with Carlo Tresca in Paterson,
New Jersey, during the silk strike of 1913. Both were devoted labor
organizers for the Industrial Workers of the World (IWW) and both
would later become committed antifascists. *Walter P. Reuther Library,
Archives of Labor and Urban Affairs, Wayne State University.*

dictate their future. Her antifascism was very much her own, and she practiced it freely. The way she acted, though, it was as if she thought it was only natural for someone not Italian to be an antifascist.

But at the time, few were. On the whole, or at least compared to what would follow, antifascism throughout its first dozen years—the period of its prehistory—remained a politics of Italian people, even when practiced outside of Italy. This was a large part of the reason why Vergnon saw these years as prelude. When—one week after Flynn's speech at the Civic Club in New York City—Uruguayan anarchists put in print their exclamation of surprise that antifascism had materialized in Montevideo, it was because local Italian émigrés had started to stir up an antifascist politics in the city. Even in these early years, antifascism beyond Italy always had to face two ways at once. To be an antifascist in a city such as New York or London or Montevideo was, of course, to defy the Mussolini regime from a distance. It was also to confront the fascisti right in front of you. Often literally so, as when Pei challenged Flynn.

Where the Italian diaspora landed, there one found Mussolini's backers ready to build up a fascist politics in their new land. Where that happened, there one also found other Italian émigrés ready to take up antifascism, spurred to do so by the fascism of both their old country and their new home. In Buenos Aires, where many Italian people had settled, it didn't take long for a portion of them to counter the fascisti among them. Fascism itself had taken form early in Buenos Aires. The fascio there may well have been one of the few established outside of Italy before the March on Rome, along with the likes of the fasci of New York and London. By the end of the 1920s, at least, it was claimed that fasci in Argentina first appeared on the "Día de la Raza," or "Day of the Race," of 1922, the October 12 holiday celebrating Christopher Columbus's landfall in 1492.[52] Whether or not it's true that fascisti in Buenos Aires organized as early as that, it is certain that by early the next year there was a fascio in the city; and there were also locals, adhering to a mix of ideological beliefs, who were determined to defy the city's fascisti. They did so collectively and sometimes violently. In May 1923, antifascisti crashed a pair of local fascist rallies. At one of them, at the historic Italian mutual aid society in the city center, a crowd of 200 antifascisti fought an even larger number of fascisti. The affair ended in gunfire.[53]

—

But neither fascism nor antifascism was to remain entirely contained within greater Italy, walled off from the rest of the world's politics. Throughout these early years, both fascism and antifascism were political forms growing like weeds out in the world's intellectual commons, there for the picking. People in all sorts of places, acting on all sorts of impulses, from all sorts of social positions and out of all sorts of ambitions, gathered what they wished and consumed what they pleased. Fascism and antifascism were not oddities in this regard. All of the isms of modern political history have grown like this. No manifesto, however programmatic it may be, ever really defines its subject so as to prevent people – on the whole stubborn and freethinking – from pursuing all the countless heresies, deviations, and misconstructions they formulate in their heads.

Take, for instance, the Londoners who called themselves the British Fascisti. They adopted the name as soon as they began meeting in the summer of 1923. Yet they weren't Italian in any sense of the word; scholars have suggested that they weren't fascists either – that they were misguided or foolish, ultimately somehow wrong, to say that they were.[54] But they were fascist in the sense that they said fascism fit how they saw things and that they tried earnestly to act as they thought fascisti ought to act. The British Fascisti had nothing to do with Bettini and Pellizzi and the rest of the fascisti of Noel Street, and they had nothing to do with the new Mussolini regime either, other than that it had inspired them to organize. Rather, in early 1923 young Rotha Lintorn-Orman had placed ads in the *Patriot,* a sixpence London sheet started up the year before to serve as a source of alternative news about the "movements threatening to the safety and welfare of the British Empire" – the news that the "established newspapers" had conspired to hide from the public. In her ads Lintorn-Orman – Kensington-born, twenty-eight years old, a skilled mechanic who had driven ambulances on the Salonika front during the war – called for British anticommunists like herself to join together in a new organization, open to those (British-born) wishing to defend the empire and monarchy from red internationalists. Another of the first British Fascisti, Nesta Helen Webster, had written in the *Patriot* that the old ideologies were "empty husks." Conservatism, liberalism, socialism – they were all "dead formulas that hold no life-giving force within them." She had argued this in early 1922, desperate to find "a

—

93

living creed" in a dying world. Her conclusion then had been simply to revivify conservatism, to enliven it beyond what it had been, even, because it had been, she thought, quite dull. She sought a conservatism open to the British masses, a mix of populism and nationalism. She had condemned internationalism already, in a 1921 work of history and political theory that had traced the unrest of the post–World War moment back to the ideas unleashed in the French Revolution. She had argued that Bolshevism derived from the notorious – the "amazing," she called it – *Protocols of the Elders of Zion,* the authenticity of which, she insisted, had "never been refuted" and which, regardless, held in its text deeper truths. By 1923, Webster was ready to turn to fascism. She was one of the first to join Lintorn-Orman's British Fascisti. The group, very small at first, grew rapidly. By October 7, they were ready for their first rally, drawing some 500 people. British Communists showed up as well, looking to interfere and cause a scene.[55]

A little more than a year later, on Armistice Sunday 1924, the British Fascisti reenacted, in their own way, the scene that Achille Bettini and the other London blackshirts had performed two years earlier. After the British Fascisti held what their enemies called a "monster mass meeting" in Trafalgar Square, they marched to the Cenotaph. The episode was, I think, the first fascist rally in Trafalgar Square; it was not to be the last. The fascisti wore black shirts and silver badges. Some stood at the foot of Nelson's Column, and others ringed the crowd of perhaps 10,000. Among the fascisti themselves were perhaps 600 women and 1,400 men. A brass band played, and the crowd cheered as Lintorn-Orman approached Nelson's Column, where a wreath waited for her, violets and white chrysanthemums, made to look like the fascisti's badge. The one interruption to the ceremony came when an old man objected to the scene and started shouting. Fascisti swarmed and struck him. As one correspondent on the scene reported, "he received severe treatment." At the end, counterdemonstrators – it's unclear who they were or what their exact politics were – tried to sing "The Red Flag," and the fascisti countered with "God Save the King." It was then that the 2,000 fascisti marched to the Cenotaph and the wreath was laid at its base. "Then," the correspondent observed, "the units marched past, giving the Fascisti salute."[56]

* * *

—

94

Sometimes martyrs know what awaits them. Giacomo Matteotti did. There were many victims of fascism before him, but all the same it's fair to think of him as the first martyr of antifascism. And antifascism was to become very much a politics haunted by its martyrs — akin in this regard to fascism.[57] Matteotti's death hardened his comrades' commitments, inspired the courage of dissidents throughout the land, and came to symbolize the suffering and sacrifice of all who resisted. Which is what martyrs do. They do so mostly by invocation. Antifascists invoke names like Giacomo Matteotti, José Guevara, Leone Ginzburg, Liselotte Herrmann, Zoltán Schönherz, Eugenio Curiel, Akber Aghayev, Norma Beatriz Melena, Sandra Neely Smith, Kalbinder Kaur Hayre, Carlo Giuliani, Brahim Bouarram, Clément Méric, Pavlos Fryssas, Heather Heyer. The list goes on, and it lengthens still. What's more, the list above is only suggestive; to point out its most obvious shortcoming, it doesn't even begin to recognize the many martyrs of the Spanish Civil War, some of whom have already appeared in this book as they were when they were young and alive, not yet martyrs. String together enough names and a certain sort of antifascist history takes form in your mind, a history stripped of context and complications, a history that reaches easily over the years and decades, across countries and continents, to tell a simple story of one heroic sacrifice after another. But invoke even one name — say, the name of Matteotti — and you can already feel the pull of martyrdom's melodrama. Because of that pull, the mourning of a martyr is a potent political act. It inspirits and rallies the living.[58] It does so in particular when the invocation is kept simple. Say much more than a martyr's name and quarrels over what the martyr's life and death signified are sure to follow. Keep the invocation direct and unadorned, and its emphasis remains on what is shared in common: the belief that the martyr's life and death held significance.

When Matteotti finished the heroic final public act of his life, he knew he had just tempted the fates. It was May 30, 1924, and the Italian chamber of deputies, the Camera dei Deputati, was opening its new session, the first since the fascisti's electoral triumph in April that had seemed to ratify Mussolini's rule. Matteotti, a socialist deputy who had been one of the most vocal antifascist politicians all along, had just given a speech fulminating against fascist violence and misdeeds. He was young — thirty-nine — and charismatic, intelligent and ambitious. He had spoken for two hours, over the shouts and threats of fascist deputies. Mussolini had been there in the Camera. After he finished his speech, Matteotti turned and said to friends at his side, "You can start writing my eulogy now." He was smiling. Eleven days later, alongside the Tiber, five men pushed him into a black automobile—a Lancia Lambda, sleek and skeletal—and took him away. "Alas!" said Pietro Nenni, the editor of *Avanti!* "He was a prophet."[59]

Where was Giacomo Matteotti? No one knew, but everyone figured what had happened. Not until weeks later was his body found, in a shallow grave outside of Rome. By then there had been memorial events held in his honor in cities around the globe. His presumed death had mobilized antifascisti not only in Italy but also out in the Italian diaspora. That in itself was predictable enough. But what was novel about the efforts to memorialize Matteotti was the extent to which they drew in people who weren't Italian. The mass mourning for Matteotti gave the cause of antifascism its first great boost toward becoming something larger than a particularism of Italy and its diaspora. It would be an overstatement to say that the mourning outright universalized the idea of antifascism, or made it a global political concept, but it pushed the idea in that direction. Far more so than Zetkin's arguments did, Matteotti's martyrdom prodded new sets of people outside of Italy to stir notions of antifascism into their political thought and to begin thinking of antifascism as a general principle.

As soon as it became apparent that Matteotti had died, antifascisti began to commemorate his life. He had been kidnapped on June 10; by late June, there had been gatherings in his honor in Geneva, Nice, and the Parisian suburb of Le-Pré-Saint-Gervais. The rally in Le-Pré-Saint-Gervais had drawn thousands—the French Communist Party's newspaper *Humanité* claimed 30,000—and it ended in gunfire, arrests, and injured protesters and police. On June 26, Flynn, Giovannitti, and Tresca spoke to an outraged crowd of 3,000 at Carnegie Hall in New York; four days later, Tresca spoke to an even bigger crowd on the Boston Common (Giovannitti had planned to come up as well but was asked to speak at another meeting in New York). Before Tresca's speech, given from the Parkman Bandstand on the Common, marchers held up a large portrait of Matteotti and made a funeral procession with a band along Tremont, Boylston, and Charles streets. On the same day, antifascisti in

São Paulo held "a solemn commemoration" in the Theatro Olympia, a minute's walk from the Praça da Sé in the center of the city. "A tragic, sorrowful, harrowing event has struck Italy and shook the world," the commemoration's organizers had written in their plea for "everyone who has faith in freedom and justice" to come and take part.[60]

The commemorative demonstration in London was a tenser affair. The leadership of the governing Labour Party was wary of alienating the Italian regime. And yet Labour members of Parliament had known Matteotti personally—he had visited London only weeks before his death and had spoken to them about the fascist terror. Among the socialists in the Independent Labour Party (which, despite its name, was at the time a part of the Labour Party), there were strong feelings of solidarity with Matteotti; they organized a demonstration to take place in Trafalgar Square on the last Saturday of June, the day before the Boston and São Paulo events. Fifteen hundred people came out, but the four Labour members of Parliament scheduled to speak didn't show up, fearful of offending Mussolini. Fascisti showed up, though, and heckled Shapurji Saklatvala, a Parsi communist who had recently represented North Battersea in the House of Commons. He hadn't been scheduled to speak but the crowd cried out for him, perhaps because so many of the scheduled speakers hadn't shown. In response to the fascisti's heckles, Saklatvala was defiant and dismissive. Referring to the park in South London where the fascisti often held forth, he gibed, "These Fascisti speak soft stuff on Clapham Common, but if they are the real article let them kidnap and murder half a dozen men like me. I am quite ready." Buoyed by cheers and laughter, he taunted, "Unless they do that we won't believe they are genuine fellows, but cowards."[61] It was no longer a very mournful scene. Saklatvala's defiance had made for a great success and lifted many spirits.

Was Sylvia Pankhurst there? It seems likely. She had a long history with the Independent Labour Party and was already by this time an outspoken antifascist (and she was also a long-standing personal comrade of Saklatvala's). Whether Pankhurst was there or not, one year later she and Silvio Corio, along with several others, planned another memorial protest for Matteotti, to mark the first anniversary of his murder. They organized themselves as the Friends of Italian Freedom and leased the St. James's Hall of the Working Men's Club in Soho, in the heart of London's Italian colony. By this point, June 1925, Pankhurst had been organizing antifascist meetings for over two years, and she had been writing antifascist polemics for even longer. During the tumultuous fall of 1922, the newspaper she had founded and edited, the *Workers' Dreadnought,* had juxtaposed news of the March on Rome with that of the blackshirted fascisti's march on Westminster Abbey in London.[62] Back in 1919, after she had traveled to Italy to attend the Italian Socialist Party's congress, she had reported on the violence of arditi, and had even mentioned Mussolini, in the *Dreadnought.*[63] She then had made her way into Germany, where she found Zetkin in her country home near Stuttgart and traveled with her to Frankfurt. The following year, Pankhurst had gone to Soviet Russia for the Comintern's second congress and had listened as Lenin critiqued her and all the others suffering from bouts of "Leftism"—his treatise, she had said, somewhat diplomatically, "was intended to confound and convert those of us who disagree with its author." Pankhurst had already been active in radical politics for a long time by then and knew well that fiercely held differences were a part of it. She was a daughter of Emmeline and Richard Pankhurst, both of whom had worked to found the Independent Labour Party. Emmeline Pankhurst had gone on to found and run the Women's Social and Political Union, the militant suffrage organization. Sylvia had organized on behalf of women's suffrage for years; she had a radical's mind, and it was in part her expansive vision of emancipation that had led to her expulsion from her mother's organization. Emmeline told Sylvia that she was unreasonable and had always been so. Another militant from the women's suffrage movement told her off by writing publicly, "I know you and your kind, Sylvia. You are of the authentic martyr stuff."[64]

The St. James's Hall meeting for Matteotti that Pankhurst and the rest of the Friends of Italian Freedom organized never happened. At least not at St. James's Hall. As Pankhurst explained it a few days later, "The meeting was to have been a public memorial . . . to commemorate the death of the murdered Italian deputy Giacomo Matteotti." Describing the Friends as "English and Italian lovers of freedom," she commented that they had paid for the hall in advance only to be told later that they would have to put down an indemnity "against violence which might arise during the meeting." Then on the day of the meeting, the hall's caretaker refused to let in anyone at all; as Pankhurst told the story,

—

the caretaker explained that the club's governors had canceled the lease "on the ground that the police had warned them that violence from persons hostile to the meeting must be anticipated, and urged them not to permit the meeting." Pankhurst and the others "repaired to a café in High Street, Soho, where resolutions of commemoration and protest were passed." But, Pankhurst noted, it was a "very grave" matter that "Fascism is now able in London to prevent the holding of so solemn a thing as a memorial meeting."[65]

Elsewhere as well, antifascists marked the one-year anniversary of Matteotti's murder. In Buenos Aires, antifascisti of different political creeds honored the day by announcing that they had come together to form the Unione Antifascista Italiana. The group published a manifesto in Matteotti's honor — "on the anniversary of the execrable crime that horrified the whole world" — and held a public meeting of remembrance at which socialists, communists, and anarchists all spoke.[66] The message was that the best way to honor the antifascist martyr was by working toward a politics of unity and preparing to fight fascism together.

The work of getting along together, however, wasn't easy; and it wasn't inevitable — it *was* work. In the days leading up to the commemoration in Buenos Aires, local anarchists argued that unlike "the so-called 'antifascisti,' pure and simple," who had bourgeois politics, they themselves had to wrestle with the stakes and strategy of antifascism because, unlike the bourgeois antifascisti, they hoped for a social revolution: "we are 'anarchists' before we are antifascisti." And yet, they concluded, they were antifascisti all the same — antifascisti *and* anarchists *and* revolutionaries; or, "better yet: we are revolutionaries and we are antifascisti, anarchistically so."[67]

In the late 1920s, the work of clearing away that sort of common ground became a lot harder. Institutional rivalries and jealousies intensified. Ideological differences sharpened. Even then, though, contemporaries didn't think that there once had been a big unified mass collectivity called "the left," now tragically rent. The idea of the left as something that encompasses all the world's communist, socialist, anarchist, and radical movements, parties, and people was something that still hadn't been worked out. But in the late 1920s and into the early 1930s, the ideological divides didn't narrow; they widened. The Comintern's social fascist thesis exemplified the trend. When French Communist

Party members organized a meeting in the summer of 1927 to observe the third anniversary of Matteotti's murder, the French Socialist Party's newspaper, the *Populaire,* couldn't help but point out that in all the Communists' talk of honoring Matteotti's memory they had neglected to consider two points. First, that Matteotti was a deputy of a socialist party.[68] And, second, that according to "bolshevik logic," socialism was "the left wing of fascism." Thus, "the communists were celebrating the memory of a fascist named Matteotti. Oh, what logic!"[69]

August 30, 1932: Clara Zetkin rose to speak. As the oldest member of the Reichstag—now seventy-four—she had the privilege of giving the opening speech following the July elections. She had been a member of the Weimar Republic's parliament since 1920. The Nazis in the Reichstag were beside themselves. They had won the most seats of any party, over one-third of the total, with 230, and they wanted the day for themselves.

Waiting for Zetkin, the Nazis sat on the right.

Where to locate Nazism on an imagined ideological spectrum has been a point of intellectual contention for decades. Sometimes the arguments are glib, sometimes they are nakedly disingenuous, and sometimes they are intellectually incandescent. They are rarely grounded in the history of what left and right meant in the era of Nazism's making. Quite forgotten in all the rhetorical crossfire is that the Nazis at the time knew left and right in quite unambiguous terms: the seats in the Reichstag building's plenary chamber. As the Nazis began to win seats, they took the ones on the right. Just like the wartime Fascio of Giretti and Centurione had done in the Italian Camera dei Deputati. And just like Mussolini and his party of fascisti had done once they entered the same chamber after the war. In 1921, when the newly elected Mussolini addressed the Camera for the first time, he began by stating outright, "I am not at all displeased, honorable colleagues, to begin my discourse from these benches on the extreme right." Indeed, he said, he was proud to take his place where few dared to go.[70] Left and right aren't where one begins. Rather, they are first encountered as a choice to be made: where will one go to make one's politics? For all the intellectual sparring over whether German Nazism and Italian fascism were, in some metaphysical sense, left or right at their birth, it explains

—

100

more to point out what's not so equivocal: where their practitioners went and took a seat.[71]

Zetkin's usual seat, of course, was on the left. On August 30, though, her place was the chamber president's chair so that she could give her opening speech. She was not well and made her way only with great difficulty. "So feebly did she move that it looked doubtful whether she would even reach that big chair," one witness wrote. She walked with a thick cane, and two women, both communists, held her. Her speech, which was recorded, began in a voice that was hard to hear. But she soon came alive and delivered a classic statement of antifascism (fig. 3).[72]

Zetkin had been through a lot by 1932. Her hopes for a Comintern-led united front had not materialized in 1923. And then the moment had gotten away. Stalin sought a harder line. When Angelo Tasca was expelled from the Comintern for siding with what Stalin had called "the Right danger" in the German Communist Party, it had been Zetkin who had been the danger. Tasca had sided with Zetkin. Zetkin had been seeking to give the United Front another try. Saddened by Stalin's takeover of the German Communist Party, she struggled with what was best to do.[73] She decided to stay in the party. In part, it was because she kept her faith in the idea of communism. In part, it was because she thought the party was necessary for fighting fascism in Germany. Now, in the summer of 1932, fascism appeared to be closing in on state power in Germany.

Her speech was a defiant plea for a politics of antifascist unity. She spoke past the members of the Reichstag and asked the masses not to forget the ultimate aim: living a life of emancipation from suffering, hunger, and exploitation. Never forget, she said, "the brutal forces of capitalism" behind "the slaughter of the people the world over." But, she said, "the necessary task in the present hour is to raise the United Front of all working people to knock back fascism." To that task, she said, "all the differences and divisions of political, labor organizing, religious, and ideological beliefs must yield."[74] The vanguard of the struggle, she still insisted, was in the Soviet Union, but she noticeably refrained from depicting her new version of the United Front as Comintern-driven, or as a revolt of rank-and-file Social Democrats away from their party. Her antifascism sounded now less tactical, less instrumental and doctrinal, than in 1923.

—

Figure 3. The German antifascist Clara Zetkin gives the opening speech in the Reichstag following the July 1932 elections. The Nazis had won 230 seats in the elections and they took their seats on the chamber's right side. Zetkin's fellow members of the German Communist Party sat on the left. With her speech, Zetkin delivered a classic statement of antifascism. *Ullstein Bild Dtl./Getty Images.*

Throughout the speech, the Nazis on the right stewed. Some hid their faces behind newspapers. The left roared. It was Clara Zetkin's final major public act. She died less than a year later, near Moscow, in exile, a little over five months into the reign of the Third Reich. She certainly hadn't given an anti-Stalinist speech, but neither had she given the speech Stalin would have chosen. Not only had she returned to her notion of the United Front, she had hinted at an antifascism unbeholden to Comintern directives. And yet she hadn't exactly come out and said so either. All of which was her way.[75] Which is to say, as the summer of 1932 drew to an end, Clara Zetkin was still trying to find her way through.

—

CHAPTER 3

FASCISM SHALL NOT PASS

Anti-fascism is not dead. The opposition is still alive. It's just that
the battlefield has expanded; yesterday it was Italy, today it is the
world. Everywhere, the fight is for or against fascism.

—BENITO MUSSOLINI, 1930

In the summer of 1934, when he was twenty-one years old, Arnold Sevareid stumbled into a larger political world without leaving his hometown. Even
in an age when unforeseen events remade people's political imaginations with
peremptory force, young Sevareid's revelation stood out, so suddenly had he
been struck, so unawares had he been taken. "Suddenly I knew," he explained
later. "I understood deep in my bones and blood what Fascism was." His shock
came amidst a series of strikes that convulsed his home city, Minneapolis, for
much of the year. A college student hired by the *Minneapolis Star* to cover the
street warfare surrounding the strikes, he was touring the local hospital with
nurses who showed him bullet holes in the bodies of injured strikers—"in the
backs of their heads, arms, legs, and shoulders"—when he decided he knew
what fascism was. It wasn't just the violence of the mass shooting that hit him.
He also was struck by the strange mix of cynicism and zeal that had led to it.
And he was unsettled, too, by the relation of the violence to its press coverage.
He saw in the hospital that the violence had been an ambush—"a deliberate
trap"—and not a haphazard disturbance as depicted in the papers. The whole
thing horrified him, and his horror deepened as he considered that he had
learned the nature of fascism not in Germany or Italy but "in the precise area

—

which is psychologically the most removed from the troubles of Europe – in the heart of the Middle West."[1]

Severeid's realization hit him harder than most, but it fit the moment all the same. Middle West, Middle East, up and down the Americas, in spots of Africa, Asia, and Australia, in port cities on islands in between, and of course in the cities of Europe, people were having the same sort of realization as the age of fascism began. They read of fascism in the newspapers; they heard it on the radio; they saw it in the newsreels at the movie palaces; then they experienced it right in front of them, where they lived. Not everywhere, but in ever more places, fascism no longer seemed like a distant menace. It certainly no longer seemed like a particularism of Italy, or even of Italy and its diaspora. The fascism that delivered unto Severeid his great revelation in the summer of 1934 had become a much larger, more fearful political beast than what Carlo Tresca and Arturo Giovannitti or the Arditi del Popolo had faced in the era of the March on Rome, much larger as well than what Clara Zetkin had conjured or what had compelled young Eric Hobsbawm into the streets of Berlin only eighteen months before. In Severeid's time, the sense that fascism had become a figure with a global reach pervaded political talk. When Mussolini had begun suggesting as much in 1930, after years of insisting that fascism was "not an article for export," it had been with some bluster.[2] But the sense had taken hold since Hitler claimed power. That opened the way to a new, more expansive idea of antifascism. Fascism's new immensity meant the need to defy it as never before. For those like Severeid who felt its sting now for the first time, fascism's new proximity meant the chance to defy it in ways more direct and meaningful – more immersive – than ever before.

It was a minority, to be sure, that absorbed the immensity of fascism and became militant antifascists, but it was by no means an insignificant minority. Enough people in enough places acted out enough antifascism to push word of it into the patter of everyday political talk. They all, whether they were conscious of it or not, shared in the work of creating yet another of those grandiose, universalized ideological abstractions that have enchanted the modern world. It was an emphatically collective labor. And it took place ever so scattered about. Just as fascism didn't "spread" from Italy into the wider world, so too with

—

antifascism. Locals all over pulled antifascism out of its Italian particularity by practicing it where they themselves were. The agency at work belonged, at bottom, to them, all those who made the presence of antifascism felt where it hadn't been felt before.

What's more, all those who picked up antifascism and applied it where they lived didn't just enlarge the form, they transformed it. Just as fascism's meaning changed from that of a particularism into that of a universal because of all the practice of fascism beyond Italy and its diaspora, so too with antifascism. People in different places made it meaningful to them, and in doing so they changed its meaning.

Hitler's triumph may have opened the way to a new antifascism, but it's still a mistake to draw a straight line from January 30, 1933, to the mass antifascism of a year or two later. It's a mistake because Hitler's triumph didn't only have an effect on those who feared fascism. Its more immediate effect was on those who took inspiration from it, those who saw it as a sublime sign of political creation. In the months after Hitler took power, what was most noticeable in the political world wasn't antifascist hostility to the new regime but rather the multiplication of movements working in the Nazis' own mode. Some of these had already been underway; some were more influenced by Mussolini and the Italian fascisti; and some drew on the wider well of paramilitary politics. But they all found that, with Hitler ascendant, a new aura of power and possibility wrapped around any endeavor with a whiff of fascism to it.

The movements made a heterogeneous bunch. And they showed up in a range of places reaching around the globe. Antun Sa'ada, a young down-and-out tutor of German in Beirut, had already begun in November 1932 to organize a Syrian nationalist party modeled in part on the Nazis; he adopted the title "Führer" for himself and a swastika-like symbol for the party. Sa'ada had only recently arrived in Beirut; he had been in Brazil, where the polymathic intellectual Plínio Salgado had been laying the groundwork for the Ação Integralista Brasileira. Salgado had met Mussolini in the palace at the Piazza Venezia in the summer of 1930 and had returned to São Paulo to proclaim that "the fascist conception of life will be the light of a new age." His paramilitaristic integralistas became known popularly as the greenshirts, as did a new

—

paramilitary group in Cairo. The greenshirts of Cairo put out their manifesto in October 1933 and soon started fighting in the city's streets and putting on public spectacles of military exercises, at least once at the pyramids of Giza. In Lima, armed blackshirts began marching in public and showing off straight-armed salutes in November 1933. Throughout 1933, reports trickled out of Canton and Shanghai of blueshirts carrying out their assassination campaign; such reports, though, were hampered, as one English-language dispatch from Shanghai noted, by the Nanjing regime's official insistence that there was no such thing as "any Fascist society known as the 'Blue Shirts.'" Also throughout 1933, news correspondence out of London shared word of constant local trouble caused by blackshirts there; the city's blackshirts marched in the streets, threw up straight-armed salutes, and provoked passers-by, as on an April night when, as one news correspondent described the scene, "a band of young Fascists" hurled antisemitic insults while hawking copies of the *Blackshirt,* a fascist newspaper, at Piccadilly Circus; that prompted an impromptu crowd "of jeering anti-Fascists" to assault the blackshirts. The following year, more of the same ensued, only in ever more places. Josslyn Hay, a British earl who lived in Nairobi, began organizing fascist meetings among white settlers in Kenya on behalf of, as he put it, "the Blackshirt Movement." Meanwhile, blueshirts in Dublin, men and women alike, staged an illegal march down Dawson Street, "arms raised," as one witness described it, "in the Fascist salute." In Newark, New Jersey, blackshirts called for a fascist dictatorship over the United States of America and marched in the streets in military formation. In Mexico City, goldshirts carried out military exercises in public, exchanged salutes, and assailed Jewish, Chinese, and Arab immigrants with the slogan "Mexico for Mexicans." Grayshirts in Johannesburg bullied black and Jewish South Africans. In Havana, the green-shirted terrorists of the ABC threatened a coup, dished out castor oil, set off bombs, and generally persecuted Afro-Cubans.[3] None of these scattered groups was identical to another. And any one of them was itself a confusion of ideas and action. They all struggled to attain any formal political power for themselves, and few of them lasted very long.

But in the moment they added up. And, in part because of their affinity for violence and spectacle, they stood out. As ever, the violence and spectacle slashed shortcuts into the news, into the public's political consciousness. What's

—

more, mass culture in the Depression era had become exceptionally interconnective, much more so than it had been even in 1927, when the Memorial Day violence in New York City had proven capable of drawing notice across the Atlantic. Consequently, the sensationalistic sort of news that these groups made was now likelier than ever to turn into international stories published far and wide. It was on the newspaper page that many of the blueshirts, greenshirts, grayshirts, and the rest achieved their greatest political recognition, even as the lot of them failed in their formal national politics.

It was also on the newspaper page that their political identity appeared most decidedly as fascist. The recognition depended on the name: call any of them by their own particularistic group name, and they became ciphers for almost anyone reading about them abroad; call them fascists and they were recognizable the world over. Making oneself into a fascist, or even just instigating the label, came at a cost, but there was also political power to be had in it, and that power became greater as more people in more places did the same. All of this worked to enlarge the meaning of fascism.

And it also worked to *change* the meaning of fascism.

Consider the implications tucked away in the news stories written about one typical outburst of political violence from the era. The incident occurred in the streets of Córdoba, Argentina, on the night of September 28, 1933. As portrayed in the press, both in and beyond Argentina, those who perpetrated "the crime of Córdoba," as it was called, were fascists and their victims were antifascists. A Reuters report published far afield put it that "fifty Fascists . . . attacked an anti-Fascist procession as it made its way through the streets." The attack actually occurred during a street meeting held at the corner of the calles Achával Rodríguez and Belgrano, in the heart of the city. Among those who had organized the meeting was the socialist provincial deputy José Guevara, well known in Córdoba as a ferocious antifascist orator with a knack for infuriating his foes. He was a marked man; in September alone, he already had brawled with several of the local gray-shirted paramilitarists known as "legionarios," had come home one day to find his house set afire, and had been assaulted on another occasion by a pair of legionarios. On the night of September 28, as soon as the street meeting began the fifty interlopers arrived and took their places; some of them went to the front of the crowd, right by the speakers

—

at the corner, and others stationed themselves across the tram tracks. When someone shouted, "Down with fascism!" at least some of the fifty cried out in reply, "Long live fascism!" Considerable back and forth followed. When someone shouted, "Death to fascism!" someone else started shooting; it seems that the only shots fired came from among the fifty called fascists. When the police had cleared the scene, Guevara lay dead on the street, shot through the head, from behind.[4]

Who had killed him? Who were the fifty fascists? And what made them all so decidedly fascist? Some of the fifty were members of the group called the Partido Fascista Argentino, or Fascismo Argentino. Italian émigrés had founded the group; its members wore black uniforms and were popularly known as blackshirts. Historians have had no problem identifying them as fascists. But others of the fifty were legionarios like those Guevara had battled earlier in the month.[5] They belonged to the Legión Cívica Argentina, a large paramilitary group associated with the ideology of nacionalismo, which was thought of as a particularism of Argentina.[6] Historians who subscribe to the idea of a fixed fascist minimum — and who thus take it as their task to judge who from the past meets or fails to meet the minimum as they themselves define it — have disagreed on whether or not to identify the Legión Cívica as fascist.[7] However, the facility with which the two groups' members worked together to commit such a consequential act is a hint that it's not as important to draw a blanket conclusion regarding each organization's formal ideological identity, decades after the fact, as it is to understand the politics that led the fifty interlopers, drawn as they were from both formal organizations, to organize themselves into a crowd that could and would interrupt an antifascist meeting, shout out, "Long live fascism!" and shoot down a notorious local antifascist.[8] In the moment — for those who were there on the scene, and for those who read news of the affair from afar — the ideological keys to unlocking the episode were the identities "fascist" and "antifascist."[9] Still, it would be a mistake to think that everyone who saw the fifty as fascists — including those among the fifty themselves, in particular, one presumes, those who shouted, "Long live fascism!" — all did so for the same reasons. Political identity is always complicated, always composite and capricious, and this is especially apparent when the identity in question is as morally fraught as fascism.

—

But suffice it to say that people in far-flung places read about and heard about fascists shooting down an antifascist in Córdoba in September 1933, a time when one could read and hear a run of such stories. They all reinforced each other. Fascists in Córdoba made more sense in a world where fascists were in Lima and London. And when fascists, or people labeled fascist, acted out in places like Córdoba, and Lima and London and Newark and Cairo, their actions worked to strip fascism of its particularistic, Italy-specific texture. The blackshirts of Fascismo Argentino notwithstanding, few of the fascists making news out in the world at the time were Italian emigrants; few depicted their organizations as fasci; few hailed Mussolini as their leader. Theirs was a fascism set afloat from Italian peculiarity, set afloat even from the European continent. It was a fascism with the universalistic air of liberalism or conservatism or any of the other of the great nineteenth-century isms. It was all quite a conceptual leap beyond what the small crew of self-described fascisti had done on Charles Street in New York City back in 1921.

Not only, then, does it misconstrue the matter of agency behind the act to say that fascism had "spread" from Italy to places like Córdoba, it also misconstrues the nature of the act itself. It implies that when people in places like Córdoba pulled fascism out into their world, they left the concept as they had found it. On the contrary, the more they pulled, the more they troubled the older, smaller meanings of fascism, and the more they fashioned a new, universalized fascism. And, sure enough, amid their storm of activity, talk of fascism as a universal boomed. None of which is to say that outside of Europe any of the fascists, or anyone playing the game of seeming fascist, achieved what they set out to do, or won state power for themselves. Rather, it's to say that their greatest effect was cumulative. And in their cumulation, they made fascism a less Eurocentric concept and a more global one.[10]

In an odd and counterintuitive way, it was on the margins of fascism that its great conceptual transformation was made.[11]

And as the universalized idea of fascism caught on, it brought on the age of fascism.

It also provoked a new sort of antifascism. Once the antifascists of Arnold Severeid's generation came to visualize fascism as a force at work the world over, universal in nature, they took to envisioning their own antifascism as

—

universal in kind. At least since 1923 there had been assorted communists, socialists, anarchists, and labor radicals trying to beat various paths toward an antifascism beyond Italian politics, but until the age of fascism they had been the exceptions. The idea of antifascism that had dominated political imaginations had been the one focused squarely on the antifascisti of Italy and its diaspora. Now, though, as notions of fascism opened up, so too did those of antifascism.

Beginning in 1933 and 1934, many more people, of many more ethnic, racial, and national identities, spoke out as antifascists. They did so even far away from Italy and Germany, but no matter where they themselves were, few if any antifascists in the age of fascism presented their politics as a form of sympathy for those suffering under fascist rule in a faraway land. Rather than *sympathy for,* time and time again those antifascists who didn't live under fascist rule expressed *solidarity with* the people who did. Time and time again they drew connections between what they saw as fascism in Italy and Germany and what they saw as fascism elsewhere – already in action if not yet in power.[12] Italy and Germany, then, weren't exceptions; they explained the shape the world was in. That this seemed so had to do with all those wide-ranging movements influenced by the Nazis and fascisti. The paramilitaries in sharply colored uniforms presented only the most easily discernible cases. Countless groups, cliques, and factions scattered about took lessons and cues from how the fascisti and now the Nazis had cut their paths to power. The tangle of violence in Minneapolis that had horrified Sevareid involved a paramilitary strikebreaking army, but it was nothing so visually audacious or ideologically expressive as a squad of blackshirts. It had its effect on him all the same. It threw him into antifascist politics, and within two years' time, he had even gone undercover, attending meetings of silvershirts in Minneapolis so as to write an exposé series of newspaper articles on fascism in his hometown.[13] (In August 1939 he took a job in Paris reporting for the Columbia Broadcasting System, and the following year he reported the "Fall of France" live on the radio; by the time CBS hired him, he went by the name Eric Sevareid.) The immediacy of fascism, his experience of it with his own eyes, was at the heart of Sevareid's antifascism. Humanitarian sympathy, offered from a place of privilege, for those suffering far away was never antifascism's guiding logic.

—

And neither was fear. There was, to be sure, no shortage of fear as the age of fascism began. Those who lived in the world of the Great Depression knew only too well their vulnerability to invisible and ungovernable forces. The economic crash had broken the nineteenth-century liberal ideal of individual manly labor yielding its just reward. The great lesson of the Great Depression had been that no one was safe from arbitrary ruin. Whatever safety was to be found was safety in numbers—hence the appeal of the mass collectivities that defined the era's politics. Those collectivities, though, quickly became the sources of yet more fear, fascism most of all. "Hope proved elusive," the scholar Ira Katznelson has written of the time. "A climate of universal fear affected political understandings and concerns."[14] What antifascists feared most of all was the multiplication of fascist regimes, the making of a world ruled by fascism. That was the tomorrow that Mussolini promised, that Salgado prophesied. Such visions of the future were so powerful as to reshape people's sense of the past; it became common after Hitler's rise to point back at Japan's 1931 invasion of Manchuria and renarrate it as part of an international turn toward fascist rule. But fear of fascist regimes hardly set antifascists apart from a good many others who never took up antifascism, and it wasn't the primary force that had driven them to become antifascists. Much of what set antifascists apart was their insistence on confronting fascist movements, even those nowhere near state power.

More so than it was a politics of fear, antifascism in the age of fascism was a politics of outrage.[15] Alive, Guevara had given voice to antifascist outrage with his oratory; after his martyrdom, antifascists in Córdoba felt the outrage all the more. They were outraged that, as one of them put it, "another victim of fascist reaction" had been claimed; outraged that the courageous Guevara would be heard no more; and outraged that the fascists had shown up "armed to the teeth" to assault "a rally of paltry proportions." Above all else, they were outraged that the one fascist had shot Guevara in the back.[16] Sevareid, too, was moved to outrage by seeing gunshot wounds inflicted from behind. None of which is to deny that fear is a potent thing in politics. There are worse ways to create your political self than to draw on your fears and work to counter them. But listen to how the antifascists of the years leading up to the Spanish Civil War explained themselves—or, better yet, watch them and see how they conducted themselves—and what comes across most isn't a fear of what fascism might do but outrage at what it was doing already.

All of which is to say that the antifascism taking form after Hitler's rise to power had certain telling qualities: people conceived of it as more of a universal than a particularism, more of a politics of solidarity than of sympathy, and more of a politics of outrage than of fear.

Also, even more so than it had been before, the new antifascism was very much a politics of unity. It marked a rejection of the enmity among rivals that had governed radical politics in the preceding years. The Comintern's social fascist thesis, which ruled the organization's policies until well into 1934, epitomized the enmity and its effects. A "suicidal policy," in Hobsbawm's later estimation, enforcing "sectarian isolation," the thesis had it that the parties of reformist socialism and social democracy—parties like British Labour and the German Social Democracy—either had secretly gone over to fascism or else had been duped by it. Either way, such parties were far from potential allies, let alone fellow antifascists. They constituted, as the *Daily Worker* of New York had suggested in 1925, "the left wing of fascism." When Hobsbawm reflected on the matter, near the twentieth century's end, he looked back and concluded that the idea of social fascism, and the go-it-alone politics it represented, had produced "spectacular setbacks for the revolutionary Left." What's more, it had done so at the very moment when the Nazis had sparked "the strengthening of the radical Right." Hobsbawm remained a communist throughout his life, but he did not hesitate to criticize the social fascist line and the general approach to politics it implied. He went so far as to say that it showed how communists, before the "call for anti-fascist unity," at least, "had been the most divisive force on the Enlightenment Left."[17]

By invoking "the Enlightenment Left," Hobsbawm had tapped once more into the idea of the left as a grand human community born in the French Revolution and enduring ever since. It was the idea of the left that he had used when he described the revolutions of 1848 as enacting the dreams of the left (and the nightmares of the right). If there already was a left made by the Enlightenment that included communists and revolutionaries and that reached across countries' frontiers, then no doubt the social fascist policy was, as Hobsbawm suggested, "divisive" in effect, cracking open a sturdy old left and breaking it apart. But "the Enlightenment Left" that he had in his head was the product of his own retrospective projection—it was an example of what Hobsbawm himself, regarding other matters, once called "invented tradition."[18] The social fascist line surely constituted a historic mistake. But there is a difference between splitting apart an old left already made, on the one hand, and simply reinforcing a state of separateness and difference, on the other. The communists who pushed the social fascist thesis didn't fracture any otherwise intact left; the left that historians have said the communists divided hadn't yet been made.

And likewise all of the manifold clusters and coteries of nationalists and paramilitarists around the world that were radicalized by the rise of Nazism had yet to be imagined into any state of collectivity called the right or, in Hobsbawm's phrase, "the radical Right." The right before the age of fascism had remained the stuff of parliamentary blocs and intraparty factions. So it wasn't a case of the radical right around the world "strengthening" after Nazism's rise, or even of the right radicalizing. What happened, rather, was that a great many miscellaneous movements radicalized and in their radicalization they came to constitute "the right."

How did they all radicalize? How did they become the right? They did so in part by taking Hitler and the Nazis as their model. In a way, they radicalized like typical German Nazis did. The great historian Ian Kershaw has used an offhand comment made by a petty Nazi official in 1934 to explain common Germans' paths to Nazism. It wasn't precisely that Hitler led them; rather, they themselves did the mental work of imagining what the leader wanted—"work towards the Führer" was what the Nazi official exhorted them to do.[19] Beyond Germany, many heterogeneous groups did the same imaginative work. The irony is that in working toward the Führer, they also all worked toward each other. They homogenized as they radicalized. From their uniforms, marching steps, and salutes to their rhetorical tropes, specific grievances, and notions of the nation, they cut a common pattern. It was no time at all before they, and others watching them, began to see the many scattered groups as adding up to a general collectivity reaching across national borders and painting over ideological and organizational differences. So many discrete little local groups, plugging away, trying to make a name for themselves in their nation's politics, now

—

catapulted themselves, in collectivity, into an advantageous position in global politics, where they suddenly wielded considerable new power. Like Sevareid, they had worked their way into a larger political world — many of them, again like Sevareid, without even leaving their hometowns.

They were working toward the making of "the modern right," the right as we know it. It meant stretching the idea of the right into something much bigger than what it had been. Instead of a bloc in a country's parliament, or a faction inside of an organization, the right was now about to be reimagined into the sort of mass global collectivity that Hobsbawm would later trick himself into thinking the right had always been since the French Revolution. As talk of fascism as a universal boomed, so did talk of all things concerning the right.

Both sorts of talk came from the same turn of events. Thus it unfolded, to take just one example out of many from the moment, that in November 1934, when news broke that a coterie of Wall Street brokers and bankers had sent a man to Europe to study fascism as part of their conspiracy to overthrow the Franklin D. Roosevelt administration and replace it with a fascist dictatorship, the figures behind the coup plot were talked of as "fascists" — and as "a right-wing movement" as well.[20] Such talk wasn't just the polemics of (to pick up on a phrase just then coming into use) "the left-wing press." You could read of the "fascist plot" and the "right-wing movement" behind it in even staid papers, or even in (as people were also just then learning to say) "the right-wing press." Talk of this sort all presupposed a "left wing" and a "right wing" out in the social world, floating freely, signifying something much more expansive than anything Lenin had dreamed of for left or right, and more expansive, too, than any particular voting bloc, left or right, in any one country's parliament. The globalized mass collectivities we know as the right and the left were taking shape in public imagination. Which is to say, some of the most basic elements of today's political world, the political world that today's left and right have inherited, were sliding into place.

When Simone Weil took that train to Barcelona, in early August 1936, the Spanish Civil War was less than a month underway. Like "the Great Fascist Plot," as the Wall Street scheme to overthrow Roosevelt was called, the war in Spain had begun with a conspiracy. Officers in the Spanish army had planned

—

a military coup against the republic (which Spain had become in 1931), and in the evening of July 17, 1936, at colonial outposts in Morocco (Spain still held onto a little of its empire), they put their plans into motion. The next day, the coup hit garrisons inside of Spain. Then, the day after that, the country's big labor organizations and working-class parties called for a general strike in protest; moreover, they called on all the people of Spain to rise up and resist. And so it was that on July 19, 1936, when the war was just begun, the Communist Party of Spain's greatest orator, Dolores Ibárruri, took to the radio in Madrid and exhorted all Spanish antifascists to get on their feet and fight "the fascist military uprising." Indeed, she said, workers and peasants throughout the land had already taken up arms and begun to fight. They also, she added, had taken up the battle cry, "Fascism shall not pass!"[21]

This was Ibárruri's legendary "¡No pasarán!" speech. It was a dramatic, crisp, and disciplined address, given when all was uncertainty and confusion. The simplicity of the historic line — "¡No pasarán!" ("They shall not pass!") — fit the simplicity of her message.[22] Ibárruri had a rare talent for oratory. And she understood well the particularities of radio address. She spoke with a poetic rhythm and she relied on cadence and repetition. She herself had not coined the shall-not-pass line; rather, the power of it was that the line was already in the air, part of the antifascist idiom that had been building, and bouncing around, the previous few years. The specific formulation "Fascism shall not pass!" she inherited from a dramatic and gloriously pacific mass demonstration that had taken place two years prior abroad in Paris. February 12, 1934, was the day when the phrase took hold in antifascist discourse — the day when it became, instantly, the core promise that antifascists made: to themselves, to each other, to the world. If you were looking for a date with which to mark the beginning of the antifascist moment — that short spell of time within the age of fascism when antifascists challenged their foes on a near global scale, and did so by practicing a politics of unity that prompted the making of the left as a global mass collectivity, a collectivity inclusive of multiple ideologies and parties and organizations and movements, a collectivity reaching easily over national and other such boundaries — you'd do well to pick February 12, 1934.

The events in Paris that day took place six days after a huge riot in the city that had led witnesses of many different sorts to the same kind of blood-and-

—

bones realization that Sevareid would experience a few months later in Minneapolis: that fascism had hit the city.

The riot of February 6, 1934, in Paris became the stuff of myth overnight. "The Sixth of February," as it was called, saw 40,000 rioters fight face to face with the city's authorities for hours, from the afternoon through midnight. The ordeal left fifteen people dead and 1,435 wounded. The violence encircled the Palais Bourbon, where the lower house of the French parliament was deliberating even as fighting approached its doors. As the night went on the ring of rioters constricted ever more tightly on this center point, threatening to seize the palace. Parliamentary deputies inside feared for their lives, the Reichstag fire of the previous year on their minds. The fighting was most intense just across the Seine, in the Place de la Concorde, where crowds repeatedly stormed the authorities' last line of defense at the bridge (the Pont de la Concorde) leading to the Palais Bourbon. Here, where police had orders to "defend the Pont de la Concorde at any cost and without retreating one step" — and to hold off the crowds "by any means" — violence persisted for longer than eight hours, with rising ferocity. Crowds in the Concorde improvised weapons out of familiar objects and raised barricades with debris produced by their attacks; they broke and weaponized garden chairs and flowerbed railings from the Jardin des Tuileries and newspaper kiosks from the Champs-Élysées. They fought with stones, fragments of iron, shards of glass, bricks, and, eventually, revolvers. When authorities arrived on horseback, rioters slashed at the horses' bellies with razor blades and tossed marbles and firecrackers at their hooves. They dragged down riders and beat them with their hands. After dark, they burned buses, cars, and kiosks and set afire a government building. When firefighters tried to put out the flames consuming a bus, crowds assaulted them; "the glow of this blaze," an inquiry report commented, "would last a long time and bestow a sinister aspect on the place."[23]

How had all this happened? Who had made the riot? Explanations varied. But they centered on the question of the city's paramilitaries. Among the rioters were thousands of men who belonged to them; many rioted in uniform. The organizations themselves made an odd mix, and if you were to try to make sense of any one of them by its official discourse, you wouldn't compare it to Nazis or fascisti. After the riot, conspiracy theories careened about accusing

—

the paramilitaries' leaders of ordering their followers to riot so as to trigger a coup.[24] But the theories were baseless—that wasn't at all how the Sixth had come about. The paramilitary heads were a cautious lot; if the crowds in the streets and squares of central Paris had followed their orders, there would have been no riot, no threat to the Palais Bourbon. However, among the paramilitary rank and file were those who had worked their way to a more visceral and violent politics. They used the paramilitary organizations as means to their own ends. And the organizations provisioned them with considerable political resources, not least of all the uniforms that expressed so well the wearers' readiness for violence. The different paramilitaries' uniforms varied but taken as a whole they made a blur of blue and gray shirts, berets and trench helmets, gray trousers, leather shoulder belts, black boots, and armbands.[25] A small band of paramilitarists could make a scene in the streets; with thousands thrown all together at once, the effect was greater than the parts.[26] What's more, on the Sixth, thousands more people on top of the paramilitarists joined in.

Anyone who tried to explain the Sixth in its aftermath had to figure out how to convey both the scale and the force of what had unfolded. The Sixth was the sort of extraordinary event that pushed all those everyday political theorists—the whole gamut of police, politicians, newspaper correspondents and headline copy editors, ideologues, and random locals—to reach for words to make sense of it.[27] For those horrified by the Sixth and all its implications, the interpretations turned on fascism. And it's true, no word with any currency at the moment fit better what had happened in the streets: the violence of the thing, the palpable radicalization induced by the violence, and the sense that a new collectivity was in the making, made out of the rioters' sharing of such an intense experience.[28] The labor newspaper the *Peuple* explained the next day that while rioters had gone into the Concorde "under many flags and had used dissimilar labels," those flags and labels didn't explain what had happened next: "Each group, taken in isolation, is nothing." The significance of those differences of institutional flags and ideological labels wore away as the night wore on. Don't confuse yourself, the labor paper was arguing, by focusing on the official doctrines and platforms of the different formal organizations represented in the Sixth; for "a lucid understanding" of what had happened, the *Peuple* insisted, recognize how the act of rioting pulled together many of the people

—

in the crowds and made them each other's comrades: "when gathered together, the groups produced a distinct force." The name the *Peuple* put to that force, matter of fact and without hand wringing, was fascism.[29]

Aside from the questions of what had happened on the Sixth and what forces had caused it, the question on people's minds was how to respond. The prime minister resigned the day after the riot, fearful that another riot would follow that night; liberal democracy and republican rule now tottered and reeled; the German and Italian regimes had become the models for much of the crowd that had made the Sixth, even among those who thought it sounded subtler, or more patriotic, to call themselves French monarchists rather than fascists. The French Communist Party came up with the first response. Much to the party's shame, its leaders had encouraged members to take part in the Sixth. Now, with such alarm and shock all around at what had unfolded, they knew they had to reframe the party's place in it all. They planned a mass demonstration to take place on February 9 in the Place de la République to "break the fascist wave." It was not an effective counter. Like the Sixth, it became a riot. The police blockaded the square, and the protest spilled into the surrounding neighborhood. Party militants fought police deep into the night. At the Gare de l'Est, rioters beat a police officer with his own club; another officer there was shot square in the head. The night also witnessed scenes of courage and defiance, and for some it evoked scenes of Paris's revolutionary past.[30] But it didn't fit the moment. The party had looked bad the morning after the Sixth; now, with what similarly became known as the "Ninth of February," it looked worse.

The events of February 12 worked out better. They too became known simply by their date, and they too quickly took on a myth-like significance. The "Twelfth of February" worked out better than the Ninth in part because it made such a contrast. The power of the Ninth had been as a show of counterforce to the Sixth: what nationalistic, paramilitaristic crowds had done, Communist militants could do as well. But there were problems with this. First, the Communists had taken part in the Sixth. Second, the Ninth was too much like the Sixth. The drawback of the Ninth, from the perspective of the wide political community about to take form and become known as "the left," was that it muddied the rationale for why the Sixth had been such a terrible and intolerable thing in the first place. It fed into the trope of fascism and communism as

—

similar and equivalent forms of "extremism." The Ninth had encouraged people to group fascism and communism close together conceptually, acting in kind. The Twelfth, by contrast, encouraged people to throw the two apart in their heads – to picture fascism standing alone off to one side and communism falling in with the other antifascist forces over on the opposite side. Which made clear a third drawback of the Ninth: the Communists had acted alone. On the Twelfth, a greater collectivity came together.

And so it was that on February 12, with Paris still on edge from the riots, thousands (likely at least 100,000) gathered along the Cours de Vincennes in the eastern part of the city, by the Place de la Nation, to make a clear statement of unified antifascism.[31]

At least, in retrospect it could look that way. But if you were to look closely at the texts that helped to organize and advertise the demonstration, what might strike you most is the absence of any explicit talk of antifascism itself. As is often the way when one's task is momentous and suddenly arrived upon, the organizers had to bumble about in search of a vocabulary to wrap around the protest. For all the certainty shared by communists, socialists, anarchists, syndicalists, and a good many liberals and republicans that the Sixth had amounted to fascism, it didn't follow naturally or effortlessly that their own riposte amounted to antifascism. Their idea of what was antifascism was still particularistic, centered on opposition to fascist Italy and Nazi Germany. There hadn't been any talk of practicing antifascism ahead of the Ninth either. The only mention of antifascism in the February 9 edition of *Humanité* had run well below the huge front-page appeal to join in the protest that night, in a little unrelated story about dockers in the North Atlantic port town of Concarneau: the dockers had just "shown their willingness to take up the antifascist struggle" in that they had refused to unload cargo from a German ship in port from Hamburg once they had seen the ship's "bloody swastika flag."[32] The dockers of Concarneau were antifascist because they had taken a stand against the Third Reich. How odd that, judged by what was written in Paris about the Ninth and Twelfth at the time, hardly anyone involved thought that they themselves were taking up the antifascist struggle and acting as antifascists – even though they had already labeled the Sixth an act of fascism.

—

The uncertainty of the moment extended beyond matters of language. Most uncertain of all was whether the demonstration would live up to the organizers' hopeful appeals to all to engage in "pacific protest." The atmosphere of riot and violence still hung over the city. Nobody was sure that the militants of the Communist Party and those of the Socialist Party would keep from attacking each other. Would the force of the parties' standing precepts, such as the social fascist thesis, overwhelm the day's aims? The organizers were apprehensive. In their plans, they didn't exactly lay out a massive interorganizational march along the Cours de Vincennes; rather, they plotted several different coincident and organizationally separate marches hopefully unfolding without missteps.[33]

But the glory of the Twelfth—what made it sublime—wasn't what was planned out ahead of time. It was the improvised organizing and logistics that the people in the crowd worked out for themselves on the fly, in the moment, as they marched along the Cours de Vincennes. The structure of the event, a mass march like the one that Hobsbawm had experienced as "mass ecstasy" in Berlin a little over a year before, lent itself to this. Out in the open, people's movement unregulated, large stretches of time free without scheduled orators—it all left the air democratically open for whatever shouts and chants anyone taking part might wish to take up.[34]

Early on in the afternoon, the crowd already was massive enough to overwhelm those watching it take form. "My pen," one participant wrote the next day, "can't recapture the impression of power and majesty that emanated from this unprecedented spectacle. It had to be seen; it can't be imagined." But what startled those present most of all wasn't the crowd's size but rather its harmony. It struck witnesses as beyond nonviolent, as serene even. Léon Blum, the head of the Socialist Party, admired its "calm and dignity." Another witness sensed universal and "unwavering willpower to remain calm, disciplined, master of one's own nerves." After so much violence in the preceding days, there was an affective power in this. It's a paradox of nonviolence that its force is greatest when it possesses the greatest threat of violence—when its practitioners are plainly seen to have the capacity for violence and yet abstain. The power to be found in the serenity of the Twelfth was a power that the Sixth and the Ninth had generated in violence; the Twelfth showed how to convert the undeniable power of political violence into its opposite.[35]

As the time to march neared, the crowd grew even larger, waves rolling upon waves, everyone restless to start, already, as one participant described it, "a human ocean."[36] The simple mass and density of the crowd in the street had the curious logistical effect of breaking down the division of marchers by their formal affiliations, reorganizing them instead among each other. The same participant observed, "The crowd is now so dense and so compact that, still before the march's start time, militants find it impossible to connect with their respective organizations." Young and old; women, men, and children; "Socialists, Communists, Pupistes [adherents to the Parti de l'Unité Proletarienne], Trotskyists, all fraternally united," and anarchists, republicans, and liberals, too; French-born and Algerian-born; members of rival labor organizations and nonunion workers as well: they all undivided themselves among the crowd.[37]

The scene showed the sort of effect that simple crowding can have on how people organize themselves. The effect was greater than simply taking participants out of their own formal organization's separate space. The one demonstrator noticed that with so many participants thrown together it no longer mattered that people couldn't find their way to their own party. The implications of the crowd had overtaken any formal organizational sense of one's proper place: among the crowd, the demonstrator explained with some astonishment, "everyone finds their place, because the place of everyone is everywhere."[38]

Were such observations romanticized? No doubt. Very. But they clearly were also sincere. My point in detailing them isn't to argue that participants were right to see things so. Or to argue, along the lines of what the historian E. P. Thompson once called "the enormous condescension of posterity," that they were wrong to do so.[39] Rather, I think it's worth recognizing that part of the value of informal politics—street politics, participatory and improvisational politics—is that they allow participants to experience their romance. That romance is a potent political resource. And that romance helps to clarify something about the variety of political experience. Even without taking such romanticisms at face value, you can still see in them how sensationally different the experience of being in a crowd is from the experience of belonging to

—

a formal organization. *Everyone finds their place, because the place of everyone is everywhere* may well have been a rank idealization of what happened inside the crowd of the Twelfth; it would still make an instructive contrast to how members of a political party might idealize their experiences — more along the lines of *everyone finds their place, because the rank and file are disciplined and committed and go to their precisely assigned place.*[40] In the contrast — again, even if each is seen as an exaggeration — there is much to be understood about how politics works, and what sort of politics works how.

The dreamy euphoria of the Twelfth only heightened as the march began. Those who took part described the events that followed in intensely emotional language. Some envisioned the movement toward the Place de la Nation as a passage of redemptive emancipation from the previous week's feelings of fatalism. In the beginning, the writer Marc Bernard noticed "the serious faces, with a kind of impatient curiosity, almost anxiety." This led to cathartic release as the crowd moved. Another marcher, Lucie Mazauric, remembered her heart "tightened with emotion" as she approached the Place de la Nation to find a mass of people already arrived. "The procession almost imperceptibly shook," she recalled, "and suddenly an enormous clamor reverberated through the place and propagated itself like a bolt of lightning along the entire length of the Cours de Vincennes."[41]

The crowd's vibe was apprehensive one moment, raucous the next. Yet in the end the emotion that carried the day was joy. The joy was only so intensely felt, though, because it had spun out of such real anxiety. The most anxious moment was when the columns that the Socialist and Communist parties had been able to keep intact approached each other, as they neared the Place de la Nation. "We were advancing," Blum remembered later, describing the scene as it looked to him among the Socialists, "and as the distance between the two columns diminished second by second, the same anxiety seized all of us. Would the convergence be a collision?" He feared a sectarian clash. Instead, the two columns melted into one effervescent crowd. Marchers joined hands. "This was no collision," he exclaimed, "this was fraternization." When the two clusters happily exchanged greetings, Mazauric described an emotional irruption, mass rapture pouring over the crowd — it began with a final "brief moment of anxiety" upon which, "to the astonishment of the party and union chiefs,

—

the exchange unleashed a delirious enthusiasm, an explosion of cries and joy." Another witness described the moment as an "outbreak of joy." Blum too felt the "sentiment of joy," as he put it, and he confirmed Mazauric's assessment that institutional leadership had been taken by surprise by the happy solidarity. Marceau Pivert, at the time a leader of the Socialist Party's left wing, was among the throng and he was described as "mad with joy."[42]

The moment when the Communist and the Socialist parties' contingents melded together ensured the Twelfth's place in leftist mythology, "proof," one classic history has put it, "that unity was possible if the will was there." A marcher recalled, "In an instant, all marched elbow to elbow, all sharing the same elan, the same heart." The Twelfth, then, meant more than a break with political violence; it was also a breaking up of the old order of radical politics: institutionally organized, siloed, densely theoretical, and vanguardist. Now marchers embraced each other across ideological and institutional lines and wept as a chant of "Unity! Unity!" rolled through the air.[43]

Also in the air were signs and banners of all sorts. Among them one could see those that read, "Fascism shall not pass."[44] Even if hardly anyone seems to have uttered the word antifascism, a mass politics of its enactment was taking form in the press of bodies in the street. Reflecting on the visual pageantry of the crowd, the socialist Barthélémy Mayéras wrote in the next day's edition of the *Populaire* that he agreed with the signs. "Fascism shall not pass!" he exclaimed, adding for emphasis: "It's decided." Recitations of *fascism shall not pass!* soon made the phrase into a creed among antifascists, but on the Twelfth it was still novel, hardly ever printed before. Two of the demonstration's organizers for the Socialist Party, Eugene Descourtieux and Emile Farinet, had used the expression in one of the first appeals, published February 8. Was that the phrase's original utterance?[45] A month and a day before Descourtieux and Farinet's appeal, the Spanish republican Santiago Casares Quiroga had said something very similar while speaking to a crowd in the Monumental, an immense bullring in Barcelona. "We must form," Casares Quiroga had said, "a tightly bound union and rise up against all those who wish to establish fascism in Spain, and we must tell them: 'You shall not pass'" ("No pasaréis").[46] Should that count? What *was* the origin of the fabled slogan? Posed so narrowly, such questions are intellectual traps. No one utterance gave the phrase all its meaning. But the bond between the Twelfth and the slogan is solid: the Twelfth was when the phrase first garnered its significance as a promise-byword to be shared among the faithful.

Within ten days of the Twelfth, in Bougie, Algeria, where French para-militarists marched and agitated, local socialists had already begun insisting, "fascism shall not pass." Over the weeks and months that followed, antifas-cist intellectuals in Paris took to punctuating their written calls to action with the expression, doing so without prefatory explanation, as if it were a familiar phrase exchanged between author and reader as easily as a handshake. And over the next three years, antifascists made the profession into a language-crossing, distance-collapsing covenant with each other the world over. With its imagery of passage and obstruction, the phrase captured the new vision of fascism as a transnational political force in motion, moving out and about in the public realm, marching on Paris and wherever—unless, that is, antifascists got in the way. Derived from Great War rallying cries in the trenches ("they shall not pass" were words heard at Verdun), the slogan retained a sense of militancy and also, more to the point, captured the physicality of politics as a battlefield to be crossed or held. Mayéras's realization—"It's decided"—had emanated from his seeing the human concatenation of so many along the Cours de Vincennes that he imagined the scene on the Twelfth as a human barricade raised against fascism's advance: "We were 150,000 along the Cours de Vincennes, there to block its path."[47]

Mayéras, though, made no mention of "antifascism" or of "the left." He only said "we." He repeated "we" time and time again in his depiction of "this day of joy." He poignantly left undefined whom that "we" may have been. Looking back at the Twelfth, it seems so obvious that it was an antifascist demonstration and that it was the left that demonstrated. The problem with leaving things there, though, is that it hides the drama of creativity and invention that was involved. It's so easy in retrospect to see the Twelfth as antifascist and its crowd as the left because the Twelfth and the events that followed pushed people to think in those terms.

For a sense of how rapidly and dramatically political language was about to change, take as an example how the *Manchester Guardian* correspondent Al-exander Werth described the Sixth, Ninth, and Twelfth in a pair of books he

—

wrote within three years' time. In the first book, written only months after February 1934, he told the tale without mentioning left or right at all, save for a handful of references to the "men of the Left in Parliament" or an "outburst of noise from the Right" – also in parliament – as "members of the Right" heckled the prime minister while in session late in the afternoon of February 6. Left and right had meaning only in the chamber of deputies inside the Palais Bourbon. The rioters outside, by contrast, were "Fascists and semi-Fascists," "Royalists," "Nationalist students," "more or less anti-parliamentary" "patriots," and "'anti-Republican'" "Reactionaries." They weren't the right. And the paramilitary organizations that many of the rioters belonged to were "patriotic organisations" and "'Reactionary' and 'Fascist' organisations." They weren't right-wing. In the second book, though, which came out in 1937, Werth recast the entire drama in terms of left and right. Now the left and the right were both in the streets. Now all those paramilitarists and royalists and veterans who rioted on the Sixth were "the Right." Now those who called the Sixth "a 'Fascist plot'" and took to the streets in protest were "the Left." Taken together, Werth's two accounts show how quickly the grammar changed. But for now, to think about 1934 alone, just consider the account that Werth wrote that year; it offers a clear example of how a well-informed observer, with an interest in and a knack for political idiom, could talk through the events of February 1934 without describing the crowds of the Sixth as the right or those of the Ninth and Twelfth as the left. The left didn't make the Twelfth; it's closer to the truth – an exaggeration, surely, but closer to the truth all the same – to say the Twelfth made the left.[48]

"It was the greatest Fascist demonstration ever held in Britain." So claimed the *Fascist Weekly* of London. A photograph of "the Leader addressing the audience of 10,000 at the Albert Hall on Sunday night" backed up the claim. The date of the demonstration was April 22, 1934, less than ten weeks since the early February drama across the channel. The "Leader" was Oswald Mosley, "in black from head to foot," as a *Daily Express* reporter put it, "relieved only by a gleaming belt buckle." The audience included blackshirts, their comrades who were not in uniform but were recognized as part of "the Blackshirt Movement," and the curious. "We shall bring Fascism by British methods!" Mosley

—

thundered. The *Daily Express* reporter wrote that "the peroration was perfect," Mosley's voice "rising and falling," booming so as to "crash around the hall," while the thousands sat rapt: "The silence in the hall was intense." One of the blackshirts present was even more effusive. "The Albert Hall will be a hallowed memory to Blackshirts in Britain," he argued, recounting the blackshirts' pride at seeing and hearing "our Leader reach the heights of what must be one of the greatest oratorical achievements in modern Britain."[49]

Among antifascists in London—and those who agitated against fascism in London had indeed by April 1934 begun to think of themselves as "antifascists"—there was a sense that they had let Mosley have his triumph too easily. There was a sense, too, that they shouldn't let him get away with it the next time.[50] Before May 1934 was out, the blackshirts made public their plans to hold another massive rally in London, scheduling it for a little more than six weeks after the Albert Hall meeting: June 7, at Olympia Hall in Kensington. Antifascists in London began to prepare.

The blackshirts who swore their allegiance to Mosley belonged to the British Union of Fascists (BUF), which Mosley had established in October 1932. The fascisti in Soho had long since drifted from view, and so too the British Fascisti of Rotha Lintorn-Orman and Nesta Helen Webster. It had been blackshirts from the BUF that had provoked the crowd of "jeering anti-Fascists" at Piccadilly Circus in the spring of 1933; and when Josslyn Hay had said that he was staging fascist meetings on the outskirts of Nairobi on behalf of "the Blackshirt Movement," he meant Mosley's movement. Already a public force by the beginning of 1934, the blackshirts' movement had boomed since January, when the London newspaper magnate Lord Rothermere published, in his *Daily Mail*, his own fascist manifesto, "Hurrah for the Blackshirts!" Rothermere argued that although fascism had "originated in Italy" the idea had since universalized, and was "not now peculiar to any nation." He added that British socialists often forgot that their own faith had begun as a peculiarity of elsewhere—that the "High Priest" of socialism was "the German Jew Karl Marx." Rothermere's manifesto ran alongside a photograph of a column of blackshirts marching in London past a line of their fellow blackshirts raising their right arms in straight-armed, open-palmed salutes. Berlin papers trumpeted the "striking manifesto" as evidence of "the strength of Fascist ideas."[51]

—

In his own way, Rothermere was proposing fascism as a global concept. He relied on a historicist explanation to do so: restrictively Italian in origin, fascism was no longer so; it had changed over time. What's more, it was because of actions out in the world, by actors like the London blackshirts he championed, that fascism had morphed in meaning and become "the spirit of the age." His conception of fascism, then, relied on events like those Sevareid was soon to witness, those in places far removed from Italy and Germany. It was in just such ways that fascism's periphery remade the idea into a universal during the first two years of the Third Reich.[52] And it was in such ways that the age of fascism was made.

Tangled with the transnational twist in fascism's meaning was the one in antifascism's. As people picked up and reworked fascism in new places — pushing themselves and others to think of it as more of a universal — so too did others reach out and grab ahold of antifascism — pushing themselves and others to think of it as more of a universal. Often the relationship between fascism's remaking and antifascism's was painfully direct. When blackshirts in Brighton held a mass meeting in the Dome, a large hall in the city center, in March 1934, antifascists turned out, too. The speaker was William Joyce, later to acquire considerable notoriety as "Lord Haw-Haw," the radio voice of Nazi propaganda broadcast into Britain during World War II. In 1934, he was already known as the only fascist orator in Britain who could rival Mosley in stirring a crowd. Among the antifascists who turned out were Jessie Stephens Faulkner and her husband Walter Faulkner; they came with their young children. At some point blackshirts surrounded the family. Whether they did so before or after Walter Faulkner started heckling — "Castor oil!" he hollered — isn't clear. Several times he raised his arm in a clenched-fist salute. The meeting ended with "God Save the King" and at the song's end the blackshirts swarmed. Faulkner, who had vision out of only one eye because of a war injury, came under a storm of blows, the first on the back of his head. The last thing he remembered was a blackshirt raising a cane over him as others held him down. Stephens Faulkner fought at the blackshirts, trying to protect her husband. It's unknown how the assault ended, though it can't have ended well.[53]

It is known that three blackshirts were arrested and put on trial. The trial revealed hints of how antifascists like Stephens Faulkner and Faulkner went about their politics in 1934. They had not been the only antifascists to crash the meeting; one man there belonged to the Communist Party of Great Britain, and one woman belonged to the Independent Labour Party; Stephens Faulkner's political affiliations aren't clear and Faulkner, who was unemployed, chaired the local branch of the National Unemployed Workers' Movement, which had come out of the Communist Party, though Faulkner himself was not a Communist. He testified that he didn't even know the words to "The Internationale." When the blackshirts' counsel questioned Faulkner about the clenched-fist salute, the lawyer did so by asking about "the sign of the Communist party." Faulkner replied, "I don't know it." Only when the lawyer clenched his hand and held it up did Faulkner acknowledge that he had made the sign at the meeting. The exchange showed how, already at winter's end 1934, the clenched fist had made a double journey out of the hands of the German Communist Party: beyond communism and beyond the continent. Still not yet known as the "antifascist salute," it signified antifascism all the same. At the trial, though, the authorities had a hard time distinguishing between antifascism and communism—and they had a hard time remembering that the antifascists had broken no laws. The prosecutor declared that the case was brought in part as "a lesson to people of political creeds, whether Fascists on the Right or Communists on the Left, that they had no right to behave in this sort of way."[54] And so fascists and antifascists in Brighton had, together, acted out a small scene of popular politics potent enough to push even a dismissive and unsympathetic bystander into talk of the right and left in a sense that was at the time still quite novel, quite unsettled, even for engaged ideologues: the prosecutor had offhandedly spoken of the left and right as forces out in the wider world, far removed from any parliament or interparty faction.

Whatever potency such episodes had, though, Olympia far outshined them.[55] At Olympia, antifascists practiced interruptive politics on a much larger scale and in a much more intricately organized fashion than what Faulkner had done in Brighton with his heckles and salutes. And the fascists at Olympia replied with a much more practiced brutality. In May, local members of the Communist Party made up a committee to organize "an anti-Fascist counter-demonstration on June 7 in the vicinity of Olympia" and invited the collaboration of the Labour Party, the Independent Labour Party, and the labor unions.

—

The organizers didn't get much institutional support from the other parties and the unions, but the counterdemonstration itself would turn out a crowd of anti-fascists well beyond Communist Party members alone. The antifascists who turned out at Olympia included, by one reckoning, "Communists, pacifists, and Left-wing members of the Labour party and the I.L.P."[56]

Olympia turned out quite differently from Albert Hall. "Cries, calls and screams started," one witness recalled, "almost immediately after Mosley began." And almost as soon, "Blackshirt squads" attacked the interrupters. "Chairs were smashed and used for weapons; shoes were thrown and clothes torn and many 'non-participants' in the audience left before the end." The antifascists relied on a consistent strategy of constant interruption; their tactics varied. "Interrupters used many devices," the same witness explained, "stench bombs, noises, faintings, screaming, scattering their own leaflets, etc."[57] A woman in the balcony chanted, "Mosley's a millionaire!" until blackshirts hauled her away. Down near the platform a man challenged one of Mosley's claims with a simple "No!" Blackshirts dealt with him as well. When Mosley, up on the platform, claimed that his right to free speech justified blackshirt violence, an interrupter shouted, "Does Hitler stand for free speech?"[58] The fascists had brought along two searchlights for the show, and each time that an antifascist caused a commotion the searchlights would swing around and illuminate the ensuing violence (the use of searchlights was already a familiar touch of fascist staging by this point).[59] According to one observer, the "culmination" of the meeting, "in point of sensationalism," wasn't anything Mosley or the blackshirts did but rather the daring performance of an antifascist duo: at one point, without any prelude, down from the girders in the hall's roof fluttered antifascist leaflets, followed by the chant "Down with Fascism!" Whereas most of the interrupters made quick outbursts, the antifascists in the girders had time to show off. Far up above, they had a degree of remove similar to what Oliver Law would enjoy the following summer in Chicago, when he took to the roof to speak during the grand Hands Off Ethiopia march down 47th Street. And as Law would find, this pair found that the safety of their perch was short-lived. But the two kept chanting their slogan over and over until blackshirts climbed up into the girders after them. The searchlights spun upwards and were trained on the chase scene that followed. An admirer of the blackshirts wrote, in Lord Rothermere's *Daily*

—

Mail, that the searchlights gave "to the scene a strange air of unreality." Mosley went on speaking as best he could, but, as another witness recounted, "all eyes were on the climbers. Chaos broke out." Much to the crowd's excitement the acrobatic antifascists escaped out of sight along the girders. The scene, the same witness suggested, would have "thrilled most people in a cinema."[60]

The blackshirts had their defenders, but many in attendance were unsettled by their violence.[61] A Conservative member of Parliament said, "I am bound to say that I was appalled by the brutal conduct of the Fascists." A priest, "horrified at the monstrously cruel treatment," saw "scenes of great brutality such as I had never thought to see in England"—one antifascist "was bleeding on the face, and was gasping for breath" when "a horde of Blackshirts" took him down; "he was beaten on the head by any Fascist who could get near him." Six blackshirts threw a man over the balcony's ledge; the fall knocked him unconscious. A witness saw "a man lying on the floor, obviously powerless and done for, being mercilessly kicked and horribly handled by a group of, certainly not fewer than 8, and more probably 10 or 12 Blackshirts."[62]

As word spread, much of the public was horrified. That said, Olympia did not break the blackshirt movement in Britain. It did, however, break the blackshirts' momentum and put them on the defensive. There would be more battles to come, but the events at Olympia had given antifascists some very hard won public sympathy and fascists some very well earned public antipathy. Even before the meeting had ended, it was clear that things had not gone well for Mosley. By ten o'clock, the general audience had, as one correspondent put it, "plainly grown tired of Sir Oswald's two-hour monologue," and many left. The endless interruptions had made it so that he hadn't finished his speech (the same correspondent wryly described Mosley as at one point "speaking during a lull in the interruptions"). As such, Mosley "was robbed of his triumphant exit." He was robbed of more than that. Olympia took away even some of the glory of Albert Hall. It was now Olympia, one news story the next day concluded, that stood out as "the most amazing meeting London has seen for two decades."[63] And the city's antifascists had stolen the spotlight.

The way that the antifascists of London had gone about fighting fascism at Olympia had in it many of the qualities that animated antifascism as a whole

—

at the moment. Despite the usual institutional feuds and ideological quarrels, a heterogeneous lot had come together and marched to the hall. Inside, the antifascists had scattered themselves throughout the crowd and then relied on tactical creativity and a clear, straightforward plan of action that trusted and empowered all its enactors to think for themselves and to improvise as they saw fit. The antifascists at Olympia had shown physical daring and a willingness to suffer. Both the daring and the suffering had an effect. The most potent political message that made its way into the press in the days after Olympia was that the blackshirts had behaved barbarously. The antifascists had provoked the blackshirts into proving their point about them. They themselves had paid a physical toll to do so.

That the stories of the fascists' violence had made it into the press was much of the point. In 1934, both fascism and antifascism fed off of the power of the press: both were forms of mass politics perfectly geared to an age of mass culture. It was no accident that Mussolini had first made a name for himself as the editor of *Avanti!* Even then, before the war, newspapers had offered the dominant form of daily political communication. Each day's new edition was another treatise of political theory in which, among other things, political abstractions came to life and commenced battle with each other anew. "Liberalism," "socialism," "the masses," "the nation," and all the rest—any faith that people might put in such concepts to speak to their everyday reality depended on some sort of sustained invocation. For any such abstraction, the newspapers either provided the daily sustenance it needed or else they sentenced it to a slow death by omission.

As much as that had been so already before the war, by 1934 the power of mass culture had multiplied. Now, not only was it the press that animated people's political imaginations, it was radio and newsreel cinema as well. The connection between mass politics and mass culture was so clear to fascists in Buenos Aires that they took to assaulting cinemas in retaliation for political representations on the screen that they disliked. In March 1934, Buenos Aires blackshirts set a theater's curtains on fire with an incendiary bomb, in a packed house, to protest the screening of the politically charged film *Hambre y libertad.* (An attack on the press of the paper that the socialist *Vanguardia* described at the time as "the antifascist organ of the German collectivity" in Buenos Aires,

—

Argentinisches Tageblatt, followed a few months later—"antifascism" hadn't been much a part of the *Vanguardia*'s vocabulary until this point; incidents such as this one now pushed the concept into its pages.) Mass culture shaped every aspect of fascism. After all, how was it that in the age of fascism people knew to throw up their arms in a straight-armed, open-palmed salute to express a certain politics? How was it that people knew to do this in cities as wide-ranging as London, Birmingham, Dublin, St. Louis, Chicago, Buenos Aires, Córdoba, Cairo, Aleppo, Damascus, Bucharest, Manila, Rio de Janeiro, and Santiago? How did they even know *how* to? Countless of fascism's practitioners had learned their craft from their encounters with mass culture. Endless images of straight-armed salutes—captioned as "fascist salutes," "Hitler salutes," "German fascist salutes," and so on—appeared in the newspapers. They were in the newsreels as well. When the journalist Mallory Browne first personally witnessed fascist-style salutes, on the Champs-Élysées in 1934, he readily recognized them. He asked, "What could they mean, those outstretched arms that one has become accustomed to see in the newsreels on the Via Romana and the Unter den Linden?" Browne's answer was straightforward: "They mean that Fascism has come to France."[64]

It was only fitting that people in the age of fascism would first become accustomed to seeing the stiff-armed, open-palmed salute in newsreels shown in movie theaters. The early fascisti had adopted the gesture from arditi led by the Italian "soldier-poet" Gabriele d'Annunzio—who had come up with the idea of using such a salute after seeing actors perform the gesture in the 1914 film he had helped write, *Cabiria,* a stylized silent epic set during the Second Punic War. Though fascists (and scholars) have called the pose "the Roman salute," it was not how anyone actually greeted each other in antiquity; it was just how modern actors imagined that ancient Romans had. The "Roman salute"—the fascist salute—was another of modernity's invented traditions; it came from the movies.[65]

At Olympia, one witness estimated that 3,000 in the crowd knew—and knew how—to raise "the Fascist salute" as Mosley strutted to the stage. It appears that just as many or more people had known the same sort of salute three weeks earlier in New York's Madison Square Garden, where 20,000 people attended a Hitler rally put on by the Friends of the New Germany. "We are not

Nazis," one speaker insisted, "nor is this a Nazi meeting." Swastikas hung all over the Garden. Eight hundred men in paramilitary uniforms with swastika-marked armbands enforced order. The meeting ended with the salutes, the singing of the Horst Wessel song, and cries of "Hail Hitler!" Outside, a "shouting column of workers and anti-Fascists," as one Trotskyist account described the scene, paraded up and down Broadway and then headed to the Garden to confront the meeting's attendees on their way out.[66]

The Friends of the New Germany had meant their rally as a reply to an anti-Nazi mass meeting in the Garden two months earlier. Twenty thousand had attended that meeting as well. The spectacle then had been to put Adolf Hitler on trial in absentia for his crimes "against civilization." When the judge asked for the verdict, a roar filled the place for a finding of guilt; opposed was one woman, high in the gallery. "I know all about you Jews!" she shouted. "We'll get our country back from you just as we got Germany back from you. We want free speech in this country." No violence followed. Nobody threw her over the balcony's ledge. The police, though, escorted her out. Another antifascist meeting drew 20,000 at Madison Square Garden in November. Among those who spoke was Arturo Giovannitti. By that point he had been an antifascist for more than a decade.[67]

It was the spectacle of these mass meetings that pushed them into the news. And intermixed in the reportage with all the sensational narratives describing the spectacle were interpretive explanations of the ideological forms that had been enacted amid the action. Fascism and antifascism continued to take form on the newsprint page; what's more, though, readers didn't just learn about the ideological abstractions from the news stories, they also could take lessons from the stories' details on how to produce the next spectacle. One often did lead to the next. Another of London's epic pairings of fascist demonstration and antifascist counterdemonstration took place just over three months after Olympia, in London's Hyde Park on September 9. The antifascists assembled "within brick shot," as one witness put it, of the blackshirts marching through the park, their arms raised in "the Hitler salute." The antifascist crowds were made of "Communists obviously . . . and there were many others, Leftists, Laborites, Pacifists and anti-Fascists," in one assessment.[68]

—

Less than a week after the confrontation in Hyde Park, fascists and antifascists in Buenos Aires clashed dramatically enough to score more headlines for fascism and antifascism. The trouble began when local legionarios broke up a students' rally with tear gas and gunfire in the Parque Romano, in the barrio of Palermo. These legionarios, however, were not of the same sort as those that had opened fire on the antifascist street meeting in Córdoba and murdered José Guevara almost an exact year before. These were members of the Légion Nacionalista, a group that had splintered from the Légion Cívica Argentina. Soon after the legionarios' attack on the meeting at the Parque Romano, a fracas began in the nearby Plaza Italia when some of the legionarios raised cheers for fascism, drawing a challenge from passing antifascists. A fistfight ensued, broken up by two gunshots. Someone, it was never clear who, shot the legionario Jacinto Lacebrón Guzmán. The twenty-year-old fell to the ground, covered in blood. He died shortly thereafter. At the funeral, his corpse's honor guard included uniformed members of multiple paramilitary organizations. Institutionally, the paramilitarists of Buenos Aires and the broader nacionalista movement were divided many times over. The funeral unified them. The funeral's fascist practices unified them. One account noted that despite "the confusion of diverse uniforms," all shared in "a single clamor" of mourning. Then legionarios — of both legion organizations — and other attendees as well all joined in raising straight-armed, open-palmed salutes, embracing Jacinto Lacebrón Guzmán as their martyr.[69] It was a season of martyrs.

And the martyrs of fascism, as well as those of antifascism, haunted the living. Giacomo Matteotti had been dead for nine years and one day when an eclectic assortment of São Paulo's antifascists met to honor his memory and promised to work together against fascism. This was not the first time that antifascists in São Paulo had gathered to mourn Matteotti. Italian émigrés in the city had organized one of the earliest commemorative events for him anywhere in the world, the very month of his death, before his body had even been found. The June 11, 1933, meeting, though, had a very different feel to it. This was in no small part because the meaning of fascism had changed so much since 1924. The antifascists gathered in a union hall across the street from

—

the northwestern corner of the Praça da Sé, the grand public square at the city's center. Italian socialists hosted. They were committed antifascisti. Matteotti was their martyr. Their section of the Brazilian Socialist Party they had named the Grupo Socialista Giacomo Matteotti. (Similarly, in Buenos Aires Italian socialist antifascisti constituted the Círculo Giacomo Matteotti.) Much of what made the meeting momentous, though, was that so many antifascists aside from Italian émigrés had come and now in the meeting took the lead in plotting out a new and broader antifascist politics for the city. A small set of local intellectuals had already launched an antifascist newspaper, the *Homem Livre,* a couple of weeks before. The purpose of the paper had been clear from the first page of the first issue: "The program of 'O Homem Livre' is to fight for the democratic ideals, against fascism." The *Homem Livre* gave what's likely the most specific account of the June 11 Matteotti memorial meeting. "For the first time," the paper's reporter claimed, "Italian antifascist groups, Brazilian antifascist groups, and proletarian organizations of different tendencies have reached a fundamental agreement on how to fight fascism." A well-known local Trotskyist named Aristides Lôbo had made the crucial speech. He had called on all to set aside their differences of ideology, affiliation, and nationality. He had called on all to make what he called "an anti-fascist united front."[70]

Lôbo's idea of a united front wasn't Zetkin's or Thälmann's. Lôbo's was in some ways analogous to what "the left" would come to mean. The participants' various ideological faiths were to be sustained, and their various parties and organizations were to be sustained as well. But a broader sense of collectivity was to span them all, and they were to work in common where special ideological commitments didn't get in the way. No one party was to dominate, and the aim wasn't to rip away a rival party's rank and file. No central committee lurked behind any curtains. Unlike in Zetkin's Action Committee Against War Danger and Fascism or Antifa as Thälmann had set it up, no specific institutional interest was at work to instrumentalize the antifascism of Lôbo's united front. During the week leading up to the São Paulo meeting, Willi Münzenberg had put on a massive conference, the European Anti-Fascist Workers' Congress, at the Salle Pleyel in Paris; for historians who have seen the mass antifascism of the years that followed as the product of the Comintern's propaganda machine—

—

and as dominated by the policy concerns of Stalin and the Soviet Union – the Pleyel congress has loomed large.[71]

The São Paulo meeting shows another path to the antifascist moment. And Lôbo sought a thoroughly horizontal, mutualistic collaboration of all antifascists and their organizations. Even in her Reichstag speech, Zetkin had still held onto notions of vanguardism. Lôbo described an antifascism of equals. While he of course had ideological aims beyond defeating fascism, no ulterior motives underlay his pleas to raise an antifascist united front. The aim, simply, was to work together against fascism.

Not only the antifascism but also the plea for unity was heartfelt. Lôbo didn't frame his idea as an ad hoc coalition of otherwise unrelated groups. From the start, he sought to create a sense of kinship among the city's antifascists. And, sure enough, from the start a genuine solidarity animated the making of São Paulo's united front. In marking fascism as their common enemy, the antifascists of the various parties and political faiths seemed to find that they had clarified their relation to each other as well. Respect for each other's independence of thought and recognition that sacrifice and compromise were being made by all solidified the solidarity.

It helped that Lôbo had the standing to make the case for unity. Likely no one had a wider reach among São Paulo's radicals. He had worked to organize the Brazilian Communist Party's youth movement in the city beginning in 1925, when he turned twenty. He then had become part of the Trotskyist "Left Opposition" in either 1928 or 1929. The idea behind the Left Opposition had been that the dissidents (the leftists) would mount a campaign of resistance to Stalinism from within the Comintern. The problem was that Stalin and his loyalists expelled them. In the middle of 1933, though, Trotskyists such as Lôbo still insisted that they belonged to the Communist International.[72] Lôbo also had connections beyond communism. Aside from his rapport with local anarchists and syndicalists, he had worked with Luís Carlos Prestes, the charismatic revolutionary of the "tenentes" revolts – the political rebellions in the 1920s associated with junior army officers such as Prestes. At one point, Lôbo even went to Buenos Aires, where Prestes was biding his time, and ghost wrote proclamations for him. One of Lôbo's hopes then had been that Prestes might

—

137

join the Communist Party and make the case for allowing the Left Opposition back into the fold. (Prestes did become a Communist, but he condemned the leftists as social fascist.) Lôbo also embodied a deeper history of Brazilian radical politics: he was the namesake of his uncle, a famous nineteenth-century Brazilian republican and abolitionist.[73]

When the antifascists of the Matteotti meeting gathered again a while later, Lôbo presented four "bases," according to the *Homem Livre*, "for the constitution of the Antifascist United Front." The new collectivity would, Lôbo proposed, counter fascist ideas and actions; insist on secular education and the separation of church and state; fight for freedoms of thought, assembly, association, and the press; and form a solid, "single bloc of action against fascism." He emphasized that antifascists could take part without distinction of political beliefs. The meeting's delegates included socialists, syndicalists, "tenentistas," Trotskyists, and anarchists. Some of the anarchists argued at the meeting that the Antifascist United Front should only be an organization of individuals. They envisioned something more like the Arditi del Popolo: an antifascist force that was ideologically diverse but set apart from individual members' other political affiliations. Lôbo insisted on the need for organizational commitment — to win the parties and other formal organizations over to a politics of unity. The debates, the *Homem Livre* reported, "were long and at times heated."[74] In the end, though, the delegates voted for Lôbo's confederative plan.

Noticeably absent, though, was anyone representing the Brazilian Communist Party. Its leaders had rejected the antifascists' invitation. And yet, before the end of the year, the party's local branch took part in the Antifascist United Front's largest demonstration to date, and its representatives agreed to sign the party's name to a manifesto (though *not* as an organizational member of the Antifascist United Front itself but rather as part of the invented "Federation of Groups in Defense of the United Front of São Paulo" — a distinction seemingly settled upon so as to save the local Communists from explicitly defying their orders from on high to stay out of social fascist organizations).[75] In a matter of months, the Antifascist United Front had pulled together practically all of the city's major radical groups into a shared campaign against fascism.

And fascism in São Paulo in 1933 meant the greenshirts of the Ação Integralista Brasileira. The integralistas had first marched in the city on March 23.

—

It was the day Mussolini celebrated as the anniversary of fascism's birth: in 1933, the day marked fourteen years since San Sepolcro. It was in response to integralismo's arrival in São Paulo that the one clique of antifascist intellectuals, including Lôbo, had launched the *Homem Livre*. And it was in response to integralismo's arrival that the representatives of so many radical groups — at each other's throats so often in the past — had signed on enthusiastically to Lôbo's proposal at the Matteotti memorial meeting. Like in Buenos Aires or in London, or Minneapolis or Paris, the antifascism that took form in São Paulo at the onset of the age of fascism hadn't derived from abstract fears or overheated propaganda; the antifascists of São Paulo had seen fascism hit the streets in their own city, and they set out to raise the alarm and fight fascism as, in Lôbo's words, a single bloc of action. The *Homem Livre*, in the paper's announcement of the Antifascist United Front's founding, argued that "fascism, as a method of repression and demagoguery, long ago crossed the border out of the country that saw its birth in blood, lies, and treachery." Fascism — "universal fascism" — had now come "to serve reactionaries around the world." And in Brazil, "those who yesterday were the most intransigent 'nationalists,' and who were sent into hysterics at the prospect of 'exotic ideologies' alien to 'our environment and our people,'" now had themselves fallen into a state of "enchantment" and had begun "to ape" Italian and German fascism, "adopting their shirts and insignias and the Roman salute."[76] The antifascists of São Paulo, in mid-1933, saw fascism — "universal fascism," they had called it — similarly to how Lord Rothermere would see it in the new year. Just as the paramilitarist Alvin Owsley and the communist Grigory Zinoviev, a little longer than a decade before, had both seen fascism as a particularism of Italy that could be understood comparatively to groups in other countries, so too now a fascist and antifascists both saw fascism as a universal that had spread around the world transnationally.

Clashes between antifascists and greenshirts became a part of São Paulo's street life. An Antifascist United Front meeting on November 14, 1933, turned violent when greenshirts tried to storm the hall shouting, "Long live fascism!" Rebuffed, the greenshirts lined up in the street to wait for the meeting's attendees to depart. More troubles followed later on in the evening, and more troubles followed in 1934, as integralismo grew. The same weekend as the Hyde Park clash, 4,000 greenshirts marched in Rio de Janeiro, offering fascist-style

—

salutes to President Getúlio Vargas, who replied in kind.[77] In the weeks that followed, the integralistas announced that they would march on the Praça da Sé and hold a rally there in front of the cathedral on October 7. The antifascists of the city began to organize for a confrontation.

Lôbo thought the organizing went in the wrong direction, toward armed violence.[78] He saw more value in continuing to build the local antifascist movement, in propaganda, mass meetings, and rallies. In the days before the integralista demonstration, leaflets appeared around São Paulo. They went out under the auspices of a dozen organizations, many of them member groups of the Antifascist United Front and also including the Brazilian Communist Party. The leaflets were addressed to "the proletariat and all oppressed people, workers, peasants, communists, legionary socialists, miguel-costistas, anarcho-syndicalists, those without party, manual laborers and intellectuals, those of all political and religious creeds, those of all nationalities, small merchants, low-level public servants, the petite bourgeoisie, labor militants of all tendencies, and people of all oppressed populations!" Such a varied roster! No wonder historians have preferred to say simply that "leftists" were mobilized to confront the integralistas.[79] In the moment, though, those who rallied to antifascism didn't describe themselves so — they lacked the right word with which to wrap up the many different social groups that organizers hoped would come; hence, perhaps, the long-winded plea.

Few doubted that the day would end in violence. Hundreds of police officers and government agents accompanied the integralista procession, 8,000 strong, on its way to the Praça da Sé. Though at least one greenshirt was to deny it afterwards, the first of the integralistas to come into the square were the "green-blouses" ("blusas-verdes"), women in full integralista uniform.[80] They took their position on the steps leading up to the cathedral, behind the platform on which Salgado and other prominent integralistas were to lead the rally.

Antifascists had set up around the square, and they began to heckle the greenshirts as they arrived. They seem to have seen in the greenshirts' choreography the cowardice of fascist men trying to hide behind a human shield of fascist women. The shooting began shortly thereafter; it's not clear how. More greenshirts arrived, and soon they and the police were working together to fight the antifascist forces. The antifascists held strategic spots around the square;

—

anarchists fired shots down at the square from up on the roof of the union hall where the antifascisti of the Grupo Socialista Giacomo Matteotti had hosted the meeting that launched São Paulo's antifascist united front sixteen months before. Grenades exploded, and the shooting spilled into the surrounding streets. Much of the worst of it was along the streets running into the square's northwest corner, along Rua Benjamin Constant and Rua Barão de Paranapiacapa, where the union hall stood, and where, as one report put it, "scenes of true brutality were enacted by all sides." During a lull, the green-blouses in front of the cathedral raised up their arms in straight-armed salutes, as if to taunt the antifascists, and they sang the Brazilian national anthem. The shooting flared up again.[81] It went on for hours and left at least a half dozen dead and three dozen severely wounded. After the violence died down, the antifascists attempted a rally of their own in the square, but the police ran them off.

The violence in the Praça da Sé of São Paulo, in October 1934, offered a sharp contrast to the serenity of the march into the Place de la Nation in Paris, in February. About violence, antifascism has had a dual aspect to it, at least since the Twelfth of February. But in other ways, the two episodes shared qualities in common. Both were spectacles in the public square; both were mass mobilizations; both drew in antifascists of multiple ideological faiths — neither could be said to have been organized, or controlled, by any one party. And neither had been the work of just Italian antifascisti. Antifascists remembered their early martyr Matteotti, but antifascism had been transformed out of its prehistory. What's more, both events were warnings of fascism as it looked to most antifascists in 1934: a transnational force on the move, a danger to all the world. Also, though, both episodes in their own ways were warnings *to* fascists — warnings that, to put it most simply, they would not pass.

And yet in 1934 those who had put their faith in fascism for the most part still saw the future as theirs. Whatever their differences, the Twelfth and Praça da Sé — and Olympia and Plaza Italia and many more such episodes — were all meant to shake that faith. It's fair to say, though, that for those who had faith in fascism, their faith remained strong. In the days that followed Praça da Sé, two badly injured integralistas lay in their hospital beds and raised their right arms to "make a fascist salute" as they were photographed for the press.[82]

—

CHAPTER 4

AGAINST WAR AND FASCISM

Addis Ababa
Across the headlines all year long.
Ethiopia —
Tragi-song for the news reels.

— Langston Hughes, "Broadcast on Ethiopia," 1936

On the morning of November 20, 1934, in a field next to the campus of the City College of New York, students burned an effigy with two heads. "One visage," the *New York Herald Tribune* reported, "was in the likeness of the college president, mortar-board and all, and the other a caricature of Mussolini." The conflagration was only the most provocative part of what the press called the students' "anti-Fascist demonstration," and it was the act that ensured that their protest made small national news.[1]

Much of how the students talked and otherwise acted that morning, and how the press then reported the affair, reflected the place and time in antifascism's history. When the students took a match to the effigy, while singing an improvised dirge, they enacted something between the older notion of "anti-Fascist" dissent targeting the Mussolini regime and the newer notion of antifascism as a sweeping universal.[2] The effigy, after all, had two heads. Compared to the magnificent displays of commitment that antifascists had already put on in 1934 in places such as São Paulo and Paris and London and Córdoba, the City College demonstration could seem a touch rudimentary. Certainly, compared to the murderous violence that had filled the Praça da Sé the month before, the make-believe violence that was the burning of an effigy could seem closer to playacting than to a political act. But in the modern political world there has

—

never been a real line between such things; the mock trial of Adolf Hitler that antifascists had conducted at Madison Square Garden a few months before was a masquerade of legal proceedings but also a very real political statement. What's more, large-puppet theater of the sort that the students performed with their effigy was to remain very much a part of the antifascist repertoire in the years, and decades, to follow.

That said, compared to the mass antifascism that would be on display before all the world within a year or two, it's true, the City College demonstration was a tentative, exploratory effort. With the mass antifascism of 1935 or 1936 in mind, one of the aspects of the incident that is most striking is the simple absence of any mention of antifascism, the thing itself in noun form, in the day's historical record. The demonstration was "anti-Fascist," yes, but it didn't follow that anyone talked of antifascism (or "anti-fascism" or "anti-Fascism," punctuated and letter-cased any which way). Based on what the students were quoted by journalists as saying and what they themselves published, as well as what the journalists wrote in their own words, the day's events didn't translate for those involved into express antifascism. It's a semantic distinction, to be sure, but it's one worth pointing out because a certain distance separates what adjectives do in people's imaginations from what fully formed abstract nouns can do. Still, at least some of the students sensed that they themselves were "anti-fascists." Their saying so — making "anti-fascist" a noun rather than only an adjective — was no doubt a step toward imagining outright antifascism. And in some ways it's more consequential to reimagine yourself into a new kind of political subject, such as an antifascist, than it is to imagine a new political form, such as antifascism.[3]

Among other things, though, the absence of any easily traceable talk of "antifascism" from the self-described antifascists of City College in the fall of 1934 hints at just how complicated the constitution of any given ideological form is likely to be. In the nineteenth century, there had been people who were liberal before there had been people who were liberals, and even then some further intellectual creativity had been needed before anyone started speaking of liberalism.[4] The same was true of "conservative," "conservatives," and "conservatism."[5] And while Mussolini could invoke a fascist movement in the spring of 1915, amid talk of fascisti, he nonetheless only absorbed the concept

—

143

of fascism itself well after San Sepolcro in 1919. Now, so too New York college students turned themselves into antifascists in 1934, and yet, it seems, they didn't draw from it any sense that they were practicing antifascism. The modern world's great ideological abstractions have only been put together through considerable scrabbling about for the right words to make sense of what people were doing at the time and why. And even the smallest twist — say, from -*ist* to -*ism* — takes some work.

The City College protest, though, did have elements in common with the mass antifascism that by then was indeed beginning to take shape in global politics. Many of the commonalities had to do with the incident being another act of popular politics, in the public square, like the euphoria of the Twelfth of February or the bloodshed in the Praça da Sé. What's more, created from what the students described as their own "joyful wave of enthusiasm," the impromptu collectivity that performed the rite of fire was informally formed, a crowd, just as had been the case in so many important events in antifascism's history up to that point, and as would be the case in the months and years to come. That the collectivity in question was nothing more formal than a crowd helped it to be inclusive, and it was in fact a demonstrably ideologically heterogeneous crowd, made of individuals with outright conflicting formal political affiliations. Also like so much of the antifascist politics of the moment, the incident relied on spectacle to communicate its message. The presence of newsreel cameras in the field, capturing the event, suggests just how intentional and well plotted a spectacle it was. The students' protest was also in keeping with a good many other antifascist demonstrations in that it turned violent. When police tried to break up the crowd surrounding the effigy, students locked their arms around a lamppost and chanted, "Cops off the campus!" Then, as one report put it, "Fists flew. Police shoved, students shoved."[6]

Aside from what the incident said about what antifascism meant at the moment, it also spoke to what fascism meant. The fascism that so incensed City College students was rooted in the old Italy-specific notion of fascism, and yet it also had branched out from it. Fascism was Mussolini's dictatorship in Italy, but fascism was also political behavior right there on campus, along Convent Avenue above West 135th Street. Again: the effigy had two heads.

—

The trouble on campus had begun the previous month during an assembly in the august Great Hall, when the college president, Frederick B. Robinson, had warmly welcomed sixteen Italian students visiting as part of a delegation sent by the Mussolini regime. When students in the audience shouted, "Down with Fascism!" Robinson "sprang from his chair," as a lively news report put it, and called the hecklers' conduct "worse than that of guttersnipes." Protesters promptly demanded a speaker of their own, which Robinson benevolently allowed. But as soon as the antifascist speaker began ("I bring anti-fascist greetings to the tricked and enslaved students of Italy"), another student charged at him and punched him in the face. "This was the gage of battle," the one news report exclaimed, and then the "spirit of battle swept the crowd and each man traded punches with his neighbor." Books "whizzed through the air," one student "was severely mauled before he was rescued by his comrades," and soon, it was estimated, 1,000 students were chanting, "Down with Fascism!" Unable to restore calm, Robinson made his way to the microphone and declared, "The chapel is dismissed."[7]

He fled with his visitors, apologizing to them for the melee. Afterwards, a philosophy professor deplored the discourtesy displayed by the protesters and the missed opportunity to affirm "our own fundamental belief in free speech."[8] New York University threw a reception for the Italian students at its Bronx campus the next day; when antifascist protesters confronted them on the steps of Gould Memorial Library, the Italian visitors responded by raising their right hands in straight-armed salutes and shouting, "Il Duce! Il Duce!"[9] A month later, City College expelled twenty-one students and disciplined sixteen more not only for their role in "the riot in the Great Hall," as the *Herald Tribune* account called it, but also as "a wholesale punishment for riotous anti-Fascist demonstrations": since the first incident, a number of "anti-Fascist rallies" had hit campus, provoking the creation of a "vigilante group" to break up any more attempts at agitation.[10] That back and forth of radicalization had led to the burning of the two-headed effigy of Robinson and Mussolini the morning of November 20.

How did all this unruliness speak to the changing meanings of fascism? The general thrust of all the talk of fascism throughout 1934 had had a universalizing spin to it. And plenty of such talk was to come. Right there in New York, the same day that the students burned the effigy, the *New York Post* went to press with its bombshell story about the Great Fascist Plot, the Wall Street scheme to raise a "Fascist army" to install a dictatorship over America.[11] The dominant implication that came of this and other such stories was that fascism could be enacted wherever one worked to bring it about. It was the same implication that had come of the rioting of the Sixth of February in Paris, or Mosley's public meetings in London throughout 1934, or the ongoing incendiarism of the blackshirts in Buenos Aires.

The irony, though, is that at the very end of 1934, events conspired to spin the idea of fascism back into Mussolini's hands. And for the next year or so, Rome again seemed very much the world's capital of fascism. Fifteen days after the effigy burning and the revelations of Wall Street's Great Fascist Plot, a confrontation half a world away from New York between Italian and Somali forces, on the one hand, and British and Ethiopian forces, on the other, turned deadly at a place called Walwal. Walwal was an oasis in the contested terrain between Somaliland, which was Italian territory, and the Ogaden, which was an Ethiopian province. Mussolini, very much wanting a war and craving a more sizable empire, seized on the incident. He began a determined, albeit slow, march to war.[12]

At the time, in December 1934, the episode didn't draw much attention. But that would change. It would change in part because a transnational protest movement would labor doggedly and imaginatively throughout the next year to bring attention to Mussolini's hunger for war and empire. The Hands Off Ethiopia movement tied together the politics of antifascism with that of anticolonialism. It also drew together antifascism with pan-Africanism, black nationalism, and black internationalism. It drew on antiwar sentiments and distilled antiwar politics. It grew out of the political efforts and ideas of people from an impressive range of places around the world. Looked upon in retrospect, it can be said to have shaped the postwar world of decolonization and to have helped to form the left of liberation, radical democracy and social equality, antiwar protest, participatory protest, and rights talk that would make its way through a great many struggles in the decades that followed.

—

To make sense of how antifascism helped to make the left as it was to be-come, the first big sprawling cause to understand is the Hands Off Ethiopia movement of 1935.

And the first thing to understand about the Hands Off Ethiopia movement of 1935 is that it got off to a bumpy start.

The reasons for this had to do with the state of radical politics as handed down from the era before the antifascist moment. The obsession of the anti-fascists in the mid-Depression years with unity and common cause was, as I've said, very much a rejection of the emphasis on rivalry and difference that had prevailed among radical organizations in the years before. In retrospect, it is easy to say, and it has been said, that "division" had dominated "the institutional left" in the years before the antifascist moment. Or that in the early 1930s the left's parties "pitted leftists against each other."[13] But it's more telling, and more accurate, to say that the very idea that the likes of common communists, an-archists, feminists, social democrats, and progressive liberals were all "leftists" hadn't been worked out yet. There was no one big left to divide or unite. And, it should be emphasized, there was at the time no equivalent imagined collectivity of such size and scope with a different name either. When I describe the making of a left that was thought of as a mass global collectivity, I'm not suggesting that antifascists labored to give an old understanding of collective effort a new name; the solidarity and unity of the antifascist moment pulled together people of different places and politics in a way that they had not been together before. The name "the left" isn't the point; the name is a guide, showing a way through the thickets of the modern political world's history. The point is that during the antifascist moment people put in the political work that made their new idea of the left make sense. Following how people used the name gives us a way of seeing the path they cut. They made the left's presence felt — and they made it feel like an omnipresence — in the same way that people had labored to make fascism's or antifascism's presence felt in places beyond Italy.

In the years before, there hadn't been anything at all like what the left would become in the antifascist moment. What had been front and center for people with radical politics in the previous era had been their own distinct ideological

—

and organizational identities. The ideas of unity and common cause that the antifascists would wield — the simple idea of "the left" as something larger than internal sects and parliamentary blocs — hadn't yet been honed. The antifascists themselves would have to do that. They had done some of the work already in 1934; already people were beginning to use the language of "the left" in new ways. Still, though, what such language was to signify had yet to be figured out. The visions of the left as a human crowd in the street, fists thrown up, voices joined in song, a shared stock of key phrases stored in everyone's mind — all that had to be taken in. Notions of vanguardism had to be given up. Notions that the party itself was the sovereign figure of radical politics had to be overthrown. Notions that one owed obedience, deference, and discipline to the party line had to be shaken off. The claim that "the people" — embodied in the street crowd, assembled and marching — should rule over "the left" had to be enacted time and again so as to sink in. People who had joined different parties had to join together and take part in mass mobilizations. Like Hands Off Ethiopia.

At first, though, there was little reason to think that Hands Off Ethiopia would amount to anything. On January 7, 1935, the primary organizers of the Union des Travailleurs Nègres (UTN) met in Paris, in a Communist meeting-house above the tracks behind the Gare de l'Est. The UTN was sponsored by the Comintern and had ties to the French Communist Party, but as that night's meeting showed the group had its own political aims, which often ran counter to Comintern directives. Having taken place only thirty-three days after the Walwal incident, the January 7 meeting stands out as one of the earliest documented attempts to organize protest against fascist Italy's aggression toward Ethiopia — its documentation thanks to the detailed notes taken, and passed on to police, by one of the meeting's participants.[14]

Those notes detailed how Pierre Kodo-Kossoul, a black naturalized French citizen from Dahomey, had already broached the question of Ethiopia at the group's December meeting, the same month as Walwal. Kossoul had proposed then that the group work with the Ligue de Défense de la Race Nègre (LDRN), the UTN's primary local rival in organizing black radical politics.[15] This was a bold proposal, and it showed just how much of the UTN's politics was made by its own members' choices, rather than by Comintern directives. It also showed

—

148

just how complicated and fraught (and at times contradictory) those choices were — in no small part because of all the many Comintern directives that the UTN's organizers had to navigate, whether they followed them or not.

The rival LDRN, by contrast, had nothing to do with the Comintern in December 1934. Its leaders held this up as a point of pride — and of distinction from the UTN. In the most recent issue of the LDRN's semiregular newspaper, the *Race Nègre,* an editorial insisted that the UTN "had alienated a part of its independence" in accepting the Communist Party's money. Any collaboration with the French Communist Party was a mistake, the editorial insisted, because it meant mixing oneself up with political problems that didn't concern black people — it meant mixing oneself up with the "white categories of right and left," two categories that had not previously been a part of the paper's discourse, even dismissively. What's more, the "soul" of black people was such that "it is in vain to speak to them of Capitalism and the Proletariat." It followed that, unlike the UTN, "our league strives exclusively to express only what affects them," the black people of the world. And yet from 1929 into 1931 the French Communist Party *had* helped to finance the LDRN. By 1931, though, the group's most engaged organizers had split into two factions, in large part because of the relationship with the Comintern. The faction that wished to remain attached to the Comintern (described in a police report as "extremist elements of the left wing" of the LDRN) split off from the group — and became the UTN.[16] Needless to say, Communist Party officials discouraged the UTN's members from having anything to do with the postschism LDRN, which Kossoul knew very well when he made his proposal.

In the years since the split, the UTN's organizers had had bumpy relations with the Comintern. They generally took a tactical, even cynical, approach to the French Communist Party and the Comintern hierarchy. At the January 7, 1935, meeting, one UTN member joked about the party's newspaper that "even before reading *Humanité* I already know the news: it's always the same."[17] At the root of the UTN organizers' frustration with the party was its inconsistent record of opposing the French Empire's colonialism. They saw in the Ethiopian crisis not only a chance to fight fascism, but also a chance to fight imperialism — French as well as Italian.[18] Indeed, they sought to combine the two fights, to make clear fascism's embeddedness in broader workings of

—

global power. Given that they held onto their connection to the Comintern, it's fair to say that the UTN's organizers considered the benefits of affiliation to outweigh the drawbacks, but they knew the costs of making use of the Comintern: in the fall of 1933, the Comintern had expelled the group's charismatic leader Tiémoko Garan Kouyaté. The group never fully recovered from Kouyaté's departure — in the most practical of terms, the loss of Kouyaté had meant the loss of the UTN's master mailing list, which Kouyaté, nobody's fool, had always kept to himself.[19]

Kouyaté's absence as the UTN began to organize in defense of Ethiopia epitomized the consequences of the many institutional quarrels that defined radical politics in those years before the antifascist moment. Kouyaté had a reputation as a gifted orator, and his reputation as a brilliant and dynamic (if undisciplined) organizer was even greater. Born in 1902 in French Sudan near the Niger River (in present-day Mali), Kouyaté attended the prestigious École normale William-Ponty on the Île de Gorée and the École normale d'Aix en Provence; in Paris, he audited classes at the Sorbonne. It is said that he was expelled from school in Aix, in 1926, for spreading communist propaganda among the other students. Within months, he had moved to Paris and joined the precursor to the LDRN, the Comité de Défense de la Race Nègre. That committee ended in its own factional split, which led to the creation of the LDRN. By the end of 1927, Kouyaté had become the new group's secretary general. He was indefatigable in the years that followed, organizing black radical students and intellectuals in Paris, and maritime workers in port cities like Marseille. He corresponded widely and traveled widely as well, spending time in Moscow and Berlin. It was likely in Frankfurt, in 1929, that he first met George Padmore, a young Trinidadian then living in the United States and making a name for himself as he exhorted black workers there to rally to "the left wing of the labor movement" as the answer to labor "jim-crowism" (racially exclusionary unionism). The two became close comrades. Kouyaté also tried in 1929 to recruit into the LDRN the prominent Congolese mutual aid organizer André Matswa and his movement, an effort foiled by Matswa's arrest. When the LDRN split in two in 1931, Emile Faure, a meticulous engineer from Senegal, led the remnant LDRN toward a more focused black nationalism. Kouyaté, the freewheeling intellectual, led the UTN toward something messier, something

—

Figure 4. Tiémoko Garan Kouyaté (right) stands with James Ford (left), who organized "Hands Off Ethiopia" protests in Harlem in 1935, and Willi Münzenberg (center), who organized the European Anti-Fascist Workers' Congress in Paris in 1933.

that disheveled any distinctions of black nationalism from black internationalism, or of either of those from communist internationalism. For that matter, Kouyaté disheveled distinctions of African radicalism from European and Southeast Asian and West Indian and North American radicalism—he worked to further all these, and to pull them together. And he disheveled distinctions of anticolonialism from antifascism as well.[20] Kouyaté reveled in mashing together causes and ideas (fig. 4).

And yet for all his wide-ranging intellectual obsessions, after Hitler came to power Kouyaté saw fascism as the most immediate threat faced by black people everywhere. Speaking at a public meeting held by the UTN in the summer of 1933, he warned that Hitler would soon colonize aggressively and "chase black people from their homes." What's more, Hitler would incite continental war, and then "working-class black people would be driven out of Europe," not only by the fascists of Germany but also by those of other countries, including

—

France. His organizing turned to "the goal of figuring out together how best to fight against fascism."[21]

Only one season later, though, in the fall, Kouyaté could tell the story of how a friend had just said to him, "So, you're a fascist now." The friend explained: "At least that's what your communist comrades say." The friend added, "There's nothing sincere in their words. We've warned you for years now not to alienate the independence of our beautiful movement. Now you see how you're rewarded." The reward of which the friend spoke was that Kouyaté was being expelled from the party. One wonders if the friend was Faure. The language — "alienate," "independence" — seems pulled straight from the pages of the *Race Nègre*. And one of the reasons that party leaders wanted to expel Kouyaté in the fall of 1933 was that he was keeping company with Faure. The larger reason, though, ironic enough, was that he had been far too independent. He had fought against the attempts of the party's hierarchy to exercise oversight of the UTN and to pry away control of its newspaper, the *Cri des Nègres*. At times, Kouyaté had relied on Padmore to give money from the Comintern funds he administered from Hamburg, where he edited the English-language *Negro Worker*. But in the first weeks of the Third Reich, Padmore was, as reported in the *Negro Worker*, "dragged out of his bed by Nazi police and imprisoned." After holding him for two weeks, Nazi authorities deported him. When the French Communist Party expelled Kouyaté, in October 1933, the other officers of the UTN fell in line and banished him from their organization as well. At the meeting of the vote, some of the harshest criticisms of Kouyaté came from Edmond Thomas Ramananjato. This is known because Ramananjato then wrote a report on the meeting and gave it to the police. Ramananjato was a police informant. He was not the only one in the group, and he was not the one who wrote notes on the January 7, 1935, meeting at which Kossoul's idea was discussed. That may have been Kossoul. He was an informant as well.[22]

Few in number — and at least one fewer than they had to be — the UTN's organizers nonetheless imagined raising a mass movement in support of Ethiopia. At their next meeting, in early February, one of the organizers, Stéphane Rosso, originally of Guadeloupe, said, "To interest the working class, we need a ferocious agitation . . . like those for Thälmann and the blacks of Scottsboro." He was referring to two epic protest movements from recent years. Thälmann

—

had been arrested shortly after Padmore, shortly after the Reichstag fire and the raid on the Karl-Liebknecht-Haus. He wasn't deported as Padmore was; he stayed in prison. In response to his detention, the Comintern pushed its militants to raise a transnational protest campaign: variations of "Free Thäl-mann and all the antifascists!" were heard in different languages and lands around the world as the antifascist moment began. Likewise, the imprisonment of nine black youths in Scottsboro, Alabama, on false charges of raping a white woman provoked protest in cities around the world, Shanghai to Accra, Sydney to Berlin. One of Clara Zetkin's last great appeals had been in solidarity with the "Scottsboro boys."[23]

The agitations for Thälmann and the Scottsboro youths were part of a series of transnational protest movements that had stirred together some initial elements of the global left to come. The first had been the movement to protest the imprisonment (and, in the end, the execution) of Sacco and Vanzetti. That movement ran from 1920 to 1927, Boston to Buenos Aires, Paris to Rio de Janeiro, and so on. It intertwined with the movement to memorialize Matteotti, the one often reinforcing the other. The Italian diaspora drove both, but in each case the sentiments spilled forth to form a wider movement. Several of the biggest protest campaigns of the era were intertwined with others. When Communists around the world agitated for Nazi Germany to release Thälmann, they also did the same for the Bulgarian Communist Georgi Dimitrov, accused of setting the Reichstag fire. And along with the transnational movement to free the "Scottsboro boys," Communists — and an ever-growing number of allies — agitated for the release of Angelo Herndon, a black Communist Party U.S.A. organizer accused of "attempting to incite insurrection" by organizing the unemployed of Atlanta. Each movement empowered the next. All of them approached global proportions; what's more, their participants came to understand their causes in global terms. This became abundantly clear by the time of the movement to liberate Herndon — "America's young Dimitroff" — whom antifascists described as a prisoner of fascism, incarcerated in Atlanta.[24] Such interpretation pulled local causes into a maelstrom of global politics.

By August 1935, at the height of the Hands Off Ethiopia movement, none other than Dimitrov himself — freed from prison, found not guilty of having set the Reichstag fire — would give a policy speech at the seventh Comintern

—

congress, calling on Communists everywhere to embrace antifascist solidarity even with those who in the previous era had been social fascists, even with those, like Kouyaté, whose quarrels with Comintern interests had made them figurative fascists. And yet the parade of Hands Off Ethiopia protests that had already taken place by then showed how countless Communists had already embraced the idea of a wider antifascist solidarity. When the protest movement first began to form, in early 1935, well before Dimitrov's speech, the Comintern did not engineer or even endorse the broad-based popular movement to defend Ethiopia. In some cases, as in Paris, the Comintern hierarchy actively got in the way: at that January 7 UTN meeting, Rosso announced that the French Communist Party had received, rejected, and condemned Kossoul's proposal from December to collaborate with Faure and the LDRN.[25]

The Comintern and the party did encourage protest, even early on, but they approached it as if it were an instrument for institution building. They sought always to regulate the protest. Such a narrow approach didn't allow for the sort of wide-ranging solidarity that Kossoul sought. As it was explained to him, the party's central committee had ruled that collaboration with Faure was "impossible" because Faure, by his opposition to the party, had "sold out to imperialism."[26]

And so without Kouyaté or Faure's LDRN, but with white Communist groups, the UTN sponsored the first mass meeting for the defense of Ethiopia in Paris, and perhaps anywhere, on February 28 at the Latin Quarter's majestic Maison de la Mutualité. The meeting disappointed its organizers: scarcely twenty black people showed up. White attendees, likely having read of the meeting in that morning's *Humanité*, outnumbered black attendees. When the UTN organizers tried to explain how the French working class had allowed itself to be coopted by imperialism, the white audience argued and defended the nation's proletariat.[27]

It was a frustrating beginning, to be sure. But the frustrations, examined in retrospect, are useful for understanding the making of Hands Off Ethiopia. Because here the Comintern's officials actively tried to limit the scope of protest, so as better to control it, and because local organizers bristled at their directives, you can see how common Communists, and others in the UTN who weren't party members, were themselves adamant about protesting fascist ambitions

—

in Ethiopia. Because the Comintern's command structure pressed against them so, you can see in relief their own initiative and volition. You can see the politics that was their own. Think about the antifascism of UTN organizers in relation to that of someone like Aristides Lôbo in São Paulo. Efforts like Lôbo's show how, in some instances, antifascism cropped up entirely outside of the Comintern and its parties—and then even pulled in Communists, made *them* "fellow travelers." Learning about antifascism in São Paulo is one way of seeing through the claims that reduce the antifascism of the mid-1930s to a corollary of the Comintern's political agenda, the fruit of its propaganda efforts. Scenarios like the one in São Paulo make the point with a satisfying simplicity. But the muddier scenes such as the one within the UTN teach crucial lessons, too. Learn of the antifascism practiced by the likes of Kossoul—Communist Party member, police informant, and genuine antifascist and anticolonialist all the same—and the lessons are harder won. To understand how mass antifascism came about in these years, though, such lessons are needed. In the case of the UTN, where Hands Off Ethiopia organizing came from within a Communist-backed organization, it nonetheless sprang from the politics of those who did the actual organizing. That is to say, Hands Off Ethiopia did not descend from the Comintern high command and did not proceed under its direction. A grassroots affair from the start, the movement worked toward internal solidarity by working toward independence from the formal organizations that sought to divide and control it.

That said, not all of the plans made in Paris in early 1935 to protest on behalf of the people of Ethiopia took place within the Comintern's ecosystem. Tiémoko Garan Kouyaté was still in Paris in February, and shortly before the meeting at the Mutualité he was plotting out protest of his own, with his comrade George Padmore by his side. Like Kouyaté, Padmore was by this point a notorious ex-Communist. A few months prior, he had been expelled from the Communist International, in part for keeping company with Kouyaté.[28]

Even with Kouyaté and Padmore organizing protest, though, in early 1935 the UTN led the way in Paris. The radicals who ran the organization continued to improvise everyday practices of protest, figuring things out as they went, searching for practices, and language, capable of expressing their cause. It was a daily challenge. On Saturday, March 16, when UTN members acted

—

out their solidarity with Ethiopia by marching to the country's legation in Paris, they presented the Ethiopian envoy with a letter of support for "the Empire of Ethiopia."[29] Even anticolonialists attempting to launch an anti-imperialist campaign, irritated by others' apologies for imperialism, sought to crown their cause with the legitimacy of empire. Political words can inspire and emancipate, but more often they are traps. The only way to find the right words is to work through the traps.

"Abyssinian Baptist Church literally rocked with the spirit of militant struggle against Italian fascism," one witness wrote after the mass meeting held there March 7, 1935. On a Thursday night, 3,000 people filled the eminent church on West 138th Street in Harlem. Their aim was to rally local support for Ethiopia. Hands Off Ethiopia protests hadn't taken off yet—this was nine days before the UTN emissaries visited the Ethiopian legation in Paris. Aside from communists and churchfolk, Garveyite black nationalists attended—offering a crowd of distinctly heterogeneous ideologies nonetheless gathering together in practice. The young Reverend Adam Clayton Powell Jr. pushed the crowd to take up the "struggle against fascism!" He insisted, "Fascism is eating into the very vitals of our people!" Drawing the national and the global together into a single transnationalized political dynamic, he added that the struggle was not against fascist Italy's aggression toward Ethiopia alone but also against those "who in America represent the spirit of fascism." After Powell finished speaking against fascism, the local Communist Party leader James Ford began speaking on the question of antifascist unity, calling on all to "stop fighting among ourselves." The call generated enthusiastic cheers. Garveyite Arthur Reid drew the two themes together, declaring amid more cheers, "We must unite, and after we unite we must fight."[30]

Those who gathered for the meeting at Abyssinian did not resolve their differences that night—Garveyism, communism, and the deliverance theology of the church remained distinct ideological strains, each maintaining its own institutional bases—but attendees nonetheless achieved a solidarity of purpose with each other that allowed them in turn to make a collective claim of solidarity with the people of faraway Ethiopia. In just such ways, assembled face to face, listening to each other and cheering each other, local people can create a global politics.

What's more, not only can local acts make global politics, global politics can lend meaning to local events. In Harlem, this was made clear less than two weeks after the meeting at Abyssinian, during the riot of March 19. At the meeting, attendees had begun planning a parade through Harlem. The goal of the provisional committee tasked with the planning was to hold "a gigantic 'Hands Off Abyssinia' Parade" on Saturday, March 30. The hope was to have "every important Negro organization in Harlem" take part, and to pull in other groups as well. As the local Communist paper the *Negro Liberator* reported regarding the provisional committee's agenda, "every effort will be made to cement the solidarity of the white workers, and particularly the Italian workers, in this common struggle against Italian fascism." After the meeting, the committee got started. But before it got anywhere, the riot of March 19 hit, throwing everything in the neighborhood up in the air. The wreckage made by the riot was impressive—almost 700 windows were broken in 300 businesses along and around 125th Street. Afterward, the police refused to issue a parade permit to the committee for the march, and it was indefinitely postponed.[31] On the face of it, local Hands Off Ethiopia agitation had stalled before it had really gotten underway.

And yet heard among the din of rioting on March 19 was the exclamation "Down with Mussolini!" What is the nature of the relationship between a transnational political movement such as Hands Off Ethiopia and something like a riot made along the way? Ford and Harry Gannes, in a Hands Off Ethiopia pamphlet they coauthored and put out shortly after the riot, argued that solidarity with Ethiopia had "seeped into the political consciousness of the American Negro people" in their "own struggle for freedom." In the wake of the riot, the *Negro Liberator* added, "A powerful fight for the independence of Abyssinia can be waged right here in Harlem against the miserable conditions forced on the Negro people."[32]

The transnational political dimensions of the riot hardly detract from the material local grievances that fueled it. The rioters, taken as a whole, didn't react to any one isolated outrage. Rather, it seems that they felt the weight of multiple, mutually reinforcing oppressions. Their own local hardships stood out most of all, yes, but the threat hanging over Ethiopia stood out as well. A similar here-and-there logic had governed the "Scottsboro riot" in Harlem

—

the previous year. Then, crowds had turned violent in twofold protest of local police brutality and the Jim Crow injustice in Scottsboro. More politically
charged riots had followed in Harlem later in 1934, all of which had bonded
together causes near and far: amid "save Herndon" demonstrations, Angelo
Herndon's brother Milton was arrested in Harlem for "inciting to riot" during
a local discrimination protest.[33] (In the spring of 1937, Milton Herndon set
out to fight fascism in Spain; in the autumn, he died in battle near the Ebro
River.) The March 19, 1935, riot showed the same sort of dual vision between
the local and far away that the 1934 riots had shown. What had changed was
that now the vision was wider, extended beyond the United States out into a
transnational zone of politics. Regardless, with the parade postponed the way
forward for Hands Off Ethiopia in Harlem remained unclear.

Not that it was clear anywhere at the time that Hands Off Ethiopia would
soon become a great cause. The early efforts in London to build up protest
against fascist Italy's imperial aims required considerable selflessness and imagination. C. L. R. James began those efforts from scratch, and, judging from his
accounts, it seems that he began them by himself, alone. Sometime early on in
1935, it's unknown just when, he established the International African Friends
of Abyssinia (IAFA). Since he arrived from Trinidad in 1932, James had produced two landmark polemics about West Indian radical politics, though in
England he was as yet mostly known for his *Manchester Guardian* reports on
cricket matches. He also had joined the Independent Labour Party and become
a Trotskyist. After three years, he still could not tolerate most English food, so
when he founded the IAFA he was in his favorite place to eat, Amy Ashwood
Garvey's new International Afro Restaurant. Ashwood Garvey's radical politics,
her skilled cooking of Caribbean cuisine, and her merciful prices made the
International Afro Restaurant "the center," in James's words, "of a good deal
of West Indian agitation." Even if James did start the IAFA alone, Ashwood
Garvey and her partner Sam Manning soon joined.[34]

James, Ashwood Garvey (from Jamaica), and Manning (like James, from
Trinidad) were all West Indians who had never even touched foot in Africa: the
African in the group's title imagined a diasporic community reaching around
the globe. This alone required a piercing social imagination, as countless forms

—

of nationalism complicated any attempt at theorizing a pan-African identity in the mid-1930s.[35] As if to prove the fluidity of identity, though, as well as the Friends' increasingly familiar identification with Ethiopia, the group soon changed the more exonymous "Abyssinia" at the end of its name to the more endonymous "Ethiopia," thus becoming the International African Friends of Ethiopia (IAFE). Meanwhile, a person born and raised in Africa soon joined, a young student from Kenya then calling himself by the name Johnstone Kenyatta. He too played with identity, as he soon traded Johnstone for Jomo.[36]

This initial cadre made something of a talented thousandth—even before Padmore showed up, which he did, at some point later in 1935—but the group's politics tended toward egalitarian, rather than elitist, principles all the same. The Friends' adamant informality enabled this egalitarianism, and it also endowed the group with a tactical flexibility to refit itself to specific circumstances. According to each event's audience, the group could present an entire slate of black orators or else include white antifascists, and at least once even an Italian antifascist exile. Likewise, when it suited their purposes, the organizers publicized simply as the International Friends of Ethiopia or the Society of International Friends of Ethiopia, dropping the "African" modifier. IAFE literature claimed a headquarters at 62 New Oxford Street—which was the address of the International Afro Restaurant. Ashwood Garvey lived upstairs. Rather than operating as a formal organization, the group organized itself as, in Padmore's words, "an *ad hoc* committee."[37]

In practice, the Friends chose an everyday politics of constant agitation over institution building. They did so within London's atmosphere of passionately participatory popular politics, at a moment when Mussolini's war mobilization was the talk of the town. A stroll through Hyde Park revealed antiwar protests at their liveliest and their least formalized. In the park, dissidents throughout the decades had carved out a customary right to speak near the Marble Arch, in what had become known as Speakers' Corner. The most famous of orators to make use of Speakers' Corner during the summer of 1935 was none other than Ashwood Garvey's ex-husband, Marcus Garvey, who had settled in London with his second wife Amy Jacques Garvey. On Sundays in Hyde Park, Marcus Garvey spoke out against fascist Italy. The most popular antifascist orator at Speakers' Corner, though, was not Garvey but his fellow West Indian known

—

as Prince Monolulu, the brightly clad horse-racing tipster who also thrilled Hyde Park crowds with his ferocious denunciations of Nazi crimes. Though not formally a Friend, Prince Monolulu took part in a mass meeting organized by the group at the historic Memorial Hall in Farringdon Street on July 28. Ashwood Garvey chaired the meeting and James, Kenyatta, and others addressed a crowd of 250 people, likely the largest showing for a meeting on Ethiopia so far in 1935. Nancy Cunard, a wealthy white heiress turned anarchist agitator, described the crowd as the largest gathering of black people in London "since the big Scottsboro protest in Shoreditch Town Hall in 1932."[38]

Around London, meetings multiplied. The Barbadian labor organizer Chris Braithwaite (also known as Chris Jones), previously active in London's Scottsboro protests, railed against Mussolini's warmongering at local unemployed workers' meetings. At the other end of London's class scale, elites also mobilized, led by groups such as the War and Peace Society at University College, London, and the Anti-Imperialist League. And Sylvia Pankhurst was hard at work. In the decade since she organized the Matteotti memorial meeting in Soho with the Friends of Italian Freedom, she had founded the Women's International Matteotti Committee; by the end of July 1935 the committee was collecting funds "for the relief," as Pankhurst explained, "of distress in Abyssinia"—distress, she added, "occasioned by the threatened unprovoked attack by the Italian Fascist Government." (Kenyatta wrote to her in August, though it's not clear anything came of it.)[39] Locally, these various sources of agitation fed off each other, even as no formal organization coordinated them. As such, the London movement as a whole maintained the informal and improvisational approach exemplified by James and Ashwood Garvey's group of many names. Likewise, though the cause of Ethiopia was drawing global attention, the London scene did not grow by networking with distant allies, but rather by agitating informally and fanatically at home—a sort of grassroots globalism.

What was true of London was true of the wider world. Locals protested here, there, and all around, and soon enough the movement had the feel of a global cause. "Everywhere now," Cunard claimed shortly after the Memorial Hall meeting, "throughout the world, people are rising and will rise against the clutching hands of Fascism that are stretching out to destroy the last black autonomy in Africa." Eleven days before the Memorial Hall meeting, on July 17, a big crowd had marched through Johannesburg and climbed the granite steps in front of the City Hall; there, framed by the building's imposing colonnade, the crowd had watched as an effigy of Mussolini burned. In Detroit, protesters outside the Italian consulate waved "Hands off Ethiopia!" signs and picketed. In Istanbul, supporters of Ethiopia held an enlistment drive for the Ethiopian army. On July 26, a public meeting of self-declared "citizens of Calcutta" condemned the march to war and called for resistance to "Fascism, War, Imperialism." Around the same time, Mohandas Gandhi made an appeal from his ashram: "India cannot ignore Benito Mussolini's threat against the colored people." Writing from London, the British Guiana-born jazz musician Rudolph Dunbar described Gandhi's plea as a hint that much of Asia, from Yemen to India, was readying to rise to Ethiopia's defense. The crew of a Greek steamship in Alexandria, Egypt, went on strike rather than deliver war materiel for fascist Italy; the local dockers supported the crew by refusing to load the ship. Likewise, dockers in Durban and in Lüderitz Bay, South West Africa (in present-day Namibia), refused to load Italian ships. In the harbor of Montreal, someone threw a rock through a large glass window in a docked Italian ship; wrapped around the rock was newspaper with "Hands off Ethiopia" written across it in red.[40]

Amid such widespread agitation, antifascists in Harlem decided that their neighborhood was ready for the parade that they had begun to plan in March. The provisional planning committee had actually pulled off a small demonstration earlier on, but now a deeper sense of purpose and community commitment animated its efforts. And on August 3 Harlem made transatlantic news with a musical, joyful parade of perhaps 20,000 people. A correspondent for the *Afro-American* of Baltimore depicted it as "one of the most colorful mass demonstrations ever given in this city of many demonstrations and many things colorful." Two processions, one with black and one with white marchers, joined at 129th Street and Seventh Avenue and integrated into one big crowd. The crowd then weaved north and west through Harlem until the marchers held a street meeting near Colonial Park. The physical act of black and white antifascists walking into solidarity, two columns intermixing to make one crowd, echoed the ecstasy of the Twelfth of February when the French Socialist and

—

Communist parties' columns had converged near the Place de la Nation in Paris. The Harlem parade was likewise a great success. Pacifists took part and Pullman porters wore their uniforms with white gloves; black and white nurses marched in their uniforms. People held signs inscribed "Hands Off Ethiopia!" "Schools – Not Battleships," "Smash Hitler!" and "DOWN WITH FASCIST OPPRESSION IN ITALY AND GERMANY." Two children, one black and one white, had their picture taken with the sign "ABBASSO LA GUERRA IMPERIALISTA" (Down with imperialist war). Marchers carried a black casket marked as "reserved for Mussolini."[41]

As the unified Harlem crowd made its way to Colonial Park, a band played and people sang out, "We'll never fight our class brothers, / We shall not be moved."[42] They were improvising on a militant union song. It came from an old slave spiritual. The key line that gives the song its title – "We shall not be moved" – has resonances with the Twelfth's slogan-promise "Fascism shall not pass!" Much like that expression, the song "We Shall Not Be Moved" later came to acquire its own considerable legacy across the global left. In 1949, when rioters attacked the antifascist singer Paul Robeson as he attempted to give a concert near Peekskill, New York, the interracial crew and concert organizers locked arms and sang the song while they were assaulted. The Freedom Singers of the Student Nonviolent Coordinating Committee (SNCC) sang the song at the Lincoln Memorial for the 1963 March on Washington for Jobs and Freedom. Then, by 1970, Spanish antifascists protesting the dictatorship of Francisco Franco were singing the song as "No nos moverán." Soon thereafter, during the September 11, 1973, military coup against Salvador Allende's socialist government in Chile, after Radio Magallanes played Allende's final address, the station played "No nos moverán" repeatedly until the military took over and shut it down.[43]

The song shares many an affinity with "Fascism shall not pass!" Like the slogan, the song lyric "We shall not be moved" is future-facing and commitment-making. And in the unique version that the Harlem marchers sang in August 1935, the promise of solidarity in the first line – to fight not against our class brothers – parallels the Twelfth's cries of "Unity! Unity!" Still, the most direct parallels have to do with what's shared between "Fascism shall not pass!" and the second line of the lyric, "We shall not be moved." Both the

---

promise that fascism shall not pass and the promise that we shall not be moved have such an intense physicality to them. Both offer up a scene of an imagined collective speaker, assembled together in person. In both cases, that collective speaker makes a negative promise of what shall *not* occur. Whether it be Mayerás's "we" from the Twelfth or the "we" here who will never fight our class brothers and who shall not be moved, the message remains one of empowerment in collectivity, and the imagery remains one of politics as a battlefield that we refuse to yield.

The Harlem parade set off a blast of protest that blazed through the final two months before Mussolini finally announced the invasion of Ethiopia. Until this period, mass meetings with broad attendance had been the exception. Now they became the rule, capturing public attention in places around the world. Kouyaté, who was as plugged in as anyone to the circuitry of protest, listed antiwar demonstrations in Japan, Egypt, Tunisia, India, Trinidad, British Guiana, England, the United States, Martinique, the British Gold Coast, and Kenya; and he pointed as well to the solidarity expressed by the Zulu kholwa chief Walter Khumalo in South Africa. There were more protests outside of Kouyaté's range: an eclectic crowd of trade unionists, students, clergy, children, and Italian expatriates in Melbourne marched; socialists in Rio de Janeiro organized "a mammoth demonstration"; in the Caribbean, there was antiwar agitation in Havana, Port au Prince, and Kingston, where Marcus and Amy Jacques Garvey, recently arrived from London, gave antiwar speeches to a large crowd on September 8.[44]

Back in London, Amy Ashwood Garvey and the International African Friends of Ethiopia paused their everyday agitations in Hyde Park to stage a mass meeting on August 25 in London's other great open-air forum of participatory politics, Trafalgar Square. "Negroes and coloured peoples from every part of the world," one detailed account related, "crowded the plinth of Nelson's Column and mixed with the large white audience." Those in the crowd ranged from small children to old black men "with white hair and beards," and those on stage included "coloured seamen, students, actors, musicians, doctors and, in his colourful costume and plumed headdress, a well-known racing tipster, waving the flag of Abyssinia." That, of course, was Prince Monolulu. Another

—

report suggested, "The statue which, chin in hand, stared gravely at the negro orators in Trafalgar Square to-day was appropriately that of Gordon of Khartum." The statue, which has long since been removed from the square, depicted Charles Gordon, martyr of the British Empire, killed at Khartoum in 1885.[45] That the Friends were subverting the symbolic power of Trafalgar Square, a monumental space meant to instill reverence for the empire, by loudly expressing their anti-imperialist message wasn't lost on the crowd.

The speeches themselves dealt, often quite deftly, with questions of race, empire, and fascism, linking them all. There's no sign that Padmore took part; it may be that he hadn't settled in London quite yet. But Ashwood Garvey, James, Kenyatta, and Braithwaite all spoke. One speech expressed hope for peace but warned that should Mussolini continue "his Imperialistic aggression, we shall rise like one man in all parts of the world, and we shall inflict such a disaster on Fascism that it will never be able to raise its head again." Arnold Ward, a member of the Friends who had come to London from Barbados, said that though Mussolini "has declared he is out for a race war" the black peoples of the world would not reply in kind: he himself sought solidarity with "the masses of white peoples." Ashwood Garvey directed her remarks to the white people in the crowd. She didn't ask them to give their sympathy to Ethiopia but rather told them to recognize that their own fate now relied on solidarity with black people. She declared, "You have talked of 'The White Man's burden.' Now we are carrying yours and standing between you and Fascism." James and Kenyatta pursued a different logic in their speeches. James argued, "It is true that Abyssinia is a backward nation." And he argued, "It is true that it needs western civilisation." But, he insisted, fascism could not deliver this. Fascism meant "sinking to barbarism." Likewise, Kenyatta said, "The sort of Western civilisation we need is not Italian Fascism, nor German Hitlerism." Their speeches had none of Ashwood Garvey's militancy; they seemed determined to say nothing to offend. And in avoiding anything that hinted of anticolonialism they relied on antifascism to carry the entirety of their arguments. Kenyatta made the antifascism of his argument explicit in an article that he wrote likely either just before or just after the meeting in Trafalgar Square; under the title "Hands Off Abyssinia!" he insisted, "To support Ethiopia is to fight Fascism."[46]

—

Halfway through the meeting, according to one witness, "pamphlets began to appear among the crowd" which were "alleged to be distributed by members of the Fascist party" — Mosley's BUF. Because of the ongoing slave trade in Ethiopia, the pamphlet argued, Emperor Haile Selassie's regime should be considered the enemy of black people everywhere: "Negroes, are you going to help a degenerate Semitic people, who enslave people of your own race? Keep out! This is no negro quarrel." Someone seized the pamphlets before they could all be passed out, and the meeting went on uninterrupted.[47]

The most dramatic part of the demonstration took the organizers by surprise. At some point, a stranger in the crowd passed forward his card and, explaining that he was Ethiopian, said that he wished to speak. He was only momentarily in London for a layover, but he had noticed an announcement for the meeting in the newspaper. His name was Ras Makonnen, like the father of the Ethiopian emperor. But Makonnen was neither from nor had ever been to Ethiopia. He was born in a British Guianese village as George Griffith, and his claim of Ethiopian identity rested on nothing more than his grandfather's stay in Ethiopia long before he himself was born. Griffith had taken an interest in Ethiopia, rather, as a student at Cornell University, where he had enrolled in 1932. While at Cornell, he would go in to New York and take part in an Africanist reading group at the 135th Street public library in Harlem.[48] A consequence of happenstance, his appearance in Trafalgar Square fit perfectly the Friends' improvisational methods. So too did his free sense of identity. He carried off his speech well.

While it was Makonnen's appearance that most startled the meeting's organizers, it was the meeting's atmosphere of calm that most startled the storied African American newspaper the *Chicago Defender*. By the time the paper published news of the London demonstration, police and protesters had since engaged each other on Chicago's South Side during an immense antiwar demonstration. The *Defender* found it worth noting that "unlike Chicago where . . . police last Saturday clubbed every suspicious looking person in the neighborhood . . . , in England there was no police interference and consequently no disorder."[49] The demonstration in Chicago was the one that Oliver Law had taken part in organizing. It was the one at which he had taken to the roof along

47th Street to give himself some distance from the police as he delivered his speech to the crowd parading past him below.

Just sixteen months later, Law would be catching a train out of Chicago, on his way to ship out to fight fascism in Spain. By the end of August 1935, the Hands Off Ethiopia movement was reaching its peak, and the history of antifascism had entered into its heroic period.

The 47th Street march that Law helped to put together was the culmination of two months of intense protest in Chicago. Hands Off Ethiopia agitations had begun there on June 22. On that day, antifascists had mounted an inspired offensive against the Italian consulate in the Loop of downtown Chicago. It began with two women walking up to the consulate and chaining themselves to a streetside post. Lillian Rabin, nineteen years old from the city's far West Side, was white; Eloise Robinson, twenty-four years old from the South Side, was black. Each wore a shirt that read: "HANDS OFF ETHIOPIA." Along with about thirty fellow demonstrators—some white, some black; some women, some men; some Communist, some not—Rabin and Robinson confounded police officers for some time by handcuffing themselves to the chain they had wrapped around the post and then padlocking the chain. Since the police found Rabin and Robinson not to have the keys to the cuffs or the padlock, a detail of officers ran off to acquire wire shears. Finally, according to one newspaper account that begged further explanation, a sergeant "brought into use a huge pair of snippers taken from an auto thief," before charging Rabin and Robinson with disorderly conduct—but not before the bound protesters had attracted an impressive gathering and smiled for a newspaper photographer. In the meantime, some of Rabin and Robinson's coconspirators had climbed the stairway to a nearby L train station and cast antiwar leaflets upon the crowd.[50]

The *Chicago Defender* ran the photo of the smiling Rabin and Robinson and took a jab at Jim Crow. The photo caption noted, "Such a scene as is here depicted could not happen below the Mason and Dixon line. These girls have forgotten the color line and staged the demonstration because of the injustice they feel is being done the Abyssinian government by Mussolini."[51] This slight to the U.S. South, though, underplayed the consequences of such a scene north of the Mason and Dixon line, and in particular the consequences of one in Chi-

—

cago. Rabin and Robinson had, after all, chained themselves to a post because they knew that the police would try to haul them off the moment they peaceably assembled. Local grievances fueled the Chicago antifascists' solidarity with Ethiopia. As one of the protesters, Harry Haywood, later put it, "the defense of Ethiopia inevitably became a fight against the growth of fascism right in Chicago against every petty persecution, Jim Crow degradation, misery and discrimination."[52]

As Chicago's South Side became a hotbed of Ethiopian solidarity, municipal authorities became every bit the persecutorial force that Haywood made them out to be. Even before Rabin and Robinson's arresting performance, the Chicago Park Board had refused to give the local antifascists a parade permit for a march. They attempted one nonetheless on August 4, only to have their march broken up by the police, "unleashed," the *Negro Liberator* surmised, by Mayor Edward J. Kelly, "whose pro-fascist leanings have brought him a decoration by Mussolini."[53]

In such an atmosphere, Chicago's antifascists improvised informal, ephemeral demonstrations, described by Haywood in his autobiography, many years later, as "flash actions." As many as 100 people strolling the Loop would simultaneously pull out posters to hold up and leaflets to pass out. Thus would a "full-sized sidewalk parade suddenly materialize seemingly from nowhere." Haywood added that such a spectacle could perplex police long enough to impress passers-by. Then, as quickly as it had materialized, the parade would vanish, posters dropped and protesters dissolved back into the bustle of the city.[54]

As delightfully clever as the "flash actions" were, Chicago's antifascists were determined to pull off a mass march. In the Depression era, mass marches could push their way beyond local news in a way that smaller protests, no matter how theatrical or creative, rarely did. The effect of a protest that could make national or even international news was multiple that of a protest that only drew local notice. Above all else, this was because the protests that made news far from where they happened made news alongside the news of other protests elsewhere. Taken in sum, they pushed people to connect them all into a single, larger movement. Intense sensations of interconnectivity, born of mass culture, had been critical to how people had universalized their notions of fascism in the two years since the age of fascism began. Likewise, people universalized

—

their notions of antifascism as they read about, saw, and heard about antifascist politics enacted seemingly all over. This had an effect on the wider public; it also helped those who protested. The broad-audience outlets mattered; and so did the left-wing press. For example, even a devout anti-Stalinist like C. L. R. James could not deny the value of the Comintern-sponsored *Negro Worker's* transoceanic circulation. The Trotskyist praised the publication for inviting agitators in small-scale movements – "there were scores of movements all over the world" – to imagine themselves into a shared global struggle. James argued that a local movement "needs a body of ideas and information to which its own efforts can be related, ideas and information in the light of which the daily grind can have some significance beyond that which is immediately visible."[55]

The light of which James spoke, the light of ideas and information generated far away and shined by the likes of the *Negro Worker,* allowed solidarities to bloom over great distances. Already, just by working together, local antifascists had begun to work out solidarities with each other. But reading about far-off protests allowed them to stretch their imaginations – to see themselves as part of much larger collectivities. By the time of the 47th Street march, local antifascists in Chicago had shared a cause with each other for over two months; and likewise in Harlem or London or Paris or Johannesburg, locals by this point had established sincere solidarities with each other. But by learning of protests in other places, Chicago's antifascists came to share a cause not just with each other in Chicago but also with Harlem's and Johannesburg's and Paris's and London's antifascists. Likewise in reverse and any which direction. Hands Off Ethiopia protesters learned, partially and piecemeal, of each other's efforts. Even then they didn't much coordinate protest. Rather, news of distant protest provided, in ways tangible and intangible, blueprints of practice that could be adapted to local conditions. What's more, though, simply knowing of distant dissent provided sustenance of inspiration for more local agitation. By imagining their way into solidarity with the people of Ethiopia, antifascists everywhere were imagining their way into solidarity also with each other.

And so, well aware of the protests against war and fascism going on in countless other places, the antifascists of Chicago's South Side planned a grand parade for Saturday, August 31, 1935. The authorities again denied them permission to march. The organizers held a mass meeting on Friday night, Au-

—

gust 30, in Abraham Lincoln Center, the historic six-story social settlement designed in part by Frank Lloyd Wright at 700 East Oakwood Boulevard. It was at Lincoln Center that Oliver Law insisted that the march take place, regardless of what the authorities had said. The question was put to a vote and the packed-in crowd agreed with Law unanimously. Tactical and logistical planning went on past midnight. Fearful that any scripted parade of a single procession would make an easy mark for the police to disperse, organizers mapped out multiple routes and plotted small, scattered direct actions such as the rooftop speeches, effigies of Mussolini, and traffic stoppages.[56]

Early the next morning, more than 500 police officers reported to the vicinity of the 47th Street L station, a half block from the parade's meeting point. Since this was a black neighborhood, officers made the broad judgment that anyone white was likely to be a demonstrator. The police began grabbing white train passengers and pressing them into patrol wagons as soon as they emerged from the L station. The *Chicago Tribune* approvingly described officers "swinging clubs to prevent formation of the parade. Heads were thumped freely and the demonstrators screamed curses at the bluecoats."[57]

Those who made it to the street formed a crowd all the same. Heads popped up from the multitude and individuals shouted out quick denunciations of fascism. The police pounced. That was the cue for the rooftop orators. Law went first. He hollered until the police hauled him away. As they did, someone started up from a roof across the street. The high-ground orators each went on for as long as fifteen minutes. Considering how long it took for the police to capture them, either they had taken care to choose particularly unapproachable perches or else the police lacked even basic knowledge of how to assert themselves upwards in the neighborhood, a working-class quarter with labyrinthine buildings, fortified by padlocked doors and metal gates. Regardless, the same detachment of officers that swept the streets below with what one observer described as "unexcelled police ferocity" appeared incompetent once it had to extend its campaign up even a couple of stories.[58]

The roofs offered other advantages. They made a stage within everyone's sight. As forceful as any message that the rooftop orators spoke, their physical liberty above the police clubs and wagons seemed to inspire the crowds the most. Whenever a new orator began, the crowds let out a joyful cheer;

—

and whenever officers finally made their way to the roof, they heckled and booed; then the next orator appeared, and the crowds could cheer again. The collective performance made tremendous political theater, greatly satisfying to the audience thanks to the organizers' cunning and the police officers' clumsiness. In Harry Haywood's turn, atop a hotel on the southwest corner of 47th Street and South Parkway, he condemned Mayor Kelly and the police "for importing Mussolini's tactics" to Chicago. And then an officer clubbed him from behind.[59]

Bloodied prisoners filled the Wabash Station's cells. In the men's block, prisoners shouted out a collective demand that the police take the severely wounded to the hospital. The scene in the women's block was even unrulier. Police had arrested at least seventy-nine women, white and black, including University of Chicago students who refused even to give their names. The *Tribune* reporter observed at the Wabash Station that the police there were "unable to maintain order among the women prisoners" and threatened to spray them with a fire hose unless they stopped singing. "The defense of Ethiopia," Haywood wrote later, reflecting on the day's events, "had now become a fight for the streets of Chicago."[60]

At the year's end, it was acknowledged in the newspaper of Emile Faure's LDRN, the *Race Nègre,* that as late as August, "the black people of Paris still had done nothing" in support of Ethiopia. Then, "in a few days everything changed." Back-to-back demonstrations provided the spark, after which: "Demonstrations in the street, meetings, protests . . . all this has been done in time to assure the black people of Paris's place at the head of the pro-Ethiopian movement." The LDRN congratulated "our adversary" the UTN for bringing together all the black radicals of Paris and "our other former adversary" Kouyaté for realizing an "entente" between black and Arab radicals. Police broke up the first demonstration, on August 21, but the one on the following day went off majestically. Protesters representing the range of the African diaspora held a mass meeting that sprawled along the Boulevard de l'Hôpital in Paris's 13th Arrondissement, a "gargantuan meeting," as the Algerian anticolonialist Messali Hadj remembered it. Paulette Nardal, from Martinique; Faure, from Senegal;

and Ludovic Lacombe, from Haiti, all spoke, as did Kouyaté. Messali affirmed the sympathy of (as police surveillance paraphrased his words) "all the Muslims in the movement for the Ethiopians. He calls for the union of all the workers and all the oppressed, regardless of party, race, or color, to mount a fierce struggle against Italian fascism." Messali's political imagination captured much of the antifascism made by Hands Off Ethiopia. It was an antifascism enlarged and reshaped from what it had been before; it was tightly entwined now with anticolonialism and a wider, world-spanning liberatory project. The following year Messali would declare in his hometown of Tlemcen, "We are antifascists, for peace, liberty, and democracy," adding, "we are also anticolonialists, and we are for democratic liberties as part of a total emancipation."[61]

A flurry of heterogeneous protests hit Paris in the final days of August and into September. The grandest of the events took place September 3 in the Maison de la Mutualité, gathering delegates of 150 organizations "of all tendencies and races." What a contrast it was to that first public meeting, on February 28, at the Mutualité that had so disappointed its UTN organizers. Attendees agreed that the September 3 conference was a triumph. Further vindication followed on September 16, when the UTN hosted another meeting, at the same spot above the tracks behind the Gare de l'Est as where, back on January 7, Pierre Kodo-Kossoul had been told that the French Communist Party had condemned his idea of working with Faure and the LDRN. And now among the organizations taking part in the September 16 meeting was, yes, the Ligue de Défense de la Race Nègre.[62] After eight months of hard work all around, Kossoul had his way.

Not entirely, of course. There was, after all, a war. On October 2, 1935, Mussolini made his call to arms from the balcony above the Piazza Venezia in Rome. Dressed in a black shirt, a shoulder belt, black pants, and black boots, he addressed the "Blackshirts of the Revolution" and "Italians scattered around the world." He described the present moment—"year XIII of the Fascist Era"—as the height of human history, a vantage onto the greatest spectacle ever beheld. Such was the enthusiasm of the crowd assembled in the piazza below that Mussolini returned to the balcony seven times to offer a succession of fascist salutes.[63] Italian forces crossed the Mareb River into Ethiopian territory at five o'clock the next morning.

Thought of as an antiwar movement, Hands Off Ethiopia, on the face of it, failed. But the movement had shifted global politics, pulling it a bit more into the streets, away from the great powers, and away from the central commands of institutional radical politics as well. Much of the world was to pay attention to the war when it began. In the narrated words of a *March of Time* newsreel shown on cinema screens just before the war, "As the Ethiopian war seems more and more certain, into Addis Ababa flock newspapermen from all over the world." The question of the war permeated everyday life in countless of the world's biggest cities. The Tokyo newspaper the *Yomiuri shinbun* reported a local blacksmith's "astonishment" at how slow business had become "because of the news from overseas in the morning and evening papers, as well as the radio broadcasts — everyone's mind was on that faraway African country, Ethiopia." Protest not only had helped to bring attention to Ethiopia's cause, it also undoubtedly shaped the news coverage. As protest had spread, press about the conflict had drifted from performative even-handedness toward open condemnation of the fascist regime's imperialistic aims. That contributed, in a small but discernible way, to a broad rethinking of empire and imperialism. Typical was the shift in coverage in *al-Muqattam* of Cairo, which early on had frequently expressed hopes that the two sides could set aside their differences and compromise; over the summer, the Cairene paper had turned to placing all blame on Italy, which had betrayed "the conscience of the entire world."[64] Hands Off Ethiopia, with its widespread and relentless battering of Italian fascism, was part of the reason for all these shifts. And by the end of 1935, fascist Italy's invasion of Ethiopia had come to signify how fascism had become a world menace, an existential danger threatening not only those who lived in countries under fascist regimes but all humanity.

Antifascism itself also looked larger than before, a world cause. In a poem that Langston Hughes had just written, he exhorted, "So get together, women! Get together men!" He had put the poem out in late September, less than a week before the war. "Let us tell the world," he said in the poem, "Fascism must end." A week later, after the crossing of the Mareb, antifascists reacted to the news with fierce outrage. Before dawn even broke in Rio de Janeiro, someone stoned the local Italian consulate and splashed its doors with paint. In the afternoon, several hundred students at the City College of New York rallied in Lewisohn Stadium, across the street from where some of the same students had burned the two-headed effigy less than eleven months before; they passed resolutions swearing to help defend Ethiopia from fascism. The next day, a crowd of about 100 women, students at Hunter College, picketed in front of the Italian consulate on New York's Upper East Side, chanting, "Down with Italian fascism!" until police intervened. A mass meeting followed the day after that in Buenos Aires, drawing 20,000 to the Plaza Italia—the same square where violence between fascists and antifascists had led to the death of Jacinto Lacebrón Guzmán. In Panama City, more than 5,000 people organized themselves into what they called the Hands Off Ethiopia Committee of Panama City; among the committee's express aims was to sabotage ships carrying war materiel for Italian forces. On Sunday, October 6, an interracial crowd of more than 1,000 people in Cape Town marched through the city's central public square, the Grand Parade, for a mass meeting put on by the local "Hands Off Abyssinia" Committee. That committee was part of the local League Against Fascism and War, which in turn answered to the Comintern-run World Committee Against War and Fascism, established in late 1933 by Willi Münzenberg—a decade after he'd joined Clara Zetkin's antifascist committee—and headed by Henri Barbusse—Zetkin's onetime cochair. A week later, a crowd just as large turned out again in the Grand Parade, and an effigy of Mussolini, as one correspondent reported, "was publicly strangled, torn to pieces and burnt."[65] It was by this point almost a year since the City College students in New York had burnt their two-headed effigy. The months in between had seen much done to make antifascism such a widely shared political cause.

The title of Hughes's poem, published first in a black newspaper, was "Ballad of Ethiopia." And in it he encouraged the people of Ethiopia to fight, somewhat like how Ibárruri would encourage the people of Spain to fight ten months later. But Hughes didn't just encourage Ethiopians to fight. He went on, calling on "all you colored peoples" to "say to Mussolini, No! You shall not pass!" It was ten months before Ibárruri's radio address, and a little less than

—

twenty months since the Twelfth of February; Hughes was making his own cry of "fascism shall not pass." Then, having called on Ethiopians and all people of color, Hughes built on his message and imagined a future of peace and liberty for all, fought for and won by people of all kinds: "the peace we want," he said, "is for all mankind" — "And," he added, "the peace we want means every man is free. Listen Mussolini, don't you mess with me!"[66]

CHAPTER 5

THE SOCIAL EXPLOSION

Not everything is possible.

—Maurice Thorez, 1936

"History stopped in 1936," George Orwell once said, reflecting on how, by that year's end, he had wound up in Spain. There are years when this can be felt to happen. History stops, human life rearranges, and then when it all starts up again, it sets out on some trajectory unlike before. Old regimes collapse; normal politics suspend; the world is turned upside down and disorder dances about; power runs in the street and so does possibility; assumptions and arrangements come undone; sentiments of dissent, some of them only whispered before, resound in the public square; solidarity abounds. They are fugitive moments, and judged against the hopeful rhetoric that accompanies them it is fair to say that they are failures all. Yet the effect they have on the shape of politics in their wake is so great that it's hard to imagine understanding the political world of today without somehow attending to those years when history has seemed to come to a stop.[1]

There have only been a handful of them in the modern world. The political theorist Aristide Zolberg was living in the aftermath of one — 1968 — when he called them moments of madness. He depicted them as strange and always unforeseen outbursts of mass transcendence, prophecy, and pentecost. They are the days that have shaken the world, and it is common enough for people to turn to the idea of revolution to interpret them and divine their consequences.

—

Conversely, it is common enough for people to ground their notions of revolution as a general concept in the specifics of these few historic intervals—to draw on them so as to piece together an idea of what makes a revolution. And it's true, without these moments of madness in our heads our conceptions of revolution would be somewhat slight. It's fair to think of 1789 as the first of them, in no small part because of those tense debates in the French National Constituent Assembly after the storming of the Bastille—those debates that led the chamber's champions of liberty, rights, and equality to band together on the assembly hall's left side, leaving their reactionary adversaries to huddle together on the right. Since 1789, the spells of extraordinary upheaval worthy of the name "moment of madness" surely include 1848; 1917–1920; 1945 and the year or two that followed; 1968 itself; 1989 (or even what might be thought of as a "long 1989" running from the Polish Solidarność strikes of 1988 through the South African Freedom Day of 1994); and 2011.[2] Then there's also, I'm suggesting (as did Zolberg), 1936.[3] Like these other periods of uprising, the year 1936 broke down the old; like the others, it stirred up visions of social revolutionary promise; and, like the others, it reoriented political life on a vast scale.

Part of what stands out about the great political events of 1936, or those of any of these modern moments of madness, is their unruliness. People outside of the usual channels of power and positions of authority assert themselves directly, without mediation. They step out of place. Politics becomes intensely participatory. Those who join in the commotion rely on a handbag of practices drawn from the world of popular politics to do so; they also rely on creativity and imagination. The politics of these moments thrive on their capacity to surprise, on their originality. It follows that a good many of those caught up in the excitement describe their experiences as a sustained high of sensations, full of intoxicating perceptions of agency and autonomy.[4]

The politics of these moments are also emphatically interconnected, even over long geographical and cultural distances. They have an electrical quality to them. In mysterious ways, the actions of people in one place suddenly have new power to inspire people in other places far away. "Speaking with tongues," Zolberg suggested, people in these moments sense affinities across great expanses and linguistic divides. The consequence is that politics becomes much more transnational in character, full of rapid-fire back and forth. And it surely relates that these are times, too, when political abstractions leap into the open, are spun into universals, and swiftly go on to sway minds and movements the world over.[5]

Antifascism, as it had come to be by 1936, fit the moment well. But antifascism did not create 1936 alone. Neither did anything called the left. It would be closer to the truth to say that the tumult of 1936 threw into form much of what antifascism has meant since, much of what the left has been since. But, like saying the Twelfth of February in 1934 made the left, this oversimplifies. It's better to think of 1936 as a hinge. It was a point that swung political thought, language, gesture, worldview, structure, and the like toward what we have now. And even if antifascism doesn't explain the moment entirely, it still surely belongs at the pivot of any explanation for the year's upheavals. Since Hitler's ascent to power three years earlier, violent, intensely nationalistic, and exclusionary political movements in countries around the world had multiplied and worked toward each other. Against them, people of many sorts and in many places had joined together to work out the new form of antifascist politics. And as they had gone about turning themselves into antifascists, they had transnationalized antifascism; they had remade it into less of an Italian particularism and into more of a political universal. More than that, in their hands, by 1936, antifascism had become one of the most potent universals in all of politics, the ism capable of facing off against fascism – itself so novel, and yet already dominating the age. In countless places, antifascists had confronted those who were – they, the antifascists, warned – turning the world toward fascism. Along the way, all the while fighting the fascists, the antifascists also had organized for political power of their own, in part to fend off the fearful advance of fascism and in part to put forth an alternative vision of human possibility.

Such a vision had especial value at the time because in those first years of the age of fascism many had begun to think that the world was passing inexorably into a fascist future. In 1936 antifascists finally found their footing and countered. They didn't slay fascism; they didn't even score many clear victories. But in waging the fight and holding their own they attested that another future

—

was possible. Fascism was not inevitable. A great contingency still governed human life.

And so in 1936 the antifascist moment hit its peak. At the same time, and in no small part because of antifascism's ascent, the left now underwent its great transformation. This was when people finally began in earnest to reimagine the left into a sum of boundless multitudes, a mass collectivity. This was when people finally began in earnest to reimagine the left into a singular force that reached around all the world, a global collectivity. Which is to say, this was when the left became what I've been insisting so stubbornly that it hadn't been in the years and decades before. Another way to put it is that this was when the left took its decisive leap toward becoming what it is today. To be sure, it was still common in 1936 to speak of the left in the older ways: to speak of specific national lefts made of parliamentary politicians and their parties; to speak of little factional lefts within particular political organizations. That was so then just as it is still today. But the new sort of left talk had the odd effect of making these older notions of the left into subsets of the new. Such a sweeping change in the meaning of a familiar political concept couldn't have come about because of any one particular episode, and no one particular person or group could be said to have made it happen. Yet, all the same, the new conception of the left rattled its way through political discourse in no time at all.

It was part of a larger reimagining of politics. Already, fascism and antifascism had grown into universals. Now, amid the political disorder of 1936, both the left and the right did as well. Long gone were the days when they were only countable, face-to-face collectivities. Now the left and the right of even just any one country were dense political bodies incorporating the multitudes. From their origins inside the bounds of formal politics, left and right now burst out into the social realm of mass politics and popular participation. It happened quickly. By September 1936 a dismayed political observer could already make the point explicit, gesturing in frustration to those "two extremisms in the social sphere—the 'Right' and the 'Left.'" How novel to place the right and left in "the social sphere," let alone to do so as if it were a familiar matter of fact. Even more striking than how the left and right now reached into the social sphere of any one country, though, was how the pair now wrapped

—

themselves around the world. The same observer now spoke easily of a global-ized left – "the 'Left' in human society" – and just as easily invoked "the 'Right'" to explain the border-leaping transnational aid given to the coup effort in Spain by people who were themselves far away from Spain.[6] These were a larger left and right than what people had had in their heads before.

The Spanish Civil War wasn't the source of all the new talk of left and right in 1936, but it had the greatest effect. The newspaper intellectual Anne O'Hare McCormick wrote in August, a month into the war, that "the Spanish conflict involves the world" because, for one reason, "every European and nearly every American takes sides, Left or Right."[7] In McCormick's mind, all those Europe-ans and Americans hadn't just sided with a left or a right that was Spanish. By taking sides, they had worked themselves into a left larger than any one nation's left, or else a right larger than any one nation's right. Those who were far away from Spain and yet took sides were the ones who transnationalized the ideas of left and right, just as fascists and antifascists and others far from Italy had been the ones who had transnationalized the ideas of fascism and antifascism. What's more, McCormick made clear that her notions of left and right were no longer restricted to politicians or to the customary political classes; the left and the right, as she now saw them, had popular social bases: it was, after all, "every" European and "nearly every" American that had, to some extent, made the civil war their own.

In such ways the political world was rearranged in 1936. Extraordinary events shook up the world and people reworked their words to make sense of the tumult. McCormick was quicker than most to work through the implica-tions of the new idiom of left and right. A seasoned and well-traveled foreign correspondent for the *New York Times,* she was an absorptive and engaged political thinker. Like a young Mussolini, she had a good ear for inventive lan-guage and any subtle twists of meaning in familiar words. She paid close at-tention to the riot of political speech that went on throughout the year. In the same August essay in which she argued that the Spanish Civil War had become rather all the world's civil war, she suggested as well that people everywhere were now "all using the same words and meaning something different." She was fascinated and unsettled by the new turns in political discourse. And like many others of her generation, she was fascinated and unsettled by the broader

—

ideological unrest. Liberalism, laid low by the Great War and then hammered by the Great Depression, still largely lay in ruins.[8] Conservatism was lifeless. Communism, which had once seemed ready to overturn the world order, had become hollow: "instead of propagating its own doctrine," she argued, communism now "has simply become a synonym for anti-fascism." Fascism itself had not turned out how she had thought it would. She had been an early admirer of Mussolini and the blackshirts in Italy in the time before the March on Rome. She had even been in the Camera, up in the balcony, in 1921 when Mussolini gave his first parliamentary speech, when he said that he was not at all displeased to speak from the benches on the right. Back then, she had considered it "one of the best political speeches I have ever heard, a little swaggering but caustic, powerful and telling." She had written at the time, "I admire the Fascisti. Their illimitable energy is the miracle of a weary world."[9]

Now a decade and a half later, McCormick saw fascism as the primary cause of an all-consuming crisis. "No one alive today," she wrote, "can escape the perception that he is living through one of the great crises of history." It was, in a way, she suggested, "the eternal conflict," but now events such as those in Spain intensified "this conflict between Right and Left" and tipped the world into an exceptional state of cataclysm.[10] The masses now rushed onto a wide ideological battlefield and took part in a political war touching almost every society.

McCormick wrote with verve, but her central point—summed up in the title of her essay, "Right *vs.* Left: A Great Struggle"—came across most vividly in the photo images and captions that ran alongside her text. To signify the left, the *Times* displayed a photo of a great crowd in France. (Seen from just above, the crowd appeared as an ocean of men's and women's working-class caps and hats, its surface punctured by countless fists punched into the air above to form antifascist salutes.) To signify the right, this was counterposed by a photo of an equally great crowd gathered in the Piazza Venezia in Rome. "The Right shows its strength in Italy," explained the caption (fig. 5).[11] In such prosaic ways the left and right took on new proportions on the newspaper page, as well as in people's political imaginations. Just as when Alexander Werth was to look back on the tumult of February 1934 from the perspective of 1937 and see the swarm in the streets as the left itself, here too the photographed crowd of people, fists up, *was* the left; the crowd under Mussolini's balcony *was* the

Figure 5. "The Right shows its strength in Italy—A demonstration in the Piazza Venezia, Rome." This photograph ran in the *New York Times* with that caption in 1936, alongside Anne O'Hare McCormick's essay "Right *vs*. Left: A Great Struggle." *Smith Archive/Alamy*.

right. What's more, the photo caption's explanation of the scene in the Piazza Venezia hadn't made the crowd there into the Italian right alone: the crowd had gathered there on behalf of a larger right—it was showing its strength, the caption read, in this instance in Italy, but the right invoked here had a wider reach than just Italy. It was the right now in its universal form. In 1936, the right could show itself anywhere, and so could the left.

The drama of the moment amounted, McCormick suggested, to a historic break.[12] Pointing to revolutionary periods from long ago—"landmarks" that "loom out of the past"—she explained that they were "revolutionary because they were climacteric": great change had come and "at last invaded the lives and minds of ordinary men." She added, "Certainly this is such a period." And it was the greatest revolution of all. "The upheavals of yesterday were limited and

—

small-scale affairs" whereas: "This is universal." She described her present as "the electric revolution, made by speed of communication – the news flash, the headline, the radio, the cinema, the tremendous organization of propaganda." All this meant that, unlike the revolutions of the past, "for the first time the thing is not only panoramic, but it is seen in panorama: people are conscious of their participation in the action and immediately aware of what goes on elsewhere."[13]

Newly self-aware, the world was wrapped together more tightly than it had been before. And it was no longer so weary as it had been when Mussolini spoke from a bench on the Camera dei Deputati's right side. The political world that McCormick now depicted, still as dangerous as ever, suddenly felt quite new.

"A pure joy," Simone Weil explained. "An unfiltered joy." She meant the strike that she had just witnessed inside the Renault factory just outside of Paris, the strike that had left her inspired and puzzled and that had made her wonder if perhaps she was witnessing a revolution. It took place very much in the thick of the madness of 1936. The Renault workers had struck on Thursday, May 28, a day when sitdown strikes began to sweep Paris and its surroundings. It was, the socialist Daniel Mayer suggested at the time, "the decisive day." The most eye-catching of the day's strikes took place in the big automobile and airplane factories along the perimeter of Paris. Along with the more than 30,000 workers at Renault, 22,000 struck at Citroën. So did thousands more at the factories of Fiat, Licorne, Gnôme et Rhône, and Farman. Strikes at the factories of Nieuport, Hotchkiss, and Lavalette-Bosch had begun a couple of days before.[14] In each case the workers seized their factory.

That act – the workers' seizure of property not their own, their insistence on occupying the place and claiming it as their own domain – ensured that contemporaries, both the sympathetic and the horrified, saw the sitdown strikes as bursting with revolutionary implications. Allusions were made to the factory occupations of September 1920 in Turin and Milan.[15] Those had ended in failure. It was said that their failure had meant the end of the socialist revolutionary movement that had flourished in Italy since the end of the Great War. It was said as well that those factory occupations had provoked the fascist terror that followed.[16] Their failure could also be said to have ended the transnational moment of madness that had begun with the February Revolution of 1917. The Italian factory occupations, though, had not been strikes; they had been attempts at continued mass production under workers' control. By contrast, the factory occupations sweeping through Paris and its surroundings at May's end 1936 meant a moment's rest from hard machine work. An atmosphere of holiday and carnival overtook the strikes — hence the joy that Weil wanted to convey.

The joy, though, didn't make the strikes frivolous. The factory workers had acted with serious, and well-calculated, political purpose. The left had just won at the polls. Ahead of the recent elections in France, the Socialist and Communist parties had allied with each other and with the (unreliably) left-of-center Radical Party. In the past, the Radicals and Socialists had made unhappy coalitions — "the Cartel of Leftists," each iteration had been called. The new effort was different. And not only because it included the Communists. Its proponents called it the "Popular Front," and unlike in the Cartel of Leftists the emphasis apparent even in the new name was on fusing the parties together into a common collectivity: unlike a cartel, the Popular Front was to possess what its early enthusiasts called "an organic unity."[17] There was a subtler shift as well, also apparent in the new name: whereas the Cartel of Leftists had been understood as a partnership of the parties, the idea of the Popular Front relied on imagining a much denser and more immense union, one that included also the masses of people who backed the parties. This was what put the "popular" in the Popular Front, its sweeping inclusion of the people. A more participatory vision of the left's politics was coming together.

And not only in France. The various parties of the left in Spain had also agreed to form a popular front, in no small part inspired by the early efforts to build the one in France. The parties of the Spanish left had agreed to join together in a campaign of antifascist unity in the months leading up to their historic victory in the elections of February 16, 1936.[18] These were the elections for which the CNT's anarchist and anarcho-syndicalist revolutionaries had finally given up their long-standing antipolitical stance and voted, for the Popular Front; in doing so, they had joined — and helped to remake — the

———

Spanish left. Though of course no one knew it at the time, these were also the last elections before the coup in July, which would end up making them the last free elections held in Spain for four decades to come.

In the moment, though, the Spanish Popular Front's victory looked like a much more promising sign of the future. Less than a week afterward, half a world away, at a local assembly put on by the Chilean Radical Party in Santiago, a parliamentary deputy named Justiniano Sotomayor called on the people of Chile to make a popular front of their own. For several months, talk of a Chilean popular front had bounced around in the country's political discourse to little effect. But Sotomayor made his plea at just the right moment, and his position in the Radical Party – the Chilean congress's swing vote – made him well placed to persuade. The party had stayed away from a 1934 attempt at left-of-center parliamentary unity called "the Block of Leftists" ("el Block de Izquierdas"). The party had also often enough pivoted to the right, so much so that it had become known by 1936 as, in the words of one close observer, the party "of complete vacillation." Sotomayor himself, however, had become known by 1936 as a firebrand of the party's rising left wing.[19] Those who gathered for the Radical Assembly of Santiago on February 21, 1936, responded to his plea for a popular front with delight. They drafted a declaration on the spot imploring the party's leadership "to lose no time in initiating the creation of the Popular Front." This was to be done by inviting the parties from the Block of Leftists and also the Communist Party of Chile, which, for reasons quite different from the Radicals', had not taken part in the Block of Leftists either. The Popular Front in Chile was to be made by combining all parties of the left – all parties opposed to fascism, reaction, and imperialism. Even beyond that, though, it was to be made by incorporating the people themselves, "without any distinction of ideologies." In this way, the Popular Front in Chile could, as in France and Spain, become far more than a parliamentary coalition: it could become, in the hopeful words of the assembly, "a vast movement of all the people." The Radicals who had assembled in Santiago also looked beyond France and Spain for inspiration. In their declaration they pointed as well to countries such as Cuba, Argentina, Colombia, and Ecuador, all countries where "the idea of the Popular Front is winning over the spirit of the crowd."[20]

The idea had caught on quickly. Where had it come from, though?

—

It's a crucial question, because having an answer for it goes a long way toward having an answer for the larger question of where the social revolutionary possibilities of 1936 had come from. In France and Spain and Chile, and in Cuba, Argentina, Colombia, and Ecuador—and in a good many other countries such as the United States, South Africa, Syria, and Indochina—the idea of the Popular Front played an important part in stirring up the social upheavals of 1936.

So where had the idea come from? The older historiographical answer, shaped by the Cold War, had it that the Comintern came up with the idea of the Popular Front in the mid-1930s as a strategic cover for Soviet foreign policy.[21] That claim still shades how historians discuss Popular Front politics.[22] And yet it never quite made sense. It relied on stripping away the agency of the majority of those involved in making the Popular Front: for instance, those who weren't attached to the Comintern at all, those such as Sotomayor and the others who took part in the Radical Assembly of Santiago. The claim also stood at odds, as a few particularly careful historians began pointing out long ago, with plain evidence to the contrary.[23]

Begin with the matter of origins. The original idea didn't come from any Moscow directive in the mid-1930s; it had come about in 1928, with what one historian calls "the improbable coalition of Catholics, Communists, autonomists, and Progressives" in the French-German borderland of Alsace. That coalition, determined to win regional autonomy for the Alsatian people, was the first to take the name "the Popular Front" ("die Volksfront" in German, "le front populaire" in French). The coalition legitimated its demand for an autonomous Alsace with the claim that the coalition was the political embodiment of the people of Alsace—and that the people were the source of sovereignty. In this way, the coalition's politics was an emphatic populism: concerned with imagining a version of "the people" into being and then with pursuing the supposed aims and interests of that imagined collectivity. Regarding the Communists who took part: they weren't acting on any orders from above, either from their party leadership or from the Comintern hierarchy; rather, they were outright renegades from the French Communist Party, and the Popular Front they helped to make was, according to those who kept to the party line, nothing but a despicable "deception."[24]

—

In that original conception, though, the Popular Front had had nothing to do with antifascism. It was only in the fall of 1934 that the two became entwined. That was when the secretary general of the French Communist Party, the ever-surprising and self-contradictory Maurice Thorez, took the populistic language of the Popular Front in Alsace and refashioned it to fit antifascism. Shaken by the Sixth of February (and stung at having been pushed into encouraging Communists to take part), startled by the success of the Twelfth (he himself, unlike Léon Blum of the Socialists, had stayed far away from the crowds marching on the Place de la Nation), Thorez now had it in mind to preside over the unification of the Communist, Socialist, and Radical parties of France in a great redemptive antifascist alliance. In an October 10, 1934, speech he called this the "Popular Front Against Fascism."[25]

Right away, this unsettled the Comintern officials tasked with minding him. The only popular front they knew was the renegade cabal in Alsace. They also suspected that Thorez's idea would whittle away at what remained of the Communist International's reputation as the vanguard of world revolution. It would mean collaborating with those with whom the French Communists had real differences – and whom they had long been calling social fascists. But Thorez insisted in that October 10 speech that his idea was worth the trouble because the Popular Front Against Fascism would allow him and his comrades "to keep the oath we took over the tombs of our fallen from the Ninth of February: '*Fascism shall not pass in France.*'"[26]

When his handlers in the Comintern told him he'd taken a "wrong step," Thorez kept his footing. When they warned him, in person on October 24, to walk back the Popular Front idea, he told them it was too late. He had, he explained, already written the speech he was to give that very evening outlining the form of the Popular Front Against Fascism, complete with the French Communist Party's offer to ally with both the Socialist and the Radical parties. Thorez meant his mind was made up. And so by the end of October 1934 the Popular Front Against Fascism was underway, in spite of outright opposition from Moscow.[27]

What the Popular Front became, though, went well beyond what Thorez had pictured in his head in the fall of 1934. He hadn't meant to set loose into the political world yet another universal abstraction running riot; he had meant

—

to explain his rationale for a specific electoral coalition in France. Nonetheless, somehow, during 1936 "Popular Front" became a watchword of global politics. "Down with fascism! Long live the Popular Front!" went one cheer heard in the streets of Beirut in July. Around the same time, in Tokyo, the creation of the Japanese Popular Front was announced by the antifascist labor radical Kanju Kato (newly elected to the House of Representatives in the country's tumultuous February elections and "rated," as one observer put it at the time, "as much a Leftist as is permitted by law to proletarians in Japan"). After the Spanish Civil War began, a perceptive observer of global politics wrote from Algeria that "national rivalries" had begun to matter less and that the world had become divided instead into "two antagonistic clans, each brought about by opposing ideals: fascism and the Popular Front." In "the war to come," the warring forces wouldn't be nations pitted against nations but rather would be partisans drawn from those two ideological blocs, fascism and the Popular Front; because the ranks of each side would be "recruited a bit from all over," the conflict would take the form of a sprawling civil war splitting every nation. As Franklin D. Roosevelt ran for reelection in the United States, his enemies in the right-wing press warned the electorate that he had radicalized in office and had now joined forces with "socialists and communists" and "radicals of all sorts in a 'popular front' against capitalism." And an anticolonialist's open letter printed in Saigon in November began, "The words 'Popular Front' are very important here."[28] In 1936, the Popular Front was ubiquitous.

That ubiquity was far enough from what Thorez had envisioned. But further yet, and far more of a problem for him, was how his idea of the Popular Front ended up undercutting the authority of the French Communist Party and the Comintern in France. He hadn't meant for it to do this. His problem, though, stemmed from something fundamental about his idea, something that had been there in the idea of the Popular Front even in its original Alsatian form: the power that it seemed to invest, quite expressly, in that most grandiose of invented collectivities, the people. By 1936 it had become clear that the idea of the Popular Front, at least as it had been worked out in practice, hadn't just included the people in the left's politics, it had posed them as the left's sovereign figure. The people's new sovereign sway was clear enough in the rhetoric surrounding the Popular Front; it was right there in the name itself. It was even

—

common during the antifascist moment for the Popular Front's name to be rendered outright in English as "the People's Front," making the point all the plainer that the front belonged to the people.[29]

A certain sort of power had changed hands. In the years before, it had been the vanguard party in its various guises that had wielded sovereignty over most of the world's radical and revolutionary politics. Even the notion of the United Front—which promised the unity of the proletariat much like the notion of the Popular Front promised the unity of all the people—hadn't crowned the proletariat as its sovereign. In the United Front the working class's role was largely to bring to bear its great heft wherever and however the vanguard party directed.[30] There was no claim in its name that the working class should lead the United Front. The party was to lead the way. Now, though, vanguardism fell away and populism took hold.[31] The left was something new and larger than before, and the people were to rule it. The idea stuck, and for better or for worse the claims and beliefs of the left since then have generally centered on a kind of populism more than on any class politics or any sort of vanguardism: since the Popular Front, visions of the people have animated the left. Even in the moment, when partisans of the Popular Front talked about popular sovereignty and democracy as general principles worth fighting for in the larger world, they relied on the people's mandate to rule within the Popular Front to make their case. To be sure, the parties and other organizations involved in Popular Front politics—such as, yes, the Comintern—never accepted the people's right to rule the left. Once the Comintern signed on to the idea of the Popular Front, the organization's propagandists spared no time in explaining that its parties were the proper vessels of the people's authority. Thorez himself would attempt to wrest back the power he'd handed away half unawares. But the people's claim to direct rule was there all the same, so solid and explicit in the rhetoric of the Popular Front that the idea wouldn't be unstuck. Such emphatic populism, of course, wasn't new to antifascist politics: as far back as the Arditi del Popolo—"the people's daring ones"—antifascists had reveled in the notion that they embodied the people.

It wasn't just rhetoric that shored up the people's sovereignty over the Popular Front. To even greater effect than the name or any of the related talk of the Popular Front, it was the show of the Popular Front's immense crowds—full

—

of charisma and creativity, full of joy — that made the case that in the Popular Front the people wielded sovereignty.[32] And so the assembly of a crowd, that simple act of informal association, became like a constitutional myth for the Popular Front. By the spring of 1936, when the French parties of the left won at the polls, there was no doubt that the reigning image of the Popular Front had become that of raucous crowds filling the streets. What's more, thanks to syndicated newspaper photography and newsreel cinema, the image of crowds in, say, Paris was reproduced in cities and towns around the world.[33] This was McCormick's "electric revolution." Visible worldwide now were the iconic scenes of bodies filling the public square, fists thrown up to signify antifascism, militancy, and leftist unity all at once. The scenes changed how people imagined the left. Those crowds in Paris now found themselves described in the international press as comprised of "Leftists, including men, women and babies."[34] Such an expansive view of the left was a revelation in an age of heavily restricted participation in formal politics; in 1936, after all, France still denied women the right to vote. How significant it was, then, to crown the open, inclusive crowd as the Popular Front's ruling figure.[35]

That figure had begun to show itself in Paris even before 1936 got underway. Right away, it became involved in the changes in the meaning of the left. Consider the public discourse that took form around Bastille Day 1935. It was the day on which the parties of the Popular Front launched their grand coalition ahead of the elections of 1936. On the eve of the holiday, Henri Barbusse promised that the date July 14 would thenceforth be known not only for the storming of the Bastille "but also as the sovereign day of the Popular Front." The main demonstration unfolded at the Place de la Bastille. The day's events — the crowds gathering and parading in the streets, people singing, carrying banners affirming that "fascism shall not pass," their fists in the air — all worked to show how public spectacle could remake the basic meanings of the political words people carry around in their heads. The meanings of antifascism, the left, and the Popular Front were all already shifting rapidly, and their meanings were all already tightly intertwined. Still, though, the political talk that surrounded the day — the various attempts of participants and observers to describe the scene and make sense of it in all its manifold grandeur — threw a bright new clarifying light on the changes. As recently as the Twelfth of

—

February, the previous year, a parade staged by Socialists, Communists, and the like to protest fascism could unfold in Paris without any talk of it as something that was "antifascist" or a show of "the left." Now, by Bastille Day 1935, it made perfect sense to even uninvolved observers to describe the demonstration at the Place de la Bastille as an "uncompromisingly anti-Fascist" mass mobilization and to describe the thousands assembled there as the city's "Leftists." Likewise, it made perfect sense to suggest that the crowd of leftists – the crowd itself – was the Popular Front, even "the Leftist 'Popular Front.'"[36] The many thousands who made up crowds such as this one and who practiced popular politics in public had laid claim to the name antifascist. They had laid claim to the name the left. And they had laid claim to the name the Popular Front. Each claim worked to reinforce the others.

A parallel change had taken place on the right. On the same day, across the city, uniformed members of the paramilitary groups that had taken part in the Sixth of February gathered, along with many others who had similar sympathies, for a demonstration of their own; gathered thus, they themselves now were the right. Whereas on the Sixth of February the right had been the reactionary politicians in parliament, and not the riotous crowds outside, now "thousands of Right Wing nationalists" could assemble under the Arc de Triomphe and embody the right all along the Champs-Élysées.[37] In the enactment of such events – out in the streets, boisterous and unpredictable, every step participatory and freewheeling – the nature of the political world came unsettled. Where politics happens, how it unfolds, who performs it – all these elements of political life were knocked loose from their old bearings and tossed about until they settled anew, recomposed askew from before in people's heads. The power of spectacular public events to alter how people conceive of the most basic political concepts – to alter how they piece together the most fundamental abstractions of their political world – is one of the most meaningful political powers that common people have at hand.[38] Such alterations were being worked out in 1934 and 1935; in 1936 they took hold.

It helped that by 1936 the antifascists of Paris had worked out their visual language in ways that they had not in 1934. The crowds of the Twelfth of February hadn't thought to identify themselves as antifascists, and neither had they thought to clench their fists as some sort of political expression; now, though, the antifascists of Paris made their way through the city's streets with their fists relentlessly up, like those of the crowds that had made their way through the Bülowplatz in Berlin in the winter of 1933. And when the leftists in the crowds raised their fists, what they were forming in the air was now, finally, explicitly and clearly, "the antifascist salute." Such a basic piece of antifascist choreography, and yet as recently as 1934 there had been no notion of such a thing. At Bülowplatz, the raised fist had been a sign of solidarity and defiance, yes, but no one at the time had described the gesture as an "antifascist salute." When Walter Faulkner had clenched his fist at the blackshirt meeting in Brighton in March 1934, it had only led to questions about "the sign of the Communist party." Since then, though, the crowds in the streets of Paris had worked out the idea. What's more, because of all those newspapers and newsreels, now the idea, and the name, would be picked up by others far away in quick succession. By the end of 1936, the antifascist salute would seem a universal practice, as if it were an expression spoken in every language. And it would seem an obvious, almost necessary, gesture for any assembly of the left. In the sharing of a simple act, crowds scattered far and wide put forth their claim that they all together formed a single body.[39]

In the months leading up to the elections of 1936, the great crowds of Paris expressed a great deal. The most obvious message they were meant to express, of course, was that of the strength of the French Popular Front's political coalition. After the elections, when the results were tallied and the left had its triumph, the multitudes that had propelled the left to victory were emboldened.

The sitdown strikes followed.

Many of those who seized their factories in late May recognized the advantage of doing so after the Popular Front coalition had won at the polls—and, more crucially, the advantage of doing so before the Popular Front government took office in early June. In this way, the problem of mass industrial unrest wouldn't be made on the new leftist government's watch; instead, it would be the new government's first problem to solve, presumably to the workers' advantage. "It was," the intellectual Janine Bouissounouse observed, "the opportune moment."[40]

It was clear that antifascism had fueled the Popular Front's electoral victory. No doubt the hard times of the Depression had made French voters more amenable to the idea of a socialist-led government, but the country's economy had actually improved since Bastille Day 1935. However, even as the economic crisis had lessened, the right-center government (which the Radicals had been a part of) had antagonized much of the public, first, with austerity measures and, second, with its appeasement of fascist Italy in Ethiopia. By 1936, even fascism elsewhere felt for many in France like a threat to their own peace and freedom. That, of course, was exactly what the antifascists of Hands Off Ethiopia had argued throughout 1935.

Coupled with the failures of the right-center government were the reassertions in Paris since mid-1935 of the paramilitary organizations that had taken part in the Sixth of February. In the summer of 1935, the head of the largest of the paramilitary groups, Colonel François de La Rocque of the Croix de Feu, had declared that he was ready for another Sixth of February. He had added that if a popular front government were formed, he would deliver a blow of some sort—a "coup"—against it. He had said this at a rally in Algiers in front of 15,000 Croix de Feu faithful, many of them standing in military formation. Thirty airplanes growled overhead as part of the program. Croix de Feu rallies had become the stuff of spectacle, complete with torches and bonfires and searchlights slicing their beams across the faces and chests of the assembled. In the streets of Paris, Croix de Feu forces marched in military style; they staged "lightning mobilizations" to give a hint of the speed with which they could carry out a coup.[41] Unlike the members of some of the city's other paramilitary groups, such as those known as the blueshirts, the Croix de Feu's rank and file didn't wear full uniforms to announce themselves; instead they relied on their armbands, each bearing a metallic emblem of a skull and fiery cross.

The other paramilitary groups, such as the Action Française, were also making their presence felt in the streets of Paris in the months before the 1936 elections. In February, youths from the Action Française beat up Léon Blum in the Boulevard Saint-Germain—"a fascist attentat," the top headline of the Socialist Party's paper howled the next day. They beat Blum so badly that he had to be rushed to the hospital, his head bashed, his life in danger.[42] He survived, and three months later, by the time of the factory occupations, he was set to head the Popular Front government once it took office. Two years before, on the Twelfth of February, Blum had worried that the columns of Communists and Socialists along the Cours de Vincennes would collide and collapse into violence; instead, it turned out that the politics of antifascist unity realized that day had propelled the Popular Front to power.

Once the sitdowns began, antifascism also animated life inside the occupied factories. In the cavernous Citroën plant, on the first day of the strike, hundreds of men and women shoved their fists into the air for a photograph. Inside the Renault complex, strikers put up effigies of Mussolini and Hitler and draped the walls with "Down with La Rocque" banners. A striker who abandoned the occupied factory was called "a false brother and a dirty Croix de Feu." At one point during the occupation, the Renault strikers put on an antifascist play that revolved around the idea of putting Colonel de La Rocque on trial. The improvised play amounted to a fantasy of retributive justice, with the colonel at one point handcuffed, locked inside a cage, able to say only, "Pity me! Pity me!" The play ended with the colonel condemned to death. Then the Renault strikers hung and immolated an effigy in his image, complete with a Croix de Feu armband and the markings of the Nazi swastika.[43]

In such ways, the strikers in the factories worked out a creative, even impish, antifascism. This antifascism, performed by the strikers themselves, on their own while they struck, had a depth to it much greater than the politics that showed up in the language of their union leaders' negotiations with management. It wasn't simply, though, that the factory occupations offered an opportunity for the workers to reveal their politics; it's more to the point to say that the factory occupations gave them a chance to create a new politics all their own, antifascist and liberatory. For that reason, Weil cherished the strikes: for what they were in and of themselves, as their own original and generative political expression, regardless of whatever gains might be won at the bargaining table because of them.[44]

For Weil, the joy of the strikes was the key. The joy came from the autonomy that the act of occupying the factories had given to the strikers. It made such a sharp contrast to the usual way of things in the factories. Weil knew this from when she had worked at Renault for a spell in 1934. She had not enjoyed the work. Most of all, she had felt the loss of personal freedom that came with a factory job.[45] The screws of factory discipline had bored into her head. Submissive impulses and timidity had taken hold of her mind. She had begun to

—

feel distant from others, from herself. Now, two years later, her memories of that misery converted into her intense joy at seeing the exuberant liberty of the strikers upon the very site of such melancholy in the past, everyone now capering about among the stilled machines. "Yes, a joy," she wrote. She explained, "Joy in passing through the gate now guarded only by a worker authorizing my entrance with a smile. Joy in finding so many smiles, so many warm words of welcome." And: "Joy in living in rhythm with human life — with the rhythm of breath, heartbeats, and the body's natural motions — amid all these machines now muted, instead of living your life in step with the cadence imposed by the timekeeper." She went on, finding joy as well in noticing that her friends and herself had taken to "passing in front of the bosses with our heads held high." Joy, too, she had found in the dignity shared by all the worker-strikers — "the dignity in our own eyes." So much joy Weil found and felt among the sitdown strikers: in her article that she wrote about her visit, ten times in one paragraph she struck upon the word, joy upon joy. The strike would end, she knew. It was only a brief escape from the normal order of things. But, she concluded, "There will be memories that give heart."[46]

Joy, for Weil, was its own social good, its own human good. And yet it is not hard to take from her ode a sense that the emotion holds political power; that it can serve as a political resource for anyone willing to accept it as such.[47] Weil saw how joy could spin together solidarities and weave a collective memory — a collective consciousness — for those who shared in the commotion. And so the strike, for Weil, was less something made by dependable or long-standing solidarities and more the maker of new solidarities all its own. Joy had helped to make a collectivity out of those who, before, had worked "side by side" without knowing each other, "without knowing each other's thoughts." Before, all had been stifled. And now, she exclaimed, "Finally, we can breathe!"[48]

Less than three months later, she was in Barcelona.

By then the notion of striking by seizing one's factory had been picked up by industrial workers in a startling array of places. The idea had also spilled out of the factories and into workplaces of all sorts, both in Paris and far beyond.

Much of what made 1936 a year of such wide-ranging social revolutionary possibility had to do with the reach of the sitdowns. Even before the factory occupations around Paris started up at the end of May, workers scattered about had been piecing the idea together. Rubberworkers had struck inside of a Firestone plant in Akron, Ohio, back in January, and already on the first day of that strike local labor organizers had decided to call it a "sitdown." Word spread. Soon more sitdowns took place around Akron, and others unfolded as far away as a rubber plant in Krakow, aviation plants in Le Havre and Toulouse, and a copper mine in the Huelva province of Spain.[49] How directly one led to another isn't clear. It is clear, though, that the idea of striking by sitdown took off after the dramatic Paris strikes made world news. All the attention given to them in the newspapers, in the newsreels, and on the radio invited people in all sorts of places around the world to picture how they themselves might seize control of where they worked, if only for a day or two.[50] Even before the Renault occupation had ended, as sitdowns began to hit the cafés and department stores of Paris, workers began occupying their factories in Casablanca.[51] A few days later, miners in Huelva again occupied their workings and hoped for the Spanish Popular Front government to take their side. Their strike led in part to a violent and blustery session in the Cortes on the evening of June 16. A ferocious right-wing deputy named Calvo Sotelo exchanged accusations with Ibárruri (she had won a seat in February, part of the Popular Front's triumph), and he called for the death of the republic and its constitution of 1931. Sotelo envisioned that a new kind of state could then rise up and put an end to such strikes and to all the social unrest and anarchy. "I don't know," he claimed, "if what I'm talking about is the fascist form of government that has everyone so alarmed, but if it is, then I declare myself fascist." He went on to speak obliquely about soldiers in the Spanish army who surely would never revolt to restore the monarchy but who just as surely would rise up, without hesitation, "to save Spain from anarchy." ("Leftist Deputies climbed over their seats, swinging fists," the Associated Press reported, but were held back "from reaching the Rightist benches.") Elsewhere, sitdowns multiplied. Workers sat down on the job in the Algerian industrial port cities of Oran, Bougie, and Djidjelli; others took over the Standard Oil compound in Bône. In late June 1,000 textile workers occupied their factory in Alexandria, Egypt, shortly after nearby oil workers had taken over their grounds. Then, still before June was out, several thousand workers in the textile mills of Pondicherry, French India, seized their

—

entire complexes. Ever more sitdowns followed in ever more places through the year's end. Laundry workers occupied their premises in Johannesburg, coal miners stayed in their pits in Scotland, dredgers in the Mekong Delta staged a pair of sitdowns (inside the dredging firm's offices, not in the river itself), shipping crews commandeered their vessels in the docks of New York, and so on.[52] The year ended with the outbreak of massive sitdowns in industrial Michigan.

All of these strikes had an explicit politics to them. Some of that had to do with the nature of the sitdown practice itself. The labor writer Louis Adamic, one of the sitdown phenomenon's most brilliant interpreters, commented at the end of 1936 that the industrial workers he called "the leftist rank-and-filers" had quickly seen "that the sitdown might have revolutionary implications or possibilities — workers stopping production, sitting down, and taking possession of plants!"[53]

Beyond their revolutionary implications and possibilities, though, much of the sitdowns' politics was expressed in the specific language of antifascism. Adamic — himself a determined antifascist — described the industrial labor insurgency behind the sitdowns in the United States as proof that the country's working people were figuring out how to express their "urge" to bring about "democracy and equality, as against absolutism or fascism, in the shop and factory." The paradox, as Adamic saw it, was that even though the sitdowns and the related outburst of labor radicalism were showing working people's antifascist commitment, they were also provoking "fascistic passion" among those terrified or enraged by the sitdowns.[54]

The idea that the sitdowns and antifascism were linked had the effect of pulling the strikes, and the multitudes of working people who took part in them, out of the particularities of their own local circumstances and into the general clash of universals defining the age. The first occupation of the mines in Huelva had been accompanied by street fighting between, as one local account put it, "fascists and leftists." A "Popular Front committee," including organizers described in the press as "antifascist militants," ran the largest of the Casablanca sitdowns, inside a vast sugar manufacturing plant. In Oran, the sitdowns led to street warfare involving what one observer depicted as armed "fascist settlers." Newspapers carried accounts of the Oran unrest far and wide: readers of the right-wing *Chicago Tribune* learned of "mobs of Popular Front parti-

—

sans" in Oran brutalizing members of "the Fascist Croix de Feu." The Croix de Feu was also an active antilabor force in Saigon and Pondicherry, as well as in Bougie, where local leftists fulminated that the paramilitary group could parade through the city with impunity.[55] One report out of Bougie described Croix de Feu shock troops marching "under their 'death's head' flag, making Roman salutes, and abusing and menacing militants of the Popular Front." Likewise, the most indefatigable of the sitdown strike organizers in Pondicherry, Varadarajulu Subbiah, described the strike committee there as "partisans of the 'Popular Front,'" organizing in deep solidarity with the striking workers of France. When automobile workers began sitting down in Michigan, in the final days of 1936, it was at the end of a year in which the flamboyantly fascist paramilitary organization known as the Black Legion had terrorized labor organizers, fomented race rioting, and murdered a public worker in the state. As the sitdowns escalated in the new year, striking workers in Michigan became radicalized by the experience and also perhaps became more willing to declare their politics explicitly. At a labor rally in Detroit, workers climbed a fence to hold up antifascist signs in the air, one of which read, "FORDISM IS FASCISM." Defying a court order to abandon their sitdown, autoworkers stood on the roof of an occupied Dodge factory and raised their fists in antifascist salutes; one of the strikers waved a sign reading, "THEY SHALL NOT PASS."[56]

Still, few of the sitdowns were as emphatically antifascist as the one that Weil had witnessed at Renault. To consider the sitdowns' role in 1936 alongside that of antifascism is to see how multiple dynamics, including those that at first were beyond the politics of antifascism, came to intermix and set off the madness of the moment. Causation didn't work in any one way, and no one at the time knew what might lead to what. What was clear was that everything in the moment had become combustible. When Léon Blum looked at the situation in France—the ascent of the left, the violent reaction of the right, the welfare-state ambitions of his incoming socialist-led government, the outburst of sitdown strikes—he fell upon the imagery of a "social explosion" to describe it all.[57] The vivid metaphor of explosion could have been used to explain the moment beyond France as well, to convey the wildfire-like sweep of events. Big outbursts of social upheaval followed one after another, each catalyzing the next.

—

This could be seen even within the confines of formal politics. The victory of the left in Spain gave meaning to the victory of the left in France; and those victories shaded the meaning of Roosevelt's reelection in November. (Not until 1938 would the Chilean Popular Front win and take power; even then, though, the aura of its connectedness to a larger left could be sensed.)

But the feeling of contagion that predominated in 1936 reached far beyond formal politics. Even aside from the sitdown strikes, labor insurgencies swelled throughout the year and gave shape to new political ideas. When Justiniano Sotomayor had picked the right moment to propose a popular front for Chile, much of the reason that it had been the right moment was that an immense railroad workers' strike had just inspired the left (and the state's ensuing repression of the strike had then also greatly incensed the left). Strikes began to stir in Saigon in August and soon swept across much of Cochinchina; by November's end the strikes had pushed the colonial government into crisis and had also provoked the local French war veteran Colonel Fernand Sée to step up his efforts to organize a paramilitary organization to put down the strikes. General strikes rolled through both the French mandate in Syria and Lebanon and the British mandate in Palestine. Both of those labor rebellions unfolded as part of wider social upheavals that ended up remaking anticolonial politics in the Middle East. The 1936 general strike in Palestine helped to set off the Arab Uprising there that would last three years, like the Spanish Civil War that it ran alongside.[58]

The Arab Uprising in Palestine threw more complications at antifascists than they could handle. But there were indeed antifascists on hand in Palestine who tried to explain the country's problems with antifascist principles and who tried to overcome them with antifascist political organizing. Among those who tried were the Arab and Jewish social revolutionaries who had created the collectivity known as Antifa of Palestine. Before the group's founding in late 1934, the word "Antifa" had still had only its first, very specific meaning. To speak of "Antifa" had been to refer to one of those two short-lived groups nicknamed Antifa that the German Communist Party had put together in succession in the years before the Third Reich, either the Antifaschistische Junge Garde established in 1929 (and banned the following year) or the better-known Antifaschistische Aktion that Thälmann set up in 1932. Antifa of Palestine wasn't

—

related to either of those. It wasn't related to the Communist International at all. Antifa of Palestine was very much its own singular collectivity. With its creation, though, the group began to stretch the word "Antifa" into something less specific and more general. The more recognition the group won, the more the word took on a broader meaning.

Today the idea of antifa is every bit the universalized abstraction that antifascism as a whole is. Today antifa is understood as a political form that anyone can pick up and practice wherever. What began as a particularism of late-Weimar German communism has become yet one more universal skittering about freely all over our political world. The first steps toward making it so were taken by a relatively small number of Arab and Jewish antifascists who sought, as they themselves put it, to bring about "the peaceful coexistence of the Jewish and Arab laboring masses in Palestine."[59] They didn't succeed, and today they themselves are all but forgotten, but they struggled and made their mark all the same.

"A left organisation of anti-Fascists," an early press account called Antifa. The account went on to detail how the organization had called for a general strike—in July 1935, well before the actual general strike in Palestine began in April 1936. The strike that Antifa wished for would have been waged by all workers of Palestine, not by Arabs alone, as was to happen with the strike of 1936. The idea was that by waging a fierce strike together the Arab and Jewish working people of Palestine would come to think of themselves as part of one shared collectivity. Together, Antifa hoped, the people of Palestine would deliver a social revolution that liberated the country from the British Empire. It would also, Antifa hoped, outpace the two major nationalist causes in Palestine—Zionism and Arab nationalism—both of which the antifascists of Antifa criticized severely. Both Zionism and Arab nationalism, they thought, had absorbed elements of fascism. In a way, fascism had taught Antifa's members to guard against all forms of nationalism. "'Antifa' rejects," the group declared, "the whole idea of 'national domination,' 'national sovereignty,' 'national privilege,' or, as Lenin called it, 'the hyper-chauvinism of the dominant.'"[60]

And yet the group's origins lay in a loosely organized labor Zionist party named Left Poale Zion. That Antifa came so directly from the world of labor

—

Zionism created an imbalance in the organization's political perspective and its group culture that it never quite overcame. From the beginning Antifa was a collectivity of both Arab and Jewish antifascists, but the group always had stronger connections to Jewish labor circles than to Arab ones. By early 1937, according to one of the group's most prominent Arab members, Nadjib Yusuf of Jaffa, Antifa had 800 members in all, 600 of whom were Jewish and 200 of whom were Arab. That said, for prominent labor Zionists such as David Ben-Gurion, the Zionism of even Left Poale Zion had seemed very suspect. Antifa drifted much further afield. Like Left Poale Zion, Antifa practiced a determinedly working-class social revolutionary politics. Also like Left Poale Zion, Antifa practiced an anti-imperialist politics, condemning British imperialism and agitating for a free and independent Palestine. However, unlike Left Poale Zion, Antifa rejected the idea of separate nation-states for the Arab and Jewish people of Palestine. "Two opposing states," Yusuf said, "would mean that neither Arabs nor Jews would get anywhere." Instead of pursuing anything like a two-state solution, Antifa focused on seeding, as the group proclaimed, "solidarity between Arab and Jewish workers." Such a task meant deep labor organizing on a local scale. The group emphasized, though, that it was also "an integral part of the global struggle against war and fascism."[61]

Of that, the antifascists of Antifa were certain. The Arab Uprising that began in April 1936, by contrast, only confounded them. "How can an antifascist explain this thing?" they asked forthrightly in a collective testimonial statement that the group put together and had published as a pamphlet about five months into the insurrection. The authors dedicated much of their pamphlet to criticisms of nationalism, both Zionist and Arab. The violence in April 1936 that sparked the unrest, the pamphlet's authors wrote, had been carried out by "Jewish fascists, overexcited by the provocations of their Arab 'coreligionists.'" Antifa and its allies—including those the pamphlet's authors called the country's "leftist workers"—tried their best to restore some measure of calm, but a series of violent episodes spun the situation away from them. By the time the authors of the testimonial pamphlet finished their work, only a few weeks after the Spanish Civil War began in July, nothing was going well for Antifa in Palestine. The group's members grasped that the politics they hoped for was becoming a more distant possibility by the day. "The events in Palestine," they wrote in the pamphlet, with an undisguised bitterness, "are a classic example of how a nationalist politics, by its nature, doesn't bring about *national and social liberation* but rather draws it into *the abyss* and drags it through the *muck*. This in the very country where two peoples, if they had practiced a politics of proletarian solidarity, could have built a *shared future* made by a *shared struggle*." It was time, Antifa decided, to begin focusing on finding allies abroad. The pamphlet itself was part of the collectivity's decision to set its sights on the larger world, on "all those in the world who fight for international social liberation," hopeful that they might come to the aid of the few who championed both "antifascism and anti-imperialism in Palestine."[62]

Antifa presented copies to prominent antifascist organizations, including the Ligue Internationale contre le Racisme et l'Antisémitisme, the Paris-based organization known as LICA.[63] Yusuf and fellow Antifa member David Kovarsky likely brought copies along with them when they went to Paris and took part in a two-day conference sponsored by LICA in September 1936. The International Conference Against Racism and Antisemitism took place in the Maison de la Mutualité, where the UTN had held its first Hands Off Ethiopia public meeting a year and a half before. The grand and intellectually ambitious gathering included delegates from as far away as Argentina. The proceedings began, as the antifascist writer René Defez reported, with "the invocation of the martyrs and victims of racism." Then Bernard Lecache spoke. Lecache had founded LICA after taking part in the campaign to free a Jewish anarchist who, in Paris in 1926, had shot to death a Ukrainian military commander whom he held responsible for a wave of pogroms during the Russian Civil War. Lecache's speech, according to Defez, "revolved around one central argument: Antisemitism equals Racism, Racism equals Fascism. Thus the absolute necessity of fighting fascism, *to the death*." And because "there exists a Fascist International," Lecache declared, the fight against it had to take the form of an antifascist international. He promised, for his part, to work to create "an international antiracist popular front." The concept of antiracism was still quite novel in 1936; LICA, however, was at the center of the political efforts to develop it and to make an active politics of it: to convert general and inchoate opposition to racism into a coherent and recognizable ism all its own. The organizers of the conference saw the gathering at the Mutualité as a step toward building a transnationally

—

meaningful antiracist politics, and they turned it into an annual event, renamed as the World Assembly Against Racism and Anti-Semitism, which they continued to host in Paris in each of the next two Septembers—scheduling them to counter the Nazis' Nuremberg rallies. A third annual meeting was planned for September 1939. In part because of these widely publicized annual assemblies, LICA stood out at the time for its efforts to fuse antifascism with antiracism. Beyond LICA as well, though, much of the early work to establish antiracism as a political and social concept came out of the discourse of antifascists. Even the conceptual structure of antifascism (not only an ism but also an "anti-," originating as an ideology of opposition and resistance to an already established ism) provided an example for early antiracism.[64]

The second day of the conference marked, according to Defez, "the first time that a Judeo-Arab delegation from Palestine has been seen at an international conference." Yusuf and Kovarsky spoke of Antifa's struggle to make Palestine into a peaceful country where Arabs and Jews lived and worked together toward a common future. They called for the abolition of the British mandate. Then Messali Hadj spoke. He argued that imperialism was the source of antisemitism among Arabs: if European imperialism had never claimed Arab lands, antisemitism would have never taken root there. Messali then spoke in defense of Amir Shakib Arslan, a skillful pan-Arabist propagandist from Syria. This sparked controversy. Messali himself was well known as an antifascist, but Arslan had gained notoriety for his many justifications of the fascist war on Ethiopia. He had met twice with Mussolini in 1935 and there were rumors that Italy funded him to cover Palestine in propaganda.[65] Messali went on to remind his audience of the miserable conditions endured by the Arab people of Palestine. At this, as Defez depicted the scene, a ruckus broke out and people began to shout.

A little later, Tiémoko Kouyaté spoke. He said that Africa was vast and great and that if the Jewish people of Europe were expelled from their homes, the people of Africa would welcome them with open arms. Kouyaté then challenged Messali's assessment of Arslan. Arslan had justified fascist Italy's invasion of Ethiopia on the grounds that the Ethiopian state had long oppressed Muslims. Kouyaté insisted all the same on the fundamental injustice of the invasion. Now the meeting's Arab delegation rose in protest. Messali demanded

—

another chance to speak. Given the chance, he defended Arslan again, and he also "took advantage of having the floor," Defez complained, "to reopen the debate on Palestine," again reminding his audience of the "appalling misery" endured by Arab Palestinians. Yet another uproar overtook the room. Messali walked out in protest, followed by the rest of the Arab delegation. Only after some diplomacy did the delegation agree to return for the conference's end. But while most of the assembly's resolutions passed unanimously, a major one proposing a pledge from all attendees to coordinate their struggles against racism and antisemitism drew considerable votes against. The members of the Arab delegation opposed the resolution because their motion for it to include a promise to fight against "that form of racist oppression called colonialism" had been rejected.[66] It was a tense, and telling, conclusion to the affair.

And yet those who had taken part in the gathering had heard radical dreams spoken aloud for two days. In his speech, Kouyaté had, as ever, drawn possibility from tragedy. He had envisioned an opportunity for fellowship at the prospect of a people's mass expulsion. He had conceived of separate destinies to be tied together by acts of kindness and welcoming. He had imagined new solidarities yet to be made.[67]

That, it could be said, was what Antifa did as well. The collectivity's attempt to build an interracial working-class politics didn't go far. All the same, its example — that its members came together to attempt such a politics at all — invites all sorts of valuable reflection. Which is much of what history does; even the failures can have their effect if they are remembered. There are things that are remembered and there are those that are lost, and what's remembered isn't yet lost.

By the time that Nadjib Yusuf and David Kovarsky spoke on behalf of Antifa in Paris, most of the major upheavals of 1936 were well underway. What was to become of them, though, remained undecided. The contingency of the moment was much of what Marceau Pivert had meant to capture with his short newspaper manifesto "Tout est possible" (Everything Is Possible).

It had gone to press back in May, on the day *before* the great Renault strike began. Even then, before most of the madness, Pivert could sense that an extraordinary interval was at hand. What did he mean when he wrote that everything is possible? He did not mean that you could do whatever you wanted. He did not mean that anything you might try might work. He meant that the ascent of the Popular Front—the potency of the newly remade left and "the masses who animate the Popular Front movement"—had cracked open unforeseen possibilities. And that this served as a reminder that political effort opens up always new possibilities that you hadn't seen before, that you hadn't even imagined before. Any one possibility leads to another and another. One never knows where it might end. So, Pivert said, begin.

It didn't matter, as he saw it, that the Popular Front electoral coalition's program had been vague and cautious. It didn't matter because "what millions and millions of men and women are calling for from the bottom of their collective conscience is *radical change, right away.*" Ever the populist, Pivert insisted that the new government's task was "to translate the will of the people." And the people of the Popular Front had not, he insisted, wished for "weak tea." They hungered for radical change because "they know that the capitalist world is dying and that a new world must be built if we want to put an end to the crisis, fascism, and war."[68]

Pivert was, no doubt about it, an idealist. He was a schoolteacher and a labor organizer, and by the summer of 1936 he had won the devotion of a sizable faction within the Socialist Party, in large part thanks to his romantic beliefs, his combative charisma, and his selfless commitment to his causes. He was blunt, gifted with epigrammatic flair, and dashing in person. After the Sixth of February, he had become a vocal antifascist. Doing so had reorganized all of his politics. Though long skeptical of the Comintern, throughout 1934 he pressed his party to join with the French Communist Party in a united front to combat fascism and, in doing so, to set off a social revolution. He worked to build what he described as "a powerful revolutionary left within the Socialist Party," and in the fall of 1935 he announced that his friends and he had indeed "constituted the 'Revolutionary Left.'" Now, as the summer of 1936 approached, he believed that the moment he had worked for had arrived. "Everything is possible, now," he promised, "so full speed ahead."[69]

Two days later, the day after the great Renault strike commenced, the French Communist Party's daily paper, *Humanité*, published its response to Pivert. Alongside a report of "50,000 metalworkers camping inside of the factories," one of the party's top officials, Marcel Gitton, rebuked Pivert. "No!" he exclaimed. "Not everything is possible."[70]

Maurice Thorez decided not to leave matters there. He was still the secretary general of the French Communist Party, as he had been in the autumn of 1934 when he had proposed that the party join with Pivert's Socialist Party as well as the Radical Party to create the Popular Front Against Fascism. But he had never meant for the idea to run so wild as it had. He had never meant for the Popular Front to mean true popular sovereignty over his political coalition. In private, he described the sitdown strikes as frightening, a threat to the party.[71] Now he worked to reassert the party's power. On June 11, when sitdowns were still underway in Paris, the secretary general spoke to an audience of party militants at the Gymnase Jean Jaurès, in the city's 19th Arrondissement. There he made his notorious declaration, "It is necessary to know how to end a strike."[72] The sitdown movement, even just in Paris, had grown beyond anyone's imagination, even Pivert's. Léon Blum's government was now in office. (Thorez's Communist Party had abstained from participating in the government itself, so as not to sully its reputation for revolutionary action.) It was time, Thorez declared at the Gymnase Jean Jaurès, for calm. In effect, it was time to let normalcy return. It was time to let history start back up again. Near the climax of his speech, he warned the party militants to ready themselves "to guard against leftist tendencies."[73] It was then that he echoed Gitton, insisting that, no, not everything is possible. At least, he said, not at this time.

Then, as if he thought that the claim had fallen flat, or just needed an extra touch of persuasion, he added, "It's true."[74]

CHAPTER 6

TODAY THE STRUGGLE

Now, at last, the forces of the left began to coalesce.

—DOROTHY THOMPSON, "Pattern of a Revolution," 1936

As 1936 came to an end, students at the City College of New York lit another effigy. This one had three heads: Mussolini, Hitler, Franco. It was a monstrous-looking thing, each of its faces grotesque and misshapen as if it were contorted into a premonitory rage over what the students were about to do to it. One arm was raised in a fascist salute, and the entire creation stood about six or seven feet in height.[1] Fascism had grown.

It was a December afternoon and the students were at least several hundred in number when they paraded their three-headed creation through campus. On their minds was the war in Spain. They went to the field where the effigy with the two heads had been burned a little over two years before, but a park worker insisted that they not start a fire there, so they crossed the street to Lewisohn Stadium and hung the effigy from a fence along Convent Avenue, just above 136th Street. Someone poured gasoline, the effigy was set afire, and then it deflagrated as the crowd roared.[2]

The spectacle's organizers took donations. They were raising funds for anti-fascist forces in the war. They were doing so even though the college dean had forbidden them from collecting anything—money, food, clothing—to send to Spain.[3] But the students paid him no mind. A handful of City College students themselves went to Spain.

—

One was Wilfred Mendelson. He had been raised in the Bronx by Jewish working-class parents from the Ukraine and Poland who had met in night school (and named their son after the hero of a book they'd read together for class, Walter Scott's *Ivanhoe*). By the time of the three-headed effigy's immolation in December 1936, Wilfred had dropped out of City College to focus on his local organizing work for the Young Communist League. Given that he had dropped out and yet was still around, he may or may not have taken part in the demonstration. He had, however, been the primary organizer behind the November 1934 rally that had seen the burning of the two-headed effigy. It had been Mendelson who had first rushed over to a lamppost and wrapped his arms around it when the police tried to break up the rally, leading to the chant of "Cops off the campus!" Mendelson had been on probation at the time because a month earlier he had also played a role in the brawl in the Great Hall—the one involving the fascist Italian visitors—and in the antifascist demonstrations on campus that had followed. A year later, when hundreds of City College students had gathered in Lewisohn Stadium on the day that Mussolini's forces invaded Ethiopia, it had been Mendelson who spoke and introduced the students' resolution to condemn the war. Within weeks, he had written an essay for a student magazine in which he declared that with the invasion fascism had chosen to shoulder "the 'white man's burden'" and that Mussolini could now claim to have brought "tanks, planes, poison gas, and every accoutrement to the 'civilizing process.'" He further argued that the war endangered "the whole equilibrium of peace," because the fascist regimes in Germany and Japan were watching to see how the world responded to Italy's imperial gambit. When the coup in Spain set off the civil war less than a year later, he saw the connection and considered volunteering right away. But his organizing, and some fear of war, kept him in New York until May 1938; he was one of the last of the antifascists from the wider world to ship out for Spain to take part in the war.[4]

Was Wilfred Mendelson the typical antifascist that went to Spain? There was no such thing. Those who went made a distinctly eclectic set. Most were young, though some were markedly older. Many more men than women went, but many women went as well. Most set out determined to fight at the front, but many others went to help the war effort in other capacities, resolved to show their solidarity somehow. Langston Hughes, who went as a journalist, reported that the volunteers' ranks included people of "all races." They spoke a number of languages. They belonged to a variety of political parties, some aligned with the Comintern and others far from it; some were without a party at all. They were intellectuals and students, manual laborers, military veterans, professional revolutionaries and party bureaucrats, preachers, nurses, cooks, labor organizers, and teachers. They were communists, socialists and social democrats, anarchists, liberals, anti-imperialists, Zionists and Arab nationalists, republicans, Wobblies and syndicalists, and even pacifists. They came from more than fifty nations. Some came from close by, such as Marcel Clouet of Toulouse. Few came from farther away than Agnes Hodgson of Sydney. Clouet, a member of the French Communist Party, fought in the International Brigades, the international people's army put together by the Comintern; Hodgson, a liberal, worked in Barcelona as a nurse.[5]

It was such a variety of people that came, and from such a variety of places. Pedro Tufró came from Montevideo; before he shipped out, the anarchist had to sell off all his belongings to pay for his passage. Zhang Ruishu, born in the Shandong region of China, had worked in the Renault factory just outside of Paris for a dozen years before he came to Spain in November 1936 (he surely was likely to have taken part in the great sitdown strike that Weil had witnessed a few months before). Pablo de la Torriente Brau, a Cuban revolutionary born in Puerto Rico who had lived in Santiago de Cuba and Havana, was in New York when the war began; before July was out, having heard how the people of Spain were rising up, he had what he called the "marvelous idea" of "going to Spain, to the Spanish revolution." He described the idea as burning its way through "the great forest of my imagination," and he began right away to make plans to get to Spain. Alberto Besouchet, a lieutenant in the Brazilian army, also decided right away in July 1936 to get to Spain; his decision, though, was spurred by problems at home. While stationed at Recife, he had taken part in the failed November 1935 military uprising organized in large part by the Brazilian Communist Party, of which he had been a member at the time. Since then he had faced considerable harassment from the state, and he also had faced the antagonism of his own party: despite his participation, he had been against the idea of the uprising, and by July 1936 he had been expelled and denounced as a Trotskyist. In Spain he sought out the militia of an anti-

—

Stalinist party. Salaria Kea of Akron, like Hodgson, came to Spain to serve as a nurse. Unlike Hodgson, she was a member of a Comintern-affiliated party. She had joined the Communist Party U.S.A. the previous year while working in Harlem amid all the Hands Off Ethiopia protests there (she herself had taken part in raising funds for an Ethiopian field hospital). Kea always insisted, though, that she decided to come to Spain "because I was a Catholic" — she felt the need to tend to the righteous suffering. She was struck by how the rules of white supremacy in the United States had kept her, a black woman, from even helping others freely: when she had tried to take part in a Red Cross flood relief campaign along the Ohio River, "they told me they had no place for me — that the color of my skin would make me more trouble than I'd be worth to them."[6] Instead she came to Spain. Adelina Abramson from Buenos Aires arrived in Spain in January 1937 and worked for the Comintern's forces in Albacete as a translator coordinating the air war. Jack Flior, a Jewish furniture maker who had made his home in Johannesburg, had already started fighting fascists before he came to Spain; in Johannesburg, he had regularly battled alongside his comrades in the Jewish Workers' Club against the city's grayshirts, even on the steps of the City Hall. Similarly, Bob Doyle of Dublin had engaged in constant brawls with blueshirts in the streets along the River Liffy before he came to fight fascists in Spain (a number of Irish blueshirts, perhaps several hundred of them, also came to fight, for the other side, the "Nationalists"). Mohamed Belaïda from Constantine (known to readers of André Malraux's classic anti-fascist novel *L'Espoir* as the mechanic Saïdi) was living in Paris when he joined an early detachment of volunteers organized by Marceau Pivert (who himself got to Barcelona before the end of August 1936, less than three months since he'd promised everything was possible; he now celebrated "this new world" being made by Barcelona's social revolution).[7] Manuel Lizárraga, a ship pilot from Manila, came to Spain in December 1936 and fought in the International Brigades. Mika Etchebéhère, an anarchist born in a colony of Russian Jews in Argentina, had arrived in Madrid less than a week before the coup; within a few months, she was the captain of a militia company. Itzchok Yoffe, a poet from Haifa known to have been a Zionist, fought on the Málaga front in the south of Spain.[8] Najati Sidqi, an intellectual from Jerusalem who was a member of the Palestine Communist Party, came to Spain to do propaganda work

—

209

for the Comintern. When someone in Barcelona mistook him for a Spaniard, he replied, "I am an Arab volunteer and I have come to defend Damascus in Guadalajara, Jerusalem in Córdoba, Baghdad in Toledo, Cairo in Zaragoza, and Tétouan in Burgos."[9]

They made such a diverse bunch, those who came; what they all had in common was their antifascism. They and others like them had fashioned that antifascism throughout the period I've been calling the antifascist moment, that spell of time that could be said to have begun with the Twelfth of February, 1934, in Paris, when people of different ideological faiths — people who at that point had not yet come to think of themselves as "antifascists" or to consider themselves in collectivity as "the left" or to call their politics "antifascism" — nonetheless had all paraded up the Cours de Vincennes as one and promised that fascism would not pass. Since then, people in Paris, and from Paris to Buenos Aires and from Cape Town to Tokyo, had come to imagine antifascism as a universalized form of politics — meaningful still in Italy, yes, but meaningful now, too, where they themselves lived, and meaningful throughout the world. Millions had come to think of themselves as antifascists and had come to recognize that there were indeed millions of others who shared their faith. That is, as Anne O'Hare McCormick might have put it, they saw their antifascism in panorama. The antifascism they'd crafted encouraged them to trust that the people of the world were with them and that fascism anywhere posed a threat, because it was so endlessly rapacious, to everyone everywhere. Antifascists who went to Spain explained time and time again that they saw their own fate as tied to that of the Spanish people. They didn't go to Spain out of sympathy alone. They went out of solidarity: it wasn't only a matter of what Franco was doing to the people of Spain; it was what fascism had done, was doing, and would do to everyone and anyone the world over. Yesterday it had been Ethiopia; today it was Spain; tomorrow it might be here, wherever that may be.

And so the students at City College had made their second effigy with yet another head. Fascism, they were saying, would surely grow more heads still; monstrosity that it was, it had to be killed in Spain before it mutated again and struck somewhere else.

Because of such beliefs, antifascism pulled together many different sorts of people and drew them to Spain. Then, in Spain, at least for a short period, anti-

—

fascism held them together. After that, it's true, the bonds broke. The politics of unity that had driven the antifascist moment and remade the left in its new, larger form didn't survive the war intact. But even so, the ideas of antifascism — and the antifascists' way of seeing the world and its politics, their way of envisioning the left and the right, their way of envisioning the pairing as engaged in a world-spanning ideological civil war — never went away.

When Simone Weil arrived in Barcelona, in early August 1936, and saw all around her what she thought of as the surprisingly calm but true revolution, she could only compare it to "those periods of history that we read about in books and that have inspired us to dream since childhood"—years, she wrote, such as 1792, 1871, and 1917. She sensed that another such moment of overwhelming social transformation was underway. "May it have," she added, "happier effects."[10]

When she wrote down her first impressions of Barcelona in her journal, she acknowledged that on the surface of things there was an odd normality to it all. "Money," she noted, "plays the same role as ever." The crucial difference, though, was that the common people of the city had taken over. The way Orwell put it in *Homage to Catalonia* was to say that, unlike anywhere else he had ever been, in revolutionary Barcelona "the working class was in the saddle." He wrote of the breaking apart of the private property regime visible in the city's built environment ("Practically every building of any size had been seized by the workers and was draped with red flags or with the red and black"), and he wrote of the breaking down of the old social hierarchy visible, and audible, in the city's everyday practices ("Nobody said 'Señor' or 'Don' or even 'Usted'; everyone called everyone else 'Comrade' and 'Thou'"; there was no tipping, for that was now too demeaning of a custom; women and men alike wore blue overalls and coarse militia gear; there were "no private motor cars," for "they had all been commandeered"). The example that Weil used and then returned to once again was that of the "seventeen-year-old kids with loaded rifles" in the place of police. But the change she had in mind was much more pervasive than just that. She saw in the present moment "one of those extraordinary periods, none of which before now has lasted long, when those who had always obeyed take charge of things."[11]

—

The social revolution in Barcelona made a deep impression on the antifascists from abroad. For some, it clarified what they were fighting for, beyond what they were fighting against. Orwell's description of it remains the most famous, but other new arrivals were struck just as sharply. "It was a whirlwind revolution," suggested Charles Orr, a young socialist from Michigan. For Orr, in the summer of 1936 "anti-fascist Spain became a crucible of social experiment." For the people of Barcelona, this meant a lot of work. In the collectivized factories and in the city's service departments, hospitals, and homes, all arrangements and relations had to be negotiated anew. Much of this work remained invisible to the newcomers, who inevitably saw more of the experimentation's romantic side. But what the antifascist volunteers from abroad could see and understand was real enough, and shouldn't be dismissed. Mary Low, a revolutionary socialist from London, walked along the Ramblas early on in the city's social revolution and described an atmosphere "of liberation, as though the city were emerging into fresh air and light." She wrote that the "air was filled with an intense din of loud-speakers and people were gathered in groups here and there under the trees," listening intently. When the oratory would pause, those gathered in the street would break into "snatches of the 'Internationale.'"[12]

The daily experience of the revolution, Orr explained, "was exhilarating: unbounded enthusiasm on the part of the common people and, it seemed, of the middle classes too." Of historical precedents, he thought that only the Paris Commune of 1871 compared; of the rest of history's revolutions, "none was so rapid, so profound, so all-embracing." He described the scene as "a headless, leaderless, but anarchist influenced revolution that emitted side-currents in all directions." By this he meant that "it was not only a matter of dress and forms of greeting," the things that Orwell accentuated. "It was an endless parade of movements, tendencies and fads for all kinds of social and economic reforms, ranging from women's rights, to Protestant sects (in Catholic Spain), through vegetarianism, pacifism, modern art, avant-guard music, nudism, Esperanto — any 'progressive['] goal that you can imagine." Barcelona was liberated in every sense, and "civil liberties reigned" ("except," that is, "for 'fascists'").[13]

Weil reveled in the commotion — this was very much her sort of revolution — but she didn't linger much before walking along the Ramblas to the office of the revolutionary socialist Julián Gorkin. She offered to carry out for his operation a far-fetched undercover mission behind enemy lines that she herself had dreamed up. Gorkin told her that she was offering herself "as a sacrifice" and rejected the idea out of hand. (Weil confessed later that she had indeed set out for the war "with some ideas of sacrifice" hanging heavily in her head.) With her plan rejected, she instead left town toward the Ebro River in Aragón to catch up with the Durruti Column, part of what were known as the CNT's "Antifascist Militias." Organized in Barcelona by the talismanic anarchist Buenaventura Durruti and his comrades in the days after they'd battled the military insurrectionaries on July 19, the column had marched out of Barcelona and headed for Aragón on July 24, determined to take the war to the fascists.[14] Weil had decided that she belonged at the front.

The decision had been a struggle for her. For all her determination to take up arms, she had long had deep pacifist convictions.[15] Since the beginning of the age of fascism, her pacifism and her antifascism had been at war in her head. Late in the first year of the Third Reich, she had written an essay, "Réflexions sur la guerre" (Reflections on War), in which she warned against waging war to fight fascism. The "human values" she cherished and hoped to bring about by revolution relied on peace to blossom. She insisted that this remained so even in lowly 1933, when peace was no longer what it once had been; "peace," she wrote, "has been less precious since the moment that it came to involve the unspeakable horrors of thousands of workers in the concentration camps of Germany."[16] Even with peace cheapened so, Weil insisted on avoiding war. Modern war, she wrote, inevitably worked to constrain liberty, to swell bureaucracy, to heighten authority, to expand the police, and to centralize power—in short, to do all the things that revolutionaries ought to fight against. "Revolutionary war," she declared, "is the tomb of revolution." She contended that Maximilien Robespierre the virtuous and egalitarian citizen of 1792 had given way to the dictatorial terrorist and war-maker of 1793, and that so too Lenin the democratic revolutionary of 1917 had succumbed to the dictates of war and became a centralizer, a despot, thereafter. War, not revolution, had given rise to "the barbaric regime of Stalin." Given the damage that war had done to revolutionary causes in the past, it seemed clear that an antifascist war would only fortify fascism. It would amount to an attempt to liberate people from one

—

213

"barbaric oppression" by piling another "even more barbaric" form on top of the first. "The absurdity of an antifascist struggle that takes war as its means of action," she wrote then, in 1933, "thus can clearly be seen."[17]

And yet in September 1936 she stood on the shores of the Ebro with a gun in her hands, wearing the CNT's militia fatigues, telling herself she was prepared to shoot fascists (fig. 6).

She was not a skilled soldier and her time with the militia did not go well. In the journal she kept, though, she wrote that she wasn't afraid ("Not me," she noted without bluster, clinically, after observing a comrade's fear). Rather, the danger of death awakened her to the glories of life surrounding her, suffusing her. "But how everything, all around me, is so intensely alive!" Weil exclaimed. In her mind this related to the sort of war she had engaged herself in: "War without prisoners. If you're captured, you're shot." She could live with this. Reflecting on it, she wrote, "I lie on my back and look at the leaves, the blue sky. Very beautiful day." She then returned to her thoughts on the mortal threat she faced, reminding herself, "If they capture me, they'll kill me." She was at peace with this because "it's deserved. Our side has shed plenty of blood. Am morally complicit. Complete calm."[18] Soon planes flew overhead and bombs fell from her blue sky.

Weil and her comrades waited out the bombing without incident. But then the next day, during a moment of peace in camp, she had a terrible accident. Weil had bad vision and she stepped into the cook's boiling oil. The fire had been dug low in the ground to make it less visible to enemy eyes. She was badly burned. Though she resisted, her comrades sent her to a militia hospital nearby. Her parents came from Paris and took her to the coastal town of Sitges to care for her there. It was in Sitges that she heard the stories – of war crimes, senseless murders of "fascists or those called such," and "punitive expeditions" – that most demoralized her. After a few stops back in Barcelona, Weil was soon on her way, with mixed feelings, back to Paris. It was less than two months since she had first arrived in Barcelona.[19]

Still, though, she had represented her corner of the left well. Pacifists, of course, shouldn't be expected to soldier well, and the antifascist war effort was a nobler and more meaningful cause for having had her as a part of it. What's more, her participation in the war complicated – but did not negate – the things

—

Figure 6. Simone Weil, in Barcelona, wearing the militia gear of the antifascist labor organization the Confederación Nacional del Trabajo (CNT). *Apic/Hulton Archive/ Getty Images*.

she had written in 1933, when she had said that an antifascist struggle that took the form of war was an absurdity. The question of what the Spanish Civil War meant for the cause of antifascism is not easy to answer. Weil, by engaging as she did, posed the question well.

Not long after Simone Weil left Barcelona, Guido Picelli of Parma arrived. He had traveled a hard path over the years since Parma's heroic stand against Balbo's squadristi in August 1922, when he had commanded the Arditi del Popolo behind the barricades. A few months after that, in October 1922, he had taken part in an effort to memorialize the martyrs of August, and he had taken advantage of the opportunity to champion the Arditi del Popolo's para-militarized vision of antifascism, declaring, "Faced with armed violence, armed violence is necessary." It was not surprising that by the end of the month, after the March on Rome, he was arrested. The Arditi del Popolo went underground and soon state repression broke the organization to pieces. Parma, as ever, made things tough for the fascisti. "Parma, generous and rebellious," Picelli wrote in March 1923 amid mass arrests in the city, "Parma, the city of the glorious days of August, once again faces a trial by fire. Our smiling people assure me we shall not fall. They are ready to fight once more. You know, in Parma you die singing, you never give up. Never." He remained a deputy in parliament, though amid the political turmoil to come he left the Socialist Party in 1923 and joined the Communist Party in 1924 (Bordiga had fallen from power and Gramsci's ideas were closer to his own). Arrested again and again (once, on May Day 1924, for hanging the red flag from the balcony of the Camera dei Deputati), Picelli was finally imprisoned after the fascist regime made opposition parties illegal in November 1926. That final time he was arrested the same night that Gramsci was. Unlike Gramsci, though, he was released in 1931, and he fled to France the following year. The authorities there soon expelled him, and he took refuge in the Soviet Union, in Moscow, where he alternately worked in a ball-bearings factory and taught courses on military theory and practice: theoretical lessons on urban warfare and practical lessons on the use of machine guns, cannons, automatic rifles, tanks, and armored cars. Late in the summer of 1936, con-temptuous of Stalin's regime and under suspicion himself, Picelli talked officials into letting him leave the country to go fight in Spain.[20]

—

On the way, in Paris, he met Julián Gorkin, whom Weil had approached in Barcelona a few months before. Gorkin was a prominent member of the POUM (Partit Obrer d'Unificació Marxista, or Partido Obrero de Unificación Marxista), which was a small revolutionary socialist and anti-Stalinist Spanish party strongest in Catalonia. The POUM ran the ragtag, poorly armed militia that Besouchet and Etchebéhère had joined and that, quite by happenstance, Orwell would soon join and then write of so admiringly in *Homage to Catalonia*. Picelli wanted to enlist. Actually, he wanted the POUM's blessing to organize an entire battalion, "of shock troops," that he himself would train and command. After listening to Picelli present his audacious proposal, Gorkin measured the man before him. Picelli was, he decided, "close to fifty, with a noble presence and an open and intelligent face." Picelli told Gorkin about his experiences fighting in Parma and teaching in Moscow. During that meeting in Paris he also stated, according to Gorkin later, "I have never been a communist. I managed to get out of Russia and I want to put my military knowledge at the service of the Spanish and the international antifascist cause." If Gorkin recounted the statement accurately, then Picelli, one of the earliest of the Italian antifascisti, had now come to envision antifascism as a cause that could be Spanish as well as Italian; and, what's more, he now envisioned beyond such national antifascisms a grander totality incorporating them all: "the international antifascist cause."[21]

Gorkin saw something impressive in Picelli and arranged for his passage to Barcelona. He set up a meeting for a few days later at the POUM Executive Building (where Weil had approached him), along the Ramblas next to the legendary Café Moka. In the meeting, Picelli explained himself to the party's military commander. He wasn't given license to raise his own battalion, but by the time Picelli stepped back out into the Ramblas he was a captain in the POUM militia, assigned to the front. Gorkin and Picelli walked out together; as Gorkin recalled the scene that followed, Picelli was climbing into their car when a foreign man approached them and asked Picelli to step away for a minute.[22] Picelli did.

And Gorkin never saw him again. Past the car was the Plaza de Cataluña and the Hotel Colón, which was the headquarters of the PSUC (Partit Socialista Unificat de Catalunya, or Partido Socialista Unificado de Cataluña), a joint socialist-communist party affiliated with the Comintern. Later, when he looked

—

back on his encounter with Picelli, Gorkin was certain he knew what had happened. Soviet secret police agents had been spying on them the whole time and then had taken Picelli to the Hotel Colón and threatened him.[23] Gorkin saw in the affair the far reach of Soviet surveillance and the unrelenting villainy of a regime obsessed with keeping its grip on those it had ensnared.

There is, however, no reason to share Gorkin's certainty about what had happened. After his experiences in Spain, Gorkin started pinning, as one historian has put it, "any evil on Communists on the basis of thin evidence and general principle." Regarding Picelli's fate, Gorkin had arrived at his conclusions with no evidence at all. And after Picelli disappeared up the Ramblas, he showed up again, in Madrid a few weeks later, in command of his own battalion—in the Comintern's International Brigades. Under his command were more than 500 volunteers from Italy, France, and Poland; he had trained them, quickly, at Albacete. It's certainly possible that he had been coerced into joining the International Brigades with "the worst threats," as Gorkin claimed, though Picelli never seemed like the sort to scare easily, and, again, Gorkin made his claims without any evidence at all. He did, however, at least come closer to the truth about Picelli's fate than did the historians who later, in the wake of the Cold War, wrote the celebrated anticommunist historical treatise *The Black Book of Communism*. They claimed that when Picelli disappeared on Gorkin in the Ramblas he "simply disappeared for good, without a trace."[24] But if Gorkin's account was closer to the truth than that, it still relied on simple speculation, very much informed by his anti-Stalinism, which, by the time he wrote about meeting Picelli, was well on the way to generalizing into outright anticommunism. During the Cold War, his commitment to anticommunism became such that the U.S. Central Intelligence Agency funded his work for years.[25]

However certain Gorkin was that Soviet secret police had picked up Picelli, a more recent, and more careful, historical account of the encounter with the stranger in the Ramblas found that the foreign man Gorkin saw wasn't a Soviet secret police agent but rather an old friend and comrade of Picelli's, Ottavio Pastore from La Spezia. Pastore had once long ago written an appreciation of the Arditi del Popolo and their glorious defense of Parma.[26] He may have appealed to old solidarities. He certainly appears to have offered Picelli a more promising post, with more soldiers, arms, and resources than Gorkin's outfit

—

did (or could). Indeed, Pastore seems to have given Picelli license to do almost the exact thing that Picelli had asked Gorkin to let him do. Again, then, there's no reason to share Gorkin's certainty. To be fair to him, though, by the time he made his accusations, he had good reason to throw a few imaginative accusations at the Comintern. But that doesn't make his story any truer.

Regardless, it was November 1936 and Guido Picelli, hero of Parma, was off once more to fight fascism, now on behalf of the international antifascist cause. If Wilfred Mendelson wasn't the typical antifascist that went to Spain, Picelli definitely wasn't. However, he also wasn't the only volunteer in Spain who had once fought fascism already in the Arditi del Popolo — among other former arditi were Ilio Barontini, who after fighting in Spain went to occupied Ethiopia to organize resistance there to fascist rule; and Armando Fedeli, who went on to take part in the Italian Resistance during World War II and to organize partisans in Rome and Umbria. Picelli wasn't even the only volunteer in Spain who had fought at Parma. At Parma, he had commanded from the district of Oltretorrente, where most of the fighting had taken place; the other theater of battle had been Naviglio, where the anarchist Antonio Cieri had commanded. Cieri was also in Spain as 1936 came to a close. He fought in an international section of one of the antifascist militias organized by the CNT, similar to the unit Weil had served in during her stint at the front.[27]

The antifascists who came to Spain came from many places and for many reasons. They included antifascisti from before the March on Rome. They included a philosopher horrified by Nazism who wished for revolution without war. And they included idealistic young students who had protested on their campuses against war and empire. They all had their reasons, all shaped by the history of antifascism.

In the final months of 1936, all antifascists' eyes were on Spain, but not all of the antifascists' battles took place there. A month before Picelli arrived in Barcelona — or about a week after Weil went back to Paris — antifascists in East London threw up the barricades and took just the sort of stand against fascism that Picelli surely would have admired.

In the first few months of the Spanish Civil War, antifascists had taken to painting on the walls of London, "They shall not pass." The phrase, of course,

—

paid homage to Dolores Ibárruri's radio address of July 19. By the end of September the phrase had become a mantra of antifascist commitment in countless places around the world. In the East End—London's dense working-class district long known as a haven for poor migrants, the dispossessed, and political radicals—the phrase could be seen painted not only on the walls but also on the pavements. The East End in 1936 was home to a fierce popular antifascism. And by September's end, "They shall not pass" was not only on the walls and pavements of the district but also, according to local Communist Party organizer Joe Jacobs, "on everyone's lips." Antifascism, however, was not the only political force at work in the East End at the moment, and other phrases, of a different sort, could also be found on the district's walls and hoardings. These included "Jews, we will have your blood," "Long live Hitler," and "Kill the Jews."[28] Not only had the East End become a stronghold of antifascism, it had become a target of ever-increasing fascist incursions. The incursions—the graffiti on the walls; men in blackshirt uniform prowling the streets ready to heckle and fight; abrasive open-air meetings full of loud antisemitic rhetoric—were much of the reason that the phrase "They shall not pass" was on everyone's lips.

And when Oswald Mosley's British Union of Fascists announced at the end of September that the blackshirts would soon march on the East End, there was little doubt that local antifascists would somehow respond.[29]

Trouble between fascists and antifascists had taken hold of the East End over the summer. One of the worst incidents in the area had happened at Victoria Park on Sunday, August 30. A new informally organized antifascist collectivity sometimes called the Ex-Servicemen's Movement Against Fascism had put together a parade through the East End, followed by a public meeting in the park, where local blackshirts liked to hold forth.[30] The new group had loose connections to the Communist Party of Great Britain, though its members insisted on their own collective autonomy—they "had their own ideas," Jacobs later commented. The Communist Party's local leadership learned to respect this. Most of the members of the group were Jewish military veterans, and the group also had loose connections to a few Zionist organizations. The idea of a Jewish antifascist collectivity, and a confrontational militant one at that, was enough to inflame London's blackshirts. Just how central to their political program antisemitism had become by 1936 was evident in their response

—

to the initial appearance of the veterans' group. "This new move is typical of Jewry," one writer sniped in the fascist newspaper the *Blackshirt,* adding that "Jewish Finance reaped from the last war," and now, with the creation of the Ex-Servicemen's Movement Against Fascism, "it has tried its level best to sow for another war." That war, the author warned, would pit the British people against Nazi Germany for no reason save "in defence of Jewish interests." On August 30, the veterans of the Ex-Servicemen's Movement Against Fascism marched through the East End, with thousands of fellow antifascists following behind (more than one witness suggested that the procession was a mile long). Soon enough, blackshirts descended on them, shouting "Hail Hitler" and "Hail Mosley" and making fascist salutes. The blackshirts eventually assaulted the marchers, once along the way and then again at the park's entrance. "The Fascists," wrote the correspondent for London's *Daily Worker,* "hurled stones, flour, eggs, mud, fireworks, and, it is stated, fired revolvers with blank shots." The procession still made it into the park and the antifascists held their rally.[31]

Among those who spoke was Sylvia Pankhurst.[32]

Who had been an antifascist longer than she in the summer of 1936? Even before she'd become an antifascist, Pankhurst had been in Italy back in 1919 and had raised alarm about the terroristic violence of the arditi. She had reported in her *Workers' Dreadnought* on the notorious assault by a gang of "the 'Arditi'" on the offices of *Avanti!* in Milan in April 1919. She had even commented at the time on the arrest of the "pro-war Socialist and editor of the social-imperialist daily *Popolo d'Italia,*" the violent-minded demagogue she identified at the time as "Benito Missolini."[33] Called out by name as a "Left" in Lenin's pamphlet in 1920 (and expelled from the Communist Party of Great Britain the following year for "breach of discipline"), she had been among the quickest in the wake of the March on Rome in 1922 to warn of the wider danger posed by fascism. As the leader of the Friends of Italian Freedom, she had organized the displaced memorial meeting for Matteotti in Soho in 1925; and she had been the main force behind the creation of the Women's International Matteotti Committee in 1932. Now in 1936 she had kept up her antifascist commitments. In May, still outraged by the fascist invasion of Ethiopia and the ongoing occupation, she had founded the antifascist newspaper *New Times and Ethiopia News.* Once the Spanish Civil War began in July, she rallied to the

—

defense of the Spanish Republic (she herself, ideologically, was a republican as well as an antifascist, socialist, feminist, and anti-imperialist). But unlike most antifascists around her at the time she also kept laboring steadfastly for Ethiopia's liberation.[34] All in all, at the end of August 1936 the fifty-four-year-old Pankhurst was outshined by few if any in antifascist history.

In Victoria Park, the fascists flung stones at her and struck her in the head. The scene fell into pandemonium but Pankhurst escaped without serious injury. And because of the assault the demonstration became international news. Much like antifascists had done at Olympia two years before, the antifascists in Victoria Park turned the fascists' violence against them and made a message out of their barbarism. "No doubt," concluded one feisty news commentary published a few days later across the Atlantic in the United States, "the attack may be attributed to youth and inexperience. Certainly no person cognizant of Miss Pankhurst's formidable past would be so bold as to chuck stones at her." After all, Pankhurst had "made herself famous in the days when British women were fighting for suffrage by breaking plate glass windows, throwing acid into mail boxes, and other tactics that completely cowed her male adversaries. A first-class fighting woman is Miss Pankhurst, as Sir Oswald Mosley's young men will learn."[35]

They learned of the fighting spirit possessed by all of the East End's antifascists five Sundays later, on October 4. That was the day of the confrontation quickly mythologized as the "Battle of Cable Street." As soon as word got around that the fascists were going to march through the district, local antifascists began figuring out how to react. The fascists had two basic goals in mind. First, they wanted to make their presence felt in the East End so as to make followers of working-class people there (at least, those who were not Jewish). Second, they wanted to provoke the Jews of the East End and all the antifascists, in a bid for publicity and controversy. Violent public spectacle was an unwieldy weapon—that, again, had been the lesson of Olympia—but it remained a potent one, and one that the fascists relied on. The antifascists of the East End understood this and didn't take the implications of it lightly. Jacobs later acknowledged that "it could be argued, and it was, that by reacting as we did"—defiantly, physically, meeting violence with violence—"it only served to help Mosley and we were playing into his hands." Jacobs, however, had concluded that in the end there was little choice: "what do you do when the local people, on whose doorsteps these Fascist meetings were being held, turned out in opposition? Were we to say, ignore them, you only play into their hands? What about the anti-semitic abuse? What about the violence?" Still, the Communist Party's leadership was reluctant to organize a counterdemonstration. The party's London District Committee wanted tactically to cede the field for the day; the party had scheduled a rally over in Trafalgar Square to raise funds for Spain. That was an honorable day's work and, the committee concluded, it also aligned better with the party's institution-building aims. More to the point, as one Communist official told Jacobs, Mosley marching in the East End was a sideshow; Spain was what mattered.[36] Jacobs, who was born and raised in a Jewish enclave in the East End — who was devoted to the East End, who loved it, who learned his politics from the communism of the poor in its neighborhoods, and who called it always "my East End" — was crushed. And angry.

According to Jacobs's idea of antifascism, Mosley mattered. In large part, Mosley mattered because he could send his blackshirts into Jacobs's East End. To be sure, the BUF wasn't about to seize state power; Mosley himself hadn't Hitler's or Mussolini's cunning; and Britain's parliamentary regime was in better shape than most. But political power comes in many forms and London's blackshirts exercised the ones they knew. The antifascism that Jacobs believed in meant fighting back and confronting them; "They shall not pass" was not just a slogan, it was a profession of commitment and responsibility. There were other days to raise funds for Spain — and other days to raise the party's profile in Trafalgar Square.

But the London District Committee informed Jacobs that his orders were to persuade people in the district to go to the Trafalgar Square rally. Only afterwards should they come back to the East End and attempt a late counterdemonstration. Even then, they should keep their distance from the fascists. "Avoid clashes," Jacobs was told in writing. "If Mosley decides to march let him" — any attempt at "a 'They shall not pass' policy" would "only be a harmful stunt."[37]

It was only after much protest from Jacobs and others on the ground that the party relented and agreed to focus on facing the fascists in the East End. The party even agreed to do so with "They shall not pass" as the policy of the day after all. Jacobs argued to party leaders that the two fights, in Spain and

—

in the East End, were the same and that their duty on October 4 was to face the fascists in front of them. How could they let antifascists in Spain fight for them without fighting the fascists descending on their own streets? In the end, only days before the event, the argument that weighed on the party's leadership the most was the point that the antifascists of the neighborhood, the militants of the Ex-Servicemen's Movement Against Fascism most of all, were going to come out regardless. The party ran the risk of losing face by missing out. And so, thanks to local antifascists such as Joe Jacobs, the Communist Party began organizing with the Independent Labour Party and the Ex-Servicemen's Movement Against Fascism to "save the East End of London from Fascism." It wasn't a Moscow directive; it wasn't a party edict to follow the official Popular Front line; it wasn't any of the things that anticommunists have said about antifascism to diminish it. It was a revolt of the party's local rank and file, a show of popular devotion to the antifascist cause. And in the final days before October 4, the campaign to promote the East End's defense swept through the district. In addition to leaflets, posters, and word of mouth, the Independent Labour Party hired a van with a loudspeaker to drive all over East London to turn out protesters on Sunday afternoon.[38]

The turnout exceeded all expectations. Estimates varied anywhere from 100,000 to nearly half a million people stuffed into the streets of the East End. Those who showed up were, as it was put in one pamphlet published shortly afterward, "East London workers irrespective of their race, or creed, irrespective of their political affiliations, Jews and Gentiles, Communists, Socialists, and Labour Party supporters." Among them, no surprise, was Sylvia Pankhurst. The crowds were densest from Gardiner's Corner (by the Aldgate East station) south along Leman Street down to Cable Street, near the blackshirts' assembly point in Royal Mint Street, behind the Tower of London at the East End's edge. The crowds, even before any confrontation took place, were ferocious, brimming with outrage. They themselves amounted to a human barricade against the blackshirts, but in Cable Street—where the fascists planned to enter into the East End—they threw up actual barricades made of ladders, boards, paving stones, and even an overturned lorry. The crowds, chanting, "They shall not pass," poured into Royal Mint Street; 3,000 to 5,000 men and women wearing blackshirt uniforms awaited them in formation. The fighting began.

—

Figure 7. Oswald Mosley exchanges fascist salutes with blackshirts in Royal Mint Street on October 4, 1936. The "Battle of Cable Street" followed. *Central Press/Hulton Archive/Getty Images.*

Antifascists fought both fascists and police. When Mosley showed up in a car, escorted by a motorcycle motorcade, he paraded around as best he could with his arm up in a fascist salute; someone threw something and cracked his windshield (fig. 7). Thousands of police were present and detachments charged into Cable Street repeatedly, trying to storm the barricades. They made little progress. The tumult went on for over two hours before the police commissioner, on the scene from New Scotland Yard, told Mosley that "it has been decided to ban your march." The police ushered the blackshirts away westward; they headed to Trafalgar Square, where the police promptly refused to let them hold a demonstration—their permit had been for the streets of the East End.[39]

—

225

Back in Cable Street, the barricades still stood.

It was a far less sanguinary affair, but something of the spirit of Parma had been at work in the East End's defense. Not only because it had relied on raising the barricades or because the Ex-Servicemen's Movement Against Fascism had about it a hint of the Arditi del Popolo, but also because of the community-based nature of the defense. Formal organizations certainly had played a big part but, as had been the case in Parma fourteen years before, the antifascist forces that took their stand in East London on October 4, 1936, had drawn directly from the community and had ended up comprising a collectivity much greater than the sum of the formal groups involved. And also as at Parma fascism had not passed.

Spain inspired antifascists in London and elsewhere, but the war itself didn't go well. Not until April 1, 1939, did Franco declare that hostilities had ended (and that 1939 was thenceforth to be known as the "Year of Victory"), but by then the antifascist war effort had been in a bad way for a long time.[40] The liberal great powers hadn't helped, which had made the antifascist coalition in Spain overly dependent on the Soviet Union. That had left Stalin with an abundance of influence without any countervailing forces. Not even Nazi Germany's and Fascist Italy's almost immediate violations of their nonintervention commitments pulled Britain or France or the United States into the war effort.[41] On the ground, in Spain, the great accomplishment of the Popular Front of 1936 had been to draw together ideologically diverse actors. But the politics of unity that had pressed together so many incongruent parts into "the left" had always been a fragile project. After 1936, it fell apart. The decisive blow could well be said to have been the "May Days" of 1937 in Barcelona. The May Days certainly became, as one historian has put it, a "symbolic end point" to revolutionary possibility and the left's semblance of unity in Spain.[42] Anarchists had operated the Telephone Exchange at the eastern corner of the Plaza de Cataluña since taking the building from the military insurrectionaries in a bloody floor-by-floor battle on July 19 the year before.[43] Now on May 3, 1937, a large unit of Spanish Republican government agents invaded the Telephone Exchange and violently expelled the anarchists. Three days of shooting in the center of the city followed. The barricades went up; this time antifascists

—

squared off against antifascists. The "tragical events of May 3–6," one anarchist wrote shortly after, had exposed the "poisoned atmosphere" settling over "the anti-fascist front."[44]

Other events poisoned "the anti-fascist front" in Spain as well. The incorporation of the unruly and democratic Antifascist Militias into a regular army under centralized governmental control didn't go over well with those faithful to the militias' egalitarian and anti-authoritarian ethos. The government's attempts to disarm the people didn't go over well with them either.[45] After the May Days, the Spanish Republic's efforts to consolidate control of the war effort led to an intensified political repression. The anarchists and the POUM wanted to press on with the revolution; the Spanish Republican government's official line, and the Comintern's, was that it was necessary to prosecute the war first. W. H. Auden, who had wandered through Barcelona in early 1937 (and who at one point was denied a travel pass from the PSUC because the "left poet," as an internal report called him, "was also getting in touch with Anarchists"), put the dilemma lyrically in his oracular poem "Spain." Auden wrote the poem right after he left the country in March, and in it he gave the impression that revolution could wait. "To-morrow, perhaps the future," he said — "But to-day the struggle."[46] It was a more beautiful phrasing than Maurice Thorez's when he had made the argument the year before that, no, not everything is possible, at least not now; tomorrow, perhaps. Still, the substance was the same. The police arrested Julián Gorkin and the other leaders of the POUM in June (long gone by this point were the days of seventeen-year-old kids with rifles maintaining revolutionary order in Barcelona). The Republican government, led by the Socialist Juan Negrín, found it convenient to blame the POUM for the May Days' street violence and promptly pronounced the party illegal.[47] The Comintern's international press went to work, accusing the POUM's leaders of "propagating an uprising against the Republic" in the service of Franco and the fascists. The idea was that the barricade warfare of the May Days had had nothing to do with any state assault on the Telephone Exchange, but rather that Gorkin had incited the anarchists into an unprovoked insurrection. And that he had done so while in the pay of the Gestapo.[48] The accusations grew more outlandish by the day. And all the while the fighting at the front went poorly. Military defeats and political deceptions added up.

—

The result was that a paradox ran through the antifascist war in Spain. The willingness — the determination — of so many thousands from all over to go and take part in the war effort gave the antifascist cause an uncommon grandeur and offered proof of the sincerity, the intensity of faith, and the moral seriousness possessed by the world's antifascists. So much so that, taken together, their sacrifices amounted to one of the great shows of human solidarity in world history. Yet the effect of the war was generally to damage the cause. The outcome of the war, of course, was decisive defeat. What's more, though, the experience of the war for the antifascist left was largely one of disillusionment and fracture. That is, the war went just about the way Weil had predicted in her 1933 essay "Réflexions sur la guerre" that an antifascist war would go.

And so in 1937 the antifascist moment came to an end. It did so not only because of what happened in Spain but because of setbacks and fiascoes for the left — the newly reimagined left — in a number of countries. Soon after a deadly street battle near Paris, in the working-class suburb of Clichy, in which antifascists squared off against the (by then outlawed) Croix de Feu, the Blum government crumbled.[49] The New Deal in the United States turned away from the left that had fueled Roosevelt's electoral triumph in 1936 and made a sharp turn to austerity politics; meanwhile, after a run of triumphant sitdowns, the industrial labor insurgency in the United States lost its momentum when local vigilante movements broke the sprawling "Little Steel" strike in the summer of 1937.[50] On July 7, the so-called "Marco Polo Bridge Incident" sparked war between China and Japan, raising the ambitions of the Japanese state. Japan's bombing of Chinese cities in September brought about a surge of transnational antifascist outrage.[51] And on November 1 an army of integralista greenshirts marched to the Brazilian presidential palace, where President Getúlio Vargas reviewed the parade; ten days later, Vargas carried out a coup and declared himself dictator of the "Estado Nôvo" (New State). Fascist Italy and Nazi Germany hailed the move.[52] Franco was moving closer to control of Spain; Japan was on the attack; Italy and Germany grew more confident by the day of their dominance in the European cockpit; and now a militaristic dictatorship had vanquished republican rule in Brazil. To speak of the right no longer meant the one side of parliamentary chambers, it meant dictatorial ambitions ("the so-called dictatorships of the right," they could now be called). Meanwhile, in 1937 in the Soviet Union (the "dictatorship of the left," as it could now be called, no doubt much to the disturbance of Lenin's ghost), the Stalin regime carried out what was later called "the Great Terror."[53] The American philosopher John Dewey chaired an international commission to challenge the Moscow show trials' claims against Leon Trotsky. Carlo Tresca was among those who took part in the inquiry.[54] The revolutionary possibilities of 1936 receded; any hopes for a left still committed to a politics of unity would have been easily disabused by even a cursory reading of the left-wing press, where rival leftist groups were denounced, often as freely and ferociously as were the fascists.

Even so, throughout 1937 more and more antifascists kept arriving in Spain ready to fight fascism. At the time, and afterwards as well, there were those who tried to diminish the volunteers' dedication to antifascism, as if they generally had been duped into going or had been ordered to go against their wills by their parties' leaders. Such skepticism of the antifascist volunteers' own determination to confront the fascists in Spain has always been unfounded. What ought to be stressed is the autonomy of the antifascists who went, as well as the depth of their commitment. As the antifascist moment dissipated antifascism meant many things, but in the end antifascism was what common people willing to fight fascism made of it. "They came of their *own free will*," Langston Hughes wrote regarding Spain, adding, "A number of them died there."[55]

Oliver Law came of his own free will. We'll do it here in Spain, he had said: stop fascism before "a great battle" becomes necessary back home, in the United States of America. Born in Texas in 1899 or 1900 and raised on a ranch, he was a teenage soldier during the Great War and then he lived in Galveston, working on a wharf, before he enlisted to rejoin the U.S. Army in 1920; he served six years in all, but in a Jim Crow army he never advanced past the rank of private first class.[56] Whether it was Mussolini's threats to invade Ethiopia that made an antifascist of him or the plight of Angelo Herndon or something else, he clearly had decided on his political commitments by August 1935, when he climbed onto that roof on the South Side of Chicago and gave his speech to the protesters marching below. He wasn't among the very first Americans to arrive in Spain for the war, but he still made part of the initial wave; his ship out of New York docked in Le Havre on January 23, 1937, and he promptly

—

Figure 8. Oliver Law in Spain. An antifascist who took part in organizing the "Hands Off Ethiopia" demonstration in Chicago in August 1935, he arrived in Spain in January 1937 and joined the Abraham Lincoln Battalion of the International Brigades. He quickly became the captain of the Tom Mooney Machine Gun Company and then the commander of the entire battalion.

made his way from there to enlist in the International Brigades (fig. 8). He probably showed up just too late to take part in the meeting at which the first American arrivals debated what to name the new (mostly) American battalion. They settled on naming it after Abraham Lincoln. It was a makeshift operation; the highest-ranking officers of the International Brigades hadn't planned on establishing an American battalion, and they treated the Americans, as one historian has put it, "as little more than adolescent dilettantes." The notorious commissar André Marty welcomed the American volunteers by telling them they were "spoiled cry babies."[57]

And yet with only the slightest of training, the new battalion was thrown into battle on February 23 and then again four days later. The Lincolns had been ordered to the valley called Jarama, just east of Madrid. In Jarama, as the Associated Press reported, "the Fascist Insurgents attacked in strength," hoping to encircle the capital city and choke it. The fighting made for a vicious

—

introduction to war. The battalion began February 27 with 263 soldiers at the ready, and ended it with about 150. The day's immediate attrition, then, worked out to a 43 percent loss. At the nearby hospital, bodies were left out in the cold, piled up in the courtyard; inside, the wounded outnumbered the beds four to one. "Group after group hopped the trenches," one of the Lincolns wrote shortly afterwards, "charging the Fascists who were only 250 meters away." But machine gunfire "created an impenetrable steel wall." Law, however, acquitted himself well. And with the battalion's officer corps shredded in its very first battle, promotions were already in order. He took command of the Tom Mooney Machine Gun Company, one of three companies in the battalion.[58] In a matter of weeks, he had been entrusted with more responsibility than in six years' service in the U.S. Army.

He faced hard days ahead in which to learn how to give orders. Many in the battalion's rank and file would never trust the brigades' command again after Jarama. There had been little reason for the assault that they had been ordered to carry out; and there had been little chance of its success. The soldiers had borne the cost. Anger and suspicion set in, and Law's promotion made him a target. This was unfair. He had fought admirably and he had more military experience than almost all of the Lincolns. The problems that began to tear at the battalion weren't Law's fault and they weren't anything he could fix. The contradiction of trench comradeship and military hierarchy is ubiquitous to modern warfare, but because the Lincolns, and the volunteers in all of the brigades' battalions, had made social equality and human freedom some of their core principles, their everyday encounters with military hierarchy, command, and discipline were especially fraught. George Orwell wrote of the challenges of building a revolutionary and democratic army over in the POUM's militia; those were challenges that stemmed from a conscious attempt to put egalitarian and social libertarian principles into practice.[59] In the International Brigades, the challenges stemmed instead from an institutional refusal to bend to such principles at all, even as many of the soldiers considered themselves part of a people's army. Many strict orders were handed down; and many strict orders went unfollowed.

Law's challenges multiplied when, in a matter of months, he became the commander of the entire battalion. Many of the challenges he faced had to do

—

with race. On the face of it, Law's rise and the devotion that many of the white soldiers expressed to him suggested a considerable collective antiracist commitment made among comrades. When a white member of the battalion told Nancy Cunard of his great love and admiration for Law, later on in 1937, she wrote that it was "typical of the fraternity that exists between the white and the Negro volunteers fighting here in Spain in the Republican lines and of course of all anti-Fascists of whatever races in America and the world over." Such an overstatement concealed a much more complicated racial dynamic at work in the battalion and, of course, among antifascists in America and the world over. But putting the battalion's racial politics in its best light was an effective way of critiquing the general politics of white supremacy that antifascists like Law and Cunard insisted was the stuff of fascism. Some Lincolns were fond of telling the story of a white visitor from the U.S. Army, the military attaché to Republican Spain, who caught sight of Law and sputtered, "Er, I see you are in a Captain's uniform?" As recounted by Eslanda Robeson, the polymathic antifascist intellectual who visited the Lincolns in 1938 and heard the story, "Law replied with dignity, 'Yes, I am, because I am a Captain.'" Law then added that he had been kept down "in your army" but "here people feel differently about race." Not all people did, though. When Law rebuked one white Lincoln, the anarchist Virgil Morris, for preferring labor duty to regular soldiering, Morris snapped, "at least in the labor company you are treated like [a] white man."[60] Even an anarchist in a communist army, fighting for a more equal world, could fall back on racial privilege when he felt cornered. Law was always being tested.

And even though the Communist Party's propagandists were intent on making a hero of him, he made mistakes just like the rest of the battalion's officers. His biggest one seems to have come early in the Brunete offensive of July 1937. This was the largest campaign that the Lincolns had been a part of since Jarama. It was an audacious attempt to seize the initiative away from the fascists: to take pressure off of Madrid and to compel Franco's forces to pull back from their advances into the north of the country. The Lincoln Battalion's first task, on July 6, was to take a village northwest of Madrid, Villanueva de la Cañada. The battalion did this, but Law seems to have fumbled his command duties somehow; it's not clear how.[61]

—

It had been a murderous battle. As the antifascists pulled out of Villanueva de la Cañada the next day, one of Law's runners, Harry Fisher of New York City, stopped to study the corpses lying along the road. They were, Fisher recalled decades later, the bodies of "mostly fascists." He "gazed at one body, a young fascist, no more than seventeen, I guessed. He seemed so young and innocent, not what a fascist was supposed to look like." Fisher looked at the other bodies. "They all looked alike, no matter which side of the road they were on." The realization sickened him. "Those on the fascist side were just youngsters," he lamented. "They hadn't been brought up to believe in hatred, bigotry, violence, or brutality, the trademarks of the fascists—they were just kids who happened to live in territory controlled by the fascists."[62] This was one of the moral problems of the war, that fighting fascism often didn't translate into fighting fascists. One didn't need to have pacifist beliefs such as Weil's to feel the weight of this.

Two days later, on the morning of July 9, Oliver Law led a charge at a place by the Guadarrama River called Mosquito Ridge. Winning the high ground along the ridge would open the path down to Brunete, due west of Madrid. The Lincolns hadn't had a meal in days and they had no water; the river had run dry. The early day's sun had made an oven of the valley, and nests of machine guns awaited them atop the ridge. As it was put in one account written soon after, "it was obvious that they were facing the heaviest sort of odds." According to those who saw the day's events unfold, Oliver Law ran out in front of his soldiers to begin the assault. There's some disagreement as to whether he, as the battalion's commanding officer, ought to have put himself in such peril. I see in the act Law's solution for his most immediate problem: how to perform the duties of a commander in an army where commands aren't always followed; how to lead when white soldiers have denigrated you. As I see it, Law had chosen to command by example, to get the others to throw themselves into enemy gunfire by leading the way. He was struck down right away. The most trustworthy account of the incident is that of the Lincoln who a short while later told Cunard how he loved Law and was devoted to him, a Canadian medic named David Smith. He said to her, "Bullets and shrapnel were flying all around us. I started to shout to him 'Don't stand up.' At that moment he was struck, hit right through the

—

middle of the body. He fell." Smith ran to Law and "picked him up and started to carry him away from the firing. He kept on saying 'Carry on, carry on, go on with the attack, carry on.'" Smith told Cunard that Law kept on speaking, repeating himself, until "his voice got fainter and fainter and stopped, and he was dead." When the gunfire came to an end, his comrades buried him nearby, with an inscription on a portion of wood: "Here lies Oliver Law, the first American Negro to command American whites in battle."[63]

Another antifascist was dead and another martyr was born.

Whatever tricks time plays, they can't match those played by mortals. Even the dead are vulnerable to the trickery of the living, and because their legacies matter so much, martyrs are the most vulnerable of all.

The living have picked at Oliver Law long after his death. In the final years of the Cold War, a writer at the *Village Voice* named Paul Berman conducted an interview with the man he considered "our American Orwell."[64] This was William Herrick, who had fought in Spain, in the Lincoln Battalion, and who later had become a committed anticommunist. In the McCarthy era he had testified against the Lincolns in a U.S. congressional committee hearing on communist subversion.[65] Since then he had become a novelist. In the interview with Berman, which appeared in the *Village Voice* in the summer of 1986, Herrick suggested among other things that Oliver Law had died on the hillside under Mosquito Ridge because his own comrades had murdered him. They were furious — Herrick said — because Law had led them — Herrick said — into an ambush on the hill as he had done — Herrick said — several times before. He added a self-contradictory accusation that Law had only become the battalion's commander because "the Party" wished to have a black man leading the Lincolns for propaganda purposes — it was, claimed Herrick, who was white, "an example of Party patronizing of blacks." But in the next breath he said that the soldier who "should have been the commander" was also black. It didn't quite make sense. Regardless, Herrick insisted that the soldiers considered Law a fool and wanted to stop him before he led them to their deaths. So they murdered him and desecrated his body.[66]

Herrick himself had only served with Law briefly. He had been in the Tom Mooney Machine Gun Company in February 1937, but he was hit by machine gunfire even before the February 23 battle at Jarama and was sent away to a frontline hospital. That was before Law was even put in charge of the company. Decades later, after Herrick made his accusations, those who had been with Law at Mosquito Ridge insisted that Herrick's accusations were false. And the simple circumstances of the incident also showed that he was wrong. There had been no ambush; the Lincolns who charged Mosquito Ridge with Law had understood very well that there were fascists waiting for them on the high ground. The whole point of their being there was to take the hill from the fascists. They even knew where the fascists were positioned; Law had diligently sent out a Canadian scouting party in advance that had done the dangerous work of surveying the hill in detail.[67] Herrick's falsehoods—complete with viciously gruesome invented details of the soldiers' supposed desecration of their fallen commander's body—added up to a contemptible violation of Oliver Law's memory.

In some ways, though, Herrick's tale was typical of the times. As the Cold War had worn on, tales of Soviet deceit and Communist treachery in the Spanish Civil War had multiplied. Julián Gorkin hinted at one such tale in his memoirs, right after his story about meeting Picelli. Though Gorkin never saw Picelli again after he disappeared up the Ramblas, he did read about him in the newspapers less than two months later, in January 1937. He read that Guido Picelli was dead. Picelli had fallen in action while heroically leading three units of the Comintern's army into battle in the defense of Madrid. It was only in reading this that Gorkin found out that, since he'd last seen him, Picelli had joined the International Brigades—under some sinister sort of duress, he was sure. "What," he asked himself, "had happened?"[68]

By the time of his death, Picelli's battalion had been incorporated into the larger Garibaldi Battalion of the Twelfth Brigade. Drawn from "all the antifascist political currents" of Italy, as one tribute to the Garibaldini put it, the battalion had begun as an independent legion organized by veteran antifascisti who hoped to inspire the people of Italy to revolt against the Mussolini regime by providing an example of antifascist resistance in Spain. Picelli became the Garibaldi Battalion's second in command. His record was a mix of dashing, devil-may-care audacity and slapdash indiscipline. After commanding one of the Garibaldini's greatest triumphs, on New Year's Day 1937 at Mirabueno

—

(northeast of Madrid, well past Guadalajara), he led a surprise assault on enemy forces atop a hill not far from there, near Algora, on January 5. Like Law six months later, Picelli himself led the charge up the hill (even though his instructions had been to not put himself in such peril). And like Law, Picelli was shot down in short order. He had advanced so far ahead that only after nightfall could his body be recovered. It was then taken to Barcelona and laid in the Hotel Colón; he received a grand funeral procession through the streets of Barcelona and his body was buried in Montjuïc Cemetery. Later, though, fascists violated his grave and disposed of his remains somewhere unknown, perhaps in an unmarked mass grave.[69] Again, the living are cruel to the dead, and to martyrs most of all.

Picelli has suffered other cruelties in death as well, lesser in degree but cruelties all the same. What Gorkin implied in his memoirs, and what other anti-communists have claimed outright, is that Picelli didn't die a hero shot down by fascists in battle. Rather, they've claimed, the Soviet secret police never forgave him for his nonconformity in Moscow and they never forgave him for his brief association with the POUM either and so they assassinated him. Picelli, some have stated as a fact, was felled by "a Stalinist bullet."[70] Even well into the twenty-first century partisans have argued over the cause of his death. As one scholar has framed the quarrel: "Had he been hit by Francoist machine guns or from behind by pro-Soviet Communists?"[71] As in the case of Law, there's no actual evidence that would suggest Communists shot Picelli from behind. The suspicions come of rumors. The Spanish Civil War gave rise to endless rumors of Stalinist betrayals. Some of the rumors are demonstrably true. Recognizing that others are baseless doesn't exonerate Stalinism or excuse the conduct of its enforcers.

What it does, rather, is open up room for an antifascist history, and a history of the left, that isn't consumed by the history of Soviet communism.[72] Picelli deserves a better telling of his death than Gorkin allowed him. An antifascist through and through, Picelli deserves to be remembered as he plainly was: one of fascism's victims, one of antifascism's heroes and martyrs. His determination to fight in Spain and the valor he displayed there increase the legacy of the Arditi del Popolo, antifascism's first army. And likewise the determination and valor of his old comrade Antonio Cieri, who died in combat, at

—

Huesca, about three months after Picelli. One memorializer wrote upon Cieri's death that "antifascism has lost a magnificent figure of revolutionary combat." Describing him as full of enthusiasm and energy, the memorializer suggested that Cieri embodied the best of "the romantic Italian tradition of anarchism," but that while he "was passionately anarchist, his passion was never sectarian; rather, he always labored so that all antifascist forces might unite in action." Like Picelli, he received a grand funeral in Barcelona. And like Picelli, he soon became, in death, the subject of rumors that he hadn't fallen in battle facing fascists but rather had been eliminated by Communists acting on behalf of the Soviet Union.[73] Like Picelli, he deserves better.

Oliver Law obviously deserves a better telling of his death than Herrick concocted for him. Herrick didn't only draw on his anticommunist imagination to depict Law's demise; he also clearly drew on an engrained sense of racial grievance to abuse his memory so freely. In one of his novels he caricatured Law as a character who "whines" all the time with "an Uncle Tom whine"; he's "blind," "dumb," "hated" by his comrades, possessed of a "panicked, frightened brain," and promoted to commander only because of what Herrick called "jimcrow upsidedown." And not only in his novels did he heap racial stereotypes upon Law. His animus was never more malicious, though, than when he graphically invented such an unbecoming demise for Law.[74]

How *should* Law be remembered? There is today little trace to be found of his specific political thought and beliefs. For Herrick, looking back from the Cold War years, Law was a symbol of Stalinism, a martyr mourned by those who remained ever Soviet apologists. However, if Law himself ever shared his thoughts on the Soviet Union, it has escaped historians' notice. It is known, though, that he spoke of democracy, racial justice, and the importance of fighting fascism. Throughout the Depression years, he had taken part in admirable causes. He had stood up against fascism and organized a large antiwar demonstration when the police had told him he couldn't. Before that, he had stood up for the poor and the unemployed, and he had endured police brutality because of it. And then later he had taken a ship across the Atlantic and had volunteered to join an army aiming to bury fascism. In such deeds one finds the substance of Oliver Law's politics, his communism as well as his antifascism. In the anticommunist fables told of the Spanish Civil War, the central drama of the war

—

appears to have been the disputes inside the antifascist coalition. Both Law's life and his death are reminders of the simple truth that antifascists went to Spain because what mattered to them most was that fascism should not pass. There were, to be sure, terrible conflicts among antifascists during the Spanish Civil War. But there were also the examples of Oliver Law and Guido Picelli, Simone Weil and Antonio Cieri, and thousands of antifascists more; antifascism was what they had made of it.

I BELONG TO THE LEFT

Let us at least learn from this brief history, beautiful dream that it was for many, nightmare that it was for a few. Dream or nightmare, there was something unreal about the year that has passed. Everything about it depended on imagination.

— SIMONE WEIL, "Méditations sur un cadavre," 1937

The most gifted of orators, Dolores Ibárruri confessed it was hard to find the words. She had to figure out how to say farewell to the International Brigades. Negotiations orchestrated in large part by Britain had produced an agreement for the withdrawal of all foreign combatants from the civil war in Spain. Juan Negrín, still the prime minister of what was left of the Republic, had told the volunteers of the International Brigades to pack up their things. His aim was, in return, to get rid of the many thousands of Nazi German and Fascist Italian troops in Franco's camp, and most of all to get rid of the Luftwaffe and the Aviazione Legionaria, which had been bombing the cities of antifascist Spain without mercy.[1]

It was late in the afternoon of October 28, 1938, and a good showing of the brigades' remaining members had marched one last time through the streets of Barcelona. They had marched with their fists up, and they had sung one final song. It was, a witness noted, "a hymn of hope and victory." Untold thousands came out to cheer for the soldiers, to mix with them a final time, and to throw flowers along the Paseo de Gracia and the Diagonal. The streets and balconies alike were packed. The parade included weary and proud volunteers from twenty-six nations. The Poles led the way; Germans marched eight abreast; English soldiers and Australian, French, and American soldiers and all the rest

—

followed behind. Pierre Mars, the correspondent for *Humanité*, exaggerated when he suggested that it was a parade of "all the continents, all the races, all the peoples," but the parade's composition was nonetheless a fitting final testament to the principle of human solidarity that had animated the brigades' mission. The great Hungarian antifascist photographer Robert Capa took some of his most iconic shots that afternoon; he had just made it to Barcelona after spending months documenting the war in China.[2] His best shots of the day captured an intermixture of sadness and joy (figs. 9 and 10). "An extraordinary vitality emits from this crowd," Mars explained to his French readers. "It could be one of our Popular Front crowds on Bastille Day," though, he added, "this

Figure 9. The great antifascist photographer Robert Capa captured some of his most iconic shots on October 28, 1938, when Barcelona bid farewell to the volunteers of the International Brigades. Here some of the assembled brigadiers raise their arms in antifascist salutes. © *Robert Capa/Magnum Photos*.

—

Figure 10. Another iconic image captured by Robert Capa during the International Brigades' final parade in Barcelona on October 28, 1938. © *Robert Capa/Magnum Photos.*

irrepressible joy, this delirious enthusiasm, surpasses anything we've experienced ourselves." It was a poignant paradox that the reason for this was likely that "here we are in a city that is suffering, a city where bombs are falling."[3]

Negrín gave a stilted speech explaining how grateful he was to have "the opportunity for the government to say, out of my mouth, what the withdrawal of these friends means at this international political moment."[4] Ibárruri, as ever, had a better feel for what the moment meant and what her audience needed to hear. "A feeling of anguish, a bottomless grief, catches my throat," she told the assembled once she found her words. "Anguish for those who now go away, soldiers of the highest ideal of human redemption, cast out of their country, persecuted by the tyranny known to all peoples. Grief for those who will remain here with us forever, moldering in the earth, though living on in the depths of our hearts, hallowed by the sentiment of our eternal gratitude."

She spoke directly to the volunteers, praising their "spirit of sacrifice," their bravery and selflessness. "You came to us from all peoples and from all races," she said, "as brothers." She invoked the familiar antifascist line about their ranks including "communists, socialists, anarchists, republicans, men of different colors, different ideologies, hostile religions," and so on. Then she gave recognition to the depth of their sacrifices. "They gave us everything," she said. She had switched from addressing the soldiers themselves to addressing everyone else in the crowd, as if to impress upon them the preciousness of the example before them. The volunteers, Ibárruri told the people of Barcelona, gave their youth and maturity, knowledge and experience, blood and life, and hopes and wishes; they had left behind their loves, their countries and homes, their fortunes, fathers, mothers, wives, brothers, sisters, and children. "And," she declared, "they asked us for nothing in return." She then clarified, adding, "Well, yes: they asked for a place in the struggle, they asked for the honor of dying for us." Overcome, she implored, "Flags of Spain! Salute these many heroes, lower yourselves before so many martyrs!"

She went on like this. Though not for long; even as inspirited as she was, she still knew the effect of keeping one's speech short. After expressing so much gratitude, she then acknowledged the deeper truth that the volunteers, as selflessly as they had carried themselves, had not come to fight for Spain alone. And, skilled speaker that she was, even this point she presented not as her own idea but rather as if the glorious example of the antifascists of the International Brigades had said it for her: "They came and said to us: 'Here we are! Your cause, Spain's cause, is our own cause, and it is the shared cause of all of advanced and progressive humanity.'" As they departed, she had a final message for them. Speaking again now to the soldiers themselves, she said, "You are history, you are legend, you are the heroic example of democracy's solidarity and universality."[5] And she sent them on their way.

So many martyrs, Ibárruri had said. The likes of Picelli, Law, Cieri. Though would Ibárruri have counted Cieri? After all, he had not been in the International Brigades. He had come to Spain with a large group of Italian antifascisti who had organized themselves in Paris; during their deliberations there, Cieri had been among those who argued most insistently that the group should not enlist in the Comintern's army but rather should join the CNT's Antifascist Militias. Cieri's side won the argument and in Spain the group formed what became known as the Italian Column of the Antifascist Militias. Later on when the Spanish Republican government introduced its scheme to place the militias under its own centralized command, the soldiers of the Italian Column resisted fiercely and Cieri became the face of their resistance. After his death, these points of contention became the subtext for the rumors that a "Stalinist bullet" had slain him.[6] Given all that, would Cieri still have counted for Ibárruri as a part of her heroic collective example of democracy's solidarity and universality? Or would he have posed an example of the limits of her rhetoric?

The politics of unity that had pulled together the antifascist left always had limits: the unity was always a project, never an accomplished fact. Ibárruri was as fiercely partisan as she was ideological. She had talked a lot about antifascist unity since the Spanish Popular Front began, but she also had done much to harm it. She always defended her party's attacks on the POUM and the anarchists of Barcelona—she placed the blame for the strife of the May Days on "anarchotrotskyist fascists." Even decades later she still insisted that certain documents "proved" that the POUM's leaders were responsible for the May Days and, what's more, that they had instigated the unrest as part of a treasonous conspiracy concocted within "the General Staff of Franco."[7] The contrast between the warm and personal universalism of Ibárruri's rhetoric and the deadly animus behind much else of her politics remains a conundrum.[8]

More her kind of martyr, no doubt, was Wilfred Mendelson, the antifascist from City College. He had been a loyal and disciplined Communist Party U.S.A. member. He had only arrived in Spain that spring, on May 29, but he

—

243

still hadn't made it to the farewell. He had died within two months of his arrival, along the Ebro. Death and martyrdom for the cause was a common fate among those who went to Spain. How many died isn't clear. Of those in the International Brigades alone, Negrín in his farewell speech suggested 5,000. Even just for the brigades that number was likely too low, perhaps considerably so.[9] The war inspired antifascists, but it delivered a lot of them to their demise as well.

It's easy to fall under the spell of disillusionment that comes of experiencing modern war. It's easy to think of the Spanish Civil War as the end of antifascist idealism and to close the book. But to do so would be to leave behind all that was generative and instructive about the antifascist cause in Spain and the era that produced it. In November 1937, when things in Spain were already not going well, the gifted Peruvian antifascist poet César Vallejo wrote a poem about the war. He began the poem with the line "At the end of the battle." At the end of the battle there lay a combatant who was both dead—already a "cadaver"—and yet also dying. First one person came along, then two more, then twenty, then 100, and 1,000, and 500,000; finally, millions gathered around the dead-and-dying combatant. They all exhorted their dead brother not to die. "But the cadaver—¡ay!—kept dying." For most of the poem, it seems to be a story about death and dying. But then, at the poem's end, in the last two lines, the cadaver slowly sits up, embraces the first person that had pleaded with him not to die, and, finally, begins to walk.[10] The poem isn't about death at all, it's about resurrection. The poem, it turns out in the end, is about a new beginning.

"I belong to the Left," George Orwell wrote in November 1945.[11] The way he meant it belonged to the age he himself had helped to make. He meant it in a sweeping, free manner, as if the left—or "the Left," if you want to capitalize it as Orwell always did—extended without limits, anywhere and everywhere. And since he then went on in his comments to include Stalinism in his idea of the left, it's safe to say that he—the one-time soldier of the POUM militia—meant "the Left" to include ideological beliefs and political organizations that were not at all his own. What had he meant? He hadn't meant the left as a voting bloc in any one country's parliament; and he hadn't meant it as a dissident faction

—

within any one party or movement. He hadn't meant it in any of the older ways that his generation had inherited. He had meant "the Left" as his generation had remade it. He had meant it as a great lumping together of different people and groups scattered all about. He had meant it as the global mass collectivity that I've argued people like him had labored to make of the left during those years when they also remade antifascism into something new and larger than what it had been before.

At the time that Orwell was writing, only three months had passed since World War II's end. Just three days before he wrote his remark, the president of the United States, Harry Truman, had proclaimed his country's thanks for "our victory, absolute and final, over German fascism and Japanese militarism." The atomic age had begun. (Only a few weeks before, an essay of Orwell's had appeared in the *Tribune*, "You and the Atom Bomb," in which Orwell had warned that nuclear weaponry threatened to subject the world to a never-ending state of existence just short of war: a "'cold war,'" he called it, coining a term.) When he declared that he belonged to the left, Orwell was writing a letter to the Duchess of Atholl. Years before, she had been a member of Parliament for the Scottish Unionist Party. She had also once served as a minister in a Conservative government. You could say that she belonged to the right (or, as Orwell would have had it, "the Right"). Orwell said as much in his letter. The duchess, though, wasn't a typical right winger. As a member of Parliament, she had gone to Spain during the civil war as an observer. The Luftwaffe's bombings had horrified her, and she wrote an antifascist book that came out in 1938, *Searchlight on Spain.* The Mosleyite fascists jeered her as the "Red Duchess" and mocked her when she lost her seat at that year's end. The fascist paper *Action* taunted that too many of her constituents were good "country people who vote Conservative," possessed of that "solid Scots commonsense," to let her ever get away with all her "warmongering on behalf of the Red sedition in Spain."[12]

Now, seven years later, the duchess had invited Orwell to speak before the League for European Freedom. Orwell, however, was on the record, in a *Tribune* piece he'd written earlier in 1945, describing her league as "dominated by the anti-Russian wing of the Tory Party." He found their ideas the worst sort of propaganda, though he'd conceded that "the Left-wing press" had long ago become just as bad: "The one is simply the other standing on its head." In the

—

Tribune article, he'd spoken of the left in the new way, as if it had come to life and become its own anthropomorphized creature, free to go wherever it pleased and do as it liked. At one point he chastised it, saying, "The Left refuses to talk in a grown-up manner," as if it, "the Left," were acting like an overgrown, petulant child prone to tantrums.[13] Which, even if he felt he belonged to it, was often how Orwell saw the left.

Perhaps his ever blunt talk of the left's failings had misled the duchess because she had written to him hopeful that he would address the league. In his reply, Orwell was blunt once more. "I cannot," he explained, "associate myself with an essentially Conservative body which claims to defend democracy in Europe but has nothing to say about British imperialism." He abhorred "the crimes now being committed in Poland, Jugoslavia etc.," but didn't want to speak on those crimes for a group that wasn't "equally insistent on ending Britain's unwanted rule in India." It was then that he explained, in closing, that he belonged to the left and "must work inside it." This was so, he added, "much as I hate Russian totalitarianism."[14]

The meaning of totalitarianism had changed a great deal since the days when the antifascisti of Italy first came up with the concept. After news broke of the Hitler-Stalin Pact in 1939, those who were repulsed by the compact had turned to the idea to explain what the Third Reich and Soviet regime had in common that had led to Stalin's betrayal of antifascists everywhere.[15] Stalin's deal with Hitler, after all, delivered yet another fierce blow to the left. Loyalists of the Comintern's parties embarrassed themselves defending it; a more common response was dismay and exit. Orwell, of course, already had an understanding of Stalinism from Spain. And yet for all his hatred of Russian totalitarianism, he didn't think that made himself any less a part of the left. I belong to the left, he'd written; part of his notion had to have been that, Russian totalitarianism notwithstanding, a part of the left still belonged to him.

The left that had been made in the antifascist moment had survived past the moment's end. And it has stuck since Orwell, too. The left has remained ever in an embattled, seemingly precarious state, but it has remained all the same. It has remained always something that belongs to the people, not to politicians, and it has remained always something that can depend on transnational solidarities to sustain it.[16] And even at those times when the left has fallen to pieces, its adherents have always had its history to affirm what the left has been and could be again. Though with that said, aside from the antifascist moment, the left has never held up a golden age of the past to look back upon and hope to return to. Such a mentality is, of course, the domain of the right. The left has, however, often looked back to recapture the emancipatory dreams and visions for the future that were held in its past. The eternal effort to recapture yesterday's dreams of tomorrow has done much to animate the left's political imagination.[17]

The left endured the harsh years of the Cold War, during which time it faced opposition not only from the right but often from liberalism as well. During the Cold War the left fought revolutionary wars that were at times liberatory and at times murderous disasters. And the left continued to oppose and protest wars of superpower policing and imperialism. The left also labored to create socially egalitarian and democratic societies, such as in Salvador Allende's Chile.[18] Through it all, leftists raised their fists in the air to express ages of political belief and commitment without saying a word. Through it all, their most constant enemy was that which they called fascism. What fascism meant, of course, changed over time and was never agreed upon at any one point, but no matter what else leftists have argued about with each other through the decades, they've agreed on their fundamental antifascism. During the Cold War years the left experienced defeat more often than not, but the defeats were by and large heroic defeats that paradoxically instilled leftists with more confidence of their eventual glory.[19] If only they kept the struggle alive. The left has given the modern political world a never-ending lesson on the meaning of struggle. That alone is a worthy gift.

Less than a year after the Berlin Wall fell in November 1989, the French socialist Max Gallo declared, "The left is dead. We all know it." It wasn't that much of the left mourned the passing of "actually existing socialism" in the Soviet bloc. Rather, leftists felt the sorrow of promise unfulfilled. Their enemies, however, could not contain their glee. A strange time followed of neoliberal triumphalism. Political struggle itself came to seem, to many, like a relic of a barbaric, totalitarian past, a sort of antisocial behavior. More than a few influential people suggested that a world without ideology was near, a new world "beyond left and right."[20]

But then the left slowly got up and began to walk again. A young, unruly, and ideologically omnivorous left confronted the institutions of neoliberalism at the century's turn. As the new century began, Porto Alegre in Brazil welcomed thousands of people from hundreds of organizations and countless countries for the first World Social Forum. Those who gathered meant their meeting as an "anti-Davos": just as LICA had scheduled its World Assemblies Against Racism and Anti-Semitism to clash with the Nazis' Nuremberg rallies in the late 1930s, the World Social Forum scheduled its annual gatherings in the 2000s to counter the meetings of the neoliberal World Economic Forum in Davos, Switzerland. Porto Alegre became the capital of the new century's left — "the global left," as it quickly became known.[21] The global left of Porto Alegre took as its primary statement of faith "Another world is possible."[22] The phrase had the spirit of Marceau Pivert in it, and it offered the perfect rejoinder to neoliberals' own profession of faith, the phrase that Margaret Thatcher often relied on to justify her aims: "There is no alternative." Slowly, the left revived.

And then a global economic collapse preceded another round of the right's radicalization. An eerie sense of affinity with the age of fascism came to hang over the political world.[23]

Right, left, fascism, and antifascism — these have all become once more words that people find worth fighting over. And now when people fight over them, they fight over what they mean in the present as well as what they meant in the past. They are worth fighting over because they have power, the power to sway people and to mobilize them. They have more power today than they had at the twentieth century's end. An understanding of their histories will shape the sorts of politics that people bring about in their names in the years to come. It won't, however, show people what those words must mean. The histories of right and left, fascism and antifascism, are histories without definitions — or perhaps it is more precise to say that they are histories with too many definitions, none of them final. If these words as used in today's political discourse all seem capricious and unsolid, it shouldn't surprise. Their meanings have always

—

been unstable and contested. There is no such thing as "what fascism was in the 1930s" or "what the antifascists were like back then." Back then, there was only restless, often pernicious, occasionally heroic and noble struggle over what to make of such words. The same is true of today. History is there to give you some ideas — it is, as Weil claimed, something to learn from, whether you see it as a beautiful dream or as a nightmare — but fascism and antifascism, right and left, they shall be what you and others make of them.

—

NOTES

PROLOGUE

Epigraph: Jacques Julliard, *Les gauches françaises: Histoire, politique et imaginaire, 1762–2012* ([Paris:] Flammarion, 2012), 17.

1. S. Galois [Simone Weil], "La vie et la grève des ouvrières métallos," *Révolution prolétarienne,* June 10, 1936, p. 4; Our Own Correspondent [Alexander Werth], "An Inside Story of the Great Paris Strikes," *Manchester Guardian,* June 2, 1936, p. 9. Simone Weil's pseudonym paid tribute to the mathematician, and romantic revolutionary, Évariste Galois.

2. Howard Whitman, "France Stops Work," *Today,* Aug. 1, 1936, p. 10; R., "Les grévistes maîtres de la rue," *Écho de Paris,* June 12, 1936, p. 1.

3. The claim of 500 deaths marked the high end of many conflicting reports. "The Barcelona Fighting," *Manchester Guardian,* July 23, 1936, p. 11; George Orwell, *Homage to Catalonia* (London: Secker and Warburg, 1938), 6; Alejandro Vitoria quoted in Ronald Fraser, *Blood of Spain: The Experience of Civil War, 1936–1939* (London: Allen Lane, 1979), 137; "¡Solidaridad, ante todo!" *Solidaridad Obrera,* Aug. 5, 1936, p. 2.

4. Simone Weil, "Journal d'Espagne," in *Écrits historiques et politiques* (Paris: Gallimard, 1960), 209.

5. Simone Weil, "Lettre à Georges Bernanos," in *Écrits historiques et politiques,* 221.

6. Weil, "Lettre à Georges Bernanos," 221.

7. "The Weather," *Chicago Tribune,* Aug. 31, 1935, p. 1; Harry Haywood, *Black Bolshevik: Autobiography of an Afro-American Communist* (Chicago: Liberator Press, 1978), 453;

Steve Nelson, *The Volunteers* (New York: Masses and Mainstream, 1953), 15–19; "Illinois Workers Urged to Write in Name of All Red Candidates on November 6," (New York) *Daily Worker,* Oct. 26, 1934, p. 3; G. Marion, "Oliver Law, Hero of Jarama Front," (New York) *Daily Worker,* April 17, 1937, p. 3. See also Joe Brandt, editor, *Black Americans in the Spanish People's War Against Fascism, 1936–1939* (New York: International Publishers, n.d.), 33–35; Danny Duncan Collum, editor, *African Americans in the Spanish Civil War: "This Ain't Ethiopia But It'll Do"* (New York: G. K. Hall, 1992), 83; Robin D. G. Kelley, "'This Ain't Ethiopia, But It'll Do': African Americans and the Spanish Civil War," in *Race Rebels: Culture, Politics, and the Black Working Class* (New York: Free Press, 1994), 123–58. An abbreviated version of Haywood's autobiography, with an excellent introduction by Gwendolyn Midlo Hall, is available as Harry Haywood, *A Black Communist in the Freedom Struggle: The Life of Harry Haywood,* ed. Gwendolyn Midlo Hall (Minneapolis: University of Minnesota Press, 2012).

8. Milton Howard, "Police Attack Chicago March," (New York) *Daily Worker,* Sept. 2, 1935, p. 2; "Police Halt Big Protest Meeting Here," *Chicago Defender,* Sept. 7, 1935, p. 2.

9. Haywood, *Black Bolshevik,* 452–57.

10. Haywood, *Black Bolshevik,* 453.

11. Collum, editor, *African Americans in the Spanish Civil War,* 83–84, 159; Marion, "Oliver Law, Hero of Jarama Front," p. 3. For a study of the historical shift to humanitarianism, see Didier Fassin, *Humanitarian Reason: A Moral History of the Present,* trans. Rachel Gomme (Berkeley: University of California Press, 2012).

12. For a classic statement on political and intellectual "convergence," see James T. Kloppenberg, *Uncertain Victory: Social Democracy and Progressivism in European and American Thought, 1870–1920* (New York: Oxford University Press, 1986), esp. 6–7.

13. It's worth making explicit that there are two separate arguments in suggesting that earlier notions of the left were "smaller and less consequential." One argument is about size and the other is about significance. It's useful to remember that just because an idea becomes larger doesn't mean that it becomes more consequential. Local concepts can outweigh global ones. Multisited histories of "global ideas," such as this book, bear an especial responsibility to recognize this. On some of the stakes behind this parsing, see Samuel Moyn, "On the Nonglobalization of Ideas," in *Global Intellectual History,* ed. Moyn and Andrew Sartori (New York: Columbia University Press, 2013), 187–204.

14. Conceptual history and the history of basic political ideologies are vast, overlapping fields. I have tried to hew in this book to the approach that the great political scientist (and historian) James C. Scott has called "radical constructionist," with special attention to how common people, most of them not socially recognized as intellectuals, shape concepts' makings and remakings. James C. Scott, *The Art of Not Being Governed: An Anarchist History of Upland Southeast Asia* (New Haven: Yale University Press, 2009), xii. For works explicitly situated as conceptual history, see Terence Ball et al., editors, *Political Innovation and*

—

Conceptual Change (Cambridge, Eng.: Cambridge University Press, 1989); Melvin Richter, "Reconstructing the History of Political Languages: Pocock, Skinner and the Geschichtliche Grundbegriffe," *History and Theory* 29, no. 1 (1990): 38–70; Michael Freeden, *Ideologies and Political Theory: A Conceptual Approach* (Oxford, Eng.: Clarendon Press, 1996); Reinhart Koselleck, *The Practice of Conceptual History: Timing History, Spacing Concepts,* trans. T. S. Presener et al. (Stanford: Stanford University Press, 2002); Martin Burke and Melvin Richter, editors, *Why Concepts Matter: Translating Social and Political Thought* (Leiden: Brill, 2012); Helena Rosenblatt, *The Lost History of Liberalism: From Ancient Rome to the Twenty-First Century* (Princeton: Princeton University Press, 2018). Classic works of scholarship outside the recognized field that are useful for thinking through how abstractions come to carry force include Benedict Anderson, *Imagined Communities: Reflections on the Origin and Spread of Nationalism* (1983; London: Verso, 2006); Daniel T. Rodgers, *Contested Truths: Keywords in American Politics since Independence* (1987; Cambridge, Mass.: Harvard University Press, 1998); Edmund S. Morgan, *Inventing the People: The Rise of Popular Sovereignty in England and America* (New York: Norton, 1988).

15. Dorothy Thompson, "Heywood Broun," *New York Herald Tribune,* Dec. 22, 1939, p. 17. See also Thompson's "Guide to Isms" in Dorothy Thompson, *Dorothy Thompson's Political Guide: A Study of American Liberalism and Its Relationship to Modern Totalitarian States* (New York: Stackpole Sons, [1938]), 11–32. Regarding Thompson's political and ideological acumen, see Nancy F. Cott, "Making and Circulating the News in an Illiberal Age," *Journal of American History* 104, no. 3 (Dec. 2017): esp. 607. Regarding Thompson's antifascism, see Nancy F. Cott, *Fighting Words: The Bold American Journalists Who Brought the World Home Between the Wars* (New York: Basic Books, 2020), 229–64.

16. See Stephanie L. Mudge, *Leftism Reinvented: Western Parties from Socialism to Neoliberalism* (Cambridge, Mass.: Harvard University Press, 2018). Mudge examines the histories of four center-left parties, in Europe and the United States, and periodizes the history of "Western leftism" by pointing to two twentieth-century "reinventions": from socialist to Keynesian (what Mudge calls "economistic"), which she dates from the 1920s to the 1960s, and then from Keynesian to "neoliberalized leftism," which she dates from the 1960s to the 1990s.

17. On history as storytelling and on the value of stories (and in particular on the value of absorbing multiple, even incongruous and oppugnant stories), see William Cronon, "A Place for Stories: Nature, History, and Narrative," *Journal of American History* 78, no. 4 (March 1992): 1347–76; Cronon, "On Totalization and Turgidity," *Antipode* 26, no. 2 (April 1994): 166–76; Cronon, "Storytelling," *American Historical Review* 118, no. 1 (Feb. 2013): 1–19.

18. And yet 1789 is not the oldest date of origin that scholars have suggested for the left. Eric Hobsbawm suggests that "the ideological basis that inspires all the manifestations of the Left" derives from the mid-seventeenth-century English revolution. Eric Hobsbawm, *On the Edge of the New Century,* trans. Allan Cameron (New York: New Press, 2000), 96. R. R. Palmer has framed "the European Left" as intact since some time before the French Revolution, arguing that the French Revolution actually marked the beginning of a divergence between "the European Left and America," leading as well to a divergence "of the European Left, or in fact the Left throughout the world, from the original ideas of the American Revolution." R. R. Palmer, "The Fading Dream: How European Revolutionaries Have Seen the American Revolution," in *The Walter Prescott Webb Memorial Lectures: Essays on Modern European Revolutionary History,* ed. Bede K. Lackner and Kenneth Roy Philip (Austin: University of Texas Press, 1977), 96–97 (quotations).

On the spatial metaphors of left and right, see J. A. Laponce, *Left and Right: The Topography of Perception* (Toronto: University of Toronto Press, 1981); Norberto Bobbio, *Left and Right: The Significance of a Political Distinction,* trans. Allan Cameron (Cambridge, Eng.: Polity Press, 1996).

19. Marcel Gauchet, "La droite et la gauche," in *Les lieux de mémoire, III: Les France,* vol. 1: *Conflits et partages,* ed. Pierre Nora (Paris: Gallimard, 1992), 394–467. See also Julliard, *Gauches françaises,* 127–209.

The chamber where the assembly met at Versailles was the hall of the Menus Plaisirs. The hall, which stood as its own distinct structure, was auctioned off in 1799 (separately from the rest of the complex) to "an individual named Dubusq," who soon demolished it and sold the materials; the remains fell into neglect, and by the revolution's centennial it could be reported, "Of the hall itself, there is nothing left." See "La salle des Menus-Plaisirs," *Monde illustré,* May 11, 1889, p. 318 (quotations); Armand Brette, *Histoire des édifices où ont siégé les assemblées parlementaires de la Révolution française et de la première République* (Paris: Imprimerie nationale, 1902), 314–15.

20. Louis-Henri-Charles de Gauville, *Journal du baron de Gauville, député de l'ordre de la noblesse aux États généraux, depuis le 4 mars 1789 jusqu'au 1er juillet 1790* (Paris: Imprimerie de Ad. Lainé et J. Havard, 1864), 20. For an argument to the contrary, that the aristocracy and the church "elected to sit to the right," see Donald Sassoon, *One Hundred Years of Socialism: The West European Left in the Twentieth Century* (London: Tauris, 1996), xxxv.

On the declaration, see Étienne Balibar, "The Proposition of Equaliberty," in *Equaliberty: Political Essays,* trans. James Ingram (Durham: Duke University Press, 2014), 35–65; Florence Gauthier, *Triomphe et mort de la révolution des droits de l'homme et du citoyen (1789–1795–1802)* (1992; Paris: Syllepse, 2014). For a sense of the significance that has been attached to the declaration, to the point of mythologizing it, see, for example, F. M. van Asbeck, *The Universal Declaration of Human Rights and Its Predecessors (1679–1948)* (Leiden: Brill, 1949); E. H. Carr, "The Rights of Man," in *Human Rights: Comments and Interpretations,* ed. UNESCO (New York: Columbia University Press, 1949), 19–23. See also Lynn Hunt, *Inventing Human Rights: A History* (New York: Norton, 2007).

—

On the assembly, see Timothy Tackett, *Becoming a Revolutionary: The Deputies of the French National Assembly and the Emergence of a Revolutionary Culture (1789–1790)* (University Park: Pennsylvania State University Press, 1996). See also Keith Michael Baker, "Fixing the French Constitution," in *Inventing the French Revolution: Essays on French Political Culture in the Eighteenth Century* (Cambridge, Eng.: Cambridge University Press, 1990), 252–305. On the assembly's ensuing seating arrangement—the likes of the priest Jean-Sifrein Maury to the right, Maximilien Robespierre to the left—once it moved in autumn to the Salle du Manège by the Tuileries garden in Paris, see Albert Soboul, *The French Revolution, 1787–1799,* vol. 1: *From the Storming of the Bastille to the Fall of the Girondins,* trans. Alan Forrest (London: NLB, 1974), 163–66.

21. The memory of the Constituent Assembly's seating and the concepts of the left and the right are discussed in Darrin M. McMahon, *Enemies of the Enlightenment: The French Counter-Enlightenment and the Making of Modernity* (Oxford, Eng.: Oxford University Press, 2001), 13.

Political theorists in particular have stressed continuity in the history of the left since the French Revolution; they also have sought to identify the left's essential values. See Leszek Kołakowski, "The Concept of the Left," in *Toward a Marxist Humanism: Essays on the Left Today,* trans. Jane Zielonko Peel (New York: Grove Press, 1968), 67–83; David Selbourne, "The Light That Failed, Again," *Times Literary Supplement,* May 10, 1991, pp. 7–8; John Keane, "What's Left of What's Left," *Times Literary Supplement,* June 21, 1991, pp. 7–8; Steven Lukes, "What Is Left?" *Times Literary Supplement,* March 27, 1992, p. 10. See also Steven Lukes, "The Grand Dichotomy of the Twentieth Century," in *The Cambridge History of Twentieth-Century Political Thought,* ed. Terence Ball and Richard Bellamy (Cambridge, Eng.: Cambridge University Press, 2003). For a fascinating study of what "the left" meant in French political culture just before the changes I trace here, see E. Beau de Loménie, *Qu'appelez-vous droite et gauche?* (Paris: Librairie du Dauphin, 1931).

22. For a similar construction of the left as a Durkheimian "représentation collective," see Lukes, "Grand Dichotomy of the Twentieth Century," 608.

23. Examples of nineteenth-century references to national, parliament-bound lefts include (Turin) *Gazzetta Piemontese,* Aug. 19, 1867, p. 1; "France.—Intended Assassination of the Empress Eugenie," (Colombo) *Overland Ceylon Observer,* May 3, 1870, p. 154; "The Crisis in France," *Saturday Review,* May 19, 1877, p. 596; "Italian Affairs," *New York Times,* Dec. 26, 1879, p. 4; Emilio Castelar, *Discursos parlamentarios y políticos de Emilio Castelar en la restauración,* vol. 4 (Madrid: Librerías de A. de San Martín, [1885?]), 173–220, 272; "The Norwegian Elections," *Minneapolis Tribune,* Nov. 27, 1894, p. 1; "Au Reichstag," (Bône) *Gazette algérienne,* May 22, 1897, p. 1.

Consider one explanation from 1877: "The *Journal of Commerce* explains briefly and with much clearness what is meant by the often recurring designation 'Right' and 'Left,'

'Right Centre' and 'Left Centre' as applied to the French Chamber of Deputies, as follows: 'The Right of the French Chamber is composed of Bonapartists, Legitimists and Orleanists, the first being in the majority of this side. The Left consists of Republicans. The Right Centre is composed of Moderate Monarchists and the Left Centre is composed of Republicans. That is the moderate men compose the Centre the right of which are at heart Monarchists and the left of which are at heart Republicans.'" *Philadelphia Inquirer,* Dec. 13, 1877, p. 3. To a certain extent, then, it follows that if one wishes to find the nineteenth-century lefts in their contemporary texts, one ought to look first of all in parliamentary records. How did each of the various lefts of the nineteenth century constitute themselves? It could be said that, as with the original left in the hall of the Menus Plaisirs at Versailles, the moments when individual deputies most decisively drew themselves together into collectivities recognized as lefts during the nineteenth century were those instances when they collectively applauded, cheered, muttered, and heckled in chamber. Consider, for example, the situation in Italian parliamentary records where the text of a Milanese deputy's rousing speech in 1848 does not include any mention of the left in the speech itself but its text does nonetheless end with the comment, italicized and in parentheses: "*(Bene! Approvazione alla sinistra.)*" *Atti del parlamento subalpino: Discussioni della camera dei deputati, sessione del 1848,* part 2: *Secondo periodo dal 16 ottobre al 28 dicembre 1848* (n.p., n.d.), 506.

24. "Francia," *Estrella de Panama,* Feb. 12, 1880, p. 5; "The Italian Elections," *Nation,* Dec. 8, 1892, p. 427; "The French Political Crisis," *Scotsman,* Dec. 13, 1877, p. 5; "Francia," (Cochabamba) *Heraldo,* Aug. 29, 1887, p. 3; "Latest Telegraphic News (By Reuter's Company)," *Allahabad Pioneer,* April 23, 1870, p. 1; "Havas Telegrams," (Cairo) *Egyptian Gazette,* May 15, 1893, p. 2.

Similarly, one could be in Mexico City in the nineteenth century and read of the "derechas" (those on the right, or "rightists," to use a word that never caught on much in English), but it would be in reference to Léon Gambetta's adversaries in France. "Noticias varias," *Monitor republicano,* Jan. 12, 1882, p. 2. For a discussion of the term, see the excellent comparative history Sandra McGee Deutsch, *Las Derechas: The Extreme Right in Argentina, Brazil, and Chile, 1890–1939* (Stanford: Stanford University Press, 1999), 4.

25. On historicizing universals: Judith Butler, Ernesto Laclau, and Slavoj Žižek argue that "universality is not a static presumption, not an a priori given," but rather, they insist, political ideas come to seem universal to people because of political labors. Judith Butler, Ernesto Laclau, and Slavoj Žižek, *Contingency, Hegemony, Universality* (London: Verso, 2000), 3. On universals and particularisms, see Anna Lowenhaupt Tsing, *Friction: An Ethnography of Global Connection* (Princeton: Princeton University Press, 2005), esp. 1–18. See also Sugata Bose, "Different Universalisms, Colorful Cosmopolitanisms: The Global Imagination of the Colonized," in *Cosmopolitan Thought Zones: South Asia and the Global Circulation of Ideas,* ed. Bose and Kris Manjapra (Basingstoke: Palgrave Macmillan, 2010), 97–111; Étienne Balibar, *On Universals: Constructing and Deconstructing Community,* trans. Joshua David Jordan (New York: Fordham University Press, 2020).

26. E. J. Hobsbawm, *The Age of Capital, 1848–1875* (London: Weidenfeld and Nicolson, 1975), 2; Geoffrey Eley, *Forging Democracy: The History of the Left in Europe, 1850–2000* (Oxford, Eng.: Oxford University Press, 2002), 31. In discussing nineteenth-century history, scholars often have suggested that there was an already-intact European left, already functioning as a continent-wide continuum. For a classic example, see David Caute, *The Left in Europe since 1789* (New York: McGraw-Hill, 1966).

My intent, to be clear, is not to wag a finger at historians who have portrayed the left as a long-enduring political tradition that already worked as a sprawling international or transnational combination before people learned to talk about "the left" in this manner. My aim, rather, is to flag where historians have done this, so that we can recognize it as an interpretive move when we see it. The value of taking conceptual terms from one's own era and applying it to previous ones—moving particular formulations of ideas out of their own historical homes and moving them around through time and space—is undoubtedly greater when writer and reader both understand that this is what is happening. The lesson is rather lost if it's assumed that nineteenth-century political actors did indeed imagine there to be such things as a European left or a universalized left. The lesson is also lost, I'd add, if the eventual act of imagining some general left—a global left, or a European left, or any sort of international or transnational left—into existence is thought of as a discovery of how it has always been rather than an invention of something new. The importance of this distinction is well put regarding the history of human rights in Samuel Moyn, *The Last Utopia: Human Rights in History* (Cambridge, Mass.: Belknap, 2010).

27. For a noteworthy work that interprets nineteenth-century abolitionists, revolutionists, utopians, and the like as the left, see Michael Kazin, *American Dreamers: How the Left Changed a Nation* (New York: Knopf, 2011). For the nineteenth-century United States, Kazin uses the idea of the left as a heuristic device. He points out that "'left' did not come into general use in the United States until the 1930s," but he finds the term useful for the pre-1930s United States nonetheless because "the egalitarian dreamers who form an unbroken chain from the 1820s to the present need a common name." However, he goes on to justify his heuristic device by making a suspect historical claim about the contemporaries of his pre-1930s American egalitarians: "'Left' is what their counterparts in other nations would call themselves" (p. xiv).

28. One way of understanding how nineteenth-century political actors thought about the left is to say that it decidedly wasn't how they thought about communism, socialism, and internationalism—those of them that thought about such things. That is, not only did nineteenth-century actors generally think of the left as a group set apart from the internationalists, communists, and socialists, they also thought of the left as occupying a different

—

sort of political space. Actually, they weren't inclined to think of internationalism, communism, and socialism as political questions so much as to think of them as social questions. And they imagined their collectivities—the internationalists, the communists, the socialists—as movements that easily sprawled transnationally across borders. For example, in 1871, Osborne Warde, "a workingman," spoke at the corner of the Bowery and Bleecker streets in New York and defined "the subject of Internationalism to be the fraternizing of all mankind on a labor basis." Warde went on to explain that "Communism would necessarily be an outgrowth of the fundamental principles advanced by the Internationals." At the meeting there was talk that "in the United States Communism could be established" and that communism could grow beyond borders by the "fraternizing of all mankind." "The Internationals," *Republican Banner,* Oct. 3, 1871, p. 3.

The left, by contrast, existed nowhere it was not part of the national parliamentary political culture. A socialist in Germany who migrated to Wisconsin was still a socialist. A leftist in France (a member of the left in the French chamber of deputies) was only a leftist in the specific context of that chamber. If he were to leave the French parliament behind and go to Wisconsin, he left the left behind as well. Even if he stayed in Paris, he wouldn't have been a leftist anymore once he'd left the left bloc in parliament.

29. "Prussia," *New-York Tribune,* May 5, 1856, p. 4. On Karl Marx's work for the *Tribune,* see Gareth Stedman Jones, *Karl Marx: Greatness and Illusion* (Cambridge, Mass.: Belknap, 2016), 344–63. Greeley's *Tribune* later merged with the *New York Herald* to yield the *New York Herald-Tribune* for which Dorothy Thompson wrote. On 1848 in the German states, see Jonathan Sperber, *Rhineland Radicals: The Democratic Movement and the Revolution of 1848–1849* (Princeton: Princeton University Press, 1991).

30. See Raymond Carr, *Modern Spain, 1875–1980* (1980; Oxford, Eng.: Oxford University Press, 2001), 74. For examples of the "famoso bloque de las izquierdas," see "Moret y Azcárate," (Barcelona) *Vanguardia,* Dec. 5, 1911, p. 7; [Manuel] García Prieto, "Los liberales democratas," (Madrid) *ABC,* Feb. 20, 1914, p. 8. Even in 1908, Emilio Sánchez Pastor, himself a proud old liberal, had grumbled when the liberal and republican parties first aligned with each other that not everyone who spoke of the Bloc of the Left knew "what they mean by that last word, not even in the figurative sense of it." A librettist as well as a liberal, Sánchez Pastor added, "The word"—left, *izquierda*—"sounds pleasant to many an ear and is being spoken because it has such a nice ring to it and not because anyone knows with scientific certainty what the word conveys or what ideas it contains within." Emilio Sánchez Pastor, "La vida política," (Barcelona) *Vanguardia,* Sept. 17, 1908, p. 4.

31. For an example of how distinctly set apart parliamentary concerns of the left were from discussions of the revolutionary strike and the social struggle, see "Y ahora, todos a luchar," *Socialista,* Oct. 23, 1917, p. 1. On the initial Spanish reception of the Russian Revolution, see Arturo Zoffmann Rodriguez, "An Uncanny Honeymoon: Spanish Anarchism and

—

the Bolshevik Dictatorship of the Proletariat, 1917–22," *International Labor and Working-Class History* 94 (Fall 2018): 5–26. See also Angel Pestaña, *Setenta días en Rusia: Lo que yo ví* (Barcelona: Tipografía Cosmos, 1924). On the strategic silence of the Spanish socialist party, the Partido Socialista Obrero Español (PSOE), regarding the Russian Revolution, see Chris Ealham, "An Impossible Unity: Revolution, Reform and Counter-Revolution and the Spanish Left, 1917–23," in *The Agony of Spanish Liberalism: From Revolution to Dictatorship, 1913–23*, ed. Francisco J. Romero Salvadó and Angel Smith (Houndsmills, Basingstoke, Hampshire: Palgrave Macmillan, 2010), 95.

32. On the violent events at the Cárcel Modelo, see "Graves sucesos en la cárcel," (Madrid) *ABC*, Aug. 17, 1917, pp. 10–11; "El orden publico," (Madrid) *ABC*, Aug. 19, 1917, p. 13; *Los Sucesos de Agosto ante el Parlamento* (Madrid: Tipografía Artística, 1918), 224–26; Gerald H. Meaker, *The Revolutionary Left in Spain, 1914–1923* (Stanford: Stanford University Press, 1974), 87. On the revolution of 1917, see, aside from Meaker's account, Francisco Largo Caballero, *Mis recuerdos: Cartas a un amigo* (Mexico, D. F.: Ediciones "Alianza," 1954), 51–64; Juan Antonio Lacomba Avellan, *La crisis española de 1917* (Madrid: Editorial Ciencia Nueva, 1970); Francisco J. Romero Salvadó, *The Foundations of Civil War: Revolution, Social Conflict and Reaction in Liberal Spain, 1916–1923* (New York: Routledge, 2008), 67–92.

33. "La huelga revolucionaria en Madrid," *Blanco y Negro*, Aug. 19, 1917, p. 19.

34. On the "revolutionary left" of World War I–era Spain, see Lacomba, *Crisis española de 1917*, 38–40. Looking back at the Spain of 1917, Lacomba sees a "petit bourgeois left," composed of the republican and socialist parties, on the one hand, and a "revolutionary left," primarily composed of revolutionary anarchists and labor socialists (socialists engaged in the big socialist labor union, the Unión General de Trabajadores, or UGT, more so than those socialists focused on party politics), on the other hand. Lacomba lays out very lucidly the 1917 political landscape as he sees it, explaining that in the early twentieth century "the groups that during the second half of the nineteenth century had been the left (the republicans and antimonarchists) were now in the center, their place [on the left] taken by socialism and anarchism." Lacomba certainly captures the dynamism of the political situation and describes well the growing power of socialists and anarchists. And there is no doubt that it is eminently reasonable to conceptualize anarchists and labor socialists retrospectively as part of the left, and a revolutionary part if it at that. The distinction that I think is worth making, however, is that in 1917 people in Spain themselves saw their political landscape in terms different from Lacomba's: in 1917, Spanish socialists still saw "the left" as concerning party politics — "electoral concerns" — for the socialists and their republican allies; and they still saw the anarchists as operating outside the world of politics. Why is this distinction worth making? Throughout this book, I argue that the now commonplace idea of the left as an immense collectivity was a political accomplishment, made by the labors of historical actors in a particular historical moment. Recognizing how they made the left into something politically more potent than what it had been is valuable for understanding how politics works in the modern world, and it is valuable for thinking about how to create new collectivities. Recognizing how people created a new sort of left at a certain point in the past — recognizing that they had to create it — requires recognizing that, earlier on, people did not have a concept of "the revolutionary left" available to them as a political resource; such an idea of the left had to be imagined and worked into being. Other historiographical formulations of a World War I–era Spanish "revolutionary left," following Lacomba, include Meaker, *Revolutionary Left in Spain;* Ealham, "Impossible Unity."

35. Oscar Pérez Solís, *El partido socialista y la acción de las izquierdas* (Valladolid: Viuda de Montero, n.d. [1918]), 21. On Pérez Solís's quicksilver political thought, see Meaker, *Revolutionary Left in Spain,* 199–206.

36. Antonio Bar, *La CNT en los años rojos (Del sindicalismo revolucionario al anarcosindicalismo, 1910–1926)* (Madrid: Akal, 1981), 111; Pierre Broué and Emile Témime, *The Revolution and the Civil War in Spain,* trans. Tony White (1970; Chicago: Haymarket, 2008), 76. Even in the 1933 elections, Benito Pabón, a lawyer for the CNT, advocated "absolute abstention." In 1936, Pabón himself ran and won a parliamentary seat. Julián Casanova, *The Spanish Republic and Civil War,* trans. Martin Douch (Cambridge, Eng.: Cambridge University Press, 2010), 91–92.

On labor radicalism in Spain, see Manuel Tuñón de Lara, *El movimiento obrero en la historia de España* (Madrid: Taurus, 1972); Benjamin Martin, *The Agony of Modernization: Labor and Industrialization in Spain* (Ithaca: IRL Press, 1990). On the CNT, see Bar, *CNT en los años rojos.* See also Carlos Forcadell, *Parlamentarismo y bolchevización: El movimiento obrero español, 1914–1918* (Barcelona: Crítica, 1978); Julián Casanova, "Terror and Violence: The Dark Face of Spanish Anarchism," *International Labor and Working-Class History,* no. 67 (Spring 2005): 79–99.

37. "The 'Left Wing' Is Clipped," *New-York Tribune,* June 8, 1919, part 9, p. 1; Ettore Cinnella, "The Tragedy of the Russian Revolution: Promise and Default of the Left Socialist Revolutionaries in 1918," *Cahiers du Monde russe* 38, nos. 1/2 (Jan. 1997): 45–82; R. Kowalski, "'Fellow Travellers' or Revolutionary Dreamers? The Left Social Revolutionaries After 1917," *Revolutionary Russia* 11, no. 2 (Dec. 1998): 1–31.

38. N. Lenin, *The Infantile Sickness of "Leftism" in Communism* (Moscow: Executive Committee of the Communist International, 1920), 55; Edward Hallett Carr, *The Bolshevik Revolution, 1917–1923,* vol. 3 (New York: Macmillan, 1953), 177–78; Sassoon, *One Hundred Years,* 33; John Riddell, editor, *Founding the Communist International: Proceedings and Documents of the First Congress, March 1919* (New York: Anchor, 1987); Nicolai Lenin, *"Left" Communism: An Infantile Disorder* (n.p.: The Toiler, n.d. [1921?]), 54; Jane Degras, editor, *The Communist International, 1919–1943: Documents,* vol. 1 (London: Oxford University Press, 1956), 133–34. See also Vladimir Oulianoff (Lenin), *The Chief Task of Our Times, and The Political Forces and Currents Facing the Russian Revolution* (London: Workers' Socialist Federation, n.d. [1918?]), 7–14.

For a contrasting interpretation of Lenin's views, see Robert Service, *Lenin: A Biography* (Cambridge, Mass.: Harvard University Press, 2000), esp. 410–11. Service interprets Lenin as having sought to use the Second Congress to claim for himself and the Bolsheviks global leadership of, specifically, "far-left" socialism.

Eric Hobsbawm writes of the Second Congress, "It was in 1920 that the Bolsheviks committed themselves to what in retrospect seems a major error," because in making the Communist International into such a stringently disciplinary mechanism, they divided the international labor movement. Eric Hobsbawm, *Age of Extremes: The Short Twentieth Century, 1914–1991* (London: Michael Joseph, 1994), 69. Sassoon, interestingly, takes up Hobsbawm's argument regarding the Second Congress and goes further, arguing that the Communist International itself "was a major political error." Sassoon, *One Hundred Years,* 32.

The pamphlet, which Lenin wrote as an opening salvo of his offensive to consolidate control of the Communist International at the Second Congress, appeared in Russian in June 1920 and in English, German, and French in the following month. Stephen Kotkin, *Stalin,* vol. 1: *Paradoxes of Power, 1878–1928* (New York: Penguin, 2014), 364. The original English translation was done by Mikhail Borodin. E. Sylvia Pankhurst, "Soviet Russia as I Saw It in 1920," *Workers' Dreadnought,* April 16, 1921, p. 5. Borodin later self-criticized: "I wanted very much to translate Lenin's text word for word and, of course, my clumsy, literal translation didn't come off well at all. It sounded heavy and even difficult to understand in English." Quoted in Vera Vladimirovna Vishnyakova-Akimova, *Two Years in Revolutionary China, 1925–1927,* trans. Steven I. Levine (Cambridge, Mass.: Harvard University Press, 1971), 156. The Toiler translation—with "disorder" instead of "sickness" in the title—was likely published in New York the year after the publication of *Infantile Sickness.* Later translations were published under a variety of titles; see for example V. I. Lenin, *"Left-Wing" Communism: An Infantile Disorder: An Attempt at a Popular Discussion on Marxist Strategy and Tactics* (New York: International Publishers, 1934).

Earlier in life, Lenin once belonged to a left: "the Zimmerwald Left," a communist faction, at a peace conference in 1915. See Nicholai Lenin, *The Proletarian Revolution and Kautsky the Renegade* (n.p.: Contemporary Publishing Association, 1920). See also R. Craig Nation, *War on War: Lenin, the Zimmerwald Left, and the Origins of Communist Internationalism* (Durham: Duke University Press, 1989).

39. "To name a period—the 'depression,' the 'thirties,' the 'New Deal,' the 'age of Roosevelt,' 'modernism,' the 'streamlined years,' the 'age of the CIO'—is already to argue about it." Michael Denning, *The Cultural Front: The Laboring of American Culture in the Twentieth Century* (London: Verso, 1997), 21. The historian Walter Laqueur depicts an "age of fascism" (ending in 1945) in "Fascism in the Twenty-First Century?" *Society* 44, no. 4 (May 2007): 52. The historian Ernst Nolte writes of "die Epoche der Weltkriege" as also "die Epoche des Faschismus," in *Der Faschismus in seiner Epoche: Die Action française, Der italienische Faschismus, Der Nationalsozialismus* (Munich: R. Piper & Coverlag, 1963), 31; these phrases are translated as "the era of the world wars" and "the era of fascism" in Nolte, *Three Faces of Fascism: Action Française, Italian Fascism, National Socialism,* trans. Leila Vennewitz (New York: Holt, Rinehart and Winston, 1966), 9. See also Hugh Seton-Watson, "The Age of Fascism and Its Legacy," in *International Fascism: New Thoughts and New Approaches,* ed. George L. Mosse (London: Sage, 1979), esp. 369; Zeev Sternhell, *Neither Right nor Left: Fascist Ideology in France,* trans. David Maisel (Berkeley: University of California Press, 1986), 28; Cláudia Ninhos, "The Estado Novo and Portuguese-German Relations in the Age of Fascism," in *Fascism Without Borders: Transnational Connections and Cooperation Between Movements and Regimes in Europe from 1918 to 1945,* ed. Arnd Bauerkämper and Grzegorz Rossoliński-Liebe (New York: Berghahn, 2017), 142-67.

40. *Opera Omnia di Benito Mussolini,* vol. 18: *Dalla conferenza di Cannes alla marcia su Roma (14 gennaio 1922-30 ottobre 1922),* ed. Edoardo and Duilio Susmel (Florence: La Fenice, 1955), 434. On the March on Rome, see Adrian Lyttelton, *The Seizure of Power: Fascism in Italy 1919-1929,* third edition (London: Routledge, 2004), 77-93; Giulia Albanese, *March on Rome: Violence and the Rise of Fascism,* trans. Sergio Knipe (London: Routledge, 2019). For a pithy explanation of Fascist myth-making propaganda about the March on Rome, cautioning against the idea of power "seizure," see Robert O. Paxton, *The Anatomy of Fascism* (New York: Knopf, 2004), 87-91. Albanese's book, however, serves as an excellent revisionist counterpoint, reinfusing the March on Rome with epoch-making power.

On the exceptional role of violence in fascist politics, see Federico Finchelstein, *From Fascism to Populism in History* (Oakland: University of California Press, 2017), 73-81. See also Simonetta Falasca-Zamponi, *Fascist Spectacle: The Aesthetics of Power in Mussolini's Italy* (Berkeley: University of California Press, 1997), 15-41; Enzo Traverso, *Fire and Blood: The European Civil War, 1914-1945,* trans. David Fernbach (London: Verso, 2016), 168-218.

41. The historian Leo Ribuffo is credited with coining the term "brown scare" in Gary Alan Fine and Terence McDonnell, "Erasing the Brown Scare: Referential Afterlife and the Power of Memory Templates," *Social Problems* 54, no. 2 (2007): 174. Fine and McDonnell point to Leo P. Ribuffo, *The Old Christian Right: The Protestant Far Right from the Great Depression to the Cold War* (Philadelphia: Temple University Press, 1983). Ribuffo also used the phrase in his dissertation "Protestants on the Right: William Dudley Pelley, Gerald B. Winrod, and Gerald L. K. Smith" (Ph.D. diss., Yale University, 1976), 125-59, 777-98. In contrast, the idea of a "red scare" was part of interwar political thought. See (not only because it includes the phrase "red scare") "Says Fake 'Anarchists' Seek Free Ride Home," *Indiana Evening Gazette,* Dec. 1, 1919, p. 4; see also "Newspapers Fool the Public and Cater to 'Big Business,'" (Des Moines) *Iowa Homestead,* May 20, 1920, p. 3; "Another 'Red' Scare

—

in America," *Manchester Guardian,* Jan. 15, 1921, p. 9; "Survey of Vernacular Press Proves Red Scare Unfounded," *Christian Science Monitor,* Aug. 18, 1923, p. 4.

42. Deutsch, *Derechas,* 218; Fabio Grobart, "The Cuban Working Class Movement from 1925 to 1933," *Science and Society* 39, no. 1 (Spring 1975): 73–103; Samuel Farber, *Revolution and Reaction in Cuba, 1933–1960: A Political Sociology from Machado to Castro* (Middletown: Wesleyan University Press, 1976), 52–59; Ariel Mae Lambe, *No Barrier Can Contain It: Cuban Antifascism and the Spanish Civil War* (Chapel Hill: University of North Carolina Press, 2019), 40–41; "Black Legion Rises as 1936 Ku-Klux Klan," *New York Herald Tribune,* May 31, 1936, sec. B, p. 1; George Morris, *The Black Legion Rides* (New York: Workers Library Publishers, 1936); Henry Kraus, *The Many and the Few: A Chronicle of the Dynamo Auto Workers* (Urbana: University of Illinois Press, 1985), 35–37; "$250,000 for Head. Alleged Offer by Chinese Blue Shirts," *South China Morning Post,* Sept. 7, 1933, p. 15; Maggie Clinton, *Revolutionary Nativism: Fascism and Culture in China, 1925–1937* (Durham: Duke University Press, 2017); "Notes from Syria and Lebanon," *Palestine Post,* Oct. 11, 1936, p. 5; "S. African Fascists Seek New Ways to Regulate the Natives," *Afro-American,* May 26, 1934, p. 4; "South African K. K. K. Arm Against Native and Jew," *Afro-American,* July 7, 1934, p. 5; African XYZ, "Afro Readers Say," *Afro-American,* Aug. 18, 1934, p. 4; Thomas E. Skidmore, *Politics in Brazil: 1930–1964: An Experiment in Democracy* (New York, 1967), 21, 26; Robert M. Levine, "The Vargas Regime and the Politics of Extremism in Brazil, 1934–1938" (Ph.D. diss., Princeton University, 1967), 120, 122.

43. See Traverso, *Fire and Blood,* 1–19.

The historiographical understandings of the era have been shaped considerably by the ideological passions of the Cold War. The classic pairing in the literature is Hobsbawm, *Age of Extremes;* and François Furet, *Le passé d'une illusion: Essai sur l'idée communiste au xxe siècle* (Paris: Robert Laffont, 1995). Both Furet's book and Hobsbawm's book appeared in the aftermath of the Cold War. Furet's work came to represent a certain liberal triumphalism for the age of neoliberalism—a declaration that liberalism, individualism, and the market had won the twentieth century—whereas Hobsbawm's became interpreted as an elegiac lament of the century's losers: the left, communism, and collectivist visions of human life. Since the Great Recession and the collapse of neoliberalism, scholars have grown bolder in their critiques of Furet. For an excellent collection of anti-Furetist scholarship on antifascism, with glimpses of what a post-Furetist literature might look like, see Hugo García, Mercedes Yusta, Xavier Tabet, and Cristina Clímaco, editors, *Rethinking Antifascism: History, Memory and Politics, 1922 to the Present* (New York: Berghahn, 2016). Also significant are Annie Kriegel, "Sur l'antifascisme," *Commentaire,* no. 50 (Summer 1990): 299–302; Maurice Agulhon, "Faut-il réviser l'histoire de l'antifascisme?" *Monde diplomatique,* June 1994, pp. 16–17. For incisive discussions of Hobsbawm, Furet, and the historiography of antifascism, see Hugo García, "Presente y futuro de una ilusión: La historiografía sobre el antifascismo desde Furet, 1996–2015," *Ayer* 100, no. 4 (2015): 233–47.

—

44. The claim, to be clear, is relative – relative to the abundance of studies of fascism or liberalism or socialism or communism or conservatism, studies of antifascism remain few. On twentieth-century political historiography's fascination with fascism, and its comparative neglect of antifascism, see the introductory remarks in the recent comparative history of World War II–era antifascism, Michael Seidman, *Transatlantic Antifascisms: From the Spanish Civil War to the End of World War II* (Cambridge, Eng.: Cambridge University Press, 2018), 1. Elsewhere, Seidman points out that this imbalance of attention is all the more remarkable given that, he argues, "fascism was a failure, and antifascism a success." Michael Seidman, "Was the French Popular Front Antifascist?" in *Rethinking Antifascism,* ed. Garcia et al., 43.

Excellent recent antifascist scholarship includes Seidman's work as well as Ricardo Pasolini, *Los marxistas liberales: Antifascismo y cultura comunista en la Argentina del siglo xx* (Buenos Aires: Sudamericana, 2013); Christopher Vials, *Haunted by Hitler: Liberals, the Left, and the Fight Against Fascism in the United States* (Amherst: University of Massachusetts Press, 2014); Didier Monciaud, "Pacifisme, antifascisme et anticolonialisme dans l'Égypte des années 1930: L'expérience de la ligue pacifiste Ansâr al Sâlam," *Cahiers d'histoire: Revue d'histoire critique* 127 (2015): 51–74; Traverso, *Fire and Blood;* Mark Bray, *Antifa: The Anti-Fascist Handbook* (Brooklyn: Melville, 2017); Nigel Copsey, *Anti-Fascism in Britain,* second edition (London: Routledge, 2017); John P. Enyeart, *Death to Fascism: Louis Adamic's Fight for Democracy* (Urbana: University of Illinois Press, 2019); Lambe, *No Barrier Can Contain It;* Hilary Moore and James Tracy, *No Fascist USA! The John Brown Anti-Klan Committee and Lessons for Today's Movements* (San Francisco: City Lights Books, 2020).

Excellent earlier works of European antifascist history include Jacques Droz, *Histoire de l'antifascisme en Europe, 1923–1939* (Paris: La Découverte, 1985); Gerd-Rainer Horn, *European Socialists Respond to Fascism: Ideology, Activism and Contingency in the 1930s* (Oxford, Eng.: Oxford University Press, 1996); Serge Wolikow and Annie Bleton-Ruget, editors, *Antifascisme et nation: Les gauches européennes au temps du Front populaire* (Dijon: Editions universitaires de Dijon, 1998); Emmanuelle Carle, "Women, Anti-Fascism and Peace in Interwar France: Gabrielle Duchêne's Itinerary," *French History* 18, no. 3 (2004): 291–314; Anson Rabinbach, "Paris, Capital of Anti-Fascism," in *The Modernist Imagination: Intellectual History and Critical Theory,* ed. Warren Breckman et al. (New York: Berghahn, 2009), 183–209; Gilles Vergnon, *L'antifascisme en France: De Mussolini à Le Pen* (Rennes: Presses universitaires de Rennes, 2009); Nigel Copsey and Andrzej Olechnowicz, editors, *Varieties of Anti-Fascism: Britain in the Inter-War Period* (Basingstoke: Palgrave Macmillan, 2010). Worthy of special attention, for its inclusion of a chapter on United States antifascism in a work of comparative history otherwise focused on antifascism in European countries, is Larry Ceplair, *Under the Shadow of War: Fascism, Anti-Fascism, and Marxists, 1918–1939* (New York: Columbia University Press, 1987).

—

45. On the concept of premature antifascism, see Peter N. Carroll, "Premature Anti-Fascists, Again," in *From Guernica to Human Rights: Essays on the Spanish Civil War* (Kent: Kent State University Press, 2015), 131–36. The term was invented in the United States during World War II. As the astute columnist Samuel Grafton wrote in 1944: "Everyone has heard the many FBI investigator jokes, about the intense fear on the part of several of our Government bureaus lest they make a slip and hire someone who was too hot an anti-Fascist, too soon, a 'premature anti-Fascist.'" Samuel Grafton, "I'd Rather Be Right," *Detroit Free Press,* March 27, 1944, p. 16.

For a sense of the sweep of antifascism's history, see Bray, *Antifa.* See also Vergnon, *Antifascisme en France;* Bernd Langer, *Antifaschistische Aktion: Geschichte einer linksradikalen Bewegung* (Münster: Unrast, 2014); Copsey, *Anti-Fascism in Britain;* García et al., editors, *Rethinking Antifascism;* Natasha Lennard, "We, Anti-Fascists," in *Being Numerous: Essays on Non-Fascist Life* (London: Verso, 2019), 7–24.

On the ways "in which the Spanish Civil War remained a live issue" in later years, see Kirsten Weld, "The Other Door: Spain and the Guatemalan Counter-Revolution, 1944–54," *Journal of Latin American Studies* 51, no. 2 (May 2019): 317 (quotation). Also packed with insight is Weld, "The Spanish Civil War and the Construction of a Reactionary Historical Consciousness in Augusto Pinochet's Chile," *Hispanic American Historical Review* 98, no. 1 (Feb. 2018): 77–115.

46. Aristide R. Zolberg, "Moments of Madness," *Politics and Society* 2, no. 2 (Winter 1972): 183–207.

47. Andreas Kalyvas, *Democracy and the Politics of the Extraordinary: Max Weber, Carl Schmitt, and Hannah Arendt* (New York: Cambridge University Press, 2008).

48. Marceau Pivert, "Tout est possible," *Populaire,* May 27, 1936, p. 6.

1. HOW TO FIGHT FASCISM

Epigraph: Guido Mazzali, "Come combattere il fascismo," *Rivoluzione Liberale,* Sept. 2, 1924, p. 131.

1. "Two Fascisti Die in Bronx, Klansmen Riot in Queens, in Memorial Day Clashes," *New York Times,* May 31, 1927, p. 1; a condensed and slightly altered version of the report ran as "Fascist Fighting Mars New York Memorial Day," *Chicago Tribune,* May 31, 1927, p. 5. See Stuart Chase, *The Tyranny of Words* (New York: Harcourt, Brace and Company, 1938).

2. "Fascist Fighting Mars New York Memorial Day," p. 5; "Greco and Carillo Found Not Guilty of Fascist Murder," *New York Times,* Dec. 24, 1927, p. 5; "Two Fascisti Assassinated on Street in New York," *St. Louis Post-Dispatch,* May 30, 1927, p. 1; "2 Fascisti Slain by N.Y. 'Red Ties,'" *Philadelphia Inquirer,* May 31, 1927, p. 2; "Two Fascisti Die in Bronx,

—

Klansmen Riot in Queens, in Memorial Day Clashes," pp. 1, 7. Other reports suggest Carisi was stabbed fourteen or fifteen or twenty or even twenty-one times. And other reports have it as a certainty that there were two assailants (yet later the police would focus on three men). See, for example, "Police Quell Fascisti Riot in New York," (Louisville) *Courier-Journal*, May 31, 1927, p. 1. In "Two Fascisti Die in Bronx, Klansmen Riot in Queens, in Memorial Day Clashes," the *Times* printed that Carisi and Amoroso were both part of "the Fascist movement in this country" – "Fascist" instead of the "Fascisti" of the *Chicago Tribune* version of the report.

3. "Fascist Fighting Mars New York Memorial Day," p. 5. For an estimate that the Klan forces outnumbered the police 1,500 to 200, see "Warren Ordered Police to Block Parade by Klan," *Brooklyn Daily Eagle*, May 31, 1927, p. 6.

4. On fascism, violence, and spectacle, see Falasca-Zamponi, *Fascist Spectacle;* Mabel Berezin, *Making the Fascist Self: The Political Culture of Interwar Italy* (Ithaca: Cornell University Press, 1997).

5. See, for example, "Dopo l'assassinio dei due fascisti a New York," *Stampa*, June 2, 1927, p. 1.

6. On the history of Memorial Day, see David W. Blight, *Race and Reunion: The Civil War in American Memory* (Cambridge, Mass.: Belknap, 2001), 64–97.

7. See, for example, John P. Diggins, *Mussolini and Fascism: The View from America* (Princeton: Princeton University Press, 1972); Philip V. Cannistraro, *Blackshirts in Little Italy: Italian Americans and Fascism, 1921–1929* (West Lafayette, Ind.: Bordighera, 1999); Nunzio Pernicone, *Carlo Tresca: Portrait of a Rebel* (Oakland: AK Press, 2010); Travis Tomchuk, *Transnational Radicals: Italian Anarchists in Canada and the U.S., 1915–1940* (Winnipeg: University of Manitoba Press, 2015); Sarah Churchwell, *Behold, America: The Entangled History of "America First" and "The American Dream"* (New York: Basic Books, 2018).

8. The story was broken by Matt Blum, "1927 News Report: Donald Trump's Dad Arrested in KKK Brawl with Cops," *Boing Boing*, Sept. 9, 2015, https://boingboing.net/2015/09/09/1927-news-report-donald-trump.html. The key (and inconclusive) evidence, citing Fred Trump as one of seven arrestees at the riot, was "Warren Criticizes 'Class' Parades," *New York Times*, June 1, 1927, p. 16. This article notes that, after being arrested and arraigned, Trump was "discharged"; the next sentence notes that the funeral for Carisi and Amoroso would soon be held. "About one thousand Fascisti will attend the service. The coffins were taken yesterday to the headquarters of the Fascio Mario Sonzini, 606 East 187th Street, where twelve Fascisti will stand guard day and night."

9. Sternhell, *Neither Right nor Left*, 3. On "the fascist minimum," see also Nolte, *Three Faces of Fascism*, 9; Stanley G. Payne, *A History of Fascism, 1914–1945* (Madison: University of Wisconsin Press, 1995), esp. 4–5; Roger Griffin, *The Nature of Fascism* (London: Pinter, 1991), esp. 13, 38–44, 141; Roger Eatwell, "On Defining the 'Fascist Minimum': The

Centrality of Ideology," *Journal of Political Ideologies* 1, no. 3 (Oct. 1996): 303–19. Among critiques, see Benjamin Zachariah, "A Voluntary Gleichschaltung? Perspectives from India Towards a Non-Eurocentric Understanding of Fascism," *Journal of Transcultural Studies* 5, no. 2 (2014): 63–100; Finchelstein, *From Fascism to Populism in History*, 45–57. For a historiographical discussion attentive to generational shifts, see Enzo Traverso, *The New Faces of Fascism: Populism and the Far Right*, trans. David Broder (London: Verso, 2019), 97–129.

10. Mazzali, "Come combattere il fascismo," p. 131; Falasca-Zamponi, *Fascist Spectacle*, 27. On making sense of fascism in 1924, see Emilio Gentile, *Le origini dell'ideologia fascista (1918-1925)* (1975; Bologna: Società editrice il Mulino, 1996), 55. The usual reference for the origin of "totalitarian" ("totalitario/a") (adj.) is a 1923 article by Giovanni Amendola in the *Monde*. On totalitarianism ("totalitarismo") (n.) as a quality of the fascist regime distinguishing it from other tyrannies—already in August 1924—see "Nuove formazioni sull'orizzonte politico," *Stampa*, Aug. 31, 1924, p. 2. For the usual reference of the noun's origin, see Prometeo Filodemo [Lelio Basso], "L'antistato," *Rivoluzione Liberale*, Jan. 2, 1925, p. 1.

On the *Rivoluzione Liberale*, see Charles F. Delzell, *Mussolini's Enemies: The Italian Anti-Fascist Resistance* (Princeton: Princeton University Press, 1961), 27–29; David Ward, *Piero Gobetti's New World: Antifascism, Liberalism, Writing* (Toronto: University of Toronto Press, 2010).

11. Mabel Berezin, "The Festival State: Celebration and Commemoration in Fascist Italy," *Journal of Modern European History* 4, no. 1 (March 2006): 66; *Scritti e discorsi di Benito Mussolini, edizione definitiva*, vol. 1: *Dall'intervento al fascismo (15 novembre 1914-23 marzo 1919)* (Milan: Ulrico Hoepli, 1934). Though dated 1934 (and XII, indicating the Anno Fascista), the volume was published in 1933. The same claim for March 23, 1919, as the "birth of fascism" is made in the heading in *Opera Omnia di Benito Mussolini*, vol. 12: *Dagli armistizi al discorso di piazza San Sepolcro (13 novembre 1918-23 marzo 1919)*, ed. Edoardo and Duilio Susmel (Florence: La Fenice, 1953), 321–27. Scholarly claims of attendance at San Sepolcro range from fifty to two hundred. See, for example, Payne, *History of Fascism*, 90; Finchelstein, *Transatlantic Fascism*, 19. Then there's Ernst Nolte's qualitative judgment that the meeting was attended "poorly." Nolte, *Three Faces of Fascism*, 180.

12. See, for example, Nolte, *Three Faces of Fascism*, 180; Zeev Sternhell with Mario Sznajder and Maia Asheri, *The Birth of Fascist Ideology: From Cultural Rebellion to Political Revolution*, trans. David Maisel (Princeton: Princeton University Press, 1994), 222; Falasca-Zamponi, *Fascist Spectacle*, 32; Paxton, *Anatomy of Fascism*, 5.

13. For a text of the proceedings, see "L'imponente 'Adunata' di ieri a Milano," *Popolo d'Italia*, March 24, 1919, p. 1. And yet so engrained by now is the notion that this meeting marked fascism's birth that it is often assumed that Mussolini did name fascism at San Sepolcro. Robert O. Paxton, perhaps the most renowned historian of fascism, and justly so, goes so far as to suggest, "If something begins when it acquires a name, we can date the beginnings of fascism precisely. It began on Sunday morning, March 23, 1919, at the meeting on the Piazza San Sepolcro in Milan." Paxton, *Anatomy of Fascism*, 24.

14. "Imponente 'Adunata' di ieri a Milano," p. 1. For an English translation of Mussolini's speech, under the heading "The Birth of the Fascist Movement (Piazza San Sepolcro 9, Milano, March 23, 1919)," see Charles F. Delzell, *Mediterranean Fascism, 1919–1945* (New York: Harper & Row, 1970), 7–11.

15. The organization's name, "Fasci di Combattimento," was already established before the meeting. See "Il Fascio Milanese di Combattimento è sorto," *Popolo d'Italia*, March 22, 1919, p. 3.

16. The fasci are discussed in numerous histories of fascism. See the fine discussion in Payne, *History of Fascism*, 81–87. The word *fascio* was derived from the Latin *fascis*, meaning a packet or bundle of things, often wood; *fasces* in the plural. Roman lictors, serving as bodyguards of a sort for magistrates, carried on their left shoulders fasces of rods made from birch or elm (in some cases, the fasces included an axe bundled with the rods); the fasces became a symbol of authority, power, and in particular the dictatorship of Julius Caesar. Geoffrey S. Sumi, *Ceremony and Power: Performing Politics in Rome Between Republic and Empire* (Ann Arbor: University of Michigan Press, 2005), 82, 226. See also Fred K. Drogula, *Commanders and Command in the Roman Republic and Early Empire* (Chapel Hill: University of North Carolina Press, 2015), 46–130; Helen Roche, "Mussolini's 'Third Rome,' Hitler's Third Reich and the Allure of Antiquity: Classicizing Chronopolitics as a Remedy for Unstable National Identity?" *Fascism* 8 (2019): 127–52. Robert O. Paxton suggests that before World War I, "the symbolism of the Roman *fasces* was usually appropriated by the Left," by which he means a general transnational left reaching beyond Italy; he notes as evidence that in the nineteenth century Marianne, the personification of French republicanism, was often shown carrying the Roman fasces (though she was not, I'd add, in the famous 1830 Eugène Delacroix painting, in which she carries the French tricolor and a gun). Paxton, *Anatomy of Fascism*, 4.

Not all groups identifying as "fasci," to be sure, were part of the war-interventionist movement. Italian political groups had made use of the term at least since the populistic Fasci Siciliani of the 1890s. The socialist party youth, established before World War I and still active after it, was called the Fascio giovanile socialista. See, for example, "Fascio giovanile socialista," *Avanti!* March 24, 1919, p. 3. Among those who had demanded intervention in 1914 and 1915, there were by early 1919 many active fasci. See, for example, "Il Fascio Femminile pro Fiume e Dalmazia," "Fascio Rivoluzionario Filippo Corridoni," "Il Fascio delle Associazioni Patriottiche," and "Per una grande dimostrazione ai Combattenti," all in *Popolo d'Italia*, Jan. 11, 1919, p. 2.

17. "Dimostrazioni senza incidenti a Milano," *Stampa*, May 16, 1915, p. 2. See also "Durante la giornata di 'sciopero,'" *Popolo d'Italia*, May 16, 1915, p. 4.

18. "La cronaca della giornata," *Popolo d'Italia,* May 14, 1915, p. 2; "Per la libertà dei popoli, per l'avvenire dell'Italia: Discorso pronunciato da Mussolini a Parma il 13 dicembre," *Popolo d'Italia,* Dec. 17, 1914, p. 2; "Il Fascio romano rivoluzionario plaude alla campagna di Mussolini," *Stampa,* Nov. 26, 1914, p. 3; "Costituite, ovunque, i 'fasci autonomi d'azione rivoluzionaria,'" *Popolo d'Italia,* Nov. 30, 1914, p. 2. That he was exhorting readers to form fasci *of their own* is my interpretation; more common in the historiography is to see Mussolini's labors as the establishing of a new formal organization of *his own.* My read of the situation is that in specifying "fasci autonomi d'azione rivoluzionaria," Mussolini wasn't advertising an actual, fully established, and freestanding organization ready to hand out charters to new branches so much as, rather, he was throwing around a handful of evocative words to encourage others – "everywhere" (ovunque) – to organize their own local protest groups. The unstructured looseness of Mussolini's intent was evident even in the name itself: "autonomi" inscribing for anyone who took up his proposal the promise of autonomy. There was no serious institutional infrastructure buttressing Mussolini's bluster, and even the specific organizational identity he had floated soon proved expendable. Within weeks, he had dropped the original phrasing and had begun calling for new fasci under another name, the "Fasci d'Azione Rivoluzionaria." The new rubric was meant – in part – to draw together "fasci autonomi d'azione rivoluzionaria" and the Fascio Rivoluzionario d'Azione Internazionalista, which had made its first public appeal October 5, 1914. It has been suggested by historians that this last group was created on October 1, but I think that is only based on a misreading of the historian Renzo De Felice's comments. See Renzo De Felice, *Mussolini il rivoluzionario, 1883–1920* (Turin: Giulio Einaudi, 1965), 272.

For a sense of the chronology of events, see "Le dimissioni di Mussolini," *Stampa,* Oct. 21, 1914, p. 4; "Un altro discorso di Mussolini contro la neutralità," *Stampa,* Nov. 11, 1914, p. 6; "La cronaca di Milano," *Popolo d'Italia,* Nov. 25, 1914, p. 4; "L'espulsione di Mussolini," *Stampa,* Nov. 26, 1914, p. 2.

19. Mussolini, "L'Adunata," *Popolo d'Italia,* Jan. 24, 1915, p. 1. For other mentions in the paper, see, for example, "Movimento fascista," *Popolo d'Italia,* Feb. 24, 1915, p. 2.

20. "Comizî e dimostrazioni in Italia," *Stampa,* April 12, 1915, p. 7; "Il 1° maggio in Italia," *Stampa,* May 3, 1915, p. 2; "L'indignazione in tutta Italia," *Popolo d'Italia,* May 15, 1915, p. 2; "Grandi dimostrazioni alla capitale e nelle altre città," (San Francisco) *Italia,* May 15, 1915, p. 1; Mussolini, "Il delitto," *Popolo d'Italia,* May 12, 1915, p. 1; "Le entusiastiche dimostrazioni di ieri," *Popolo d'Italia,* May 15, 1915, p. 4; Mussolini, "Abbasso il Parlamento!" *Popolo d'Italia,* May 11, 1915, p. 1.

21. "Cronaca della giornata," p. 2; De Felice, *Mussolini il rivoluzionario,* 679–81. On the manifesto and the emphasis of national revolutions, see Sternhell, *Birth of Fascist Ideology,* 205. See also Norberto Bobbio, *Ideological Profile of Twentieth-Century Italy,* trans. Lydia G. Cochrane (Princeton: Princeton University Press, 1995), 62-63, 91-102. On revolutionary syndicalism, see Marcel van der Linden and Wayne Thorpe, editors, *Revolutionary Syndicalism: An International Perspective* (Aldershot: Scolar, 1990). For a contemporary critique, see J. A. Estey, *Revolutionary Syndicalism: An Exposition and a Criticism* (London: King, 1913). On its relation to fascism, see David D. Roberts, *The Syndicalist Tradition and Italian Fascism* (Chapel Hill: University of North Carolina Press, 1979). Benito Mussolini's relation to revolutionary syndicalism is a matter of great scholarly contention. See Nolte, *Three Faces of Fascism*, 164; Sternhell, *Birth of Fascist Ideology*, 195–206. Mussolini on occasion called himself a revolutionary syndicalist. Falasca-Zamponi, *Fascist Spectacle*, 31. On other occasions, he insisted he wasn't one. R. J. B. Bosworth, *Mussolini* (London: Bloomsbury, 2010), 70.

22. "Cronaca della giornata," p. 2. See Herbert W. Schneider, *Making the Fascist State* (New York: Oxford University Press, 1928), 13–15.

23. "Fascio d'Azione rivoluzionaria," *Popolo d'Italia*, May 19, 1915, p. 4.

24. A. Rossi, *La naissance du Fascisme, L'Italie de 1918 à 1922* (Paris: Gallimard, 1938), 33; A. Rossi, *The Rise of Italian Fascism, 1918–1922*, trans. Peter and Dorothy Wait (London: Methuen and Co., 1938), 33; Sternhell, *Birth of Fascist Ideology*, 223; Dylan Riley, *The Civic Foundations of Fascism in Europe: Italy, Spain, and Romania, 1870–1945* (2010; London: Verso, 2019), 43. For similar examples, see Emilio Gentile, *Fascismo: Storia e interpretazione* (Roma: GLF Editori Laterza, 2002), 9; Payne, *History of Fascism*, 81. For an even more assertive claim than what appears in the translated *Birth of Fascist Ideology*, see Zeev Sternhell, Mario Sznajder, and Maia Ashéri, *Naissance de l'idéologie fasciste* (Paris: Fayard, 1989), 300.

A. Rossi was one of several pseudonyms Angelo Tasca used. Others were Serra, André Leroux, and XX.

25. Emanuel Rota, *A Pact with Vichy: Angelo Tasca from Italian Socialism to French Collaboration* (New York: Fordham University Press, 2013), 52, 57. On Tasca, see also Alexander De Grand, *In Stalin's Shadow: Angelo Tasca and the Crisis of the Left in Italy and France, 1910–1945* (DeKalb: Northern Illinois University Press, 1986). On Josef Stalin's machinations regarding the German Communist Party (involving the suspended secretary Ernst Thälmann) during the 1928 "Wittorf Affair," see Sean McMeekin, *The Red Millionaire: A Political Biography of Willi Münzenberg, Moscow's Secret Propaganda Tsar in the West* (New Haven: Yale University Press, 2003), 215–17. On the theory of social fascism, see Lea Haro, "Entering a Theoretical Void: The Theory of Social Fascism and Stalinism in the German Communist Party," *Critique* 39, no. 4 (2011): 563–82. See also Sidney Hook, "The Fallacy of the Theory of Social Fascism," *Modern Monthly* 8, no. 6 (July 1934): 342–52; "U.S. Communist Party," *Fortune*, Sept. 1934, p. 154; O. Tanin and E. Yohan, *Militarism and Fascism in Japan* (New York: International Publishers, 1934), 228–48; Franz Borkenau, *World Communism: A History of the Communist International* (New York: Norton, 1939), 341–42; Theodore Draper, "The Ghost of Social-Fascism," *Commentary* 47, no. 2 (Feb. 1969): 29–42.

—

26. André Leroux, "La crise catalane et la situation en Espagne," *Populaire,* April 5, 1937, p. 3. On Tasca's wartime politics, see Rota, *Pact with Vichy,* 121–53, esp. 149–50. Also illuminating is Denis Peschanski, editor, *Vichy, 1940–1944: Quaderni e docomunti inediti di Angelo Tasca: Archives de guerre d'Angelo Tasca* (Milan: Fondazione Giangiacomo Feltrinelli, 1986). Tasca's relation to Vichy was complicated, made all the more so by the aid he gave to the Belgian resistance.

27. For example, see the comments of Michele Bianchi, quoted at length in De Felice, *Mussolini il rivoluzionario,* 569. Speaking in late 1919 with an eye on the approaching elections, Bianchi (a prominent fascist who had given a speech at the San Sepolcro meeting) advocated that the fascisti support both "left-wing interventisti" and "right-wing interventisti": the left and right referred to their position in parliamentary politics; regardless of whether they were left-wing or right-wing deputies, what mattered, Bianchi insisted, was their willingness to keep the interventista mentality of war alive in domestic politics even after the war had ended, to fend off any return to a politics of normalcy.

28. Sternhell, *Birth of Fascist Ideology,* 204, 206; Donald Sassoon, *Mussolini and the Rise of Fascism* (London: HarperPress, 2007), 44. On Mussolini's ideological trajectory, see Gentile, *Origini dell'ideologia fascista,* 61–110; Sternhell, *Birth of Fascist Ideology,* 195–232.

29. "La sepoltura del Fascio," *Stampa,* July 15, 1919, p. 1.

30. See Francesco Ciccotti, "La dittatura della menzogna," *Stampa,* Aug. 27, 1919, p. 1.

31. "Sepoltura del Fascio," p. 1. On the parliamentary Fascio, known formally as the Fascio Parlamentare di Difesa Nazionale, see Charles S. Maier, *Recasting Bourgeois Europe: Stabilization in France, Germany, and Italy in the Decade after World War I* (Princeton: Princeton University Press, 1975), 110–11.

32. "La discussione sulla politica del Governo," *Stampa,* Dec. 21, 1917, p. 1; "I diritti del Parlamento," *Avanti!* Oct. 20, 1918, p. 1; "La fine del Gruppo piemontese del Fascio parlamentare," *Stampa,* Nov. 22, 1919, p. 2; "L'esposizione finanziaria alla Camera," *Stampa,* Dec. 20, 1917, p. 2. On Edoardo Giretti's pacifism, see Sandi E. Cooper, *Patriotic Pacifism: Waging War on War in Europe, 1815–1914* (New York: Oxford University Press, 1991). Giretti later initially supported Benito Mussolini's dictatorship with a rationale akin to that of certain neoliberals later on, as he explained that Mussolini's "political dictatorship will give us a regime of greater economic freedom." Giretti explained, "I am more than ever convinced that without economic liberty, liberalism is an abstraction devoid of any real content." Quoted in Ralph Raico, *Classical Liberalism and the Austrian School* (Auburn, Ala.: Mises Institute, 2012), 281. See also Edoardo Giretti, "Lotta di classe industriale," *Rivoluzione Liberale,* Feb. 12, 1924, p. 4.

33. "Una mascalzonata dell'on. Centurione alla Camera dei Deputati," *Stampa,* Nov. 24, 1918, p. 1; "L'aggressione e la fuga dei fascisti alla Camera," *Avanti!* Nov. 24, 1918, p. 1; "Il naufragio dei fascisti alla Camera," *Avanti!* Nov. 25, 1918, p. 1.

—

34. See Federico Finchelstein, *A Brief History of Fascist Lies* (Oakland: University of California Press, 2020).

35. "Note alla seduta," *Avanti!* Nov. 24, 1918, p. 1. See also "Mascalzonata dell'on. Centurione alla Camera dei Deputati," p. 1.

36. "Naufragio dei fascisti alla Camera," p. 1; "Note alla seduta," p. 1.

37. Mussolini, "I fantasmi di Turati," *Popolo d'Italia*, April 1, 1919. It is commonplace in the historiography of fascism to posit that the trenches were the seeding grounds for fascism; this is true of studies of Italian fascism, the classic works of generic and comparative fascism, and the recent works of transnational fascism, too. See, for example, Finchelstein, *Fascism to Populism in History*, 32. On the modern warrior ethic, see Joanna Bourke, *An Intimate Portrait of Killing: Face to Face Killing in Twentieth-Century Warfare* (New York: Basic Books, 1999), 32-56.

38. Mussolini, "23 marzo," *Popolo d'Italia*, March 18, 1919, p. 1; Maria Rygier, "Il nemico interno d'Italia," *Popolo d'Italia*, May 12, 1915, p. 2. Regarding Rygier's participation in the fasci interventisti, see "La grande adunata interventista," *Popolo d'Italia,* Jan. 25, 1915, p. 1. In the past she herself had been one of Italy's most notorious antimilitarists (she even, like Mussolini, suffered imprisonment for protesting against the campaign into Libya). Her early-twentieth-century speeches in Apulia, on topics such as anarchism, feminism, and workers' emancipation, were "so powerful that even landlords came out of curiosity to hear her." Frank M. Snowden, *Violence and the Great Estates in the South of Italy: Apulia, 1900-1922* (Cambridge, Eng.: Cambridge University Press, 1986), 115. See also Michael Miller Topp, "The Transnationalism of the Italian-American Left: The Lawrence Strike of 1912 and the Italian Chamber of Labor of New York City," *Journal of American Ethnic History* 17, no. 1 (Fall 1997): 47. Rygier later was an outspoken, though untrusted, antifascist. See, for example, Maria Rygier, "Le fascisme et l'étranger," (Paris) *Radical*, Sept. 29, 1929, p. 4. See also Christopher Duggan, *Fascist Voices: An Intimate History of Mussolini's Italy* (London: Bodley Head, 2012), 159-60.

39. For a sense of the era's political grammar, see, for example, "Dimostrazioni pro e contro la guerra," *Stampa*, May 15, 1915, p. 6; "L'Unione Parlamentare e le libertà," *Avanti!* Nov. 1, 1918, p. 1; "I socialisti alla seduta storica," *Avanti!* Nov. 22, 1918, p. 1; "Note alla seduta," p. 1.

40. George Orwell, "Politics and the English Language," *Horizon*, no. 76 (April 1946): 255. Historians of fascism have often relied on the metaphor of diffusion to explain fascism's presence outside of Italy. See, for example, Payne, *History of Fascism*, 290. For an interpretation favoring diffusion by institutional means, see Emilio Gentile, "La politica estera del partito fascista. Ideologia e organizzazione dei Fasci italiani all'estero (1920-1930)," *Storia contemporanea* 26, no. 6 (Dec. 1995): esp. 899.

41. "Gli Italiani negli Stati Uniti," *Carroccio* 13, no. 6 (June 1921): 679 (address and Cesare Passamonte's first name); Mussolini, "L'avvenimento," *Popolo d'Italia*, May 3, 1921, p. 1 (quotation and men's surnames). On Agostino De Biasi and Umberto Menicucci, see Cannistraro, *Blackshirts in Little Italy*, 11–16. Passamonte's first name previously eluded historians, likely in part because it has been believed that his first initial was "G." His surname also occasionally appeared in print spelled differently. See, for example, "Italy to Fight Communism by Fascisti in U.S.," *New-York Tribune*, July 24, 1921, p. 3. The telegram appears in Mussolini's article as dated May 1 and suggests that the New York fascio met "today." Shortly thereafter, though, it was suggested that the meeting had occurred on April 30. "Il Fascio del Nord-America," *Carroccio* 13, no. 5 (May 1921): 543.

42. *Popolo d'Italia*, May 3, 1921, p. 1.

43. Mussolini, "Avvenimento," p. 1; "Dal Plaustro," *Carroccio* 13, no. 2 (Feb. 1921): 256; "Fascio del Nord-America," 543; Philip V. Cannistraro, "Per una storia dei Fasci negli Stati Uniti (1921–1929)," *Storia Contemporanea* 26, no. 6 (Dec. 1995): 1069; Cannistraro, *Blackshirts in Little Italy*, 29; Maria Luiza Tucci Carneiro, "Fascistas à brasileira encontros e confrontos," in *Tempos de fascismos: Ideologia, intolerância, imaginário*, ed. Carneiro and Federico Croci (São Paulo: Editora da Universidad de São Paulo, 2010), 434; Ronald C. Newton, "*Ducini, Prominenti, Antifascisti*: Italian Fascism and the Italo-Argentine Collectivity," *Americas* 51, no. 1 (July 1994): 46; María Victoria Grillo, "Creer en Mussolini: La proyección exterior del fascismo italiano (Argentina, 1930–1939)," *Ayer*, no. 62 (2006): 231–55.

44. Agostino De Biasi, "La vita de Fasci in America," *Carroccio* 17, no. 4 (April 1923): 399, 401; "Fascisti in America to Fight Radicalism," *New York Times*, March 21, 1923, p. 20; "Italian Unions Join in War on Fascism," *New York Times*, April 11, 1923, p. 36.

45. Marcello Gallian, *Il Ventennale: Gli uomini delle squadre nella Rivoluzione delle Camicie nere* (Rome: Azione letteraria italiana, 1941), 61–62, 65. The most recent generation of scholarship on early Italian fascism has accentuated violence and suggested that earlier scholarship on early Italian fascism had, for a variety of reasons, gone out of its way to neglect it. See Michael Ebner, *Ordinary Violence in Mussolini's Italy* (Cambridge, Eng.: Cambridge University Press, 2011); Matteo Millan, "Origins," in *The Politics of Everyday Life in Fascist Italy: Outside the State?* ed. Joshua Arthurs, Michael Ebner, and Kate Ferris (New York: Palgrave Macmillan, 2017), 19–49; Albanese, *March on Rome;* and Alessandro Saluppo, "Paramilitary Violence and Fascism: Imaginaries and Practices of Squadrismo, 1919–1925," *Contemporary European History* 29, no. 3 (Aug. 2020): 289–308. See also Barbara Spackman, *Fascist Virilities: Rhetoric, Ideology, and Social Fantasy in Italy* (Minneapolis: University of Minnesota Press, 1996); Roberta Suzzi Valli, "The Myth of Squadrismo in the Fascist Regime," *Journal of Contemporary History* 35, no. 2 (April 2000): 131–50.

46. *Fascismo: Inchiesta socialista sulle gesta dei fascisti in Italia* (1922; Milan: Edizione Avanti! 1963). See Arthurs, Ebner, and Ferris, editors, *Politics of Everyday Life.*

47. Gallian, *Ventennale,* 61. For a sublime analysis of violence's place in fascism, see Finchelstein, *From Fascism to Populism in History,* 73–81.

48. "Le fortune del fascismo," *Stampa,* Jan. 30, 1921, p. 1.

49. "I particolari del conflitto di Parma," *Stampa,* March 30, 1922, p. 5.

50. "Particolari del conflitto di Parma," p. 5. Regarding the newspaper, the fascist Italo Balbo wrote: "*Il Piccolo,* velenosissimo contro Mussolini e contro di noi." Italo Balbo, *Diario 1922* (Milan: A. Mondadori, 1932), 116. The *Piccolo* hadn't always taken an antifascist stance. See, for example, "Assemblea al Fascio di Combattimento," *Piccolo di Parma,* March 23, 1920, p. 4; "Fasci Italiani di combattimento," *Piccolo di Parma,* May 25, 1920, p. 3; "Fasci Italiani di Combattimento: Sezione di Parma," *Piccolo di Parma,* Nov. 21, 1920, p. 3.

51. Stanislao G. Pugliese, editor, *Fascism, Anti-Fascism, and the Resistance in Italy: 1919 to the Present* (Lanham, Md.: Rowman & Littlefield, 2004), 55; Bray, *Antifa,* 13; Tom Behan, *The Resistible Rise of Benito Mussolini* (London: Bookmarks, 2003), 2. On the Arditi del Popolo, see Paolo Spriano, *Storia del Partito comunista italiano,* vol. 1: *Da Bordiga a Gramsci* (Turin: Einaudi, 1967), 139–51; Fernando Cordova, *Arditi e legionari dannunziani* (Padova: Marsiglio, 1969); Ivan Fuschini, *Gli Arditi del popolo* (Ravenna, Longo, 1994); Eros Francescangeli, *Arditi del popolo: Argo Secondari e la prima organizzazione antifascista (1917-1922)* (Rome: Odradek, 2000); Behan, *Resistible Rise of Benito Mussolini;* Giancarlo Bocchi, *Il ribelle: Guido Picelli; Una vita da rivoluzionario* (Parma: IMP, 2013); Andrea Staid, *Gli arditi del popolo: La prima lotta armata al fascismo 1921-22* (Milan: Milieu, 2015). On the historiography, see Staid, *Arditi del Popolo,* 15–25.

52. Benedetto Migliore, *Le convulsioni dell'arditismo* (Milan: Treves, 1921); Günter Berghaus, *Futurism and Politics: Between Anarchist Rebellion and Fascist Reaction, 1909-1944* (Providence: Berghahn, 1996), 101; Giuseppe Bottai, quoted in MacGregor Knox, *To the Threshold of Power, 1922/33: Origins and Dynamics of the Fascist and National Socialist Dictatorships,* vol. 1 (Cambridge, Eng.: Cambridge University Press, 2007), 221.

53. Behan, *Resistible Rise of Benito Mussolini,* 56-58; Francescangeli, *Arditi del popolo,* 55 *n*28, 59; Maier, *Recasting Bourgeois Europe,* 330. Born into a bourgeois family in Rome, Argo Secondari had traveled to South America before the war and trained as a boxer; he then fought during the war in one of the army's "arditi" assault units and was decorated more than once for his valor; after the war, amid the strikes, riots, protests over food prices, and desperate hunger of 1919 in Rome, he put together, with fellow anarchists and republicans, the "Pietralata Plot" to seize weapons from a fortress and use them to revolutionize the food supply in the city's grocery markets; the plot failed, and the authorities accused the conspirators of attempting to seize not grocery markets but rather the parliamentary palaces and other key sites of state power in Rome, in an attempt to overthrow the government. The authorities' accusations have led to some confusion in the historiography. See Marco Grispigni, "Gli Arditi del popolo a Roma. Due aspetti particolari della loro storia," *Storia* *contemporanea* 17, no. 5 (Oct. 1986): 853–74; Francescangeli, *Arditi del popolo,* 47; Behan, *Resistible Rise of Benito Mussolini,* 56–57; Ángel Alcalde, *War Veterans and Fascism in Interwar Europe* (Cambridge, Eng.: Cambridge University Press, 2017), 56.

The ways that historiography has inscribed a long-lived, inherited left are manifold. Translation is one of them. Consider a translation of Argo Secondari's words from an interview of the Arditi del Popolo cofounder given around the time of the Proletarian Day demonstration of 1921. In his (superb) 2003 history of the Arditi del Popolo, the historian Tom Behan quoted Secondari as having said that because of a fascist monopoly on political violence "today it is no longer appropriate to talk about left-wing violence." Look at the original text of the interview, though, from the July 12, 1921, issue of the *Ordine Nuovo,* and see that Secondari's words were: "Oggi però non è più il caso di parlare di violenza rossa." Behan had translated "rossa" (red) as "left-wing." A political world that Secondari had interpreted by coding it in color in 1921 Behan had reinterpreted by using the coding that made sense to him in 2003, the topography of left and right. Behan, *Resistible Rise of Benito Mussolini,* 61.

54. Behan, *Resistible Rise of Benito Mussolini,* 91.

55. Giovanni Giglio, "The Situation in Italy," *Nation,* Aug. 10, 1921, p. 149.

56. "La 'giornata proletaria' a Roma," *Stampa,* July 7, 1921, p. 1; Giglio, "Situation in Italy," p. 149. Erected to honor Titus for his part in suppressing revolution in Jerusalem, the Arch of Titus includes a notorious relief depiction of sacred objects sacked from the Temple of Jerusalem, which the Romans destroyed; opposite this is another relief, depicting Titus driving a chariot, in glory, attended by lictors bearing fasces.

57. "'Giornata proletaria' a Roma," p. 1; "Una grandiosa dimostrazione al Duce," *Stampa,* Oct. 29, 1931, p. 1. On the regime's uses of Piazza Venezia, see Paul Baxa, *Roads and Ruins: The Symbolic Landscape of Fascist Rome* (Toronto: University of Toronto Press, 2010), 90–100. On the Vittoriano, see Catherine Brice, *Monumentalité publique et politique à Rome: Le Vittoriano* (Rome: École française de Rome, 1998); Bruno Tobia, *L'Altare della Patria* (Bologna: Il Mulino, 1998). Regarding "participatory dictatorship," see Mary Fulbrook, *The People's State: East German Society from Hitler to Honecker* (New Haven: Yale University Press, 2005).

58. "Il Congresso fascista," *Stampa,* Nov. 9, 1921, p. 2; "Duemila fascisti trattenuti a Roma dai capi finchè non finisca lo sciopero," *Stampa,* Nov. 12, 1921, p. 1; "Un'altra giornata di conflitti con morti e feriti a Roma," *Stampa,* Nov. 11, 1921, p. 1. See also the fascinating account in Alessandro Portelli, *The Order Has Been Carried Out: History, Memory, and Meaning of a Nazi Massacre in Rome* (New York: Palgrave Macmillan, 2003), 53.

59. For an incisive discussion of the parties' resistance to antifascist unity, see Behan, *Resistible Rise of Benito Mussolini,* 91–108.

60. Guido Picelli, "La rivolta di Parma," *Stato operaio* 8, no. 10 (Oct. 1934): 754; Tasca, *Rise of Italian Fascism,* 229; Balbo, *Diario,* 113–15, 118.

—

61. Picelli, "Rivolta di Parma," 758.

62. See Francescangeli, *Arditi del popolo,* 204. The remarkable anarchist Elena Melli was an official member of the Arditi del Popolo. See Francescangeli, *Arditi del popolo,* 299. More scholarship on Melli would be welcome.

63. Isabelle Richet points out the challenges of "studying women's antifascist activities because they were expressed in a multitude of ways, mostly informal and poorly documented." Isabelle Richet, "Marion Cave Rosselli and the Transnational Women's Antifascist Networks," *Journal of Women's History* 24, no. 3 (Fall 2012): 118. See also Giovanni De Luna, *Donne in oggetto: L'antifascismo nella società italiana (1922–1939)* (Turin: Bollati Boringhieri, 1995); Sara Galli, *Le tre sorelle Seidenfeld: Donne nell'emigrazione politica antifascista* (Florence: Giunti, 2005); Patrizia Gabrielli, *Tempio di virilità: L'antifascismo, il genere, la storia* (Milan: Franco Angeli, 2008).

64. Staid, *Arditi del popolo,* 75; Balbo, *Diario,* 117; Picelli, "Rivolta di Parma," 755–57.

65. See "Parma eroica," *Martello,* Oct. 21, 1922, p. 1.

66. "Italian Unions Join in War on Fascism," p. 36; "Contro il fascismo," *Martello,* Oct. 7, 1922, p. 3; Ego Sum [Carlo Tresca], "Il fascismo," *Martello,* Feb. 12, 1921, p. 1; Carlo Tresca, "Fascismo e Fascisti," *Martello,* March 12, 1921, p. 1; Arturo Giovannitti, "Let Justice Be Done," in *Who Killed Carlo Tresca?* (New York: Tresca Memorial Committee, 1945), 3. On Tresca's life, see Dorothy Gallagher, *All the Right Enemies: The Life and Murder of Carlo Tresca* (New Brunswick: Rutgers University Press, 1988); Pernicone, *Carlo Tresca.* On Lawrence, see also Ggi, "Questa no, Carluccio!" *Cronaca sovversiva,* March 20, 1915, p. 3. Ggi was the anarchist Luigi Galleani. On Arturo Giovannitti, see Marcella Bencivenni, *Italian Immigrant Radical Culture: The Idealism of the Sovversivi in the United States, 1890–1940* (New York: New York University Press, 2011), 155–86. Helen Keller wrote a delightful biographical sketch of him as well. Helen Keller, "Introduction," in Arturo Giovannitti, *Arrows in the Gale* (Riverside, Conn.: Hillacre Bookhouse, 1914), 9–16.

67. "Bar Tresca Sixth Time, One Arrested," *Boston Globe,* March 26, 1923, p. 5; "Red Orator Arrested After Fiery Address," *Hartford Courant,* March 26, 1923, p. 1; *Omaggio alla memoria imperitura di Carlo Tresca* (New York: Martello, 1943), 31; "Waterbury Conn.!" *Martello,* March 17, 1923, p. 3; Gallagher, *All the Right Enemies,* 103; "Anti-Fascismo Orator Is Held for Sedition," *New York Times,* March 26, 1923, p. 2. On the effect of "the 'Waterbury incident,'" see Robert Cresswell, "Labor Conflict Feared Here as Fascisti Spread," *New-York Tribune,* April 15, 1923, p. 6.

68. "Italian Unions Join in War on Fascism," p. 36; Giuseppe Cannato, "Italian Labor Unites in War on Fascism," *Worker,* April 21, 1923, p. 5; Cannistraro, *Blackshirts in Little Italy,* 36–37; Topp, "Transnationalism of the Italian-American Left," 39, 49. The plan for the Anti-Fascisti Alliance of North America was to incorporate "the anti-Fascisti organizations of Canada and Mexico." "Union Labor Starts War on Fascism," *New York Times,*

—

April 9, 1923, p. 10. On the Italian Labor Center, see Rudolph J. Vecoli, "The Making and Un-Making of the Italian American Working Class," in *The Lost World of Italian-American Radicalism*, ed. Philip Cannistraro and Gerald Meyer (Westport, Conn.: Praeger, 2003), 51. Regarding Tresca's "aloof" attitude toward AFANA in 1923 (and his change in attitude two years later), see Pernicone, *Carlo Tresca*, 145, 175–81.

For a depiction of the alliance's problems as rooted in "the faction-ridden Italo-American Left," see John P. Diggins, "The Italo-American Anti-Fascist Opposition," *Journal of American History* 54, no. 3 (Dec. 1967): 580–81.

69. "Gli Italiani negli Stati Uniti," *Carroccio* 18, no. 10 (Oct. 1923): 405. At Carnegie Hall, Agostino de Biasi gave a speech, the propaganda film *I figli d'Italia* was screened, and "fascist squads in black shirt" sang the fascist anthem "Giovinezza." See also Il Consiglio Centrale Fascista, "Nel Iº Anniversario della Marcia di Roma," *Carroccio* 18, no. 10 (Oct. 1923): 335–36; Gaetano Salvemini, *Italian Fascist Activities in the United States,* ed. Philip V. Cannistraro (New York: Center for Migration Studies, 1977), 39. Gaetano Salvemini was among the antifascist Italian exiles who formed the Concentrazione Antifascista in 1927.

In 1921, the organizers of the New York fascio had told the press that members of the fasci would neither receive nor possess uniforms. Whether this was the actual institutional intent or a convenient public transcript is unclear. See "Italy to Fight Communism by Fascisti in U.S.," p. 3.

70. Quoted in "Fascisti in the United States," *Nation*, April 25, 1923, p. 503.

71. Charles Yale Harrison, "The Long Arm of Mussolini," *Labor Defender* (Nov. 1927), 166; Charles Yale Harrison, *Next Please! The Story of Greco and Carillo* (New York: International Labor Defense, 1927), 20–21; Carlo Tresca, "A bandiere spiegate," *Martello*, Aug. 6, 1927, p. 1; "Greco on Stand Offers an Alibi," *New York Times,* Dec. 20, 1927, p. 21; Lisa McGirr, "The Passion of Sacco and Vanzetti: A Global History," *Journal of American History* 93, no. 4 (March 2007): 1085–1115.

72. See Harrison, *Next Please!*; "Greco on Stand Offers an Alibi," p. 21. For a sense of direct action in the age of propaganda by the deed, see Beverly Gage, *The Day Wall Street Exploded: A Story of America in Its First Age of Terror* (New York: Oxford University Press, 2009), 41–68. See also Eric Rauchway, *Murdering McKinley: The Making of Theodore Roosevelt's America* (New York: Hill and Wang, 2003); John M. Merriman, *The Dynamite Club: How a Bombing in Fin-de-Siècle Paris Ignited the Age of Modern Terror* (2009; New Haven: Yale University Press, 2016); Nunzio Pernicone and Fraser M. Ottanelli, *Assassins Against the Old Order: Italian Anarchist Violence in Fin de Siècle Europe* (Urbana: University of Illinois Press, 2018).

73. "L'efferato assassinio dei due fascisti a New York," *Popolo d'Italia*, June 1, 1927, p. 1; "Fascisti Will Bury Slain Men in Italy," *New York Times,* June 2, 1927, p. 5; "10,000 at Funeral of Slain Fascisti," *New York Times,* June 5, 1927, p. 12; "Italy Honors 2 Fascisti

Slain Here On Arrival of Bodies at Naples," *New York Herald Tribune,* June 25, 1927, p. 1; "Neapolitans Honor Fascisti Slain Here," *New York Times,* June 25, 1927, p. 2; Diggins, *Mussolini and Fascism,* 129.

2. A PREHISTORY OF ANTIFASCISM

Epigraph: "De Montevideo: Crónica semanal," *Protesta* (Buenos Aires), April 15, 1924, p. 2.

1. Eric Hobsbawm, *Interesting Times: A Twentieth-Century Life* (London: Allen Lane, 2002), 68, 73–74; A.-G. Leroux, "Le froid continue a sévir sur toute l'Europe," *Paris-Soir,* Jan. 26, 1933, p. 1; "9 Reds Killed by Police Fire in Dresden Riot," *New York Herald Tribune,* Jan. 26, 1933, p. 5; N., "Cent mille prolétaires ont manifesté hier à Berlin," *Humanité,* Jan. 26, 1933, p. 1; Richard J. Evans, *Eric Hobsbawm: A Life in History* (New York: Oxford University Press, 2019), 38; "Berlin Workers in Huge Protest," (New York) *Daily Worker,* Jan. 26, 1933, p. 3; "Unter Polizei-Schutz," *Berliner Tageblatt,* Jan. 23, 1933, p. 1; "Après la parade fasciste de la Bülowplatz," *Humanité,* Jan. 24, 1933, p. 1; Richard J. Evans, *The Coming of the Third Reich* (New York: Penguin, 2003), 267; Peter Fritzsche, *Hitler's First Hundred Days: When Germans Embraced the Third Reich* (New York: Basic Books, 2020), 85; "9 Reds Killed by Police Fire in Dresden Riot," p. 5.

2. "Die K.P.D. demonstriert," *Berliner Tageblatt,* Jan. 26, 1933, p. 10; Hobsbawm, *Interesting Times,* 73–74; N., "Cent mille prolétaires ont manifesté hier à Berlin," p. 1. For an assessment of the two demonstrations critical of the German Communist Party, see S. Weil, "La situation en Allemagne," *École Émancipée,* Feb. 19, 1933, p. 331. Considering Simone Weil's critique, see "Face à la police et aux provocateurs nazzis les ouvriers de Berlin dressent des barricades," *Humanité,* Jan. 23, 1933, p. 1. See also Ronald Friedmann, *Die Zentrale: Geschichte des Berliner Karl-Liebknecht-Hauses* (Berlin: Dietz, 2011), 71–82.

3. Today the Karl-Liebknecht-Haus is the headquarters of Die Linke, the German "Left Party," and the square is the Rosa-Luxemburg-Platz.

4. N., "Cent mille prolétaires ont manifesté hier à Berlin," p. 1.

5. "Antifaschistische Junge Garde in Berlin gegründet," *Rote Fahne,* July 21, 1929, p. 12; "Braunes Hemd – blaues Hemd," *Berliner Volks-Zeitung,* Oct. 22, 1930, p. 3; "Der Eid der 'Antifa,'" *Berliner Börsen-Zeitung,* Nov. 19, 1930, p. 3; Eve Rosenhaft, *Beating the Fascists? The German Communists and Political Violence, 1929-1933* (Cambridge, Eng.: Cambridge University Press, 1983), 90, 155. On the Iron Front, see Donna Harsch, *German Social Democracy and the Rise of Nazism* (Chapel Hill: University of North Carolina Press, 1993), 169–202.

6. Rosenhaft, *Beating the Fascists?* 97–99.

7. Quoted in Heinz Karl and Erika Küklich, editors, *Die Antifaschistische Aktion: Dokumentation und Chronik Mai 1932 bis Januar 1933* (Berlin: Dietz, 1965), 71. On Antifaschistische Aktion, see also Erika Kücklich and Elfriede Liening, "Die Antifaschistische Aktion,"

—

Beiträge zur Geschichte der deutschen Arbeiterbewegung 4 (1962): 872–97; Rosenhaft, *Beating the Fascists?* 97–99; Langer, *Antifaschistische Aktion,* 69–73.

8. Langer, *Antifaschistische Aktion,* 73; Karl and Küklich, editors, *Antifaschistische Aktion,* 169.

9. Serge Tchakhotine, *Le viol des foules par la Propagande Politique* (Paris: Gallimard, 1939), 102. Sergei Chakhotin wrote that crossing a street in Heidelberg, perhaps on November 30, 1931, he "was struck all of a sudden as if by lightning. Near the corner of a wall a swastika was painted, scratched over by thick lines of white chalk. A thought struck me: But this is the symbol of struggle of our own that I have been seeking! This is precisely what we need!" When his comrades began drawing graffiti of the three arrows over swastikas "a curious guerrilla war broke out in the city." He went on to explain some of the emblem's brilliance: "This symbol, so easy to draw that any child could do it, had the further advantage that it could not be destroyed: our enemies couldn't superimpose their symbol over ours, like we could do to theirs, because in that case it would still leave the impression that it was the swastika that had been barred in by our three arrows." Tchakhotine, *Viol des foules par la Propagande Politique,* 102–04.

On the astonishing Sergei Chakhotin, see Dan S. White, *Lost Comrades: Socialists and the Front Generation, 1918–1945* (Cambridge, Mass.: Harvard University Press, 1992), 94–96; Harsch, *German Social Democracy and the Rise of Nazism,* 177–90; Wolfgang Schivelbusch, *Three New Deals: Reflections on Roosevelt's America, Mussolini's Italy, and Hitler's Germany, 1933–1939,* trans. Jefferson Chase (New York: Metropolitan, 2006), 73–103; Bray, *Antifa,* 24; Charlie E. Krautwald, "Three Arrows Against the Swastika: Militant Social Democracy and Radical Opposition to Fascism in Denmark, 1932–1934," in *Anti-Fascism in the Nordic Countries: New Perspectives, Comparisons and Transnational Connections,* ed. Kasper Braskén, Nigel Copsey, and Johan A. Lundin (London: Routledge, 2019), 101–02.

10. Sergej Tschachotin, "Die Technik der politischen Propaganda," *Sozialistische Monatshefte,* May 9, 1932, p. 426; White, *Lost Comrades,* 97; Langer, *Antifaschistische Aktion,* 101.

11. "Berlin Workers in Huge Protest," p. 3; Tchakhotine, *Viol des foules par la Propagande Politique,* 253.

12. Vergnon, *Antifascisme en France,* 21–42.

13. Evans, *Eric Hobsbawm,* 38.

14. Gottfried Korff, "Rote Fahnen und geballte Faust: Zur Symbolik der Arbeiterbewegung in der Weimarer Republik," in *Transformation der Arbeiterkultur,* ed. Peter Assion (Marburg: Jonas, 1986), 93; Tschachotin, "Technik der politischen Propaganda," 427. See also Philippe Burrin, "Poings levés et bras tendus: La contagion des symboles au temps du Front populaire," *Vingtième siècle,* no. 11 (July 1986): 5–20; Gottfried Korff, "From Brotherly Handshake to Militant Clenched Fist: On Political Metaphors for the Worker's

—

Hand," *International Labor and Working-Class History*, no. 42 (Fall 1992): 70–81; Gilles Vergnon, "Le 'poing levé', du rite soldatique au rite de masse: Jalons pour l'histoire d'un rite politique," *Mouvement social*, no. 212 (July 2005): 77–91.

15. Tchakhotine, *Viol des foules par la Propagande Politique*, 106.

16. "Paraders Hail Hitler as Head of Third Reich," *Christian Science Monitor*, Jan. 31, 1933, p. 1. On wireless news and its political ramifications, see the excellent Heidi J. S. Tworek, *News from Germany: The Competition to Control World Communications, 1900–1945* (Cambridge, Mass.: Harvard University Press, 2019).

17. "A imprensa de Roma recebeu bem a ascenção do sr. Hitler," *Correio da Manhã*, Jan. 31, 1933, p. 1; Kriegel, "Sur l'antifascisme," 299.

18. For a terrific intellectual history of the Munich revolution, see Sterling Fishman, "Prophets, Poets and Priests: A Study of the Men and Ideas that Made the Munich Revolution of 1918/1919" (Ph.D. diss., University of Wisconsin, 1960).

19. Ian Kershaw, *Hitler, 1889–1936: Hubris*, (1998; New York: Norton, 1999), 193, 689 *n*222. See also Tilman Allert, *The Hitler Salute: On the Meaning of a Gesture*, trans. Jefferson Chase (New York: Metropolitan, 2008).

20. The Nazis' paramilitary organization, the Sturmabteilung, or SA, first adopted brown shirts, in 1924. Georg Franz-Willing, *Ursprung der Hitlerbewegung 1919–1922* (Schütz: Preussisch Oldendorf, 1974), 127; Evans, *Coming of the Third Reich*, 181; Daniel Siemens, *Stormtroopers: A New History of Hitler's Brownshirts* (New Haven: Yale University Press, 2017), 14. Georg Franz-Willing writes that when Ernst Röhm was considering how to outfit the paramilitary at a 1924 meeting in Salzburg, another SA leader, Gerhard Rossbach, suggested the brown khaki shirt he himself was wearing, and Röhm replied: "That looks good!" Franz-Willing, *Ursprung der Hitlerbewegung*, 127.

21. "Erfasst den Putschisten-Geldsack!" *Berliner Volks-Zeitung*, Aug. 6, 1929, p. 1; Karl H. von Wiegand, "Bavarian Reds Rout Fascisti; 12 Wounded," *Washington Post*, Dec. 14, 1922, p. 2; Cyril Brown, "New Popular Idol Rises in Bavaria," *New York Times*, Nov. 21, 1922, p. 18; Andres Revesz, "El fascismo fuera de Italia," (Madrid) *ABC*, Nov. 24, 1922, p. 5.

22. Hermann Shützinger, "Der deutsche Fascismus," *Berliner Volks-Zeitung*, Nov. 28, 1922, p. 1; beyond Germany, see "German Fascisti," (London) *Times*, Oct. 18, 1922, p. 11; "El general Litwiz ultima los preparativos antirrepublicanos en Munich," (Buenos Aires) *Crítica*, Nov. 5, 1922, p. 4; "La agitación monárquica en Alemania," (Valparaíso) *Mercurio*, Nov. 7, 1922, p. 10; "Los socialistas alemanes están dispuestos a no permitir el avance de los fascistas bávaros," (Buenos Aires) *Vanguardia*, Nov. 11, 1922, p. 3; "Fascisti Plan New Coup," *Los Angeles Times*, Nov. 18, 1922, p. 11; Revesz, "Fascismo fuera de Italia," p. 5; "Help from America to Bavarian Fascisti," *New York Times*, Dec. 11, 1922, p. 3; "Bavarian Fascisti Censuring Berlin," *Toronto Globe*, Dec. 2, 1922, p. 7; "Germany Is Centre of

—

Tightening Ring Formed by Fascisti," *Philadelphia Inquirer,* Dec. 31, 1922, p. 1; "Confusion and Chaos in Germany," *Daily Express,* Sept. 28, 1923, p. 1; "Les nationalistes bavarois prétendent entrer, le 9, à Berlin," *Paris-Soir,* Nov. 6, 1923, p. 1.

23. "The White Guard in Italy," *Workers' Dreadnought,* Dec. 13, 1919, p. 1570. On the paramilitaries of the era, see Sandra McGee Deutsch, "The Right Under Radicalism, 1916–1930," in *The Argentine Right: Its History and Intellectual Origins, 1910 to the Present,* ed. Deutsch and Ronald H. Dolkart (Lanham, Md.: SR Books, 1993), 37–47; Christopher Capozzola, "The Only Badge Needed Is Your Patriotic Fervor: Vigilance, Coercion, and the Law in World War I America," *Journal of American History* 88, no. 4 (March 2002): 1354–82; Robert Gerwarth, "The Central European Counter-Revolution: Paramilitary Violence in Germany, Austria and Hungary After the Great War," *Past and Present* 200, no. 1 (Aug. 2008): 175–209; Robert Gerwarth and John Horne, editors, *War in Peace: Paramilitary Violence in Europe After the Great War* (Oxford, Eng.: Oxford University Press, 2012); Alcalde, *War Veterans and Fascism in Interwar Europe;* Richard Steigman-Gall, "Star-Spangled Fascism: American Interwar Political Extremism in Comparative Perspective," *Social History* 42, no. 1 (Jan. 2017): 94–119; Béla Bodó, *The White Terror: Antisemitic and Political Violence in Hungary, 1919–1921* (Abingdon, Eng.: Routledge, 2019); Larry Eugene Jones, *The German Right, 1918–1930: Political Parties, Organized Interests, and Patriotic Associations in the Struggle Against Weimar Democracy* (Cambridge, Eng.: Cambridge University Press, 2020).

On the "white guard" paramilitarism of the "Tragic Week" of January 1919 in Buenos Aires and the formation of the Liga Patriótica Argentina less than a week later, see Julio Godio, *La semana trágica de enero de 1919* (Buenos Aires: Granica, 1972), 179–86; Victor A. Mirelman, "The Semana Trágica of 1919 and the Jews in Argentina," *Jewish Social Studies* 37, no. 1 (Winter 1975): 61–73; Deutsch, *Derechas,* 82–84; Finchelstein, *Transatlantic Fascism,* 66. On the Liga Patriótica Argentina, see Sandra F. McGee, "The Visible and Invisible Liga Patriótica Argentina, 1919–28: Gender Roles and the Right Wing," *Hispanic American Historical Review* 64, no. 2 (May 1984): 233–58. See also "Guardia cívica," *Prensa,* Jan. 20, 1919, p. 8. On the Comité Nacional de la Juventud and the Tragic Week, see "Movimiento político," *Nación,* Jan. 9, 1919, p. 9; "Agitación obrera—El paro general," *Nación,* Jan. 12, 1919, p. 6.

24. Scholarly sensibilities change over time, too. My point is that historians do well to wed their method, be it comparative or transnational, to the peculiarities of their period of study. Fascism studies took off in the high Cold War era, when developmentalist social thought encouraged scholars to think in comparative terms: early Italian fascism was imagined largely as its own contained national species of fascism; it could be usefully compared to German, French, and Spanish fascism, and so on, which were all evolving by parallel stages, but separately, each at its own stage and pace in any given era. Twenty-first-century scholarship has been more likely to present transnational connections between places, to think of fascism as a general conceptual project built out of the back and forth of intellectual

—

exchange between the various movements (and other actors). Exemplary of the comparative method is Payne, *History of Fascism;* exemplary of the transnational method is Finchelstein, *Transatlantic Fascism.* For a plea for further transnational studies of antifascism, see the excellent Hugo García, "Transnational History: A New Paradigm for Anti-Fascist Studies?" *Contemporary European History* 25, no. 4 (Nov. 2016): 563–72.

For an insightful examination of comparative and transnational (and global) historical methods, see the instant classic Sebastian Conrad, *What Is Global History?* (Princeton: Princeton University Press, 2016).

25. Gerwarth, "Central European Counter-Revolution," 178; G. Zinoviev, "The Tactics of the Communists," *Toiler,* Dec. 24, 1921, p. 10. "Orguesch" is an alternate spelling of Orgesch, which itself is a portmanteau for Organisation Escherich; Georg Escherich organized the Bavarian paramilitary.

26. For example, Edward Thierry, "Legion Will Become U.S. Fascisti if Reds Peril Nation, Says Owsley," *Helena Daily Independent,* Dec. 12, 1922, p. 5. On the American Legion and paramilitarism, see Capozzola, "Only Badge Needed Is Your Patriotic Fervor."

27. "New Popular Idol Rises in Bavaria," p. 18; "Anti-Semite American Money Said to Aid Bavaria Fascisti," *New-York Tribune,* Dec. 11, 1922, p. 1; "German Fascisti Pour into Munich," *Philadelphia Inquirer,* Dec. 18, 1922, p. 8; "Germany Is Centre of Tightening Ring Formed by Fascisti," p. 1; Leo Spitzer, "La vie du mot 'nazi' en français," *Français moderne* 2, no. 3 (June 1934): 263–69; Franz H. Mautner, "*Nazi* und *Sozi*," *Modern Language Notes* 59, no. 2 (Feb. 1944): 93–100; John Elliott, "New Reichstag Coalition May Upset Fascists," *New York Herald Tribune,* Sept. 16, 1930, pp. 1, 8.

28. See Kasper Braskén, "Making Anti-Fascism Transnational: The Origins of Communist and Socialist Articulations of Resistance in Europe, 1923–1924," *Contemporary European History* 25, no. 4 (Nov. 2016): 573–96. See also Anson Rabinbach, "Staging Antifascism: *The Brown Book of the Reichstag Fire and Hitler Terror*," *New German Critique* 35, no. 1 (Spring 2008): 97–126; Anson Rabinbach, "Freedom for Thälmann! The Comintern and the Orchestration of the Campaign to Free Ernst Thälmann, 1933–39," in *Rethinking Antifascism*, ed. Garcia et al., 23–42. Though Rabinbach is focused on the 1930s, his analysis is useful for thinking through earlier Geman antifascism. On Zetkin's election to the executive committee, at the 1922 Comintern Congress, see John Riddell, editor, *Toward the United Front: Proceedings of the Fourth Congress of the Communist International, 1922,* trans. Riddell (Leiden: Brill, 2012), 64.

29. Fritz Heckert, in *To the Masses: Proceedings of the Third Congress of the Communist International, 1921,* ed. and trans. John Riddell (Leiden: Brill, 2015), 652 (Heckert was not always so admiring of Zetkin; see *To the Masses,* 493); Carl E. Schorske, *German Social Democracy, 1905–1917: The Development of the Great Schism* (1955; New York: Russell & Russell, 1970); Pierre Broué, *The German Revolution, 1917–1923,* trans. John Archer

(Chicago: Haymarket, 2006), 27–40; Eric D. Weitz, *Creating German Communism, 1890–1990: From Popular Protests to Socialist State* (Princeton: Princeton University Press, 1997), 79–80; J. P. Nettl, *Rosa Luxemburg: The Biography* (1966; London: Verso, 2019), 193–99, 793–95; Gilbert Badia, *Clara Zetkin, féministe sans frontières* (Paris: Éditions ouvrières, 1993), 203.

30. Sassoon, *One Hundred Years of Socialism,* 5–31; Mudge, *Leftism Reinvented,* 75–86; "La Conférence des Femmes socialistes," *Humanité,* Aug. 30, 1910, p. 2; Choi Chatterjee, *Celebrating Women: Gender, Festival Culture, and Bolshevik Ideology, 1910–1939* (Pittsburgh: University of Pittsburgh Press, 2002), 19.

On Clara Zetkin's life, see Karen Honeycutt, "Clara Zetkin: A Left-wing Socialist and Feminist in Wilhelmian Germany" (Ph.D. diss., Columbia University, 1975); Philip S. Foner, "Introduction," in *Clara Zetkin: Selected Writings,* ed. Foner (New York: International Publishers, 1984), 17–42; Badia, *Clara Zetkin;* Tânia Puschnerat, *Clara Zetkin: Burgerlichkeit und Marxismus* (Essen: Klartext Verlag, 2003); Tânia Ünlüdağ-Puschnerat, "A German Communist: Clara Zetkin (1857–1933)," in *Agents of the Revolution: New Biographical Approaches to the History of International Communism in the Age of Lenin and Stalin,* ed. Kevin Morgan, Gidon Cohen, and Andrew Flinn (Oxford: Peter Lang, 2005), 93–110. On Zetkin's thought, see Honeycutt, "Clara Zetkin"; Richard J. Evans, "Theory and Practice in German Social Democracy, 1880–1914: Clara Zetkin and the Socialist Theory of Women's Emancipation," *History of Political Thought* 3, no. 2 (Summer 1982): 285–304; Angela Y. Davis, "Foreword," in *Clara Zetkin,* ed. Foner, 9–16; Soma Marik, *Revolutionary Democracy: Emancipation in Classical Marxism* (Chicago: Haymarket, 2018).

Karen Honeycutt points out that it's unclear when Clara Eissner (later Zetkin) joined the party that would become the German Social Democratic Party. She points out as well the ways that relying on formal membership status to define people's political identities runs the risk of uncritically reproducing the limits on formal political participation and recognition that all historical social and political orders—all of them repressive and inducive of domination in their own ways—have imposed. It has been claimed that Eissner joined the party in 1878—a time when it would have been illegal for a woman to do so. Honeycutt asks, was it possible for Zetkin to have joined in 1878? It has also been claimed that she joined in 1881, when the organization was entirely illegal—was it possible for a woman to join then? And if so what would that say about the possibility, or supposed impossibility, of belonging when the party had been still legal? Political belonging is a problem not a fact. See Honeycutt, "Clara Zetkin," 43 *n*71.

31. On the history of the Communist International (Comintern), see F. Borkenau, *World Communism: A History of The Communist International* (1939; [Ann Arbor:] University of Michigan Press, 1962); E. H. Carr, *Twilight of the Comintern, 1930–1935* (New York: Pantheon, 1983); Kevin McDermott and Jeremy Agnew, *The Comintern: A History of International Communism from Lenin to Stalin* (Houndsmills, Basingstoke: Macmillan,

1996). The executive committee of the Comintern called for an international united front against fascism on January 3, 1923. It's unclear to me whether the provisional committee was established at this point, with Zetkin appointed as chairwoman, or whether that happened shortly thereafter. See Mike Taber, editor, *The Communist Movement at a Crossroads: Plenums of the Communist International's Executive Committee, 1922–1923*, trans. John Riddell (Leiden: Brill, 2018), 21.

32. *Protokoll des Vierten Kongresses der Kommunistischen Internationale* (Hamburg: Verlag der Kommunistischen Internationale, 1923), 1.

33. "It is hard to be sufficiently critical of Amadeo Bordiga in this period." Behan, *Resistible Rise of Benito Mussolini*, 91.

34. "Rapport de Bordiga sur le fascisme. Débats sur l'offensive du capital," *Correspondance internationale: Supplement (documentaire)* no. 36 (Dec. 22, 1922): 1; Mussolini, "Il 'Vigente sistema,'" *Popolo d'Italia*, March 1, 1919, p. 1. (I've made my translations of Amadeo Bordiga's report from the *Correspondance internationale* because he gave his report in French. See Riddell, editor, *Toward the United Front*, 416 n7.) See also, at the same congress, Bordiga's reference to the "left tendency" and Nikolai Bukharin's depiction of the Comintern as split into various currents, including, among others, the faction comprised of "the actual lefts" as well as a faction of semi-reformists who "wear a 'left' mask" and hide behind the left's phraseology. *Protokoll des Vierten Kongresses der Kommunistischen Internationale*, 112, 136.

35. "Rapport de Bordiga sur le fascisme," 3; Ceplair, *Under the Shadow of War*, 42; Mike Taber and John Riddell, "Introduction," in Clara Zetkin, *Fighting Fascism: How to Struggle and How to Win*, ed. and trans. Taber and Riddell (Chicago: Haymarket, 2017), 5; Alexander De Grand, *The Italian Left in the Twentieth Century: A History of the Socialist and Communist Parties* (Bloomington: Indiana University Press, 1989), 38–40, 45–46, 49, 52–53; Spriano, *Storia del Partito comunista italiano*, 1: 11–16, 139–51, 237–42; Behan, *Resistible Rise of Benito Mussolini*, 67.

36. Zetkin, *Fighting Fascism*, 23; "Auf zum kampf gegen den Faschismus!" *Rote Fahne*, March 10, 1923, p. 3; "La Conférence de Francfort," *Humanité*, March 21, 1923, p. 3. The primary purpose of the Frankfurt conference wasn't to challenge fascism but rather to agitate against French imperialism. The French military had begun occupying the Ruhr valley to Frankfurt's north in January, after Germany had fallen behind in war reparation payments. On the conference, see Braskén, "Making Anti-fascism Transnational"; Zetkin, *Fighting Fascism*, 77.

37. Zetkin, *Fighting Fascism*, 82–83; "Organisiert den Kampf gegen Faschismus und Kriegsgefahr," *Rote Fahne*, April 7, 1923, p. 3. See also "Die internationale Propagandawoche gegen Krieg und Faschismus," *Rote Fahne*, April 7, 1923, p. 7.

38. "Pour le front unique contre le fascisme," *Humanité*, Feb. 5, 1923, p. 3; "Die Kommunisten und die Ruhrfrage," *Berliner Tageblatt*, March 22, 1923, p. 3.

—

39. "Préparons méthodiquement l'action," *Humanité*, March 19, 1923, p. 1. For early debates on the United Front, see Ernst Meyer, "K.A.P. und Bereinigte Kommunistische Partei," *Internationale* (Unabhängigen Sozialdemokratischen Partei Deutschlands), Nov. 20, 1920, p. 1; "Die nationale Einheitsfront," *Internationale* (Unabhängigen Sozialdemokratischen Partei Deutschlands), Nov. 25, 1920, p. 1; "Fronte unico?" *Martello*, Aug. 13, 1921, p. 4; "Communistes et indépendants allemands," *Humanité*, Dec. 28, 1921, p. 3; G. Zinoviev, "Pour l'Unité du Front prolétarien!" *Correspondance Internationale*, Jan. 4, 1922, pp. 1-3 (speech at the December 4, 1921, meeting of the Comintern executive committee); William F. Dunne, "The United Front in America," *Worker*, March 18, 1922, p. 6; Leon Trotsky, "On the United Front," in *The First Five Years of the Communist International*, vol. 2 (New York: Pioneer, 1953), 91-104; Delegation of the Executive Committee of the Communist International, "Second International Smashes Efforts of Commission of Nine," *Worker*, July 8, 1922, pp. 1, 4; John Pepper, "Limits of the United Front," *Worker*, April 28, 1923, p. 5; "El anarquismo internacional es unionista," (Buenos Aires) *Libertario*, Aug. 10, 1923, p. 1. See also Borkenau, *World Communism*, 221-37; Broué, *German Revolution*, 468-73 and 667-71; Ceplair, *Under the Shadow of War*, 33-46; Larry Peterson, *German Communism, Workers' Protest, and Labour Unions: The Politics of the United Front in Rhineland-Westphalia, 1920-1924* (Dordrecht: Kluwer Academic Publishers, 1993); McDermott and Agnew, *Comintern*, 27-40.

40. McMeekin, *Red Millionaire*, 149; Helmut Gruber, "Willi Münzenberg's German Communist Propaganda Empire 1921-1933," *Journal of Modern History* 38, no. 3 (Sept. 1966): 278-97; Furet, *Passé d'une illusion*, 254, 255.

41. Braskén, "Making Anti-Fascism Transnational," 585, 587-88.

42. Clara Zetkin, *Ausgewählte Reden und Schriften*, vol. 2: *Auswahl aus den Jahren 1918 bis 1923* (Berlin: Dietz, 1960), 729.

43. This is a point made well in Braskén, "Making Anti-Fascism Transnational," 575.

44. Furet, *Passé d'une illusion*, 250, 258.

45. Roberta Suzzi Valli, "Il fascio italiano a Londra. L'attività politica di Camillo Pellizzi," *Storia contemporanea* 26, no. 6 (Dec. 1995): 957-58, 961; Alfio Bernabei, *Esuli ed emigrati italiani nel Regno Unito, 1920-1940* (Milan: Mursia, 1997), 53; "Fascisti in London," *Daily Mirror*, Nov. 6, 1922, p. 9; "Fascisti of Soho," *London Daily Express*, Aug. 25, 1922, p. 2. The founding meeting of the London fascio took place in an ornate house at 27 Holland Park that still stands.

Regarding insignias of skull and crossbone in New York ("the death symbol of piracy"), see "Fascisti in the United States," 503. The first Disperata ("Desperate") squad was made up of unruly, informally organized bodyguards in Fiume dedicated to Gabriele d'Annunzio, established in September 1919. G. A. Chiurco, *Storia della Rivoluzione fascista*, vol. 1: *Anno 1919* (Florence: Vallecchi, n.d. [1929]), 288-89. Shortly thereafter, an elite squad known as the Disperata led punitive expeditions in Tuscany. Frank M. Snowden, *The Fascist Revolution in Tuscany, 1919–1922* (Cambridge, Eng.: Cambridge University Press, 1989), 208.

46. "Fascisti in London," p. 9; "March of Fascisti in London," (London) *Times*, Nov. 6, 1922, p. 11; George L. Mosse, *Fallen Soldiers: Reshaping the Memory of the World Wars* (New York: Oxford University Press, 1990), 95–96. See also "I morti d'Italia esaltati sull'Altare della Patria nell'apoteosi del Soldato ignoto," *Stampa*, Nov. 5, 1921, p. 1.

47. "Dal plaustro," *Carroccio* 17, no. 4 (April 1923): 507; for example, Bosworth, *Mussolini*, 109.

48. Bernabei, *Esuli ed emigrati italiani nel Regno Unito*, 46, 63, 69; P. Di Paola, "Emidio Recchioni," in *Dizionario biografico degli anarchici italiani*, vol. 2, ed. Maurizio Antonioli et al. (Pisa: BFS, 2005), 418–20; Judith R. Walkowitz, *Nights Out: Life in Cosmopolitan London* (New Haven: Yale University Press, 2012), 129; Pietro Di Paola, *The Knights Errant of Anarchy: London and the Italian Anarchist Diaspora* (Liverpool: Liverpool University Press, 2013), 209; Stefania Rampello, "Italian Anti-Fascism in London, 1922–1934," *Modern Italy* 20, no. 4 (Nov. 2015): 352.

49. "Calls Radicals to Save U.S. from Legion and Klan," *New York Herald Tribune*, April 7, 1924, p. 4; "Warns of Fascisti as a Menace to US," *New York Times*, April 7, 1924, p. 2. See also Pietro Allegra, "Fascismo e Klu Klux Klan," *Martello*, Jan. 27, 1923, p. 3.

50. "L'agitazione antifascista," *Martello*, June 9, 1923, p. 3; "To Address Protest Meeting," *Baltimore Sun*, Feb. 16, 1924, p. 7; "Girl Anarchist to Speak," *Detroit Free Press*, April 6, 1908, p. 5. On the life of Elizabeth Gurley Flynn, see, first of all, Elizabeth Gurley Flynn, *The Rebel Girl: An Autobiography: My First Life (1906–1926)* (New York: International, 1973). See also Rosalyn Fraad Baxandall, editor, *Words on Fire: The Life and Writings of Elizabeth Gurley Flynn* (New Brunswick: Rutgers University Press, 1987); Helen C. Camp, *Iron in her Soul: Elizabeth Gurley Flynn and the American Left* (Pullman: Washington State University Press, 1995); Lara Vapnek, *Elizabeth Gurley Flynn: Modern American Revolutionary* (Boulder: Westview Press, 2015); Elizabeth Gurley Flynn, *My Life as a Political Prisoner: The Rebel Girl Becomes "No. 11710,"* second edition (New York: International, 2019). See also Elizabeth Gurley Flynn, *Sabotage: The Conscious Withdrawal of the Workers' Efficiency* (Cleveland: I.W.W. Pub. Bureau, 1915); reprinted in Elizabeth Gurley Flynn, Walker C. Smith, and William E. Trautman, *Direct Action and Sabotage: Three Classic IWW Pamphlets from the 1910s*, ed. Salvatore Salerno (Oakland: PM, 2014).

51. "Gli Italiani negli Stati Uniti: Il movimento fascista," *Carroccio* 17, no. 4 (April 1923): 501. Mario Pei later became a professor at Columbia University and taught there for decades. He wrote linguistic studies and polemics. See, for example, Mario Pei, *The America We Lost: The Concerns of a Conservative* (New York: World, 1968); Mario Pei, *Words in Sheep's Clothing* (New York: Hawthorn, 1969); see also Mario A. Pei, "Freedom Under Fascism," *Annals of the American Academy of Political and Social Science* 180, no. 1 (July

1935): 9–13. Pei's academic admirers have not recognized, or at least have not acknowledged, his fascism. "The new Fascist regime (in its initially mild form) was in those years extremely popular with Italo-Americans, so there was nothing startling about Pei's willingness to translate Vittorio E. de Fiori's Mussolini biography." "From Rome to New York City: Necrology – Mario Andrew Pei (1901–78)," *Romance Philology* 32, no. 4 (May 1979): 496. See also John Fisher and Paul A. Gaeng, editors, *Studies in Honor of Mario A. Pei* (Chapel Hill: University of North Carolina Press, 1972).

52. "Argentina," in *Enciclopedia italiana di scienze, lettere ed arti,* vol. 8, ed. Giovanni Gentile and Calogero Tumminelli (Milan: Rizzoli, 1929), 219. I don't find any reference in 1922 sources to the appearance of fasci in Argentina. Specialists have relied on the 1929 encyclopedia entry to posit the October 12, 1922, origin date. For example, see Newton, *"Ducini, prominenti, antifascisti,"* 46; Katharina Schembs, "Fascist Youth Organizations and Propaganda in a Transnational Perspective: *Balilla* and *Gioventù italiana del Littorio all'estero* in Argentina (1922–1955)," *Amnis* [online] 12 (2013), http://journals.openedition.org/amnis/2021. On early fascism in Argentina, see also Grillo, "Creer en Mussolini," 231–56. And see also Deutsch, *Derechas;* Fernando J. Devoto, *Nacionalismo, fascismo y tradicionalismo en la Argentina moderna: Una historia* (Buenos Aires: Siglo Veintiuno de Argentina, 2002); Daniel Lvovich, *Nacionalismo y antisemitismo en la Argentina* (Buenos Aires: Vergara, 2003); Daniel Lvovich, *El nacionalismo de derecha: Desde sus orígenes a Tacuara* (Buenos Aires: Capital Intelectual, 2006); Finchelstein, *Transatlantic Fascism;* Elina Tranchini, *Granja y arado: Spenglerianos y fascistas en la pampa 1910–1940* (Buenos Aires: Editorial Dunken, 2013).

On early antifascism in Argentina, see Maria de Lujàn Leiva, "Il movimento antifascista in Argentina (1922–1945)," in *Gli italiani fuori d'Italia: Gli emigrati italiani nei movimenti operai dei paesi d'adozione 1880–1940,* ed. Bruno Bezza (Milan: Angeli, 1983), 549–82; Pietro Rinaldo Fanesi, "El anti-fascismo italiano en Argentina (1922–1945)," *Estudios migratorios latinoamericanos* 12 (Aug. 1989): 319–52; Andrés Bisso, editor, *El antifascismo argentino: Selección documental y estudio preliminar* (Buenos Aires: Buenos Libros, 2007); Andrés Bisso, "The Argentine Antifascist Movement and the Building of a Tempting Domestic Appeal, 1922–46," in *Rethinking Antifascism,* ed. Garcia et al., 133–51.

On the Día de la Raza and its political significance, see Marcela García Sebastiani, "Nacionalismo español y celebraciones hispánicas en Argentina: El 12 de octubre, una aproximación," *Anuario IEHS* 31, no. 2 (2016): 159–79; Weld, "Spanish Civil War and the Construction of a Reactionary Historical Consciousness in Augusto Pinochet's Chile," 89.

53. Newton, *"Ducini, prominenti, antifascisti,"* 47.

54. See Keith O. Hodgson, *Fighting Fascism: The British Left and the Rise of Fascism, 1919–39* (Manchester: Manchester University Press, 2010), 100–101.

55. "Introduction," *Patriot,* Feb. 9, 1922, p. 1; Nesta H. Webster, "Conservatism a Living Creed," *Patriot,* Feb. 9, 1922, pp. 8–9; Nesta H. Webster, *World Revolution: The Plot*

Against Civilization (London: Constable, 1921), 296–312. See also Nesta H. Webster, *The French Revolution: A Study in Democracy,* second edition (London: Constable, 1919). The Communists who challenged the British Fascisti's October 7, 1923, meeting caused such a scene that the leading historian of British antifascism, Nigel Copsey, has argued that the "roots of Britain's anti-fascist tradition can be traced back" to that rally. He also calls the British Fascisti "Britain's first fascist organisation." I think it is important to recognize the earlier King Bomba crowd (Emidio Recchioni, Sylvia Pankhurst, Pietro Gualducci, Silvio Corio, and the like) as part of Britain's antifascist tradition and the earlier London fascio (Achille Bettini, Camillo Pellizzi, Antonio Cippico, and the like) as Britain's first fascist organization, but Copsey's point about the informal, direct-action–driven nature of early British antifascism is well taken. Copsey, *Anti-Fascism in Britain,* 1.

56. "Fascisti Plan March in London," (London) *Daily Worker,* Nov. 11, 1924, p. 1; "British Fascists' Procession," *Manchester Guardian,* Nov. 10, 1924, p. 7; "Armistice Memorial Services," *Scotsman,* Nov. 10, 1924, p. 7.

57. See Anson Rabinbach, "George Mosse and the Culture of Antifascism," *German Politics and Society* 18, no. 4 (Winter 2000): 40–41.

58. See Enzo Traverso, *Left-Wing Melancholia: Marxism, History, and Memory* (New York: Columbia University Press, 2016).

59. Pietro Nenni, *Sei anni di guerra civile,* trans. Giuliana Emiliani (Milan: Rizzoli, 1945), 178.

60. "Malgré les chefs réformistes le prolétariat manifestera en masse contre le fascisme assassin," *Humanité,* June 21, 1924, p. 1; "Great Geneva Meeting Denounces Fascismo," *New York Times,* June 22, 1924, p. 16; "Une manifestation à Nice," *Humanité,* June 22, 1924, p. 2; "Malgré Herriot-Blum et leurs flics plus de 30.000 travailleurs ont clamé hier leur haine du fascisme," *Humanité,* June 23, 1924, p. 1; "Une manifestation communiste," *Écho de Paris,* June 23, 1924, p. 2; "Il Comizio internazionale in memoria di Giacomo Matteotti," *Martello,* June 21, 1924, p. 1; "3,000 N.Y. Italians Want Envoy Ousted," *Baltimore Sun,* June 27, 1924, p. 5; "Slaying of Matteotti Protested, Resignation of Mussolini Demanded," *Boston Globe,* June 30, 1924, p. 2; "La grande manifestazione internazionale di N.Y.," and "Grande dimostrazione antifascista a Boston, Mass.," *Martello,* July 5, 1924, p. 1; "Cittadini, Connazionali," (São Paulo) *Difesa,* June 29, 1924, p. 1; "Uma solenne commemoração no Theatro Olympia," (São Paulo) *Combate,* June 27, 1924, p. 4.

61. Our Own Correspondent, "Rome and British Socialists," *Daily Mail,* June 23, 1927, p. 10; Alan Cassels, *Mussolini's Early Diplomacy* (Princeton: Princeton University Press, 1970), 249–50; Lucio Sponza, *Divided Loyalties: Italians in Britain During the Second World War* (Bern: Peter Lang, 2000), 35; "International Fascism," *New Leader,* July 4, 1924, p. 3; "British Labour and the Matteotti Affair," *Manchester Guardian,* June 30, 1924, p. 12. Regarding Shapurji Saklatvala, see Susan D. Pennybacker, *From Scottsboro to Munich: Race and*

Political Culture in 1930s Britain (Princeton: Princeton University Press, 2009). Regarding Saklatvala's political beliefs and various organizational affiliations during the post–October Revolution shuffle, see "Communism in Great Britain," *Manchester Guardian*, Dec. 5, 1922, p. 16. See also Sehri Saklatvala, *The Fifth Commandment: A Biography of Shapurji Saklatvala* (Calcutta: National Book Agency, 1996).

62. "The Fascisti Menace," *Workers' Dreadnought,* Nov. 11, 1922, p. 1. On Sylvia Pankhurst's work with Saklatvala, see Pennybacker, *From Scottsboro to Munich,* 9.

63. "White Guard in Italy," p. 1570. Sylvia Pankhurst's historians have generally depicted this article by Pankhurst as her first testimony against fascism. Her own son, a serious historian, has written that her "introduction to fascism" took place when she traveled to Italy in 1919 and "witnessed fascist *squadristi,* or thugs, beating up the people. This turned her overnight into a passionate anti-fascist." Richard Pankhurst, "Sylvia Pankhurst and the Italian Anti-Fascist Movement: The Women's International Matteotti Committee," *Socialist History* 19 (2001): 1. The situation was more complicated. When Pankhurst went to Italy in 1919 she didn't code the violence she saw as fascist. It wouldn't have made sense for her to have done so at the time. She wrote instead about the violence of "the 'Arditi.'" It's a mistake, I'm suggesting, to think that her experiences in Italy in 1919 made her, or even could have made her, an antifascist overnight. She could comment in 1919, though, that "the 'Arditi'" were "in the strictest sense a White Guard."

64. E. Sylvia Pankhurst, "In the Red Twilight," manuscript, p. v, Estelle Sylvia Pankhurst Papers, International Institute of Social History, Amsterdam (accessed online, image 18, item 146, collection ARCH01029); Katherine Connelly, *Sylvia Pankhurst: Suffragette, Socialist and Scourge of Empire* (London: Pluto, 2013), 58, 105–06; Pankhurst, "Soviet Russia as I Saw It in 1920," 6; Patricia W. Romero, *E. Sylvia Pankhurst: Portrait of a Radical* (New Haven: Yale University Press, 1987), 149. On the life of Sylvia Pankhurst, see also Ian Bullock and Richard Pankhurst, editors, *Sylvia Pankhurst: From Artist to Anti-Fascist* (Houndsmills: Macmillan, 1992); Martin Pugh, *The Pankhursts: The History of One Radical Family* (London: Vintage, 2008); E. Sylvia Pankhurst, *A Suffragette in America: Reflections on Prisoners, Pickets and Political Change,* ed. Katherine Connelly (London: Pluto, 2019); Rachel Holmes, *Sylvia Pankhurst: Natural Born Rebel* (London: Bloomsbury, 2020).

65. "A Prohibited Memorial Meeting," *Manchester Guardian,* June 17, 1925, p. 20.

66. Bisso, editor, *Antifascismo argentino,* 103; Fanesi, "Anti-fascismo italiano en Argentina," 324.

67. Quoted in Leiva, "Movimento antifascista italiano in Argentina," 561.

68. To be clear, though, Giacomo Matteotti had not been in the Italian Socialist Party (Partito Socialista Italiano, PSI) since 1922; he was the face of the Unitary Socialist Party (Partito Socialista Unitario, PSU), created in 1922. Amadeo Bordiga had led the extreme left of the Italian Socialist Party to split off and create the Communist Party of Italy (Partito

Comunista d'Italia, PCd'I) in 1921; that was the party that would become the Italian Communist Party of great renown during and after World War II (Partito Comunista Italiano, PCI). See De Grand, *Italian Left in the Twentieth Century,* 45–61.

69. "Le 'fasciste Matteotti,'" *Populaire,* Aug. 2, 1927, p. 1.

70. *Atti parlamentari: Discussioni della camera, sessione 1921,* part 1–1a della XXVI legislatura dall'11 giugno al 31 iuglio 1921 ([Turin: Tip. E. Botta,] n.d.), 89.

71. See Sternhell, *Neither Right nor Left,* 302.

72. Frederick T. Birchall, "When the Reichstag Heard a Hymn of Hate," *New York Times,* Sept. 18, 1932, sec. 8, p. 2. For a critical assessment of Zetkin's speech, see Antonia Grunenberg, *Antifaschismus, ein deutscher Mythos* (Reinbek: Rowohlt, 1993), 22–23.

73. Badia, *Clara Zetkin,* 271–304; John Riddell, "Zetkin's Appeal for a United Front Against Nazism," in Zetkin, *Fighting Fascism,* 95–101.

74. Clara Zetkin, *Ausgewählte Reden und Schriften,* vol. 3: *Auswahl aus den Jahren 1924 bis 1933* (Berlin: Dietz, 1960), 417–18.

75. See Riddell, "Zetkin's Appeal for a United Front Against Nazism," 101.

3. FASCISM SHALL NOT PASS

Epigraph: "'Il Fascismo è all'ordine del giorno in tutti i paesi,'" *Stampa,* Oct. 28, 1930, p. 1.

1. Eric Sevareid, *Not So Wild a Dream* (New York: Knopf, 1946), 58.

2. T. W. [Theodor Wolff], "Bei Mussolini," *Berliner Tageblatt,* May 11, 1930, p. 2.

3. Patrick Seale, *The Struggle for Syria: A Study of Post-War Arab Politics, 1945–1958* (London: Oxford University Press, 1965), 64; Elizabeth Thompson, *Colonial Citizens: Republican Rights, Paternal Privilege, and Gender in French Syria and Lebanon* (New York: Columbia University Press, 2000), 192; Deutsch, *Derechas,* 252; Plínio Salgado, "Como eu vi a Itália," *Hierarchia,* March 1932, p. 205; "Fascists in Egypt," *Palestine Post,* March 14, 1934, p. 4; "Labour Trouble in Egypt—Green Shirts Arrested," *Palestine Post,* July 3, 1934, p. 7; Israel Gershoni and James Jankowski, *Confronting Fascism in Egypt: Dictatorship Versus Democracy in the 1930s* (Stanford: Stanford University Press, 2010), 234–39; Adám Anderle, *Los movimientos políticos en el Perú entre las dos guerras mundiales* (Havana: Editorial Casa de las Américas, 1985), 297; Tirso Aníbal Molinari Morales, *El fascismo en el Perú: La Unión Revolucionaria, 1931–1936* (Lima: Fondo Editorial de la Facultad de Ciencias Sociales, 2006); "'Blue Shirts' Again," *North-China Herald,* Aug. 23, 1933, p. 281; "Alleged Offer by Chinese Blue Shirts," *South China Morning Post,* Sept. 1933, p. 15; Eugene Speck, "London Rioters Beat Fascisti for Baiting Jews," *Chicago Tribune,* May 1, 1933, p. 2; "Earl of Erroll as Blackshirt Delegate to Kenya," *Blackshirt,* June 29, 1934, p. 10; "A Fascist Earl," (London) *Daily Worker,* July 3, 1934, p. 4; "Irish Blue Shirts Re-elect O'Duffy," *New York*

Times, Feb. 9, 1934, p. 3; "Jersey Fascists Organize," *New York Times,* March 14, 1934, p. 9; "Newark Fascists Get Permit to March in Uniforms, with Arms," (New York) *Daily Worker,* May 19, 1934, p. 1; "Mexico Asked by 'Gold Shirts' to Oust Aliens," *New York Herald Tribune,* June 24, 1934, sec. 2, p. 7; Ricardo Pérez Montfort, *"Por la patria y por la raza": La derecha secular en el sexenio de Lázaro Cárdenas* (Mexico City: Facultad de Filosofía y Letras, UNAM, 1993), 19; Gustavo Reno, "11 Bombs Rock Havana in War Over Labor Law," *Chicago Tribune,* Dec. 20, 1933, p. 10; J. D. Phillips, "Havana Students Shot by Soldiers," *New York Times,* Feb. 7, 1934, p. 8; "Mutiny on Gunboat in Cuba Harbor," (New York) *Daily Worker,* June 26, 1934, p. 6; Grobart, "Cuban Working Class Movement from 1925 to 1933," esp. 94; Frank Andre Guridy, "'War on the Negro': Race and the Revolution of 1933," *Cuban Studies* 40 (2010): 49–73.

The slogan "México para los mexicanos" was older, and could be used in a variety of ways. Woodrow Wilson's emissary to Mexico wrote to Wilson that Pancho Villa embodied the notion by opposing foreign *capital.* Friedrich Katz, "De la alianza a la dependencia. Formación y deformación de una alianza entre Villa y Estados Unidos," in *Nuevos ensayos mexicanos* (Mexico City: Ediciones Era, 2006), 243.

4. "El crimen de Córdoba," (Buenos Aires) *Vanguardia,* Oct. 21, 1933, p. 1; "Riot in Argentine City," *Scotsman,* Sept. 30, 1933, p. 14; "Sangriente choque entre socialistas y fascistas," (Madrid) *ABC,* Sept. 30, 1933, p. 36; "La Barbarie Fascista en Córdoba," (Buenos Aires) *Vanguardia,* Oct. 24, 1933, p. 5; "Cómo Asesinaron al Dip. Guevara," (Buenos Aires) *Vanguardia,* Oct. 1, 1933, p. 2; Hernán M. Capizzano, *Presencia fascista en Argentina: Relatos y apuntes, 1930–1945* (Buenos Aires: Memoria y Archivo, 2013), 77–78; Deutsch, *Derechas,* 210; Finchelstein, *Transatlantic Fascism,* 76. See also "11 Wounded in Clash at Socialist Parley," *Austin Statesman,* Sept. 29, 1933, p. 1; Hernán M. Capizzano, *Legión Cívica Argentina: Del uriburismo al nacionalismo* (Buenos Aires: Editorial Santiago Apóstol, 2007), 168.

5. Capizzano, *Presencia fascista en Argentina,* 77–79.

6. On the relationship of nacionalismo to fascism, see Finchelstein, *Transatlantic Fascism.*

7. On the historiographical debate, see Deutsch, *Derechas,* 245.

8. For an explanation of why one should be wary of reifying a formal organization such as the Legión Cívica Argentina and assigning it the identity of fascism wholesale (or rejecting the identity wholesale), see Finchelstein, *Transatlantic Fascism,* 71.

9. At the time of Guevara's murder, the legionarios were often identified as fascists. One account of the assault on the antifascist rally, published in Madrid's *ABC,* had it that legionarios alone had assailed the antifascists and assessed that they *were* "Argentine fascists," *called* "legionarios" ("fascistas argentinos, llamados legionarios"). "Sangriente choque entre socialistas y fascistas," p. 36. The person accused of shooting José Guevara was a legionario. Deutsch, *Derechas,* 211.

10. It's worth stressing as well that there was nothing inevitable or predetermined about people imagining fascism into a political universal. There was no "logic" inherent to the idea of fascism pushing it toward the universal. Rather, people put the idea of fascism to work in places beyond where the particularity of the idea, as people had fashioned it before, suggested it should be, and this work (not anything inherent in the concept itself) pushed people to reimagine. People take some particularisms and remake them into universals; others they don't. There are different reasons for this; much of it has to do with cultural power rather than the ingenuity of the concept. This line of argument is laid out well in Moyn, "On the Nonglobalization of Ideas."

And since this is a history of how abstractions became something like global concepts and how they came to appear to people as universals, it's worth stating that there's nothing about global concepts or universal abstractions that is superior to local concepts and particularistic abstractions. There's nothing inherently more valuable or significant or noble in universalism. It's closer to my line of thought to say that it's valuable to trace the construction of universals to better recognize their constructedness. See Butler, Laclau, and Žižek, *Contingency, Hegemony, Universality;* Balibar, *On Universals.*

11. This argument derives from the claims advanced since the transnational turn in fascist historiography, and departs from the arguments made in the comparative historiography that dominated fascist studies before then. See Finchelstein, *From Fascism to Populism in History,* 53–66.

12. "Solidariedade pelas vitimas do fascismo internacional," *Homem Livre,* July 24, 1933, p. 2.

13. Arnold Sevareid, "New Silver Shirt Clan with Incredible Credo Secretly Organized Here," *Minneapolis Journal,* Sept. 11, 1936, pp. 1, 14; Arnold Sevareid, "Silvershirts Meet Secretly Here but Come Out Openly in Pacific Coast Drive," *Minneapolis Journal,* Sept. 12, 1936, pp. 1–2; Arnold Sevareid, "Silvershirts Hoard Food in Readiness for Siege Foretold by Pyramids," *Minneapolis Journal,* Sept. 13, 1936, pp. 1, 4; Arnold Sevareid, "Silvershirts Here Elevate Maurice Rose to Status of International Banker," *Minneapolis Journal,* Sept. 14, 1936, pp. 1, 8; Arnold Sevareid, "Silvershirts Say Quarters Are Bought by Morgenthau in Russia at 5 Cents Each," *Minneapolis Journal,* Sept. 15, 1936, pp. 1, 6; Arnold Sevareid, "Silvershirts' Dire Prophecy Falls Flat," *Minneapolis Journal,* Sept. 16, 1936, pp. 1, 11.

14. Ira Katznelson, *Fear Itself: The New Deal and the Origins of Our Time* (New York: Liveright, 2013), 12.

15. On antifascism and the politics of outrage, see Stéphane Hessel, *Indignez-vous!* (Montpellier: Indigène, 2011), translated into English as Stéphane Hessel, *Time for Outrage,* trans. Damion Searls with Alba Arrikha (London: Quartet Books, 2011).

16. "El País Marcha Hacia el Caos," (Buenos Aires) *Vanguardia,* Oct. 24, 1933, p. 5.

17. Hobsbawm, *Age of Extremes,* 104, 147; (New York) *Daily Worker,* Jan. 14, 1925, p. 6.

—

18. Eric Hobsbawm, "Introduction: Inventing Traditions," in *The Invention of Tradition*, ed. Hobsbawm and Terence Ranger (1983; Cambridge, Eng.: Cambridge University Press, 2003), 1.

19. On the idea of "working towards the Führer," see Kershaw, *Hitler, 1889–1936*, 527–91. See also Ian Kershaw, "'Working Towards the Führer': Reflections on the Nature of the Hitler Dictatorship," *Contemporary European History* 2, no. 2 (July 1993): 103–18.

20. "Fascist Coup Planned, Says Smedley Butler," *Los Angeles Times*, Nov. 21, 1934, p. 1.

21. "The Great Fascist Plot," *New Republic*, Dec. 5, 1934, p. 87; Dolores Ibárruri, *En la lucha: Palabras y hechos, 1936–1939* (Moscow: Editorial Progreso, 1968), 36.

22. Ibárruri, *En la lucha*, 36–37.

23. Alexander Werth, *Which Way France?* (New York: Harper, 1937), 47–63; Pierre Appell, *Rapport fait au nom de la commission d'enquête chargée de rechercher les causes et les origines des événements du 6 février 1934 (La soirée du 6 février 1934 à la Concorde)*, no. 3386 (Paris: Impr. de la Chambre des députés, 1934), 2–16; Laurent Bonnevay, *Les journées sanglantes de février 1934: Pages d'histoire* (Paris: Flammarion, 1935), 138; "Les bagarres dans la rue," *Matin*, Feb. 7, 1934, p. 6; La Commission d'enquête parlementaire, *Rapport fait au nom de la Commission chargée d'enquêter sur les événements survenus en France de 1933 à 1945: Témoignages et documents recueillis par la Commission d'enquête parlementaire* (Paris: Presses universitaires de France, 1947), 123; Alexander Werth, *France in Ferment* (New York: Harper & Brothers, 1935), 151; Lucien Rottée to Directeur Général de la Police Municipale, Feb. 9, 1934, p. 1, document 15092, série C, Archives Nationales d'Outre Mer, Aix-en-Provence, France (hereafter, sources from this archive appear in the form: Lucien Rottée to Directeur Général de la Police Municipale, Feb. 9, 1934, p. 1, ANOM C 15092); Lucie Mazauric, *Vive le Front populaire! 1934–1939* (Paris: Plon, 1976), 25; Max Beloff, "The Sixth of February," in *The Decline of the Third Republic*, ed. James Joll (London: Chatto & Windus, 1959), 24; Untitled report, Feb. 6, 1934, document 13308, série F7, Archives Nationales, Paris (hereafter, in the form: Untitled report, Feb. 6, 1934, AN F7 13308).

The contentious historiography of the February 6, 1934, riot is explained at length in Brian Jenkins and Chris Millington, *France and Fascism: February 1934 and the Dynamics of Political Crisis* (London: Routledge, 2015).

24. See, for example, Werth, *France in Ferment*, 142; Bonnevay, *Journées sanglantes*, 85–103.

25. The literature on the paramilitary groups of interwar France is immense. An excellent comparative history of the different organizations is Robert Soucy, *French Fascism: The Second Wave, 1933–1939* (New Haven: Yale University Press, 1995).

26. Regarding the everyday public violence of Paris's paramilitary organizations, see the endlessly fascinating police reports in the AN F7 series, including, for example, AN F7 13238, AN F7 13305, AN F7 13983, AN F7 14795. For a persuasive discussion of the veracity of these reports, see Soucy, *French Fascism*, 11, 323–24 *n*27.

---

27. For a theory of events and how they shift perception, see William H. Sewell, Jr., *Logics of History: Social Theory and Social Transformation* (Chicago: University of Chicago Press, 2005). Regarding the category of the extraordinary, see Kalyvas, *Democracy and the Politics of the Extraordinary.*

28. See Elias Canetti, *Crowds and Power,* trans. Carol Stewart (1962; New York: Farrar, Straus and Giroux, 1984).

29. "Paris et province," *Peuple,* Feb. 7, 1934, p. 1.

30. "Brisez la vague fasciste!" *Humanité,* Feb. 9, 1934, p. 1; Ernest de Framond, *Rapport fait au nom de la commission d'enquête chargée de rechercher les causes et les origines des événements du 6 février 1934 et jours suivants (La journée communiste du 9 février et les incidents communistes du 12 en banlieue),* no. 3392 (Paris: Impr. de la Chambre des députés, 1934), 22; Report, 12:20 a.m., Feb. 10, 1934, AN F7 13308; "La manifestation communiste à d'hier soir," *Populaire,* Feb. 10, 1934, p. 3; "Les troubles communistes d'hier," *Temps,* Feb. 11, 1934, p. 5; Jacques Duclos, *Mémoires,* vol. 1: *1896–1934: Le chemin que j'ai choisi: De Verdun au Parti communiste* (Paris: Fayard, 1968), 402; Daniel Guérin, *Front Populaire: Revolution manquée: Témoignage militant* (Paris: Maspero, 1970), 53.

31. Estimates ranged from 100,000 to 150,000. Werth, *Which Way France?* 62; "Nous étions 150.000 . . . ," *Populaire,* Feb. 13, 1934, p. 2.

32. "Les dockers de Concarneau s'opposent au déchargement d'un bateau hitlérien," *Humanité,* Feb. 9, 1934, p. 1.

33. "Au Peuple de Paris!" *Populaire,* Feb. 11, 1934, p. 1; Pétrus Faure, *Rapport fait au nom de la commission d'enquête chargée de rechercher les causes et les origines des événements du 6 février et les jours suivants (Les manifestations du 12 février 1934 – La grève générale),* no. 3393 (Paris: Impr. de la Chambre des députés, 1934), 4–7, 84–85.

34. On "the *open* crowd" (the "natural crowd"), see Canetti, *Crowds and Power,* 16–17. The flip side of such open-ended organizing is seen in top-down choreographed events – staged events. See Rabinbach, "Staging Antifascism." For an extended discussion of staging politics, see Grunenberg, *Antifaschismus,* 171–86. For a theoretical discussion of the creative powers of human action, see Hans Joas, *The Creativity of Action,* trans. Jeremy Gaines and Paul Keast (Cambridge, Eng.: Polity Press, 1996).

35. "La manifestation monstre au Cours de Vincennes," *Populaire,* Feb. 13, 1934, p. 3; "Le fascisme ne passera pas!" *Populaire,* Feb. 13, 1934, p. 1; Faisal Devji, "The Paradox of Nonviolence," *Public Culture* 23, no. 2 (Spring 2011): 269–74. Much of the literature in nonviolence studies argues that nonviolence largely proves its efficacy as a general rule – that it works *better than* violence, when adopted *instead of* and *without* violence. See Erica Chenoweth and Maria J. Stephan, *Why Civil Resistance Works: The Strategic Logic of Nonviolent Conflict* (New York: Columbia University Press, 2012); Michael N. Nagler, *The Nonviolence Handbook: A Guide for Practical Action* (San Francisco: Berrett-Koehler, 2014). See also

—

Dustin Ells Howes, "The Failure of Pacifism and the Success of Nonviolence," *Perspectives on Politics* 11, no. 2 (June 2013): 427–46; Sharon Erickson Nepstad, *Nonviolent Struggle: Theories, Strategies, and Dynamics* (New York: Oxford University Press, 2015); Mario López Martínez, "La resistencia civil examinada: De Thoreau a Chenoweth," *Polis* 15, no. 43 (April 2016): 41–65. For a critique of certain nonviolence studies, see Bray, *Antifa*, 178–87.

On the "conversion of violence," see Étienne Balibar, *Violence and Civility: On the Limits of Political Philosophy*, trans. G. M. Goshgarian (New York: Columbia University Press, 2015), 25–92. See also the essay on Lenin and Gandhi not included in the English translation of *Violence et civilité* (Paris: Galilée, 2010), 305–21. And see Gene Sharp, *Gandhi Wields the Weapon of Moral Power* (Ahmedabad: Navajivan Publishing House, 1960), esp. 3–9; Wendy Pearlman, *Violence, Nonviolence, and the Palestinian National Movement* (Cambridge, Eng.: Cambridge University Press, 2011); Faisal Devji, *The Impossible Indian: Gandhi and the Temptation of Violence* (Cambridge, Mass.: Harvard University Press, 2012), esp. 119–50.

36. "Manifestation monstre au Cours de Vincennes," p. 3.

37. "Manifestation monstre au Cours de Vincennes," p. 3; "Ce que fut la journée," *Populaire*, Feb. 13, 1934, p. 2.

38. "Manifestation monstre au Cours de Vincennes," p. 3.

39. E. P. Thompson, *The Making of the English Working Class* (1963; New York: Pantheon, 1964), 12.

40. For a deeper examination of this sort of argument, see the study in contrasts between Vladimir Lenin's theory of political action, on the one hand, and Rosa Luxemburg's and Aleksandra Kollontay's, on the other, in James C. Scott, *Seeing Like a State: How Certain Schemes to Improve the Human Condition Have Failed* (New Haven: Yale University Press, 1998), 147–79.

41. Mazauric, *Vive le Front populaire!* 43.

42. Léon Blum, *L'Œuvre*, vol. 6: *1934–1937* (Paris: Éditions Albin Michel, 1964), 16–17; B. Mayeras, "Nous étions 150.000 . . . ," *Populaire*, Feb. 13, 1934, p. 2; Léon Blum, "12 février 1934," *Populaire*, Feb. 13, 1934, p. 2; Werth, *Which Way France?* 62. For a learned ode to joy, see Lynne Segal, *Radical Happiness: Moments of Collective Joy* (London: Verso, 2017).

43. Julian Jackson, *The Popular Front in France: Defending Democracy, 1934–1938* (Cambridge, Eng.: Cambridge University Press, 1987), 6; "Manifestation monstre au Cours de Vincennes," p. 3; "Nous étions 150.000 . . . ," p. 2.

44. Werth, *Which Way France?* 62.

45. Already on February 6, 1934, Léon Blum had said in the deputies' chamber inside the Palais Bourbon, *during* the riots outside, quite similar words: "fascist reaction shall not pass." Another appeal, put out on the Saturday before the Twelfth, signed "CGT," had pleaded for a mass turnout Monday to ensure that "odious and barbarous fascism shall not pass!" "La réaction fasciste ne passera pas!" *Populaire*, Feb. 7, 1934, p. 1; "Le fascisme ne passera pas!" *Peuple*, Feb. 10, 1934, p. 1.

46. The historian Hugo García, whose work has been crucial to the transnational turn in the study of antifascist history, has pointed out this speech by Santiago Casares Quiroga. See Hugo García, "Was There an Antifascist Culture in Spain During the 1930s?" in *Rethinking Antifascism*, ed. Garcia et al., 101. The discourse in and around Casares Quiroga's oratory conveyed well the dynamics of antifascism and ideas of the left at the moment. The Spanish elections that would bring to power the antifascist Popular Front government were one month away when Casares Quiroga spoke at the Monumental. Thousands attended and there was much talk of "the left" and "leftists" — but all the leftists who were present were onstage, not in the stands. The account in the *Voz* of Madrid (García's cited source) described the thousands of people arriving to hear the speeches from "the leaders of the left"; then, "personalities of the Catalan Left" ("personalidades de la Esquerra") arrived and took their places on the stage, in the ring. Casares Quiroga said his goal was "to republicanize the republic," and he called for a "grand front of leftists to serve as a bulwark against the aggressions of those on the right." Regarding "leftists" and "those on the right," he meant parliamentarians. His notions of left and right in January 1934 remained squarely in parliament. He set up his "No pasaréis" line by referring to the battle cries used in the Great War: "Just as in the European war, a group of heroes, including many Catalans, stood up in front of the Germans to tell them, 'You shall not pass,' so too we must form a tightly bound union and rise up against all those who wish to establish fascism in Spain, and we must tell them: 'You shall not pass.'" "El importante mitin de ayer en Barcelona," *Voz*, Jan. 8, 1934, p. 2.

47. "Contre le fascisme," *Avenir de Bougie*, Feb. 22, 1934, p. 2; Frank H. Simonds, *They Shall Not Pass* (Garden City: Doubleday, Page and Company, 1916); Mayeras, "Nous étions 150.000 . . . ," p. 2.

48. Werth, *France in Ferment*, 142, 143, 144, 145, 147, 153, 161, 162, 165; Werth, *Which Way France?* 51–52, 59. On Paris's centrality to the antifascist left, see Rabinbach, "Paris, Capital of Anti-Fascism."

49. "The Leader at the Albert Hall," *Fascist Week*, April 27, 1934, p. 3; "6,000 Cheering Blackshirts," *Daily Express*, April 23, 1934, p. 2; W. J. Leaper, "Leader's Inspired Speech," *Blackshirt*, April 27, 1934, p. 1.

50. Copsey, *Anti-Fascism in Britain*, 17–18.

51. Viscount Rothermere, "Hurrah for the Blackshirts!" *Daily Mail*, Jan. 15, 1934, p. 10; Our Own Correspondent, "Sign of the Times," *Daily Mail*, Jan. 16, 1934, p. 12. On the British Union of Fascists, see Martin Pugh, *'Hurrah for the Blackshirts!' Fascists and Fascism in Britain Between the Wars* (London: Pimlico, 2006).

52. See Benjamin Zachariah, "Global Fascisms and the *Volk*: The Framing of Narratives and the Crossing of Lines," *South Asia: Journal of South Asian Studies* 38, no. 4 (Dec. 2015):

—

608–12; Finchelstein, *From Fascism to Populism,* 53–66. Federico Finchelstein in particular plays with methods of global history and transnational history to show how thinking through the history of fascism from outside of Europe isn't additive to a Europe-centric history of fascism (as implied by the comparative historians) but rather is transformative of how the whole of fascism looks.

53. "William Joyce," *Fascist Week,* Dec. 1, 1933, p. 4; "Scene at a Blackshirt Meeting," *Daily Express,* March 15, 1934, p. 7; "Three Fascists Charged," *Manchester Guardian,* March 15, 1934, p. 14; "Fascist Fined After Scene at Meeting," *Daily Express,* April 10, 1934, p. 7; "Fascists Charged with Assault," *Yorkshire Post,* April 10, 1934, p. 5. See Colin Holmes, *Searching for Lord Haw-Haw: The Political Lives of William Joyce* (London: Routledge, 2016).

54. "Three Fascists Charged," p. 14.

55. It's only fair to note, since my argument is that spectacular events such as Olympia had the capacity to break through into a broader public consciousness and boost antifascism in an immense transnational arena, that historians of British antifascism, prompted by an admirable iconoclasm, have worked to decenter legendary episodes such as Olympia and Cable Street (and to decenter London in general) in their narratives. Keith O. Hodgson wrote that clashes of a "spectacular nature . . . have overshadowed many of the smaller events, and have perhaps contributed to an underestimation of the scale and intensity [of] British anti-fascism." Hodgson, *Fighting Fascism,* 137. And since my argument is that considerable informal organization went into making events of popular politics into spectacles, even those that might look to some like "spontaneity," it's only fair to note as well that Nigel Copsey has written that "emphasis on the 'popular' and the 'spontaneous' obscures antifascism's organisational features." Copsey, *Anti-Fascism in Britain,* 7. See also Copsey and Olechnowicz, editors, *Varieties of Anti-Fascism;* Tom Buchanan, "'Beyond Cable Street': New Approaches to the Historiography of Antifascism in Britain in the 1930s," in *Rethinking Antifascism,* ed. Garcia et al., 61–75.

56. "Communists and Fascists," *Manchester Guardian,* May 26, 1934, p. 5; "Chase in the Roof," *Manchester Guardian,* June 8, 1934, p. 6.

57. A. D. Emmart, "Huge Fascist Rally in London Is Marked by Wild Disorders," *Baltimore Sun,* June 8, 1934, p. 1.

58. Vindicator, *Fascists at Olympia: A Record of Eye-Witnesses and Victims* (London: Victor Gollancz, 1934), 22–23. At Olympia, antifascists incessantly interrupted, which doesn't necessarily amount to no platforming but does relate to it; on the antifascist ethics of no platforming and free speech, see Bray, *Antifa,* 143–65. After Olympia, the Conservative member of Parliament Geoffrey Lloyd wrote to "definitely challenge Sir Oswald Mosley's whole attitude to the interruption of meetings." Against Mosley's argument that the violence protected his freedom to speak on the platform, Lloyd suggested that "heckling and rough interruptions" were themselves forms of speech protected by customary right. He added that "only by incompetent or conceited speakers" was such speech resented – those "who expect every word of theirs to be listened to in an obsequious silence." Lloyd also pointed out the inequality posed by the technology of loudspeakers: "a speaker is almost proof against effective interruption when using a battery of loudspeakers, because the human voice cannot prevail against the enormous power of the apparatus." He added, "In my experience, in nine times out of ten the meeting gets along pretty well by reasonable and good-natured give-and-take between speaker and audience" – except "when a band of Socialist hooligans used to infest Conservative meetings in Birmingham, when Sir Oswald Mosley was a prominent Labour leader in that city." (Mosley had indeed been a Labourite earlier in life; he also had been a Conservative for a spell.) Vindicator, *Fascists at Olympia*, 9–10.

59. German Nazis already used searchlights for their public spectacles by the time British blackshirts did, though the "cathedral of light" – Albert Speer's use of searchlight beams as surrealistic visual pillars, endowing the proceedings with a scale of monumentality – began later in 1934, in September at the Nuremberg rally filmed for Leni Riefenstahl's propaganda film *Triumph of the Will* (1935). See Albert Speer, *Inside the Third Reich*, trans. Clara and Richard Winston (New York: Simon and Schuster, 1970), 58–59.

60. G. Ward Price, "Reds' Futile Protests," *Daily Mail*, June 8, 1934, p. 13; "Chase in the Roof," *Manchester Guardian*, June 8, 1934, p. 6.

61. G. Ward Price, of Lord Rothermere's *Daily Mail*, wrote of the interrupters, "They got what they deserved." Price, "Reds' Futile Protests," *Daily Mail*, p. 13. See also "The Truth About the Olympia Disorder," *Blackshirt*, June 15, 1934, p. 1.

62. Vindicator, *Fascists at Olympia*, 9, 11, 14, 29. On the brutality of the blackshirts at Olympia, see also "Fascists Beat Up Women," (London) *Daily Worker*, June 8, 1934, p. 1.

63. "Chase in the Roof," p. 6; "Baton Charges in London Riots," *Daily Express*, June 8, 1934, p. 1.

64. "Escándalo Fascista en un Cine," (Buenos Aires) *Vanguardia*, March 11, 1934, p. 2; "Nuevo Atentado Fascista," (Buenos Aires) *Vanguardia*, March 12, 1934, p. 1; Deutsch, *Derechas*, 210; "Criminal Atentado," (Buenos Aires) *Vanguardia*, Sept. 15, 1934, p. 1; "Philippine Youth Organize," *Chicago Tribune*, Jan. 8, 1934, p. 11; "Mosley Opens Drive for Fascist Britain," *New York Times*, Jan. 22, 1934, p. 7; "Irish Blue Shirts Re-elect O'Duffy," *New York Times*, Feb. 9, 1934, p. 3; "Els feixistes d'Egipte," *Rambla*, Feb. 12, 1936, p. 1; M. O'Zoux, "Les Insignes et Saluts de la jeunesse en Syrie et au Liban," *Entretiens sur l'évolution des pays de civilization arabe* 2 (1937): 96–104; "Oppose Chilean Fascists," *New York Times*, March 12, 1939, p. 39; Mallory Browne, "Fascism in France," *Times of India*, May 1, 1934, p. 8. On mass culture and class-based politics, see Matthew B. Karush, *Culture of Class: Radio and Cinema in the Making of a Divided Argentina, 1920–1946* (Durham: Duke University Press, 2012).

65. Before the "Roman salute" appeared in silent films, it appeared in nineteenth-century "toga plays." The practice, then, is specifically an invented tradition of the nineteenth-century popular stage. See the revelatory Martin M. Winkler, *The Roman Salute: Cinema, History, Ideology* (Columbus: Ohio State University Press, 2009). Regarding Gabriele d'Annunzio, see Lucy Hughes-Hallett, *Gabriele d'Annunzio: Poet, Seducer, and Preacher of War* (New York: Knopf, 2013).

66. Charles A. Selden, "Fists Fly at Big Fascist Gathering Held in London," (Kingston) *Daily Gleaner,* June 14, 1934, p. 21; "20,000 Nazi Friends at a Rally Here Denounce Boycott," *New York Times,* May 18, 1934, pp. 1, 3; "Anti-Nazi Demonstration in N.Y.," *Militant,* May 26, 1934, p. 4.

67. "Garden Rally Indicts Hitler," *New York Herald Tribune,* March 8, 1934, pp. 1, 20; "20,000 Pledge Fight on Fascist Regimes," *New York Times* Nov. 29, 1934, p. 25.

68. Charles A. Selden, "Rival Rallies Pass Quietly in London," *New York Times,* Sept. 10, 1934, p. 9; A. D. Emmart, "Huge Fascist Rally in London Is Marked by Wild Disorders," *Baltimore Sun,* June 8, 1934, p. 1. See also "Mosley's Rally an Utter Fiasco," (London) *Daily Worker,* Sept. 10, 1934, p. 1. Regarding the sorts of creative organizing labors that went into making the antifascist counterdemonstration a success, see "Raid on Dance Band Microphone," *Daily Mirror,* Sept. 7, 1934, p. 2.

69. "Fué Brutalmente Disuelto por la Policía el Mitin de la F.U.A.," (Buenos Aires) *Vanguardia,* Sept. 16, 1934, p. 3; Hernán M. Capizzano, *Jacinto Lacebrón Guzmán: Primer caído del Nacionalismo Argentino* (Buenos Aires: Editorial Santiago Apóstol, 2001), 42 (photo of salutes), 48 (quotation, from the newspaper the *Bandera Argentina*).

70. "A comemoração de Matteotti e os seus resultados praticos," *Homem Livre,* June 17, 1933, p. 3; Fanesi, "Anti-fascismo italiano en Argentina," 324; "Contra o fascismo," *Homem Livre,* May 27, 1933, p. 1. On antifascism among Italian émigrés, see João Fábio Bertonha, *Fascismo e Antifascismo Italianos: Ensaios* (Caixos do Sul: EDUCS, 2017).

71. The European Anti-Fascist Workers' Congress, at the Salle Pleyel in June 1933, has loomed large in the historiography of antifascism in part because of the confusing way that Communists started talking about it afterward. After Pleyel, Comintern officials and Communists in multiple countries took to speaking of the "Amsterdam-Pleyel movement," linking the congress at the Pleyel with an earlier congress, held the previous summer in Amsterdam (and organized by none other than Willi Münzenberg). Likely in large part because Communists started linking the two together, after the fact, historians inclined to emphasize the Comintern's role in antifascist politics have described not only the congress at the Pleyel as an example of Comintern-orchestrated antifascism but also the previous congress at Amsterdam as an example of it. François Furet, for example, argued that the crucial turn in the Comintern's policy occurred before Hitler took power: when the Amsterdam conference opened on August 27, 1932, it opened, Furet wrote, under what he called a "double watchword": a call to stand "against fascism and war." Furet mistakenly thought that the title of the Amsterdam conference was the "Congrès international contre le fascisme et la guerre" (International Congress Against Fascism and War). In fact, it was the "Congrès mondial

—

contre la guerre" (World Congress Against War). The Amsterdam meeting of August 1932, that is, wasn't a congress dedicated to fighting fascism. (As Münzenberg's biographer put it, the congress avoided focusing on fascism and did so "stunningly in light of Hitler's electoral triumphs that year." McMeekin, *Red Millionaire,* 202.) Only later, after Pleyel, did the antiwar committee that had come out of Amsterdam (the World Committee Against Imperialist War) merge with the antifascist organization that came out of Pleyel to form the World Committee Against War and Fascism. And it was at that point that Communists began to talk of the "Amsterdam-Pleyel movement"; only then did the Amsterdam congress become, retrospectively, linked to antifascism in Communists' minds. Far from an example of the Comintern leading the way on antifascist politics, as Furet understood it to be, the Amsterdam conference of 1932 is evidence that the Comintern's propaganda machine was geared toward other matters in the months before the Nazis took power. See Furet, *Passé d'une illusion,* 254–63.

Even the antifascism that followed, though, didn't all unfold from Comintern directives given from above. Consider London in the summer of 1934, the summer of Olympia and Hyde Park: the Communist Party of Great Britain established an antifascist committee, as the historian Larry Ceplair put it, "under the auspices of the World Committee Against War and Fascism (Amsterdam-Pleyel)." Ceplair, *Under the Shadow of War,* 164. This, the establishment of the Co-ordinating Committee for Anti-Fascist Activities headed by John Strachey, happened on July 25, 1934—which is to say, after Olympia. The committee didn't create mass antifascism in London, it reacted to it. (For more along this line of argument, see the discussion of the Union des Travailleurs Nègres in Chapter 4.) On the origin of the Co-ordinating Committee for Anti-Fascist Activities, see Nigel Copsey, "'Every Time They Made a Communist, They Made a Fascist': The Labour Party and Popular Anti-Fascism in the 1930s," in *Varieties of Anti-Fascism,* ed. Copsey and Olechnowicz, 60.

72. John W. F. Dulles, *Anarchists and Communists in Brazil, 1900–1935* (Austin: University of Texas Press, 1973), 337; Ricardo Figueiredo de Castro, "O movimento trotskista brasileiro nos anos 30," in *Izquierdas, movimientos sociales y cultura política en América Latina* ed. Lazar Jeifets et al. (Morelia: Instituto de Investigaciones Históricas, 2016), 129–36; James P. Woodard, *A Place in Politics: São Paulo, Brazil, from Seigneurial Republicanism to Regionalist Revolt* (Durham: Duke University Press, 2009), 235; Ricardo Figueiredo de Castro, "A Frente Única Antifascista (FUA) e o antifascismo no Brasil (1933–1934)," *Topoi* 3, no. 5 (Dec. 2002): 362–63. See also Fulvio Abramo and Dainis Karepovs, editors, *Na contracorrente da História: Documentos do trotskismo brasileiro (1930–1940),* second edition (São Paulo: Sundermann, 2015).

73. Robert J. Alexander, *Trotskyism in Latin America* (Stanford: Hoover Institution Press, 1973), 70, 72. On the republican and abolitionist Aristides Lôbo, see Moreno Brandão, *Aristides Lobo* (Rio de Janeiro: A Noite Editora, 1938).

74. *Jornal do Recife,* June 28, 1933, p. 1; "A Constituição da Frente Unica Antifascista," *Homem Livre,* July 2, 1933, pp. 1–2.

75. "Manifesto das organizações coligadas em frente única antifascista," *Homem Livre,* Dec. 14, 1933, p. 1; "Um manifesto da F. G. D. da F. U. A.," *Homem Livre,* Jan. 3, 1934, p. 4; Castro, "Frente Única Antifascista (FUA) e o antifascismo no Brasil," 360–61. See also Ângela Meirelles de Oliveira, "El antifascismo en Brasil en los años 30: Un panorama de la lucha de los intelectuales," *Trabajos y los días,* no. 3 (2012): 166. For an argument crediting the Brazilian Communist Party as the "fundamental nucleus of the united front" and the "motor" driving "the formation of the antiintegralista united front," see Eduardo Maffei, *A batalha da Praça da Sé* (Rio de Janeiro: Philobiblion, 1984), 57 and 75.

The Antifascist United Front had its own manifesto, based on Aristides Lôbo's original proposal. See "Manifesto da Frente Unica Anti-Fascista ao Povo do Brasil," *Homem Livre,* July 17, 1933, p. 6. Lôbo's uncle cowrote the manifesto of the Confederação Abolicionista. *Manifesto da Confederação Abolicionista do Rio de Janeiro* (Rio de Janeiro: Typ. Da "Gazeta da Tarde," 1883).

76. Castro, "Frente Única Antifascista," 359; "Frente Unica," *Homem Livre,* July 2, 1933, p. 1.

77. "A manifestação anti-integralista do dia 14 de Novembro," *Homem Livre,* Nov. 20, 1933, p. 1; Deutsch, *Derechas,* 259.

78. Disagreements over the violence at the Praça da Sé led to the expulsion of Lôbo from the Brazilian Trotskyists' organization the Liga Comunista Internacionalista (Bolcheviques-Leninistas). Robert J. Alexander, *International Trotskyism, 1929–1985: A Documented Analysis of the Movement* (Durham: Duke University Press, 1991), 132.

79. "A capital paulista foi theatro, ante-hontem, de graves acontecimentos," *Correio da Manhã,* Oct. 9, 1934, p. 1; Deutsch, *Derechas,* 260.

80. "São Paulo viveu horas sangrentas de pavor," *Nação,* Oct. 9, 1934, p. 1.

81. Sandra McGee Deutsch, "Spartan Mothers: Fascist Women in Brazil in the 1930s," in *Right-Wing Women: From Conservatives to Extremists Around the World,* ed. Paola Bacchetta and Margaret Power (New York: Routledge, 2002), 161; Dulles, *Anarchists and Communists in Brazil,* 519; "Capital paulista foi theatro, ante-hontem, de graves acontecimentos," p. 1; Deutsch, *Derechas,* 260.

82. "O conflicto da praça da Sé," *Noite,* Oct. 9, 1934, p. 1.

4. AGAINST WAR AND FASCISM

Epigraph: Langston Hughes, "Broadcast on Ethiopia," *American Spectator* 4, no. 43 (July 1936): 16.

1. "C.C.N.Y. Rioters Burn 2-Headed Prexy in Effigy," *New York Herald Tribune,* Nov. 21, 1934, p. 3; "New York College Students Incite Strike," *Washington Post,* Nov. 21, 1934,

p. 4. This chapter includes material originally published in the journal *Diplomatic History*. Joseph Fronczak, "Local People's Global Politics: A Transnational History of the Hands Off Ethiopia Movement of 1935," *Diplomatic History* 39, no. 2 (April 2015): 245–74.

2. "Students Rout Police in Riot at N.Y. College," *Chicago Tribune*, Nov. 21, 1934, p. 5; "C.C.N.Y. Rioters Burn 2-Headed Prexy in Effigy," p. 3.

3. "Strike Against Fascism!" *Student News*, Nov. 19, 1934, p. 1. In general, antifascists in the age of fascism began calling their actions antifascist before they began identifying themselves as antifascists; and they began identifying themselves as antifascists before they began articulating antifascism itself, in noun form. They also began using the abstract noun "fascism" before they used the abstract noun "antifascism." When faculty at the City College of New York formalized an organization less than two months after the effigy burning, with the stated intent of "studying the manifestations of Fascism" and pledging "to assist the forces fighting against Fascism" on campus, they only used "anti-Fascist" as an adjective, as in the group's formal name, the Anti-Fascist Association. See "Preamble," *Bulletin of the Anti-Fascist Association* 1, no. 1 (January 1935): 1.

4. The political concept of liberalism originated in the Spain of Napoleon's occupation, when constitutionalist deputies in the Cortes, gathered at Cadiz, took on the label "los liberales." The "gran sistema" proposed by the liberales quickly became known as "liberalismo." Javier Fernández Sebastián, "Liberalismo en España (1810–1850): La construcción de un concepto y la forja de una identidad política," in *La aurora de la libertad: Los primeros liberalismos en el mundo iberoamericano*, ed. Fernández Sebastián (Madrid: Marcial Pons Historia, 2012), 261. See also Isabel Burdiel, "Myths of Failure, Myths of Success: New Perspectives on Nineteenth-Century Spanish Liberalism," *Journal of Modern History* 70, no. 4 (Dec. 1998): 899–900.

5. The 1832 Reform Act in Britain threw into existence new political worlds of mass politics, popular sovereignty, and ideology. The Whigs emerged as the dominant force of British politics. The Tories were left to plot out new ways of imagining themselves, as America's politics-obsessed newspaper readers were quick to learn: the *New-York Spectator* shared with its readers that the familiar English "tories" had become "conservatives, as they are now called." "England," *New-York Spectator*, June 6, 1833, p. 1. Conceptions of "conservatism" came only later. For an early example, see *London Morning Chronicle*, July 13, 1836, p. 3. For another early example, posing "a question between conservatism and locofocoism," see "New Features of the Revolution," *New York Morning Herald*, Oct. 30, 1837, p. 2.

6. "Rally, March by Torchlight at 8 Tonight," *Student News*, Nov. 19, 1934, p. 1; Joseph Dorman, *Arguing the World: The New York Intellectuals in Their Own Words* (2000; Chicago: University of Chicago Press, 2001), 42; "Students Rout Police in Riot at N.Y. College," p. 5. For footage of New York students' protests (shot a few years later), see the fascinating student-produced film *We Want Peace*, dir. Marvin Rothenberg and Elias S. Wilentz (American Student Union, 1937).

7. "Riot and Fight Greet Italians at City College," *New York Herald Tribune,* Oct. 10, 1934, pp. 1, 14; Joseph Leeds, *Let My People Know: The Story of Wilfred Mendelson, "Mendy," August 17, 1915–July 28, 1938* (n.p., 1942), 20; "Riot and Fight Greet Italians at City College," pp. 1, 14. After the college president's outburst, the antifascist students took to wearing buttons that read, "I AM A guttersnipe / I FIGHT fascism."

8. "Riot and Fight Greet Italians at City College," p. 14; "Italian Students Defy N.Y.U. Protest," *New York Times,* Oct. 11, 1934, p. 25. Though it had been a student sympathetic to fascism — a member of the Italian visitors' welcoming committee — who had punched the antifascist speaker, the professor's comments on campus free speech were intended to condemn the initial antifascist hecklers — whose interruptions had been their means to extract an opportunity of speech for their own contingent.

9. "Italian Students Defy N.Y.U. Protest," p. 25. Another detachment of the students sent by the fascist regime (there were 350 students in all on the tour of United States campuses) visited Princeton University. The administration held an official welcoming ceremony for the fascist students in the Faculty Room of Nassau Hall. The fascists' leader thanked the university for the courteous welcome, and Dean of the Faculty Robert K. Root welcomed them "in the name of the university," as the *New York Herald Tribune* put it. When the visitors raised a fascist salute and sang a song (likely "Giovinezza"), Clarence Di Donato (identified as a "local Communist" by the *Daily Princetonian*) heckled them from the back of the room, directly underneath a famous Charles Willson Peale portrait of George Washington. Di Donato began to shout out antifascist rhetoric. Some of the fascists charged at him, restrained only by their leader. The reporter for the *Daily Princetonian* admitted to having been bored until Di Donato had piped up. Now, "the ceremony took on a new lease of life" as the fascists pushed toward him, replying "in fiery language." The reporter concluded that "there was no doubt in the minds of the spectators" that Di Donato "had stolen the show from under the nose of the star performers, and had put some life and color into an otherwise drab affair." Di Donato was arraigned and barred from campus. "Communist Livens Italian Reception," *Daily Princetonian,* Oct. 10, 1934, pp. 1, 3; "Italian Students Defy N.Y.U. Protest," p. 25. The *Daily Princetonian* editorialized that the fascist campus tour "seems to be leaving behind it at every step a reinforced sentiment against the Fascists who sponsored the tour." The student paper credited antifascists for this. The editorial added that the antifascist heckling entitled the fascists to some resentment, but "the thing which has prejudiced observers against them is the manner in which they have received these hecklings, which are perhaps unavoidable in a country as heterogeneous as ours. The riot methods employed to silence criticism have only proved what the anti-Fascists have contended: that Fascism aims to silence and expunge all individual liberties." The editorial acknowledged that "the anti-Fascists have not covered themselves in glory in their exercise of the right of free speech," but they had made their point. "Fascist Intellectuals," *Daily Princetonian,* Oct. 10, 1934, p. 2.

—

10. "Ex-Dean Dies After C.C.N.Y. Ousts Rioters," *New York Herald Tribune*, Nov. 14, 1934, p. 1.

11. Paul Comly French, "Gen. Butler Accuses N.Y. Brokers of Plotting Dictatorship in U.S.," *New York Post*, Nov. 20, 1934, p. 1.

12. On the Walwal incident, see George W. Baer, *The Coming of the Italian-Ethiopian War* (Cambridge, Mass.: Harvard University Press, 1967), 45–61.

13. My rebuke here is a humble exercise in the very practice, self-criticism, that Lenin insisted upon as an imperative duty in *The Infantile Sickness of "Leftism" in Communism*. The offending quotations are drawn from Fronczak, "Local People's Global Politics," 249–50.

14. Handwritten report, Jan. 7, 1935, document 53, série 3, Service de liaison avec les originaires des territoires français d'outre-mer, Fonds ministériels, Archives Nationales d'Outre Mer, Aix-en-Provence, France (hereafter cited in the form: Handwritten report, Jan. 7, 1935, ANOM FM 3 SLOTFOM 53). The office most responsible for policing people of color in Depression-era Paris was the Centre des Affaires Indigènes, which collaborated with the Sûreté Générale and local police prefectures. The bureaucratic structure of the policing, and its racializing force, is explained well in Jennifer Anne Boittin, *Colonial Metropolis: The Urban Grounds of Anti-Imperialism and Feminism in Interwar Paris* (Lincoln: University of Nebraska Press, 2010), xxv.

Regarding early documented attempts at organizing protest against fascist Italy's aggression toward Ethiopia: a December 13, 1934, letter from the Women's International League for Peace and Freedom to the League of Nations is noted in Brenda Gayle Plummer, *Rising Wind: Black Americans and U.S. Foreign Affairs, 1935–1960* (Chapel Hill: University of North Carolina Press, 1996), 40.

15. Handwritten report, Jan. 7, 1935, ANOM FM 3 SLOTFOM 53.

16. L. D. R. N., "Notre ligne politique," *Race Nègre*, Nov. 1934, p. 1; Brent Hayes Edwards, *The Practice of Diaspora: Literature, Translation, and the Rise of Black Internationalism* (Cambridge, Mass.: Harvard University Press, 2003), 251; J. S. Spiegler, "Aspects of Nationalist Thought Among French-Speaking West Africans, 1921–39" (D.Phil. thesis, Oxford University, 1968), 176; report, n.d., ANOM FM 3 SLOTFOM 78. On the split, see Spiegler, "Aspects of Nationalist Thought," 173–78. The name Union des Travailleurs Nègres was established in 1932.

17. Report, Jan. 7, 1935, ANOM FM 3 SLOTFOM 53.

18. The Union des Travailleurs Nègres had already fashioned this logic. See, for example, "Fascisme et colonialisme," *Cri des Nègres*, July 1933, p. 1.

19. "Exclusions," *Humanité*, Oct. 31, 1933, p. 4; report, Oct. 9, 1933, ANOM FM 3 SLOTFOM 53. George Padmore also refused to hand over his prodigious contacts list when he was expelled from the Comintern. "Expulsion of George Padmore from the Revolutionary Movement," *Negro Worker*, June 1934, p. 15.

20. Report, May 1, 1937, ANOM FM 5 SLOTFOM 42; Spiegler, "Aspects of Nationalist Thought," 167–68, 178; Joyce Moore Turner, *Caribbean Crusaders and the Harlem Renaissance* (Urbana: University of Illinois Press, 2005), 212; Edwards, *Practice of Diaspora,* 250–51; George Padmore, "The Trade Unity Convention and the Negro Masses," (New York) *Daily Worker,* Aug. 27, 1929, p. 6. For a sense of the range of the UTN's radical imagination, see the issues of the *Cri des Nègres.* The group's politics of solidarity, though, extended well beyond the newspaper page. On the group's 1933 "Fête du Tết," shared with the Étudiants Indochinois de France, see report, Jan. 14, 1933, ANOM FM 3 SLOTFOM 78. After meeting for perhaps the first time, in Frankfurt in 1929, Kouyaté and Padmore were together again in July 1930 for "an international conference of Negro workers" that came out of the 1929 Frankfurt conference. See V. Chattopadhyaya, "First International Conference of Negro Workers," (New York) *Daily Worker,* Aug. 7, 1930, p. 4. On Kouyaté and Padmore, see Edwards, *Practice of Diaspora,* 241–305. See also Turner, *Caribbean Crusaders and the Harlem Renaissance,* 210–13. Other Padmore studies include James R. Hooker, *Black Revolutionary: George Padmore's Path from Communism to Pan-Africanism* (London: Pall Mall, 1967); Leslie James, *George Padmore and Decolonization from Below: Pan-Africanism, the Cold War, and the End of Empire* (Houndsmills, Basingstoke: Palgrave Macmillan, 2015). Other studies attentive to Kouyaté include Spiegler, "Aspects of Nationalist Thought"; Philippe Dewitte, *Les mouvements nègres en France, 1919–1939* (Paris: Harmattan, 1985); Pennybacker, *From Scottsboro to Munich;* Hakim Adi, *Pan-Africanism and Communism: The Communist International, Africa, and the Diaspora, 1919–1939* (Trenton: Africa World Press, 2013); Boittin, *Colonial Metropolis;* Robbie Aitken and Eve Rosenhaft, *Black Germany: The Making and Unmaking of a Diaspora Community, 1884–1960* (Cambridge, Eng.: Cambridge University Press, 2013).

21. Report, June 19, 1933, ANOM FM 3 SLOTFOM 53.

22. Kouyaté, "À l'Assemblée Générale de l'U.T.N.," Nov. 4, 1933, ANOM FM 3 SLOTFOM 53; report, Nov. 4, 1932, ANOM FM 3 SLOTFOM 53; "Fascist Terror Against Negroes in Germany," *Negro Worker,* April 1933, p. 2; "Hitler Expels Africans from Germany in Race Hate Tilt," *Chicago Defender,* April 15, 1933, p. 1; report, Nov. 7, 1933, ANOM FM 3 SLOTFOM 53. On Edmond Thomas Ramananjato's informant role, see Boittin, *Colonial Metropolis,* xxiv–xxviii. On Pierre Kodo-Kossoul's informant role, see Michael Goebel, *Anti-imperial Metropolis: Interwar Paris and the Seeds of Third World Nationalism* (New York: Cambridge University Press, 2015), 47 *n*84.

23. Report, Réunion de la sous-section du Parti Cte, Feb. 12, 1935, ANOM FM 3 SLOTFOM 53; "Police Refuse Permit for N. Y. Thaelmann March," (New York) *Daily Worker,* June 22, 1934, p. 1; "Action commune contre le fascisme!" *Humanité,* June 24, 1934, p. 3; "The Fight to Free Thaelmann," (London) *Daily Worker,* July 13, 1934, p. 1; "Increase and Spread the Scottsboro Defense," *Negro Worker,* July 1931, pp. 3–4; "Scottsboro Appeal a Tremendous Success," *Times of West Africa,* Feb. 8, 1934, p. 3; James A.

Miller, Susan D. Pennybacker, and Eve Rosenhaft, "Mother Ada Wright and the International Campaign to Free the Scottsboro Boys, 1931–1934," *American Historical Review* 106, no. 2 (April 2001): 401; Glenda Elizabeth Gilmore, *Defying Dixie: The Radical Roots of Civil Rights, 1919–1950* (New York: Norton, 2008), 118–24, 159–61; Zetkin, *Selected Writings,* 167–69.

24. McGirr, "Passion of Sacco and Vanzetti," 1091, 1096; Denning, *Cultural Front,* 13–15; "Raise $1500 to Aid Sacco and Vanzetti," *Boston Globe,* Feb. 2, 1921, p. 2; "Comité de agitación pro Lacco y Vanzetti," (Buenos Aires) *Vanguardia,* Oct. 20, 1921, p. 6; "La manifestation a atteint son but," *Humanité,* Oct. 24, 1921, p. 1; Miller et al., "Mother Ada Wright and the International Campaign to Free the Scottsboro Boys," 401; Gilmore, *Defying Dixie,* 161, 173.

25. Report, Jan. 7, 1935, ANOM FM 3 SLOTFOM 53.

26. Report, Jan. 7, 1935, ANOM FM 3 SLOTFOM 53.

27. "Un meeting de protestation contre la guerre en Abyssinie," *Humanité,* Feb. 28, 1935, p. 3; handwritten report, March 2, 1935, ANOM FM 3 SLOTFOM 53.

28. Handwritten report, n.d., ANOM FM 3 SLOTFOM 53; Gilmore, *Defying Dixie,* 57. On the role that Padmore's relationship with Kouyaté played in his own expulsion, see Turner, *Caribbean Crusaders and the Harlem Renaissance,* 213.

29. "L'Union des Travailleurs Nègres communique," *Cri des Nègres,* March 1935, p. 1.

30. "Ethiopia Unity Rallies Harlem," *Negro Liberator,* March 15, 1935, p. 1; "Gigantic Ethiopian United Front Rallies Harlem Masses," *Negro Liberator,* March 15, 1935, p. 4; "3,000 Strike at Mussolini," *New York Amsterdam News,* March 9, 1935, p. 15. On the founding of the Abyssinian Baptist Church, and the legend explaining "Abyssinian" in the name, see Genna Rae McNeil et al., *Witness: Two Hundred Years of African-American Faith and Practice at the Abyssinian Baptist Church of Harlem, New York* (Grand Rapids, Mich.: Wm. B. Eerdmans, 2013), 2–3. Such comity between black churches and local Communists as was witnessed at Abyssinian on March 7, 1935, was not uncommon in the Depression-era United States. In Alabama, Robin D. G. Kelley argues, black working-class faith radicalized the local Communist organization (rather than vice versa) with its "collectivist values." Robin D. G. Kelley, "'We Are Not What We Seem': Rethinking Black Working-Class Opposition in the Jim Crow South," *Journal of American History* 80, no. 1 (June 1993): 83. See also Robin D. G. Kelley, *Hammer and Hoe: Alabama Communists During the Great Depression* (Chapel Hill: University of North Carolina Press, 1990); Michael K. Honey, *Southern Labor and Black Civil Rights: Organizing Memphis Workers* (Urbana: University of Illinois Press, 1993); Brenda McCallum, "Songs of Work and Songs of Worship: Sanctifying Black Unionism in the Southern City of Steel," *New York Folklore* 14, nos. 1–2 (1988): 9–33.

31. "Bulletin: Provisional Committee for Defense of Ethiopia (Abyssinia)," *Negro Liberator,* March 15, 1935, p. 4; "Gigantic Ethiopian United Front Rallies Harlem Masses,"

p. 4; "Hands Off Abyssinia!" *Negro Liberator,* March 15, 1935, p. 4; An Eye-Witness, "What Caused the Harlem Upsurge Is Vividly Told," *Negro Liberator,* April 1, 1935, p. 1; "Riot Glass Loss $147,315," *New York Times,* March 30, 1935, p. 17; "Harlemites Stage 'Hands Off Ethiopia' Parade," *Chicago Defender,* April 13, 1935, p. 4. See Mark Naison, *Communists in Harlem During the Depression* (Urbana: University of Illinois Press, 1983), 141–50.

32. James W. Ford and Harry Gannes, *War in Africa: Italian Fascism Prepares to Enslave Ethiopia* (New York: Workers Library Publishers, 1935), 3; "Ethiopia and America," *Negro Liberator,* April 1, 1935, p. 4. For a theoretical discussion of rioting as collective politics, see Joshua Clover, *Riot. Strike. Riot: The New Era of Uprisings* (London: Verso, 2016).

33. Mayor's Commission on Conditions in Harlem, *The Complete Report of Mayor La-Guardia's Commission on the Harlem Riot of March 19, 1935* (New York: Arno Press & the New York Times, 1969); "5,000 Fight Police in Harlem Streets," *New York Times,* March 18, 1934, p. 1; "Harlem Police Face Dismissal or Suspension for Tear Gas Attack on Scottsboro Meeting," "Scottsboro Parade Which Ended in Riot," *New York Amsterdam News,* March 24, 1934, p. 1; "1,500 in Harlem Protest," *New York Times,* Sept. 1, 1934, p. 16.

34. C. L. R. James, *The Life of Captain Cipriani: An Account of British Government in the West Indies* (Nelson, Lancashire: Coulton, 1932); James, *The Case for West-Indian Self Government* (London: Hogarth, 1933) (*Case for West-Indian Self Government* is an abridgment of *Life of Captain Cipriani*); Paul Buhle, *C. L. R. James: The Artist as Revolutionary* (London: Verso, 1988), 38–65; Tony Martin, *Amy Ashwood Garvey: Pan-Africanist, Feminist and Mrs. Marcus Garvey No. 1, or, A Tale of Two Amies* (Dover, Mass.: Majority, 2007), 138, 140–41.

Often described as founded in August, C. L. R. James and Amy Ashwood Garvey's group was recognized already in July, as the International African Friends of Abyssinia, organized and holding meetings; see "Africans' Pride in Abyssinia," *Manchester Guardian,* July 29, 1935, p. 13. The group laid the foundation for the later pan-African, populist, and antifascist organization the International African Service Bureau, established in March 1937. See Pennybacker, *From Scottsboro to Munich,* 90–91.

For an example of James's cricket journalism, see C. L. R. James, "Nichols, Human, and Townsend Save Their Side from Ignominy," *Manchester Guardian,* Sept. 11, 1934, p. 3.

On the thought and activities of Amy Ashwood Garvey, see Keisha N. Blain, *Set the World on Fire: Black Nationalist Women and the Global Struggle for Freedom* (Philadelphia: University of Pennsylvania Press, 2018).

35. See Cedric J. Robinson, "The African Diaspora and the Italo-Ethiopian Crisis," *Race & Class* 27, no. 2 (Oct. 1985): 51–65; see also Robert A. Hill, "In England, 1932–38," in *C. L. R. James: His Life and Work,* ed. Paul Buhle (London: Allison and Busby, 1986), esp. 69; Tiffany Ruby Patterson and Robin D. G. Kelley, "Unfinished Migrations: Reflections on the African Diaspora and the Making of the Modern World," *African Studies Review* 43, no. 1 (April 2000): 11–45; Brent Hayes Edwards, "The Uses of *Diaspora*," *Social Text* 19, no. 1 (Spring 2001): 45–73.

36. Nancy Cunard, "For Abyssinia," *Atlanta Daily World*, Sept. 7, 1935, p. 6; Kenyatta's classic work three years later was published as Jomo Kenyatta, *Facing Mount Kenya: The Tribal Life of the Gikuyu* (London: Secker and Warburg, 1938).

37. Jonathan Derrick, *Africa's 'Agitators': Militant Anti-Colonialism in Africa and the West, 1918–1939* (New York: Columbia University Press, 2008), 336; Minkah Makalani, *In the Cause of Freedom: Radical Black Internationalism from Harlem to London, 1917–1939* (Chapel Hill: University of North Carolina Press, 2011), 202; George Padmore, *Pan-Africanism or Communism? The Coming Struggle for Africa* (London: D. Dobson, 1956), 144–45.

38. Nancy Cunard, "25,000 Natives Demonstrate in South Africa," *Afro-American*, Aug. 24, 1935, p. 2; Cunard, "For Abyssinia," p. 6; "International Actions in Support of Abyssinia," *Negro Worker*, Sept. 1935, p. 12. On Hyde Park and political speech, see Lisa Keller, *Triumph of Order: Democracy and Public Space in New York and London* (New York: Columbia University Press, 2009), esp. 99. On Marcus Garvey and Garveyism, see Adam Ewing, *The Age of Garvey: How a Jamaican Activist Created a Mass Movement and Changed Global Black Politics* (Princeton: Princeton University Press, 2014); Blain, *Set the World on Fire*.

39. Cunard, "25,000 Natives Demonstrate in South Africa," p. 1; "Letters to the Editor," *Manchester Guardian*, July 24, 1935, p. 18; Richard Pankhurst, *Sylvia Pankhurst: Counsel for Ethiopia* (Hollywood: Tsehai, 2003), 11–12.

40. Activities of the International Trade Union Committee, n.d., delo 60, opis' 14, fond 495, Russian Government Archive of Social-Political History (RGASPI), Moscow (hereafter in the form: RGASPI, f. 495, op. 14, d. 60); Cunard, "25,000 Natives Demonstrate in South Africa," p. 2; "Pickets Assail Ethiopia War," (New York) *Daily Worker*, July 16, 1935, p. 1; Martin Dwyer, "Conflict in Africa Stirs Entire World," *Chicago Defender*, July 20, 1935, p. 2; "Indian Opinion on the Italo-Abyssinian Conflict," *Negro Worker*, Dec. 1935, p. 16; "'India Cannot Ignore Mussolini's Threat Against the Colored People'—Gandhi," *Pittsburgh Courier*, Aug. 3, 1935, p. 1; Rudolph Dunbar, "Asiatics Seek Way to Assist Ethiopia," *Pittsburgh Courier*, Aug. 10, 1935, sec. A, p. 10; "Effective Answer of Dockers to Appeal," *Negro Worker*, Sept. 1935, p. 6; "Picked Up in Passing," *Lethbridge Herald*, Aug. 26, 1935, p. 4; "International Actions in Support of Abyssinia," p. 13.

41. "Ethiopian Defense Parade Held in N.Y.," *Chicago Defender*, May 18, 1935, p. 3; "'Respectable' Organizations Snub N.Y.'s Biggest Turn-out," *Afro-American*, Aug. 10, 1935, p. 7; "White and Negro Join Peace Rally," *New York Times*, Aug. 4, 1935, p. 28; Robert Conway, "15,000 Protest Duce's War in Harlem Rally," (New York) *Sunday News*, Aug. 4, 1935, p. 2; Ruth James, "Ethiopia Rallies Harlem," *Negro Liberator*, Aug. 15, 1935, p. 5.

42. James, "Ethiopia Rallies Harlem," p. 5.

43. See the marvelous David Spener, *We Shall Not Be Moved/No nos moverán: Biography of a Song of Struggle* (Philadelphia: Temple University Press, 2016).

44. Spiegler, "Aspects of Nationalist Thought," 249 *n3*; "Les nègres d'Afrique soli-daires," *Humanité*, Aug. 22, 1935, p. 3; Our Haitian Correspondent, "Haitian Intellectu-als Rap League of Nations," *Chicago Defender*, Aug. 17, 1935, p. 12 (in Port au Prince, Dr. François Duvalier, one year out of medical school, signed a proclamation of solidarity with Ethiopia); "Anti-Mussolini Demonstrations," *Manchester Guardian*, Aug. 23, 1935, p. 4; "2,000 Cubans Mass to Aid Ethiopia," *Chicago Defender*, Sept. 1, 1935, p. 13; "Bra-zilian Blacks Are Restless," *Chicago Defender*, Sept. 7, 1935, p. 22; "The Negro and Italian 'War' with Ethiopia," (Kingston) *Daily Gleaner*, Sept. 11, 1935, p. 10; "Vibrante protesto dos anti-fascistas italianos do Brasil, contra a terrível aventura Abyssinica," *Manhã*, Sept. 11, 1935, p. 1.

45. "Meeting of White and Coloured Peoples in London Protests Against Arms Em-bargo," (Kingston) *Daily Gleaner*, Sept. 11, 1935, p. 18; "Our London Correspondence," *Manchester Guardian*, Aug. 26, 1935, p. 8. Regarding Trafalgar Square's legacy as a forum of participatory politics, see Rodney Mace, *Trafalgar Square: Emblem of Empire*, second edi-tion (London: Lawrence and Wishart, 2005), 11–21. Regarding the martyrdom of Charles Gordon, see the account of the "memorial service" held for him after a brutal battle in Ernest N. Bennett, *The Downfall of the Dervishes: Being a Sketch of the Final Soudan Campaign of 1898* (London: Methuen, 1898), 231–32.

46. "Meeting of White and Coloured Peoples in London," pp. 18, 20; J. M. Kenyatta, "Hands Off Abyssinia!" *Labour Monthly* 17, no. 9 (Sept. 1935): 536. For extended analy-sis of Ashwood Garvey's speech and her political thought, see Blain, *Set the World on Fire*, 147–50.

47. "Meeting of White and Coloured Peoples in London," p. 20.

48. Ras Makonnen, *Pan-Africanism from Within* (Nairobi: Oxford University Press, 1973), 91–103.

49. "Londoners Demonstrate in Favor of Ethiopia," *Chicago Defender*, Sept. 14, 1935, p. 1.

50. "Chicago Girls Are Strong for King Selassie," *Pittsburgh Courier*, July 6, 1935, p. 18; "Chain Selves to Post," *New York Times*, June 23, 1935, p. 27; "Girls in Demonstration," *Chicago Defender*, July 6, 1935, p. 18; Haywood, *Black Bolshevik*, 450–51.

51. "Girls in Demonstration," p. 18. And yet interracial antifascism did form in the U.S. South: see Gilmore, *Defying Dixie*, 157–246.

52. Haywood, *Black Bolshevik*, 449.

53. "Chicago Girls Are Strong," p. 18; Ellen Jones, "Police Terror Rages on 'South Side,'" *Negro Liberator*, Sept. 2, 1935, p. 2.

54. Haywood, *Black Bolshevik*, 451.

55. James quoted in Carol Polsgrove, *Ending British Rule in Africa: Writers in a Common Cause* (Manchester: Manchester University Press, 2009), 3.

56. "Jail 300 Rioters to Balk Parade Aimed at Italy," *Chicago Tribune,* Sept. 1, 1935, p. 4; Haywood, *Black Bolshevik,* 452. By 1934, Lincoln Center had enough of a reputation for radicalism that Elizabeth Dilling, the anticommunist polemicist from Chicago's suburbs, included it in her 1934 *Red Network* list of 460 anti-American organizations (silvershirts treated her book as a bible and the New York police commissioner kept a copy in his secret files, "apparently not disturbed," Dwight Macdonald observed in *Fortune,* "by the fact that one of the 1,450 names it lists is that of Fiorello H. La Guardia"). See Elizabeth Kirkpatrick Dilling, *The Red Network: A "Who's Who" and Handbook of Radicalism for Patriots* (Chicago: Dilling, 1934), 101; "Draft letter to Walter S. Steele, General Manager, National Republic, Wash. D.C.," Dies Committee folder, box 59, Research File, Vito Marcantonio Papers, Manuscripts and Archives Division, New York Public Library; "U. S. Communist Party," *Fortune,* Sept. 1934, p. 73.

57. "Police Halt Big Protest Meeting Here," *Chicago Defender,* Sept. 7, 1935, p. 2; Haywood, *Black Bolshevik,* 452; "Jail 300 Rioters to Balk Parade Aimed at Italy," p. 4.

58. Haywood, *Black Bolshevik,* 454; "Police Halt Big Protest Meeting Here," p. 2. On state forces' difficulties climbing much greater heights, see Scott, *Art of Not Being Governed,* 50-58.

59. Haywood, *Black Bolshevik,* 453-54. South Parkway today is Martin Luther King Drive, renamed in 1968.

60. "Jail 300 Rioters to Balk Parade Aimed at Italy," p. 4; Haywood, *Black Bolshevik,* 451.

61. "En France," *Race Nègre,* Jan. 1936, p. 4; police report, Aug. 18, 1935, AN F7 13423; "Une manifestation des nègres en faveur de l'Ethiopie," *Humanité,* Aug. 22, 1935, p. 4; "Anti-Mussolini Demonstrations," *Manchester Guardian,* Aug. 23, 1935, p. 4; Messali Hadj, *Les mémoires de Messali Hadj, 1898-1938* (Paris: Lattès, 1982), 193; Spiegler, "Aspects of Nationalist Thought," 248; Derrick, *Africa's 'Agitators,'* 341; police report, Aug. 23, 1935, AN F7 13423; Jacques Simon, *Messali Hadj (1898-1974): La passion de l'Algérie Libre* (Paris: Editions Tirésias, 1998), 77-78. On Paulette Nardal, see Imaobong D. Umoren, "Anti-Fascism and the Development of Global Race Women, 1928-1945," *Callaloo* 39, no. 1 (Winter 2016): 151-65; Imaobong D. Umoren, *Race Women Internationalists: Activist-Intellectuals and Global Freedom Struggles* (Oakland: University of California Press, 2018), 40-46.

62. "International Conference in Paris in Defense of Abyssinia," *Negro Worker,* Sept. 1935, p. 3; "Moscou 3/9/35, 12H.40," AN F7 13423; police report, Sept. 17, 1935, AN F7 13423; "Les Nègres manifestent en faveur de l'Abyssinie," *Cri des Nègres,* Sept. 1935, p. 1.

63. "Il discorso della mobilitazione," in *Scritti e discorsi di Benito Mussolini,* vol. 9: *Scritti e discorsi dal Gennaio 1934 al 4 Novembre 1935 (XII-XIV E.F.)* (Milan: U. Hoepli Editore, 1935), 218; Arnaldo Cortesi, "Italy Will Fight, Mussolini Asserts," *New York Times,* Oct. 3,

1935, p. 1; Frank Iezzi, "Selected Political Addresses of Benito Mussolini: Translations, Notes and Rhetorical Analysis" (Ph.D. diss., University of Wisconsin, 1954), 511-18.

64. Newsreel, "Ethiopia," *March of Time* 1, episode 6 (New York: Home Box Office, 1935); Reto Hofmann, *The Fascist Effect: Japan and Italy, 1915-1952* (Ithaca: Cornell University Press, 2015), 89; Gershoni and Jankowski, *Confronting Fascism in Egypt*, 59-60.

65. "Italian Consulate Stoned," *Manchester Guardian*, Oct. 4, 1935, p. 15; "Students Decry Invasion," *New York Times*, Oct. 4, 1935, p. 6; Leeds, *Let My People Know*, 23; "Girls Picket Consulate," *New York Times*, Oct. 5, 1935, p. 6; Fanesi, "Anti-fascismo italiano en Argentina," 340; "W.I. Boycott of Italian Goods," (Kingston) *Daily Gleaner*, Oct. 28, 1935, p. 18; "Native Sympathy for Ethiopia," *Rand Daily Mail*, Oct. 7, 1935, p. 9; Our Own Correspondent, "Mussolini Effigy Burnt," *Rand Daily Mail*, Oct. 14, 1935, p. 9. The October 6, 1935, mass meeting in Cape Town was not the city's first for Ethiopia; an interracial group made of "representatives," according to the report received by the Comintern, "of 23 Labour and other mass organizations of native white, coloured and Malay workers" demonstrated in August. RGASPI, f. 495, op. 14, d. 60.

66. Langston Hughes, "Mussolini, Don't You 'Mess' with Me: Ballad of Ethiopia," *Afro-American*, Sept. 28, 1935, p. 3. The poem also was published as Langston Hughes, "Ballad of Ethiopia," *Indianapolis Recorder*, Sept. 28, 1935, p. 9. It doesn't appear in Arnold Rampersad, editor, *The Collected Poems of Langston Hughes* (New York: Knopf, 1994). I first read of the poem in the work of scholarship that inspired the research for this chapter, the classic Kelley, "'This Ain't Ethiopia, But It'll Do.'"

5. THE SOCIAL EXPLOSION

Epigraph: "Importantes déclarations de Maurice Thorez à l'assemblée des communistes parisiens," *Humanité*, June 12, 1936, p. 1.

1. George Orwell, "Looking Back on the Spanish War," in *Such, Such Were the Joys* (New York: Harcourt, Brace and Company, 1953), 139. The point about such moments' powers to constitute new political orders is made well in Kalyvas, *Democracy and the Politics of the Extraordinary*. For Kalyvas, such moments aren't simply extraordinary moments that show "another world is possible" before normalcy settles back in; they are constitutional moments and the normalcy that inevitably "returns" is different from what had been before.

2. Aristide Zolberg framed the question in terms of French history and listed 1848, 1871, 1936, 1944, and 1968. Zolberg, "Moments of Madness," 184. For a sense of the magnitude of the social and political madness of such moments, as well as the deep political work behind their making, see Suzanne Desan, Lynn Hunt, and William Max Nelson, editors, *The French Revolution in Global Perspective* (Ithaca: Cornell University Press, 2013); Kurt Weyland, "The Diffusion of Revolution: '1848' in Europe and Latin America,"

International Organization 63, no. 3 (Summer 2009): 391–423; Immanuel Wallerstein, "1968, Revolution in the World-System," *Theory and Society* 18, no. 4 (July 1989): 431–49; Luisa Passerini, *Autobiography of a Generation: Italy, 1968,* trans. Lisa Erdberg (Hanover: University Press of New England, 1996); Jeremi Suri, *Power and Protest: Global Revolution and the Rise of Detente* (Cambridge, Mass.: Harvard University Press, 2003); Gerd-Rainer Horn, *The Spirit of '68: Rebellion in Western Europe and North America, 1956–1976* (Oxford, Eng.: Oxford University Press, 2007); Lawrence Goodwyn, *Breaking the Barrier: The Rise of Solidarity in Poland* (New York: Oxford University Press, 1991); Roman Laba, *The Roots of Solidarity: A Political Sociology of Poland's Working-Class Democratization* (Princeton: Princeton University Press, 1991); Patrick Bond, *Elite Transition: From Apartheid to Neoliberalism in South Africa* (London: Pluto, 2000); Susan Watkins, "Oppositions," *New Left Review* 98 (March 2016): 5–30; Marwan M. Kraidy, *The Naked Blogger of Cairo: Creative Insurgency in the Arab World* (Cambridge, Mass.: Harvard University Press, 2016); Asef Bayat, *Revolution Without Revolutionaries: Making Sense of the Arab Spring* (Stanford: Stanford University Press, 2017).

3. See Serge Berstein, *1936: Année décisive en Europe* (Paris: Armand Colin, 1969).

4. James C. Scott, *Domination and the Arts of Resistance: Hidden Transcripts* (New Haven: Yale University Press, 1990), 202–27.

5. Zolberg, "Moments of Madness," 183. See Sewell, *Logics of History,* 225–46.

6. "The Pope on Communism," (Regina, Sask.) *Leader-Post,* Sept. 17, 1936, p. 4.

7. Anne O'Hare McCormick, "Right *vs.* Left: A Great Struggle," *New York Times,* Aug. 30, 1936, sec. 7, p. 2.

8. On the plight of liberalism, and its gradual, greatly compromised recuperation in the United States, see Katznelson, *Fear Itself.*

9. McCormick, "Right *vs.* Left," sec. 7, pp. 1–2; Anne O'Hare McCormick, "Italy and Popes and Parliaments," *New York Times,* July 24, 1921, sec. 3, p. 8.

10. McCormick, "Right *vs.* Left," sec. 7, pp. 1–2.

11. McCormick, "Right *vs.* Left," sec. 7, pp. 2, 14.

12. For a theory of historical breaks, or ruptures, see, again, Sewell, *Logics of History,* 225–46.

13. McCormick, "Right *vs.* Left," sec. 7, p. 1.

14. Galois [Weil], "Vie et la grève des ouvrières métallos," p. 7; Daniel Mayer, "Le patronat de la métallurgie parisienne accepte de négocier un contrat collectif," *Populaire,* May 29, 1936, p. 1; [Werth,] "Inside Story of the Great Paris Strikes," p. 9; "Hier, 107 victoires!" *Humanité,* June 6, 1936, p. 1; report, May 30, 1936, AN F7 13983. On the strikes, see Bertrand Badie, "Les grèves du Front populaire aux usines Renault," *Mouvement social,* no. 81 (Oct. 1972): 69–109; Herrick Chapman, *State Capitalism and Working-Class Radicalism in the French Aircraft Industry* (Berkeley: University of California Press, 1991); Michael Seidman, *Workers Against Work: Labor in Paris and Barcelona During the Popular Fronts* (Berkeley: University of California Press, 1991), 212–30.

15. For example, "Comment fut brisé le magnifique élan des ouvriers italiens maîtres des usines (septembre–octobre 1920)," *Militant* (Saigon), Sept. 8, 1936, p. 8; Henri Prouteau, *Les occupations d'usines en Italie et en France, 1920–1936* (Paris: Librairie technique et économique, 1938).

16. See Paolo Spriano, *The Occupation of the Factories: Italy 1920,* trans. Gwyn A. Williams (London: Pluto, 1975).

17. J. Lebas, "Pour l'information sur l'Unité organique," *Populaire,* Jan. 2, 1936, p. 1.

18. Horn, *European Socialists Respond to Fascism,* 147–49.

19. Juan F. Fernández C., *Pedro Aguirre Cerda y el Frente Popular Chileno* (Santiago: Ediciones Ercilla, 1938), 49; Pedro Milos, *Frente Popular en Chile: Su configuración: 1935–1938* (Santiago: LOM Ediciones, 2008), 35, 47, 51; John Reese Stevenson, *The Chilean Popular Front* (Philadelphia: University of Pennsylvania Press, 1942), 63. The Socialist Party (el Partido Socialista), the Radical Socialist Party (el Partido Radical Socialista), the Democratic Party (el Partido Democrático), and the Trotskyist Communist Left (la Izquierda Comunista) all took part in "el Block de Izquierdas," created in December 1934. (Neither the Radical Party nor the Communist Party of Chile took part.) This collaboration of the Socialist Party with the Trotskyist "comunistas de Izquierda" caused trouble for the efforts by the Socialist and Communist parties to establish a united front. On the rise of the Radical Party's left, see Julio Faúndez, *Marxism and Democracy in Chile: From 1932 to the Fall of Allende* (New Haven: Yale University Press, 1988), 39–40.

20. Alfredo Guillermo Bravo, "El Partido Radical y el Frente Popular," in Darío Poblete N. and Alfredo Guillermo Bravo, *Historia del Partido Radical y del Frente Popular* (Santiago: Imp. La República Independencia, 1936), 68, 70. A comparative history that examines the Popular Front idea's uses in the Americas is Mark Falcoff and Fredrick B. Pike, editors, *The Spanish Civil War, 1936–39: American Hemispheric Perspectives* (Lincoln: University of Nebraska Press, 1982); an excellent transnational history that does likewise is Katherine M. Marino, *Feminism for the Americas: The Making of an International Human Rights Movement* (Chapel Hill: University of North Carolina Press, 2019), 120–44.

21. For an influential example, see Célie and Albert Vassart, "The Moscow Origin of the French 'Popular Front,'" in *The Comintern: Historical Highlights,* ed. Milorad M. Drachkovitch and Branko Lazitch (New York: Praeger, 1966), 234–52.

22. For a presentation of the Popular Front as an entirely Moscow-derived policy, see Richard Pipes, *Communism: A History* (New York: Modern Library, 2001), 107. The historian Robert Service suggests that when the French Communist Party "concluded a pact with socialists and liberals for the formation of a Popular Front in July 1935," it was "at Stalin's instigation." Robert Service, *Comrades: A World History of Communism* (London: Macmillan,

2007), 173. See also Kevin McDermott and Jeremy Agnew, *The Comintern: A History of International Communism from Lenin to Stalin* (Houndsmills, Basingstoke: Macmillan, 1996), 120–57; Archie Brown, *The Rise and Fall of Communism* (New York: Ecco, 2009), 88; David Priestland, *The Red Flag: A History of Communism* (New York: Grove, 2009); A. James McAdams, *Vanguard of the Revolution: The Global Idea of the Communist Party* (Princeton: Princeton University Press, 2017), 236–45.

23. Miloš Hájek, *Storia dell'Internazionale comunista, 1921–1935: La politica del fronte unico* (Rome: Editori Riuniti, 1969), 252–53; Jonathan Haslam, "The Comintern and the Origins of the Popular Front 1934–1935," *Historical Journal* 22, no. 3 (Sept. 1979): 689.

24. Christopher J. Fischer, *Alsace to the Alsatians? Visions and Divisions of Alsatian Regionalism, 1870–1939* (New York: Berghahn, 2010), 179; Rotelslot, "Pour leur droit de libre disposition les travailleurs alsaciens-lorrains voteront communiste!" *Humanité*, April 27, 1932, p. 2; Rotelslot, "Ennemis des travailleurs," *Humanité*, June 23, 1932, p. 5. On populism as a politics of inventing "the people" and making claims on behalf of the thus invented collectivity, see Ernesto Laclau, *On Populist Reason* (London: Verso, 2005); Balibar, *Equaliberty;* Chantal Mouffe, *For a Left Populism* (London: Verso, 2018).

25. John Bulaitis, *Maurice Thorez: A Biography* (London: I. B. Tauris, 2018), 108.

26. "A tout prix, battre le fascisme: Pour un large front populaire antifasciste," *Humanité*, Oct. 12, 1934, p. 4. See also M. Thorez, "Pourquoi retarder l'unité syndicale?" *Humanité*, Oct. 14, 1934, p. 1.

27. Bulaitis, *Maurice Thorez*, 100–110, esp. 109; Haslam, "Comintern and the Origins of the Popular Front," 688–89; Marcel Cachin, "Front populaire contre le fascisme," *Humanité*, Oct. 22, 1934, p. 1; "Élargissons le front populaire!" *Humanité*, Oct. 24, 1934, p. 1. See also Georges Lefranc, *Histoire du front populaire (1934–1938)*, second edition (Paris: Payot, 1974), 66–71.

To varying degrees, many historians of communism and the Comintern have underplayed the extent to which Thorez was at odds with the Comintern hierarchy. Of the large-scale general histories of communism and the Comintern, the account given by Kevin McDermott and Jeremy Agnew stands out for the general accuracy and detail with which the authors depict the origins of the Popular Front. But even McDermott and Agnew explain away Thorez's move by arguing that "he seems to have anticipated developments in the Comintern." Likewise, their claim that Thorez was simply enacting a "logical extension of recent thinking in Moscow" and that it was just a matter of "tempo" that "caused alarm" in the Comintern's executive committee assumes far too much. McDermott and Agnew, *Comintern*, 127.

Leading the delegation dispatched by the Comintern to visit Thorez was none other than Palmiro Togliatti. Regarding Togliatti's later defenses of the Popular Front, see, for example,

M. Ercoli [Palmiro Togliatti], *The Fight for Peace: Report on the Preparations for Imperialist War and the Tasks of the Communist International, Delivered August 13, 1935* (New York: Workers Library Publishers, 1935), 34–35.

28. "Les chefs fascistes de la police de Beyrouth font charger sauvagement au cortège paisible," *Humanité*, July 7, 1936, p. 3; Wilfrid Fleisher, "People's Front Starts in Tokio; to Hit Fascism," *New York Herald Tribune*, July 6, 1936, p. 30; J. Skikda, "Comme en 14," *Echo de Bougie*, Aug. 30, 1936, p. 1; Arthur Sears Henning, "Radicals Stage New York Rally for Roosevelt," *Chicago Tribune*, Oct. 28, 1936, p. 9; "Nach Roosevelt – die 'Volksfront'!" *Deutscher Weckruf und Beobachter*, Nov. 12, 1936, p. 1; "Annexe II à l'Envoi no. 4993-SG du 5 decembre 1936," p. 2, ANOM FM 3 SLOTFOM 101. Kanju Kato became a "noted leader of the Legal Left in Japan." Elias Tobenkin, *The Peoples Want Peace* (New York: Putnam, 1938), 55. He was arrested the next year when militarists in the government decided on "cracking down on leftist elements." "Japanese Police Conduct Wholesale Arrests of 'Leftists,'" *China Weekly Review* 83, no. 5 (Jan. 1, 1938): 130.

29. For example, "The People's Front," *Negro Worker*, July 1936, pp. 4–5.

30. See Scott, *Seeing Like a State*, 150.

31. See Lefranc, *Histoire du front populaire*, 68.

32. On collective charisma and its relation to constitutional moments, see Kalyvas, *Democracy and the Politics of the Extraordinary*, 27.

33. On the attention antifascists elsewhere paid to Paris at the time, see Rabinbach, "Paris, Capital of Anti-Fascism." On the assembly of crowds and its implications, see Judith Butler, *Notes Toward a Performative Theory of Assembly* (Cambridge, Mass.: Harvard University Press, 2015).

34. "Paris Reds Pile Floral Tower to Honor Dead," *New York Herald Tribune*, Feb. 11, 1935, p. 17.

35. See Canetti, *Crowds and Power*, 16–17.

36. Henri Barbusse, "L'ère du Front populaire," *Humanité*, July 13, 1935, p. 1; "Un fleuve d'hommes de la Bastille à Vincennes," *Humanité*, July 15, 1935, p. 2; Leland Stowe, "French Leftists Unite to Wage War on Fascists," *New York Herald Tribune*, July 1, 1935, p. 1; Stowe, "French Fascist 'Plot' to Seize Rule 'Exposed,'" *New York Herald Tribune*, July 2, 1935, p. 15; Stowe, "Right and Left Rally Strength in Paris Today," *New York Herald Tribune*, July 14, 1935, p. 1.

37. Stowe, "Right and Left Rally Strength in Paris Today," p. 1.

38. On the power of events to "signify something new and surprising," see Sewell, *Logics of History*, 245.

39. "Paris Reds Pile Floral Tower to Honor Dead," p. 17. On the unity of crowds, see Canetti, *Crowds and Power*, 15–90.

40. J. Bouissounouse, "Paris Sets a Strike Style," *Survey Graphic*, Sept. 1936, p. 516.

41. Jackson, *Popular Front in France*, 7; "Les menaces de La Rocque à Alger," *Humanité*, June 16, 1935, p. 2; AN F7 13314; Alexander Werth, "French Fascism," *Foreign Affairs* 15, no. 1 (Oct. 1936): 146; newsreel, "Croix de Feu," *March of Time* 1, episode 5 (New York: Home Box Office, 1935).

42. "Léon Blum victime d'un attentat fasciste," *Populaire*, Feb. 14, 1936, p. 1.

43. Mayer, "Patronat de la métallurgie parisienne accepte de négocier un contrat collectif," p. 1; "L'occupation par des grévistes d'usines de la région parisienne," *Temps*, May 30, 1936, p. 4; Our Own Correspondent [Alexander Werth], "Stay-In Strikers' Life in a Factory," *Manchester Guardian,* June 13, 1936, p. 13.

44. Galois [Weil], "Vie et la grève des ouvrières métallos," pp. 4–8.

45. See Elizabeth Anderson, *Private Government: How Employers Rule Our Lives (and Why We Don't Talk About It)* (Princeton: Princeton University Press, 2017).

46. Simone Weil, "Journal d'Usine," in *La condition ouvrière* (Paris: Gallimard, 1951), 35–108; Galois [Weil], "Vie et la grève des ouvrières métallos," p. 7.

47. See Segal, *Radical Happiness*.

48. Galois [Weil], "Vie et la grève des ouvrières métallos," pp. 4, 7.

49. "1,000 Men Halt Work at Firestone Plant," *Akron Beacon Journal*, Jan. 29, 1936, p. 1; "Colisión por motivos políticos," (Barcelona) *Vanguardia*, April 23, 1936, p. 24; "Strike Closes Goodyear Plants" and "Raise Denied, 500 Sit Down at Columbia Chemical Co.," *Akron Beacon Journal*, Feb. 19, 1936, p. 1; Feliks Gross, *The Polish Worker: A Study of a Social Stratum* (New York: Roy, 1945), 140–41.

50. For newsreel coverage, see, for example, "Revolt in France," *March of Time* 2, episode 7 (New York: Home Box Office, 1936). Leon Trotsky, in exile in a Norwegian village, wrote of following the sitdowns on the radio. "Never did the radio seem so precious as during these days," he commented, before claiming, "The French revolution has begun." Leon Trotsky, "The French Revolution Has Begun," *Nation*, July 4, 1936, p. 12.

51. "Les grèves à Casablanca," *Humanité*, June 17, 1936, p. 2. The Renault workers had briefly returned to work on June 2; by the end of June 5, the strike, and the factory occupation, was renewed.

52. "Importante debate sobre el Orden Público," (Barcelona) *Vanguardia*, June 17, 1936, p. 26; "3,000 Miners in Spain Hold Pits in Strike," *Baltimore Sun*, June 17, 1936, p. 14; report, Department of Constantine, "État statistique des grèves subvenues pendant les mois de Juin à Juillet 1936," Sept. 29, 1936, ANOM GGA 9H/41 (GGA: fonds du Gouvernement général d'Algérie); "800 Strikers Arrested," *Times of India*, June 27, 1936, p. 13; "Stay-In Strike in Egypt," *Manchester Guardian*, June 27, 1936, p. 13; "Untimely End to 'Stay-In' Strike," *Palestine Post*, June 29, 1936, p. 3; Joel Beinin and Zachary Lockman, *Workers on the Nile: Nationalism, Communism, Islam, and the Egyptian Working Class, 1882–1954* (Princeton: Princeton University Press, 1987), 220–21; report, "Pour comprendre . . . ce qui se passe à Pondichery," ANOM FM 1 AFFPOL 2888/4 (AFFPOL: fonds des Affaires politiques); Solomiac, telegrams 72 and 73, June 30 and July 1, 1936, ANOM FM 1 AFFPOL 2888/3; "Pondicherry Strike," *Times of India,* July 4, 1936, p. 12; "Stay-in Strike in Pondicherry," *Times of India,* July 29, 1936, p. 6; V. Subbiah, *Saga of Freedom of French India (Testament Of My Life)* (Madras: New Century Book House Private Ltd., 1990), 55–78 (Varadarajulu Subbiah's account is invaluable); "Stay-In Strike near Glasgow," *Manchester Guardian,* Sept. 11, 1936, p. 12; "Natives' 'Stay -- In-Strike,[']" *Negro Worker,* Nov. 1936, p. 27; "Strike Holds Crack Liner at N. Y. Pier," *Baltimore Sun,* Nov. 3, 1936, p. 1; "Grève des bras croisés à la Société des Dragages," *Lutte* (Saigon), Nov. 22, 1936, p. 1; "État recapitulatif des grèves survenues en Cochinchine du 1er août au 5 décembre 1936," ANOM Indochine GGI 64348 (GGI: fonds du Gouvernement général de l'Indochine).

    53. Louis Adamic, "Sitdown," *Nation,* Dec. 5, 1936, p. 653.

    54. Louis Adamic, *My America, 1928–1938* (New York: Harper & Brothers, 1938), 427. On the antifascism of Louis Adamic, see Enyeart, *Death to Fascism.* Louis Adamic influenced the remarkable antifascist Carey McWilliams. See Daniel Geary, "Carey McWilliams and Antifascism, 1934–1943," *Journal of American History* 90, no. 3 (Dec. 2003): 912–34. On the antifascism of the industrial labor insurgency in the United States (concentrated in the campaigns of the Committee for Industrial Organization, or CIO), see Denning, *Cultural Front.*

    55. "Colisión por motivos políticos," p. 24; "Nouvelles grèves en province," *Humanité,* June 17, 1936, p. 2; "Peyrouton veut employer les gaz lacrymogènes contre les grévistes," *Humanité,* June 20, 1936, p. 2; "À Oran, 10.000 travailleurs sont en grève," *Humanité,* June 25, 1936, p. 2; "Arabs Attack Jews in French African Cities," *Chicago Tribune,* July 1, 1936, p. 4; report, "Pour comprendre . . . ce qui se passe à Pondichery"; "Nouvelles du camarade Mai," *Lutte* (Saigon), Nov. 29, 1936, p. 2; "Les fascistes locaux s'organisent militairement," *Lutte* (Saigon), Oct. 22, 1936, p. 1. The Croix de Feu elements in Saigon kept wearing the skull-and-bones insignia after Léon Blum's government dissolved the French paramilitary groups. "Pour un Rassemblement populaire en Indochine," *Lutte* (Saigon), Oct. 15, 1936, p. 1.

    56. "Les antifascistes de Bougie demandent la dissolution des ligues fascistes," *Humanité,* May 15, 1936, p. 4; Va. Soubbaya, "Mon avis aux ouvriers de l'Inde française," March 22, 1937, ANOM FM 1 AFFPOL 2888/4; "Black Legion Rises as 1936 Ku-Klux Klan," sec. B, p. 1; "New Plot Revealed in Black Legion Probe," *Detroit Tribune,* July 4, 1936, p. 1; William Hazzard, "Black Hoods of Terror," *Today,* Aug. 1, 1936, pp. 4–7, 28; Peter H. Amann, "Vigilante Fascism: The Black Legion as an American Hybrid," *Comparative Studies in Society and History* 25, no. 3 (July 1983): 490–524; "Union Claims 'Fordism is Fascism,'" (Moberly, Mo.,) *Monitor-Index and Democrat,* June 9, 1937, p. 6; "'They Shall Not Pass'—Strikers Declare," *Asheville Citizen,* March 20, 1937, p. 1.

—

57. Georges Lefranc, *Juin 36: "L'explosion sociale"* (Paris: Julliard, 1966); Jackson, *Popular Front in France,* 86.

58. "L'état de siège au Chili," *Humanité,* Feb. 13, 1936, p. 3; Faúndez, *Marxism and Democracy in Chile;* Jody Pavilack, *Mining for the Nation: The Politics of Chile's Coal Communities from the Popular Front to the Cold War* (University Park: Pennsylvania State University Press, 2011), 81–82; Mario Garcés Durán, *El movimiento obrero y el Frente Popular (1936–1939)* (Santiago: LOM Ediciones, 2018); "État recapitulatif des grèves survenues en Cochinchine du 1er aoüt au 5 décembre 1936"; "Note sur l'activité révolutionnaire pendant le mois de novembre 1936," p. 1, ANOM FM 3 SLOTFOM 59; "Fascistes locaux s'organisent militairement," p. 1; Trân-van-Thach [Trần Văn Thạch], "Laissera-t-on les fascistes d'Indochine s'organiser librement?" *Lutte* (Saigon), Nov. 5, 1936, p. 1; "Les fascistes bougent!!" *Lutte* (Saigon), Nov. 29, 1936, p. 1. See also "Le Fascisme à Saigon," *Lutte* (Saigon), July 1, 1936, p. 1. Also see Daniel Hémery, *Révolutionnaires vietnamiens et pouvoir colonial en Indochine: Communistes, trotskystes, nationalistes à Saigon de 1932 à 1937* (Paris: Maspero, 1975); Chau Tran, *Trần Văn Thạch (1905–1945): Une plume contre l'oppression* (Paris: Indes savantes, 2020). For a study that ties together the Arab uprising in Palestine and the civil war in Spain, see Marc Matera and Susan Kingsley Kent, *The Global 1930s: The International Decade* (Abingdon: Routledge, 2017), 197–207.

59. "Antifa" Palestine, *Les Troubles Sanglants en Palestine 1936* (Brussels: Imprimerie Polyglotte, 1936), 103.

60. "Two Week Hunger-Strike," *Palestine Post,* July 30, 1935, p. 5; "Antifa" Palestine, *Troubles Sanglants en Palestine,* 101–02.

61. J. C. Royle, "Arab Missionary of Peace Won't Have Picture Taken, Fearing Attack Back Home," *Winnipeg Evening Tribune,* April 9, 1937, p. 1; Zachary Lockman, *Comrades and Enemies: Arab and Jewish Workers in Palestine, 1906-1948* (Berkeley: University of California Press, 1996), 83; "Antifa" Palestine, *Troubles Sanglants en Palestine,* 4. An emphasis on the need for "the establishment of Jewish Arab proletarian unity" was shared among those who saw themselves as "the Left of the Jewish working class movement." Mordekhai Orenstein, *Jews, Arabs and British in Palestine: A Left Socialist View* (London: I. Narodiczky, 1936), 15, 21.

On Left Poale Zion, see Lockman, *Comrades and Enemies,* esp. 80–85. The party Left Poale Zion was organized after the May Day 1921 demonstration in Jaffa ended in rioting and interracial violence; the authorities then banned the Socialist Workers' Party. One remnant became Left Poale Zion (not to be confused with the left wing of the Poale Zion movement) and another became the Palestine Communist Party. For pieces of this history, see Mario Offenberg, *Kommunismus in Palästina: Nation und Klasse in der antikolonialen Revolution* (Meisenheim am Glan: Anton Hain, 1975); Musa Budeiri, *The Palestine Communist Party, 1919-1948: Arab and Jew in the Struggle for Internationalism* (Chicago: Haymarket, 1979), 3–6; Nathan Weinstock, *Le pain de misère: Histoire du mouvement ouvrier juif en*

—

Europe, vol. 3: *L'Europe centrale et occidentale, 1914–1945* (Paris: Éditions La Découverte, 1986), 58–67, 95–96. On the riots see *Palestine. Disturbances in May, 1921. Reports of the Commission of Inquiry with Correspondence Relating Thereto* (London: His Majesty's Stationery Office, 1921). On the contested, and shifting, meanings of Zionism in the era, see Dmitry Shumsky, *Beyond the Nation-State: The Zionist Political Imagination from Pinsker to Ben-Gurion* (New Haven: Yale University Press, 2018).

62. "Antifa" Palestine, *Troubles Sanglants en Palestine*, 47, 55, 97–98, 102. On the violence that set off the Palestinian uprising in Palestine, see *Palestine Royal Commission Report* (London: His Majesty's Stationery Office, 1937), 95–96.

63. "Antifa" Palestine, *Troubles Sanglants en Palestine*, 2. The Ligue Internationale contre le Racisme et l'Antisémitisme was established as the Ligue Internationale contre l'Antisémitisme, hence the acronym LICA; the group decided to include opposition to racism in its formal title in 1934 because it sought to combat Hitlerian racism, but kept the acronym by which it was already known. Today the venerable organization goes by LICRA.

64. "La conférence contre le racisme et l'antisémitisme," *Œuvre*, Sept. 21, 1936, p. 5; René Defez, "La Conférence internationale contre le racisme et l'antisémitisme," *Univers Israelite*, Oct. 2, 1936, p. 54; Emmanuel Debono, *Aux origines de l'antiracisme: La LICA, 1927–1940* (Paris: CNRS, 2012), 25–58; Catherine Lloyd, *Discourses of Antiracism in France* (Aldershot: Ashgate, 1998), 105.

On the episode that led to the founding of LICA, see also Elie Dobkowski, *Affaire Petliura-Schwarzbard* (Champigny: Union fédérative socialiste, n.d. [1927?]); *Documents sur les pogromes en Ukraine et l'assassinat de Simon Petlura à Paris (1917–1921–1926)* (Paris: Trident, 1927); Samuel Schwarzbard, *Mémoires d'un anarchiste juif* (Paris: Éditions Syllepse, 2010); Carolyn J. Dean, *The Moral Witness: Trials and Testimony after Genocide* (Ithaca: Cornell University Press, 2019), 26–60.

Léon Blum had written in 1934 of rallying "the French popular masses" around "the idea of an antifascist or antiracist struggle," by which he meant in part a struggle against "Hitlerian racism." Léon Blum, "La défense internationale contre le fascisme," *Populaire*, July 13, 1934, p. 1.

In September 1937, LICA held the first annual World Assembly Against Racism and Anti-Semitism at the Maison de la Mutualité (it was also advertised in English as the World Congress Against Racism and Anti-Semitism; in some references, the continuity from the 1936 conference was made explicit and it was called the Second World Congress Against Racism and Anti-Semitism). For an early example of the word "anti-racism" in English, see the depiction of the 1937 assembly in "Anti-Racism Group Convenes in Paris," *Chicago Defender,* Sept. 25, 1937, p. 9. As an example of how unsettled the concept of antiracism was, a banner hung at the 1938 meeting translated the French word "antiracistes" into English as "Antiracialists." Debono, *Aux origines de l'antiracisme*, 282 (photograph).

For an apt history of antiracism, see Todd Shepard, "Algeria, France, Mexico, UNESCO: A Transnational History of Anti-Racism and Decolonization, 1932–1962," *Journal of Global History* 6, no. 2 (July 2011): 273–97. See also Rebecca Herman, "The Global Politics of Anti-Racism: A View from the Canal Zone," *American Historical Review* 125, no. 2 (April 2020): 460–86.

65. "Conférence contre le racisme et l'antisémitisme," p. 5; Defez, "Conférence internationale contre le racisme et l'antisémitisme," p. 54; Haggai Erlich, "The Tiger and the Lion: Fascism and Ethiopia in Arab Eyes," in *Arab Responses to Fascism and Nazism: Attraction and Repulsion*, ed. Israel Gershoni (Austin: University of Texas Press, 2014), 281–86; William L. Cleveland, *Islam Against the West: Shakib Arslan and the Campaign for Islamic Nationalism* (Austin: University of Texas Press, 1985), 150.

66. Defez, "Conférence internationale contre le racisme et l'antisémitisme," pp. 54–55; Erlich, "Tiger and the Lion," 282.

67. Tiémoko Garan Kouyaté was arrested by the Gestapo in 1943 and then held as a political prisoner; he died in the concentration camp at Mauthausen in July 1944. Pennybacker, *From Scottsboro to Munich,* 262; Boittin, *Colonial Metropolis,* 216; Aitken and Rosenhaft, *Black Germany,* 309. Kouyaté's wartime politics has been the subject of much speculation, and the circumstances of his death were only ascertained thanks to the efforts of the historian Eve Rosenhaft and the scholars of the International Tracing Service. Regarding the speculation, see Hooker, *Black Revolutionary,* 37; Dewitte, *Mouvements nègres en France,* 381–86.

68. Pivert, "Tout est possible," p. 6.

69. Guérin, *Front populaire,* 23; Marceau Pivert, "Entre nous, très sérieusement . . . ," *Populaire,* Sept. 10, 1935, p. 6; Pivert, "Une lettre de Marceau Pivert," *Populaire,* Oct. 18, 1935, p. 6; Pivert, "Tout est possible," p. 6. See Jean Rabaut, *Tout est possible! Les "gauchistes" français, 1929–1944* (Paris: Éditions Denoël, 1974), esp. 134; Jean-Paul Joubert, *Révolutionnaires de la S.F.I.O.: Marceau Pivert et le pivertisme* (Paris: Presses de la Fondation nationale des sciences politiques, 1977); Jacques Kergoat, *Marceau Pivert, "socialiste de gauche"* (Paris: Éditions de l'Atelier, 1994), esp. 93–108.

70. "50.000 métallurgistes campent dans les usines," *Humanité,* May 29, 1936, p. 2; Marcel Gitton, "Tout n'est pas possible," *Humanité,* May 29, 1936, pp. 1–2.

71. Bulaitis, *Maurice Thorez,* 116.

72. The exact wording of Thorez's speech remains unclear. It seems clear that the phrases I translate and quote here were in the speech, but the surrounding text is uncertain, so his exact intent remains difficult to decipher. For slightly different wordings, see "Importantes déclarations de Maurice Thorez à l'assemblée des communistes parisiens," p. 1; P. Vaillant-Couturier, "La Chambre a voté la semaine de 40 heures," *Humanité,* June 13, 1936, p. 1; "La Lutte pour le pain," *Humanité,* June 13, 1936, p. 4; Lefranc, *Histoire du front populaire,*

164. The June 13 *Humanité* text is what appears in Maurice Thorez, *Œuvres: Livre troisième, tome douzième (Mai–Octobre 1936)* (Paris: Éditions Sociales, 1954).

73. "Lutte pour le pain," p. 4.

74. "Lutte pour le pain," p. 4.

6. TODAY THE STRUGGLE

Epigraph: Dorothy Thompson, "Pattern of a Revolution," *New York Herald Tribune,* July 30, 1936, p. 17.

1. "C.C.N.Y. Students Burn 3-Headed Fascist Effigy," (New York) *Daily Worker,* Dec. 4, 1936, p. 2; "Students Burn Effigy," *New York Times,* Dec. 4, 1936, p. 51.

2. "C.C.N.Y. Students Burn 3-Headed Fascist Effigy," p. 2; "Students Burn Effigy," p. 51. For context, see Peter N. Carroll and James D. Fernandez, editors, *Facing Fascism: New York and the Spanish Civil War* (New York: Museum of the City of New York, 2007).

3. "C.C.N.Y. Students Burn 3-Headed Fascist Effigy," p. 2.

4. Leeds, *Let My People Know,* 11–12, 20, 23, 41–44, and 79–80.

5. Langston Hughes, "Fighters from Other Lands Look to Ohio Man for Food," *Afro-American,* Jan. 8, 1938, p. 2; Hobsbawm, *Age of Extremes,* 160; Judith Keene, *The Last Mile to Huesca: An Australian Nurse in the Spanish Civil War* (Kensington: New South Wales University Press, 1988); Jean-Yves Boursier, *La guerre de partisans dans le sud-ouest de la France 1942–1944* (Paris: Harmattan, 1992), 119; Bruno Bermezel, *Resistants à Lyon* (Lyon: Editions BGA Permezel, 1995), 523. On the International Brigades, see Michel Lefebvre and Rémi Skoutelsky, *Les brigades internationales: Images retrouvées* (Paris: Seuil, 2003); Giles Tremlett, *Las Brigadas Internacionales: Fascismo, libertad y la Guerra Civil española,* trans. Jordi Ainaud (Barcelona: Debate, 2020).

6. Sergio Yanes Torrado, Carlos Marín Suárez, and María Cantabrana Carassou, *Papeles de plomo: Los voluntarios uruguayos en la Guerra Civil española* (Montevideo: Banda Oriental, 2017), 103; Hwei-Ru Tsou and Len Tsou, *Los brigadistas chinos en la guerra civil: La llamada de España (1936–1939),* trans. Laureano Ramírez Bellerín (Madrid: Catarata, 2013), 172–83; Pablo de la Torriente Brau, "Nueva York, 6-8-936," in *Cartas y crónicas de España* (Havana: Centro Cultural Pablo de la Torriente Brau, 1999), 55; Lambe, *No Barrier Can Contain It,* 32–53, 76–100; Thaís Battibugli, *A solidariedade antifascista: Brasileiros na guerra civil espanhola (1936–1939)* (Campinas: Autores Associados, 2004), 29, 97–98, 116–17; Dulles, *Anarchists and Communists in Brazil,* 526; John Gerassi, *The Premature Antifascists: North American Volunteers in the Spanish Civil War, 1936–39: An Oral History* (New York: Praeger, 1986), 43; Blake Green, "The Angels of the Last 'Pure War,'" *San Francisco Chronicle,* Feb. 10, 1977, p. 22. Regarding Salaria Kea's antifascism, see also *A Negro Nurse in Republican Spain* (New York: The Negro Committee to Aid Spain, n.d. [1938]);

—

Salaria Kea O'Reilly, "While Passing Through," manuscript, Salaria Kea (O'Reilly) Papers, file D, box D-2, International Brigade Memorial Archive, Marx Memorial Library, London (hereafter IBMA MML); "While Passing Through," *Health and Medicine* 5, no. 1 (Spring 1987): 11–13. The scholar Anne Donlon has found that the primary author of *A Negro Nurse in Republican Spain* was Thyra Edwards, an African American labor organizer, journalist, and antifascist. See Anne Donlon, "Thyra Edwards's Spanish Civil War Scrapbook: Black Women's Internationalist Writing," in *To Turn the Whole World Over: Black Women and Internationalism*, ed. Keisha N. Blain and Tiffany M. Gill (Champaign: University of Illinois Press, 2019), 101–22.

    7. Jerónimo E. Boragina and Ernesto R. Sommaro, *Voluntarios judeoargentinos en la Guerra Civil Española* (Buenos Aires: Ediciones del CCC, 2016), 241; Taffy Adler, "Lithuania's Diaspora: The Johannesburg Jewish Workers' Club, 1928–1948," *Journal of Southern African Studies* 6, no. 1 (Oct. 1979): 85; Immanuel Suttner, editor, *Cutting through the Mountain: Interviews with South African Jewish Activists* (London: Viking, 1997), 289, 302; Bob Doyle, *Brigadista: An Irishman's Fight Against Fascism* (Dublin: Currach, 2006), 27–41; Judith Keene, *Fighting for Franco: International Volunteers in Nationalist Spain During the Spanish Civil War* (London: Hambledon Continuum, 2007), 119; "Notre camarade Jean Belaïdt de la 7ᵉ Section est mort en héros le 28 décembre en Espagne," *Populaire*, Jan. 6, 1937, p. 2; Abdellatif Bensalem, "Los voluntarios árabes en las brigadas internacionales (España, 1936–1939)," *Revista internacional de sociología*, no. 4 (1988): 554; Stanley G. Payne, *The Spanish Civil War, the Soviet Union, and Communism* (New Haven: Yale University Press, 2004), 133 (quotation). Payne suggests that Pivert "shrilled" his words.

    8. *The Book of the XV Brigade: Records of British, American, Canadian and Irish Volunteers in the XV International Brigade in Spain 1936–1938* (1938; Newcastle upon Tyne: Frank Graham, 1975), 52; Tsou and Tsou, *Brigadistas chinos en la guerra civil*, 267; Mika Etchebéhère, *Ma guerre d'Espagne à moi* (Paris: Denoël, 1976); Gina Medem, *Los Judios voluntarios de la libertad (Un año de la lucha en las Brigadas Internacionales)* (Madrid: Ediciones del Comisariado de las Brigadas Internacionales, 1937), 39. Itzchok Yoffe, as he was known to Gina Medem, has also been referred to as Jechok Joffe and Isaac Ioffe. See Maxim D. Shrayer, editor, *Voices of Jewish-Russian Literature* (Brighton, Mass.: Academic Studies Press, 2018), 308.

    9. Nayati Sidqi, "Recuerdos de un comunista palestino en la Guerra de España," trans. Nieves Paradela, *Nación árabe*, no. 52 (Summer 2004): 140. For a slightly different translation of Najati Sidqi's declaration, see Mustafa Kabha, "The Spanish Civil War as Reflected in Contemporary Palestinian Press," in *Arab Responses to Fascism and Nazism*, ed. Gershoni, 133.

    10. Weil, "Journal d'Espagne," 209.

    11. Weil, "Journal d'Espagne," 209; Orwell, *Homage to Catalonia*, 4–5. On the ethics and operation of auto appropriations, see, for example, "Sobre los autos requisados," *Soli-*

—

daridad Obrera, July 25, 1936, p. 2; "Autos requisados que deben ser devueltos," *Solidaridad Obrera,* July 28, 1936, p. 3.

12. Charles A. Orr, "The Spanish Revolution – 1936–37," manuscript, p. 10, Charles A. Orr Papers, Hoover Institution Library and Archives, Stanford University, Stanford, Calif.; Mary Low and Juan Breá, *Red Spanish Notebook: The First Six Months of the Revolution and the Civil War* (London: Martin Secker and Warburg, 1937), 18, 20. On the challenges that the social revolution posed in Barcelona, see, for example, "reunión del Pleno del Comité Central de Control Obrero, del Ramo de Gas y Electricidad," BAR 182/1: 181, Archivo Histórico Nacional (Sección Guerra Civil), Salamanca (hereafter AHN-SGC); "General Motors Peninsular, S.A.," BAR 1329/1:3, AHN-SGC; "Segunda reunión del Consejo de Empresa de General Motors Colectivizada," BAR 1329/6:11, AHN-SGC.

13. Orr, "Spanish Revolution," pp. 10–12.

14. Simone Pétrement, *Simone Weil: A Life,* trans. Raymond Rosenthal (New York: Pantheon, 1976), 270–71; Weil, "Lettre à Georges Bernanos," 224; "¡Salud y suerte, hermanos!" *Solidaridad Obrera,* July 25, 1936, p. 1. On the Durruti column, see José Mira, *Los guerrilleros confederales. Un hombre: Durruti* (Barcelona: Ediciones del Comité Regional de la C.N.T., n.d. [1938?]). On Buenaventura Durruti, see Abel Paz, *Durruti in the Spanish Revolution,* trans. Chuck Morse (Oakland: AK Press, 2007). On Civil War–era Aragón, see Julián Casanova, *Anarquismo y revolución en la sociedad rural aragonesa, 1936–1938* (Madrid: Siglo Veintiuno, 1985).

15. See Athanasios Moulakis, *Simone Weil and the Politics of Self-Denial,* trans. Ruth Hein (Columbia, Mo.: University of Missouri Press, 1998), 169–77; E. Jane Doering, *Simone Weil and the Specter of Self-Perpetuating Force* (Notre Dame, Ind.: University of Notre Dame Press, 2010), 13–40.

16. Simone Weil, "Réflexions sur la guerre," in *Écrits historiques et politiques,* 232. On the establishment, and international public knowledge, of the concentration camps in 1933, see "Communists to Be Interned," *Manchester Guardian,* March 21, 1933, p. 9; G. E. R. Gedye, "Nazis to Hold 5,000 in Camp at Dachau," *New York Times,* April 5, 1933, p. 10; "A Visit to a Nazi Concentration Camp," *Palestine Post,* Aug. 28, 1933, p. 6. "Three victims of the Hitlerite terror, three antifascists and Jews who have known the Hitlerite concentration camps, will speak today . . . at the Palais de la Mutualité." "Une réunion sur la terreur hitlérienne," *Humanité,* Nov. 27, 1933, p. 3.

17. Weil, "Réflexions sur la guerre," 236–38.

18. Weil, "Journal d'Espagne," 214.

19. Weil, "Lettre à Georges Bernanos," 221, 222.

20. Francescangeli, *Arditi del popolo,* 142–144; "Les communistes résistent à Parme," *Humanité,* Nov. 2, 1922, p. 3; Spriano, *Storia del Partito comunista italiano* 1: 233 *n*3, 339–41; "Il Primo Maggio i lavoratori italiani riaffermano la loro fede nella riscossa proletaria,"

Humanité: Supplemento settimanale in lingua italiana, May 10, 1924, p. 6; Paolo Spriano, *Storia del Partito comunista italiano,* vol. 2: *Gli anni della clandestinità* (Turin: Giulio Einaudi, 1969), 62; Fiamma Lussana, "A scuola di comunismo. Emigrati italiani nelle scuole del Comintern," *Studi storici* 46, no. 4 (Oct. 2005): 1020–21; Bocchi, *Ribelle,* 101–10. For a precise account of Guido Picelli's life after Parma, see Francescangeli, *Arditi del popolo,* 140–44. See also Bocchi, *Ribelle,* 74–119. Palmiro Togliatti's memorial narrative is misleading and contains factual errors. M. Ercoli [Palmiro Togliatti], "To the Memory of Guido Picelli," *Communist International* 14, no. 2 (Feb. 1937): 146–47.

21. Julián Gorkin, *El proceso de Moscú en Barcelona: El sacrificio de Andrés Nin* (Barcelona: Aymá, 1974), 54. The episode is also related in Julián Gorkin, *Canibales políticos: Hitler y Stalin en España* (Mexico City: Ediciones Quetzal, 1941), 94–95. The two accounts differ on a few particulars.

22. Gorkin, *Proceso de Moscú en Barcelona,* 54.

23. Gorkin, *Proceso de Moscú en Barcelona,* 54.

24. Patrick Iber, *Neither Peace nor Freedom: The Cultural Cold War in Latin America* (Cambridge, Mass.: Harvard University Press, 2015), 48; Marco Puppini, *Garibaldini in Spagna: Storia della XII Brigata Internazionale nella guerra di Spagna* (Udine: Kappa Vu, 2019), 64; Gorkin, *Proceso de Moscú en Barcelona,* 54; Stéphane Courtois and Jean-Louis Panné, "The Shadow of the NKVD in Spain," in Stéphane Courtois et al., *The Black Book of Communism: Crimes, Terror, Repression,* trans. Jonathan Murphy and Mark Kramer (Cambridge, Mass.: Harvard University Press, 1999), 341. Why the rush to write off Picelli? The historian Anson Rabinbach has described the *Black Book* as a "questionable effort to produce a moral arithmetic according to which communism was responsible for 'four times as many' deaths as Nazism." Anson Rabinbach, "Moments of Totalitarianism," *History and Theory* 45, no. 1 (Feb. 2006): 77.

25. Herbert R. Southworth, *Conspiracy and the Spanish Civil War: The Brainwashing of Francisco Franco* (London: Routledge, 2002), 80. See also Herbert R. Southworth, "'The Grand Camouflage': Julián Gorkin, Burnett Bolloten and the Spanish Civil War," in *The Republic Besieged: Civil War in Spain, 1936–1939* ed. Paul Preston and Ann L. Mackenzie (Edinburgh: Edinburgh University Press, 1996), 261–310.

26. Bocchi, *Ribelle,* 111–12.

27. Francescangeli, *Arditi del popolo,* 155; Neelam Srivastava, "Anti-colonialism and the Italian Left: Resistances to the Fascist Invasion of Ethiopia," *Interventions* 8, no. 3 (Nov. 2006): 413–29; "Armando Fedeli," *Enciclopedia dell'antifascismo e della Resistenza,* vol. 2 (Milan: La Pietra, 1971), 300–301; "L'eroica morte di Antonio Cieri sul fronte di Huesca," *Giustizia e Libertà,* April 16, 1937, p. 1.

28. Joe Jacobs, *Out of the Ghetto: My Youth in the East End, Communism and Fascism, 1913–1939* (London: Janet Simon, 1978), 238; "East-End Fascists Call for Blood," (Lon-

—

don) *Daily Worker,* Sept. 28, 1936, p. 1; *They Did* Not *Pass: 300,000 Workers Say NO to Mosley* (London: Independent Labour Party, n.d. [1936]), 3.

29. *Blackshirt,* Sept. 26, 1936, p. 2; "Fascist March in East End," *Yorkshire Post,* Sept. 30, 1936, p. 3; *Action,* Oct. 1, 1936, p. 3.

30. "Anti-Fascist Demonstrators Attacked," *Manchester Guardian,* Aug. 31, 1936, p. 9. Other identities included "the Ex-Servicemen's Anti-Fascist Movement," "the Ex-Servicemen's Anti-Fascist Organisation," and "the Ex-Servicemen's Anti-Fascist Association." Our Special Correspondent, "Veterans of War Stoned by Fascists," (London) *Daily Worker,* Aug. 31, 1936, p. 1; *They Did* Not *Pass,* p. 6; "Ex-Soldiers 'Asked' to Give Way to Mosley," (London) *Daily Worker,* Sept. 30, 1936, p. 5.

31. Jacobs, *Out of the Ghetto,* 204–05; Daniel Tilles, *British Fascist Antisemitism and Jewish Responses, 1932–40* (London: Bloomsbury, 2014), 127; "Jew Farce in East London," *Blackshirt,* Sept. 5, 1936, p. 1; "Parade Uproar," *Daily Express,* Aug. 31, 1936, p. 11; "Anti-Fascist Demonstrators Attacked," *Manchester Guardian,* Aug. 31, 1936, p. 9; "Baton Threat to Restore Order," *Yorkshire Post,* Aug. 31, 1936, p. 10.

32. "18 Arrests at Meetings," *Daily Mail,* Aug. 31, 1936, p. 9; "Fascist Stone Hits Sylvia Pankhurst," (New York) *Sunday News,* Sept. 6, 1936, p. 2.

33. "White Guard in Italy," p. 1570. In her unpublished manuscript "In the Red Twilight," Sylvia Pankhurst also wrote of being present when people in Bologna were "attacked by the Arditi." Pankhurst, "In the Red Twilight," p. iva, Pankhurst Papers (accessed online, image 19, item 146, collection ARCH01029).

34. Mary Davis, *Sylvia Pankhurst: A Life in Radical Politics* (Sterling, Va.: Pluto, 1999), 88, 107–16; Connelly, *Sylvia Pankhurst,* 133–37.

35. "A First-Class Fighting Woman," *St. Louis Post-Dispatch,* Sept. 3, 1936, sec. C, p. 2.

36. Jacobs, *Out of the Ghetto,* 205, 237; Copsey, *Anti-fascism in Britain,* 49. On the "Battle of Cable Street," see Tony Kushner and Nadia Valman, *Remembering Cable Street: Fascism and Anti-Fascism in British Society* (London: Vallentine Mitchell, 2000); Copsey, *Anti-fascism in Britain,* 45–55.

37. Jacobs, *Out of the Ghetto,* 238. But on the Communist Party of Great Britain's perspective, see also Kevin Marsh and Robert Griffiths, *Granite and Honey: The Story of Phil Piratin, Communist MP* (Croydon: Manifesto Press, 2012).

38. Jacobs, *Out of the Ghetto,* 238–42; (London) *Daily Worker,* Oct. 3, 1936, supplement; *They Did* Not *Pass,* 6.

39. Ferdinand Kuhn, Jr., "Enraged Anti-Fascists in London Force Mosley to Cancel Parade," *Montreal Gazette,* Oct. 5, 1936, p. 1; "Londoners Smash Fascist Parade," *Toronto Globe,* Oct. 5, 1936, p. 1; *They Did* Not *Pass,* 3, 8; Holmes, *Sylvia Pankhurst,* 685; "Barricades in the East End," *Daily Express,* Oct. 5, 1936, p. 1; "Mosley Did Not Pass: East London Routs the Fascists," (London) *Daily Worker,* Oct. 5, 1936, p. 1.

—

40. "El día de la victoria," (Madrid) *ABC*, April 2, 1939, p. 1. On the war's end, see Sandi Holguín, "How Did the Spanish Civil War End? . . . Not So Well," *American Historical Review* 120, no. 5 (Dec. 2015): 1767–83.

41. See Michael Alpert, *A New International History of the Spanish Civil War*, second edition (Houndsmills, Basingstoke: Palgrave Macmillan, 2004).

42. Gerd-Rainer Horn, "The Catalan Revolution," in Lois Orr, *Letters from Barcelona: An American Woman in Revolution and Civil War*, ed. Horn (Houndsmills, Basingstoke: Palgrave Macmillan, 2009), 8. On the "May Days," see, of course, Orwell, *Homage to Catalonia*, 121–79. See also "Las fuerzas armadas traiaron de apoderarse, ayer tarde, del edificio de la Telefónica," *Solidaridad Obrera*, May 4, 1937, p. 8; Broué and Témime, *Revolution and the Civil War in Spain*, 281–89; Vernon Richards, *Lessons of the Spanish Revolution (1936–1939)* (London: Freedom Press, 1972), 120–34; Frank Mintz and Miguel Peciña, *Los Amigos de Durruti: Los trotsquistas y los sucesos de mayo* (Madrid: Campo Abierto Ediciones, 1978); Burnett Bolloten, *The Spanish Revolution: The Left and the Struggle for Power During the Civil War* (Chapel Hill: University of North Carolina Press, 1979), 403–30; Helen Graham, *The Spanish Republic at War, 1936–1939* (Cambridge, Eng.: Cambridge University Press, 2002), 254–315; Ferran Aisa, *Contrarevolució: Els Fets de Maig de 1937* (Barcelona: Edicions de 1984, 2007); Ferran Gallego, *Barcelona, mayo de 1937: La crisis del antifascismo en Cataluña* (Barcelona: Debate, 2007).

43. On the fight for the Telephone Exchange on July 19, 1936, see "Episodis de la lluita sagnant de diumenge," *Rambla*, July 22, 1936, p. 2; Pere Ardiace Martí, interview by Ronald Fraser, Dec. 10, 1973, transcript, p. 3, Col·lecció Ronald Fraser, Departaments de Fonts Orals, Arxiu Històric de la Ciutat de Barcelona, Barcelona (hereafter, collection cited as CRF); Manuel Andújar Muñoz, interview by Ronald Fraser, June 5, 1974, transcript, p. 4, CRF; Paz, *Durruti in the Spanish Revolution*, 442. The Telephone Exchange building still stands, at the corner of Carrer de Fontanella and Portal de l'Àngel.

44. Juan Andrade Rodríguez, interview by Ronald Fraser, Nov. 15, 1973, transcript, p. 12, CRF; "Workers War to Stop Fascism," *One Big Union Monthly* 1, no. 7 (July 1937): 24, 26.

45. See Broué and Témime, *Revolution and the Civil War in Spain*, 219–23, 296–315. See also Richards, *Lessons of the Spanish Revolution*, 155–62.

46. "Case of Comrade O'Donnel," manuscript, file 12/3, box C, IBMA MML; W. H. Auden, *Spain* (London: Faber and Faber, 1937), 7, 11. In his rebuke of the poem, George Orwell did not seem to see it as a critique of the POUM's insistence on revolution first. The criticism Orwell offered was based on a misunderstanding of Auden's use of the phrase "necessary murder." Auden was actually making a point that Orwell would have been likely to appreciate if he'd understood; Auden meant, he himself later explained, "To kill another human being is always murder and should never be called anything else." He was saying

that war is murder and that this shouldn't be hidden by any euphemisms; and yet, he was suggesting, some wars are necessary. Orwell thought Auden was basically excusing political assassination. Monroe K. Spears, *The Poetry of W. H. Auden: The Disenchanted Island* (New York: Oxford University Press, 1963), 157 *n*10. See George Orwell, "Inside the Whale," in *Inside the Whale and Other Essays* (London: Victor Gollancz, 1940), 131–88. See also Nicholas Jenkins, "Appendix: Auden and Spain," in *W. H. Auden: "The Map of All My Youth": Early Works, Friends and Influences* ed. Katherine Bucknell and Nicholas Jenkins (Oxford, Eng.: Clarendon Press, 1990), 92.

47. Gorkin, *Proceso de Moscú en Barcelona*, 106–20. Especially effective at letting her readers see "the error of seeing the POUM's post-May 1937 experience as part of a seamless whole of imported and monolithic stalinist persecution" is Graham, *Spanish Republic at War*, 346 (quote). Graham means in particular to counter Gorkin's notion of the trial of the POUM's leaders (including himself) as a Moscow show trial in Spain. See Graham, *Spanish Republic at War*, 385.

48. "Franco's Spies and Trotskyists Plotted Strife in Barcelona," (New York) *Daily Worker*, May 8, 1937, p. 1; Georges Soria, "Spanish Fascists Shielding Nin, POUM Chief, Arrested by Loyalists for Trotzkyist Plots," (New York) *Daily Worker*, Nov. 26, 1937, p. 2; "La Gestapo Trotski et ses lieutenants," *Humanité*, July 13, 1937, p. 1.

49. On Clichy, see Alexandre Zévaès, *Clichy en Deuil* (Paris: Editions du "Secours Populaire de France," 1937).

50. On the New Deal's turn, see Alan Brinkley, *The End of Reform: New Deal Liberalism in Recession and War* (New York: Knopf, 1995); on the breaking of the Little Steel strike, see Joseph Fronczak, "The Fascist Game: Transnational Political Transmission and the Genesis of the U.S. Modern Right," *Journal of American History* 105, no. 3 (Dec. 2018): 583–86.

51. See Tom Buchanan, *East Wind: China and the British Left, 1925–1976* (Oxford, Eng.: Oxford University Press, 2012), 48–80.

52. "Brazil Goes Fascist," *Fortune*, Dec. 1937, insert; Robert M. Levine, *Father of the Poor? Vargas and His Era* (Cambridge, Eng.: Cambridge University Press, 1998), 120.

53. "Put Americanism First," *Shreveport Times*, Oct. 6, 1936, p. 4. See Karl Schlögel, *Moscow, 1937*, trans. Rodney Livingstone (Cambridge, Eng.: Polity, 2012).

54. *Not Guilty: Report of the Commission of Inquiry into the Charges Made Against Leon Trotsky in the Moscow Trials* (New York: Harper, 1938); Pernicone, *Carlo Tresca*, 230–32.

55. Langston Hughes, *I Wonder as I Wander: An Autobiographical Journey* (1956; New York: Hill and Wang, 1964), 384.

56. Some records list a 1900 birth year for Oliver Law; his Veterans' Administration master index card lists Oct. 23, 1899. (This card also dates his enlistment.) A photocopy of the card is available on the database *FamilySearch*. For his raising on a ranch, see Marion, "Oliver Law, Hero of Jarama Front," p. 3. For his time as a wharf worker, see Bureau of

—

the Census, *Fourteenth Census of the United States: 1920–Population*, Galveston City, Texas, sheet no. 8A. On the length of his military service and his rank, see Peter N. Carroll, *The Odyssey of the Abraham Lincoln Brigade: Americans in the Spanish Civil War* (Stanford: Stanford University Press, 1994), 135–36. On the area's black military culture in the era, and the Houston Riot of 1917, see Tyina Steptoe, *Houston Bound: Culture and Color in a Jim Crow City* (Oakland: University of California Press, 2016).

57. Carroll, *Odyssey of the Abraham Lincoln Brigade*, 94; R. Dan Richardson, *Comintern Army: The International Brigades and the Spanish Civil War* (Lexington: University of Kentucky Press, 1982), 77–78.

58. "Fascists Advance in Drive on Madrid," *Baltimore Sun*, Feb. 7, 1937, p. 16; Carroll, *Odyssey of the Abraham Lincoln Brigade*, 102, 136; Lini de Vries, *Up from the Cellar* (Minneapolis: Vanilla Press, 1979), 207; Edwin Rolfe, *The Lincoln Battalion: The Story of the Americans Who Fought in Spain in the International Brigades* (New York: Random House, 1939), 55; Richardson, *Comintern Army*, 79. On the Battle of Jarama, see Tremlett, *Brigadas Internacionales*, 220–57.

59. Orwell, *Homage to Catalonia*, 26–29, 55.

60. Nancy Cunard, "Negro Captain of Spanish Unit Killed in Battle," *Atlanta Daily World*, Dec. 20, 1937, p. 1; Brandt, editor, *Black Americans in the Spanish People's War Against Fascism*, 35; Carroll, *Odyssey of the Abraham Lincoln Brigade*, 137.

61. Tremlett, *Brigadas Internacionales*, 347–400.

62. Harry Fisher, *Comrades: Tales of a Brigadista in the Spanish Civil War* (Lincoln: University of Nebraska Press, 1998), 58–59, 166.

63. Herbert L. Matthews, *Two Wars and More to Come* (New York: Carrick and Evans, 1938), 232; Cunard, "Negro Captain of Spanish Unit Killed in Battle," p. 1; Fisher, *Comrades*, 62.

64. Paul Berman, "William Herrick: An Introduction," in William Herrick, *Jumping the Line: The Adventures and Misadventures of an American Radical* (Madison: University of Wisconsin Press, 1998), xi.

65. Lisa A. Kirschenbaum, *International Communism and the Spanish Civil War: Solidarity and Suspicion* (New York: Cambridge University Press, 2015), 234.

66. "Spanish Betrayals: A Lincoln Vet Remembers," *Village Voice*, July 22, 1986, pp. 23–25. Earlier, William Herrick had told his invented narrative of Oliver Law's death to Bernard Wolfe, who had been a secretary to Leon Trotsky in Mexico. Wolfe wrote a novel that included a character based on Herrick's perceptions of Law, *The Great Prince Died* (the prince being Trotsky). See Bernard Wolfe, *The Great Prince Died: A Novel* (New York: Charles Scribner's Sons, 1959), 192–200. It appears likely that Herrick was also the sole source for the flawed discussion in Cecil Eby, *Between the Bullet and the Lie: American Volunteers in the Spanish Civil War* (New York: Holt, Rinehart and Winston, 1969), 134–35.

—

67. See the testimony of the Canadian Lincoln William Brennan in William C. Beeching, *Canadian Volunteers in Spain, 1936–1939* (Regina: Canadian Plains Research Center, 1989), 49.

68. Gorkin, *Proceso de Moscú en Barcelona,* 54. For press coverage of the death, see, for example, "Guido Picelli, ancien député au Parlement italien tombé en héros sur le front de Siguenza," *Humanité,* Jan. 12, 1937, p. 3.

69. "El partido Comunista de Italia à los combatientes italianos de la libertad," list 23, delo 74, opis' 1, fond 545, Russian Government Archive of Social-Political History (RGASPI), Moscow, microfilm edition (hereafter in the form: RGASPI, microfilm, f. 545, op. 1, d. 74, l. 23); Francescangeli, *Arditi del popolo,* 144; Puppini, *Garibaldini in Spagna,* 66–67, 69; RGASPI, microfilm, f. 545, op. 1, d. 74, l. 23; Puppini, *Garibaldini in Spagna,* 66; Andreu Castells, *Las Brigadas Internacionales de la guerra de España* (Barcelona: Editorial Ariel, 1974), 136. On the Italian Legion and the creation of the Garibaldi Battalion, see Richardson, *Comintern Army,* 62–64; Puppini, *Garibaldini in Spagna,* 42–54. See also Pietro Nenni, *La guerre d'Espagne,* trans. Jean Baumier (Paris: François Maspero, 1960), esp. 135–82.

70. See Dante Corneli, *Scritti storico-politici di D. Corneli,* vol. 3: *Dal leninismo allo stalinismo* (Bolsena: Massari, 2019), 250. See also Guelfo Zaccaria, *200 comunisti italiani tra le vittime dello stalinismo: Appello del Comitato italiano per la verità sui misfatti dello stalinismo* (Milan: Edizioni Azione Comune, n.d. [1964]), 54–56.

71. Puppini, *Garibaldini in Spagna,* 68.

72. The historian of fascism George L. Mosse, who late in life described himself as having been "active in the antifascist movement" in the era of the Spanish Civil War, wrote: "The antifascist movement, despite its importance, has not yet found its historian, and those who have written about it have tended to look at it through the prism of the Cold War. Antifascism looked at in this manner turns into something like a Communist front, and the issue of whether or not it was dominated by the Communists becomes the central focus. This is looking at history backwards from a time after the Second World War when 'antifascism' was no longer a true political movement but in effect became a Communist slogan." George L. Mosse, *Confronting History: A Memoir* (Madison: University of Wisconsin Press, 2000), 104.

73. "Eroica morte di Antonio Cieri sul fronte di Huesca," p. 1. See Gianni Furlotti, *Parma libertaria* (Pisa: BFS, 2001), 154–58; Luigi Di Lembo, *Guerra di classe e lotta umana: L'anarchismo in Italia dal Biennio rosso alla Guerra di Spagna (1919–1939)* (Pisa: BFS, 2001), 199, 211.

74. William Herrick, *¡Hermanos!* (New York: Simon and Schuster, 1969), 302, 303, 305, 315, 318, 327, 329, and 330; see also Eby, *Between the Bullet and the Lie,* 122.

—

EPILOGUE

Epigraph: Simone Weil, "Méditations sur un cadavre," in *Écrits historiques et politiques,* 324.

1. Ibárruri, *En la lucha,* 354; Broué and Témime, *Revolution and the Civil War in Spain,* 484–503; Thomas, *Spanish Civil War,* 554–57.

2. "L'adieu des volontaires," *Regards,* Nov. 10, 1938, p. 13; Pierre Mars, "Une foule ardente exprime son admiration et sa gratitude aux héroïques défenseurs de la liberté," *Humanité,* Oct. 29, 1938, p. 3; Peter Wyden, *The Passionate War: A Narrative History of the Spanish Civil War, 1936–1939* (New York: Simon and Schuster, 1983), 493. Historians have dated the farewell parade October 28, October 29, November 1, and even November 15. Influential, one presumes, for the suggestions of November 15 was Thomas, *Spanish Civil War,* 558. The parade took place on Friday, October 28, 1938. For Robert Capa's work from that day, see "Les volontaires quittent l'Espagne," *Ce Soir,* Oct. 29, 1938, p. 8; "Adieu des volontaires," pp. 12–13; "International Brigade Dismiss!" *Picture Post,* Nov. 12, 1938, pp. 34–37. See also Richard Whelan, *Robert Capa: A Biography* (New York: Knopf, 1985), 148; Richard Whelan, *Robert Capa: The Definitive Collection* (London: Phaidon, 2001).

3. Mars, "Foule ardente exprime son admiration et sa gratitude aux héroïques défenseurs de la liberté," p. 3.

4. "El jefe del Gobierno despide a los internacionales," (Barcelona) *Vanguardia,* Oct. 28, 1938, p. 1.

5. Ibárruri, *En la lucha,* 354–56.

6. See Furlotti, *Parma libertaria,* 153–54; also useful for understanding the political debates within the Italian Column, and Cieri's position on them, is Umberto Marzocchi, *Remembering Spain: Italian Anarchist Volunteers in the Spanish Civil War* (London: Kate Sharpley Library, 2005).

7. Dolores Ibárruri, *El único camino* (Buenos Aires: Editorial Sendero, 1963), 370. To compare to the English translation, see Dolores Ibárruri, *They Shall Not Pass: The Autobiography of La Pasionaria* ([New York:] International Publishers, 1966), 285. For an explanation of the documents that Ibárruri mentions (and misconstrues), see Burnett Bolloten, *The Spanish Civil War: Revolution and Counterrevolution* (Chapel Hill: University of North Carolina Press, 1991), 446.

8. Kevin O'Donnell, "The New Marianism of Dolores Ibárruri's *El único camino,*" *Arizona Journal of Hispanic Cultural Studies* 6 (2002): 29.

9. "Jefe del Gobierno despide a los internacionales," p. 1. For an estimate of 8,750 (one quarter of their estimate of 35,000 total volunteers in the International Brigades), see Lefebvre and Skoutelsky, *Brigades internationales,* 132.

10. César Vallejo, "Masa," *Poemas humanos* (1939; Lima: Editora Peru Nuevo, 1959), 139.

—

11. George Orwell, *Complete Works*, vol. 17: *I Belong to the Left, 1945*, ed. Peter Davison (London: Secker and Warburg, 1998), 385.

12. "Truman Urges All to Give Thanks for 'Exceeding Blessing of Victory,'" *New York Times*, Nov. 13, 1945, p. 23; George Orwell, "You and the Atom Bomb," *Tribune*, Oct. 19, 1945, p. 8; Duchess of Atholl, *Searchlight on Spain* (Harmondsworth: Penguin, 1938); "Red Duchess Out," *Action*, Dec. 31, 1938, p. 10. For an assessment of World War II emphasizing the vitality of antifascist ideas, see Seidman, *Transatlantic Antifascisms*. On antifascist resistance, see Henri Michel, *Les courants de pensée de la Résistance* (Paris: Presses universitaires de France, 1962); Claudio Pavone, *A Civil War: A History of the Italian Resistance*, trans. Peter Levy (London: Verso, 2013).

13. Orwell, *Complete Works*, 17: 29–30.

14. Orwell, *Complete Works*, 17: 384–85.

15. On the idea of totalitarianism, see Enzo Traverso, editor, *Le totalitarisme: Le xxe siècle en débat* (Paris: Seuil, 2001); Rabinbach, "Moments of Totalitarianism"; Traverso, *New Faces of Fascism*, 151–82.

16. See Mouffe, *For a Left Populism*.

17. Traverso, *Left-Wing Melancholia*, 52.

18. Marian E. Schlotterbeck, *Beyond the Vanguard: Everyday Revolutionaries in Allende's Chile* (Oakland: University of California Press, 2018).

19. Traverso, *Left-Wing Melancholia*, 22–53, 92. For another study attentive to the legacy of 1930s antifascism for later leftists, see Vials, *Haunted by Hitler*.

20. Max Gallo, *La gauche est morte. Vive la gauche!* (Paris: Éditions Odile Jacob, 1990), 15; Anthony Giddens, *Beyond Left and Right: The Future of Radical Politics* (Cambridge, Eng.: Polity, 1994).

21. Boaventura de Sous Santos, *The Rise of the Global Left: The World Social Forum and Beyond* (London: Zed, 2006). Other works valuable for conceptualizing the twenty-first-century left and its relation to the left of the twentieth century include John D. French, *Lula and His Politics of Cunning: From Metalworker to President of Brazil* (Chapel Hill: University of North Carolina Press, 2020); Ewa Majewska, *Feminist Antifascism: Counterpublics of the Common* (London: Verso, 2021).

22. John L. Hammond, "Another World Is Possible: Report from Porto Alegre," *Latin American Perspectives* 30, no. 3 (May 2003): 3–11; Tom Mertes, editor, *A Movement of Movements: Is Another World Really Possible?* (London: Verso, 2004).

23. See Finchelstein, *From Fascism to Populism in History*; Traverso, *New Faces of Fascism*.

ACKNOWLEDGMENTS

Woody Guthrie, an admirable antifascist, once wrote that the amount that we owe is all that we have. Writing a book such as this one has helped me to see how this could be so.

Thanks first must go to Ana Minian. High in the mountains of Michoacán, Ana suggested the dissertation topic that led to this book. I owe Ana more than this, though. I certainly would have lost my way without her in Michoacán, and the same is true of graduate school, where she shared her intellectual incandescence and ideological seriousness, not to mention her friendship, every step of the way.

Several institutions funded the research behind this book. I'd like to thank the Hoover Institution at Stanford University; the MacMillan Center at Yale University; the Gilder Lehrman Institute of American History; the Agrarian Studies Program at Yale University; and the Department of History at Princeton University. I'd like to thank Ian Shapiro in particular for awarding the funds that I relied on the most during my research.

This book derives from the dissertation I wrote in the Department of History at Yale University. My committee deserves endless praise for encouraging my experiments and challenging my results. Michael Denning, Joanne Meyerowitz, and John Merriman are all model mentors who teach with purpose, brilliance,

—

and kindness. At Yale my work also benefited from the examples of Drew Hannon, Dodie McDow, Kathleen Belew, David Huyssen, Kirsten Weld, Victor McFarland, Simeon Man, Sam Schaffer, Betty Luther, Katherine Mooney, Ryan Brasseaux, Sara Hudson, Tim Retzloff, Jennifer Wellington, Kevin Fogg, Joseph Yannielli, and Alison Greene and Jason Ward, who welcomed me when I first arrived in New Haven very green. Helen Veit and Charles Keith welcomed me both in New Haven and in Aix-en-Provence, where they brought me in from the damp cold and housed and fed me. Charles also showed me how to navigate the archives in Aix. My work benefited as well from the insights of George Chauncey, Seth Fein, Bev Gage, Matt Jacobson, Steve Pitti, Anders Winroth, K. Sivaramakrishnan, Jon Butler, and John Demos. Tim Snyder told me to pick up some languages; Ben Kiernan kindly invited me to his seminar; Jennifer Klein shaped the way I think about history; and David Blight was and is an inspiration in all things. Jim Scott deserves three cheers for cultivating my ideas, reading my work, and sharing his insights.

The Mahindra Humanities Center at Harvard University was the ideal postdoctoral home. Steve Biel, Suzanne Smith, and Mary Halpenny-Killip welcomed the fellows to the Warren House and guided us through a dazzling year of intellectual growth. Homi Bhabha nurtured my work a great deal and encouraged my theoretical commitments. Charles Maier, as ever, challenged my claims, and Partha Chatterjee talked me through them. Mahindra fellows-for-life shaped this book in countless ways even as they delayed its writing: Hiba Bou Akar, Sam Anderson, Thiemo Breyer, Sakura Christmas, Alex Fattal, Tae-Yeoun Keum, Murad Idris, and Ram Nadarajan, many thanks to you my beloved comrades. I returned to Harvard a few years later to begin another project; alas, I couldn't quite put this one aside. I am grateful to Fred Logevall, Erez Manela, Vince Brown, and Walter Johnson for inviting me to the Warren Center and giving me another splendid year in Cambridge. Thanks are in order as well to Chris Capozzola, a wonderful friendly presence in Cambridge whose smallest comments are filled with wisdom. And thanks most of all to Nancy Cott, a hero of mine who has taken my work seriously and has shared her ideas and time generously.

In Princeton, many people have read and nurtured my work. I'd like to thank in particular Ed Baring, David Bell, Vera Candiani, Divya Cherian,

ACKNOWLEDGMENTS

Angela Creager, Jacob Dlamini, Shel Garon, Michael Gordin, Molly Greene, Katja Guenther, Judy Hanson, Rob Karl, Matt Karp, Regina Kunzel, Michael Laffan, Jon Levy, Beth Lew-Williams, Rosina Lozano, Federico Marcon, Erika Milam, Paul Miles, Yair Mintzker, Isadora Mota, Randall Pippenger, Ronny Regev, Keith Wailoo, Natasha Wheatley, Peter Wirzbicki, and Julian Zelizer. Special thanks are due to Sean Wilentz. Thanks as well to Miranda Lida and Michael Dickman and Phoebe Nobles.

My students' ideas, interests, and principles have shaped my writing a great deal. The students of my seminar on fascism and antifascism in global history sparred with me in spirited weekly sessions as we tried to make sense of the first century or so of fascist and antifascist history. Judie Miller is due a special note of gratitude for granting my sentimental request that the seminar inherit the course number of Andy Rabinbach's legendary seminar on the history of European fascism. Andy himself has my gratitude for sharing his learning, wisdom, and stories. Of my students, all of whom have my devotion, I'd like to acknowledge in particular Christian Bischoff, Julia Case-Levine, Aida Garrido, Mikaela Gerwin, Ararat Gocmen, Ian Iverson, Cai Markham, Nathaniel Moses, Joshua Porter, Hannah Srajer, and Joshua Leifer, who deserves special thanks for sharing with me some of his deep knowledge of Palestine's interwar political history as I began to dig into my research of Antifa of Palestine.

Writing on antifascism has led me to encounter a small band of generous and talented historians. It is an honor to be among Kasper Braskén, John Bulaitis, Anna Duensing, Alexander Dunphy, John Enyeart, Michael Seidman, Clayton Vaughn-Roberson, Christopher Vials, Serge Wolikow, and Glennys Young. Writing this book also led me to Yale University Press, which has been special to me ever since I pulled *Domination and the Arts of Resistance* off the shelves of Helen C. White Library and read it in one sitting on the shore of Lake Mendota many years ago. I am grateful to Adina Berk for taking an interest in the book and for advising me in its writing. Thanks as well to Harry Haskell, Ann-Marie Imbornoni, and Ash Lago.

I would like to thank my parents and my sister for so many years of love and shared family life. And I would like to thank my children, each of them my ideal reader, perhaps tomorrow if not yet. Hawthorne, a poet before he could speak; Rosemary, with a storm in each eye; and Asa, whose laughter is for the

—

ages: in these pages are stories of joy, solidarity, and purpose; may you enact your own.

Glenda Gilmore was my adviser when I was in graduate school and remains my most trusted adviser still. I first read her work years ago and decided on the spot that what I wanted to do was to go to graduate school at Yale and learn from her. Life is full of choices and I consider myself blessed that my life has been shaped so much by this one.

Bill Jordan hired me as a lecturer at Princeton and made sure that I could keep the job long enough to finish the book. I wouldn't have been able to do so without his generosity and faith. He has my gratitude for these and other things.

And Wendy Warren has kept the faith as well. This book devoured so much time, and I relied on her left and right. I disappeared into my head for long stretches and it wasn't always clear that anything would come of it. Other times I relied on the ideas in her head. She has my unbounded gratitude for all the proofs of solidarity through the years. She would have my unbounded love, though, any which way. What's next? We shall see, together.

INDEX

References to figures are indicated by an italic "f."

—

—